Recollections of a Romanian Diplomat 1918–1969

VOLUME ONE

Recollections of a Romanian Diplomat 1918–1969

Diaries and Memoirs of Raoul V. Bossy

VOLUME ONE

EDITED AND TRANSLATED BY
G. H. and M.-A. Bossy

HOOVER INSTITUTION PRESS
STANFORD UNIVERSITY STANFORD, CALIFORNIA

The Hoover Institution on War, Revolution and Peace, founded at Stanford University in 1919 by Herbert Hoover, who went on to become the thirty-first president of the United States, is an interdisciplinary research center for advanced study on domestic and international affairs. The views expressed in its publications are entirely those of the authors and do not necessarily reflect the views of the staff, officers, or Board of Overseers of the Hoover Institution.

www.hoover.org

Hoover Institution Press Publication No. 507

First printing, 2003
09 08 07 06 05 04 03 9 8 7 6 5 4 3 2 1

Manufactured in the United States of America

Cover and frontispiece photo by Ernst Schnaider, Berlin.
Book design by Kelly J. Applegate, Publication Services.

The paper used in this publication meets the minimum requirements of the American National Standard for Information Sciences—Permanence of Paper for Printed Library Materials, ANSI Z39.48–1984.

Library of Congress Cataloging-in-Publication Data

Bossy, Raoul V., 1894–1975
[Souvenirs d'un diplomate. English]
Recollections of a Romanian diplomat, 1918–1969: diaries and memoirs of Raoul V. Bossy / edited and translated by G. H. and M.-A. Bossy.
p.cm. — (Archival documentary)
Includes bibliographical references and index.
ISBN 0-8179-2951-7 (alk. paper)
1. Romania—Foreign relations—1914–1944. 2. Bossy, Raoul V., 1894–1975—Diaries. 3. Diplomats—Romania—Diaries. I. Bossy, George H. II. Bossy, Michel-André, III. Bossy, Raoul V., 1894–1975. Memoirs of a diplomat. IV. Title. V. Series.

DR264 .B67413 2003
327.498092—dc21
[B]

2002017255

Contents

Volume One

Director's Foreword, by John Raisian xi
Foreword, by Stephen Fischer-Galati xiii
Preface xix

1. FIRST STEPS IN DIPLOMACY (1918–1921) 1
   - Student in Paris 2
   - Joining the Diplomatic Service 3
   - Chief of Take Ionescu's Cabinet 7
   - Alliances and Royal Weddings 14
2. ROME (1921–1923) 17
   - The Romanian Legation in Rome 17
   - The Italian Government and Royal Court 19
   - The Diplomatic Corps Accredited to the Quirinal 22
   - The First Months of My Assignment 27
   - The Genoa Conference (April 10–May 19, 1922) 29
   - Chargé d'Affaires at the Age of 27; the Fascists Come to Power 35
   - Other Recollections from My First Posting Abroad 38
3. POLITICAL DIRECTOR OF THE PRESIDENCY OF THE COUNCIL OF MINISTERS (1923–1926) 43
   - Domestic Political Fights 46
   - Official Visits 47
   - Carol's Renouncement of the Throne 55
   - Brătianu Goes, Averescu Comes 59
4. SECOND TOUR IN ROME (1926–1927) 63

5. SECRETARY-GENERAL OF THE REGENCY (1927–1930) 67
The Death of King Ferdinand and the Setting Up of the Regency 67
The Death of Ion I.C. Brătianu 76
Change of Government and Change in the Regency 82
Carol's Return 94

6. CABINET DIRECTOR OF THE MINISTRY OF FOREIGN AFFAIRS (1931) 103
Carol Settles Accounts 103
A Parenthesis: Diamandy's Mission to Paris (1926–1930) 105
Carol Seeks a New Government 107
Bucharest Conference of the Little Entente 110
Princess Ileana's Marriage 111
Twelfth Meeting of the Assembly of the League of Nations 112
End of the Iorga Government; Increasing Strains within the Royal Family 116

7. VIENNA (1931–1934) 119
First Impressions 119
Queen Marie on Royal Family Tensions 123
Austrian Domestic Politics 125
Conversations with Titulescu 126
Queen Helen Stands Up for Her Rights 131
Queen Marie's Renewed Complaints 133
Further Conversations with Titulescu 136
The End of a Pleasant Mission 141

8. HELSINGFORS (1934–1936) 143
Briefings in Bucharest 144
First Days in Helsingfors 145
Finnish Commemorations and Romanian Exhibition 150
Discovering Finland and Its Neighbors 152
Meanwhile, Back at Home . . . 156
A Serene Chapter Comes to an End 158

9. BUDAPEST (1936–1939) 161
I. 1936–1937 161
First Steps 162
Sketches of Hungarian Officials and Foreign Envoys 165
Hungary's Internal and External Situations 170

Hungary and the Little Entente 173
Hungary's Relations with Germany 182
Hungarian Advances toward Romania 183
Domestic Turbulence and Nazi Threat in Hungary 187
Austria and Hungary's Relations with Italy 189
Endeavors to Improve Relations between Hungary and the Little Entente 192
Relations between Hungary and Nazi Germany 195
Goga's Views on Hungary 196
Negotiations between the Little Entente and Hungary 197
II. 1938 203
Rome Protocol Meeting in Budapest 204
Finis Austriae and Its Impact on Hungary 207
Discussions with Romanian Statesmen at the Time of the Sinaia Meeting of the Little Entente (May 4–5) 220
Government Reshuffle in Hungary 222
Meeting with Regent Horthy 224
The International Eucharistic Congress (May 22–29) 225
The Imrédy Government and Its Relations with Germany 227
Romano-Hungarian Negotiations Continue 233
The Little Entente's Last Meeting 234
Slide Toward Munich 238
Spat with Kánya and Continued Negotiations 245
Futile Drive for a Common Border between Hungary and Poland 249
New Visit by Ciano to Budapest 263
III. 1939 265
Proposed Talks with Count Istvan Bethlen 267
Csáky's Foreign Policy 269
New Prime Ministers in Hungary and Romania 272
The March Crisis: Subcarpathian Russia and the Hungarian Mobilization 274
Cooling of Relations between Hungary and Romania 280
April 1939 284
Late Spring, Early Summer 1939 290
The Ribbentrop-Molotov Pact 295
War Breaks Out 298
Transfer to Rome and Farewells 303

Volume Two

10. ROME (1939–1940) 311
I. 1939 311
First Contacts 312
Foreign Colleagues in Rome 319
The "Neutral Bloc" 325
II. 1940 335
Italy's Stance in the War 335
A War of Two Weeks 341
The Soviet Ultimatum to Romania and the Loss of Bessarabia and Northern Bukovina 346
Pressure on Romania Increases 350
Semi-Official Mission to Budapest 357
Return to My Post in Rome 361
The Vienna Diktat and the Nazi-Fascist Double Cross 363
Queen Mother Helen's Return to Romania 371
Hungarian Atrocities in Transylvania 375
The End of My Mission to Rome 380

11. BERNE (1940–1941) 383
November 1940–February 1941 383

12. BERLIN AND COPENHAGEN (1941–1943) 391
I. 1941 391
Prelude 391
Yugoslavia Joins the Tripartite Pact 399
Yugoslav About-Face; Germany Attacks Yugoslavia and Greece 403
On the Brink of the German-Russian War 406
The German-Russian War 413
Danish Interlude 420
Back in Berlin 421
Mihai Antonescu's Visit to Berlin 422
America Is Swept into the War 424
II. 1942 427
Field Marshal Antonescu's Visit to Germany 427
Conversations in Bucharest and Unfolding Events 432
Oasis: An Anachronistic Princely Wedding 434
Difficult Dealings with the Germans 435
A Separate German Peace with Russia? 436
End of My Mission 438
III. 1943 443
End of My Mission (cont.) 443

13. THE END OF A CAREER (1943–1946) 453
1943 453
1944 460
1945 465
1946 467

14. EXILE (1947–1975) 471

Appendix A: *The Life of Ferdinand I* 477

Appendix B: *Bárdossy's Draft of a Secret Romano-Hungarian Protocol* 481

Appendix C: *Bossy's Report of August 19, 1938, to the Romanian Minister of Foreign Affairs on the Latest Negotiations with Kánya* 485

Appendix D: *Kánya's Counterproposal of August 11, 1938* 491

Appendix E: *Draft of a Romano-Yugoslavo-Hungarian Declaration* 495

Index 497

Director's Foreword

The Hoover Institution is pleased to publish Romanian diplomat Raoul Bossy's commentary on the events he witnessed in Central Europe during, before, and after the tumultuous era of World War II. A microfilm copy of Mr. Bossy's memoirs and diaries are held at the Hoover Archives; this volume, based in part on that material, is a significant addition to the Hoover Press's Archival Documentary series.

The Hoover Archives began collecting rare historical documentation on Romania in 1921, when Institution representative Frank Golder traveled to Bucharest. Golder was initially frustrated in his attempts to acquire papers on Romania's experience during World War I, but after he met with the eminent Romanian historian Nicolae Iorga, many doors were opened. Golder was able to acquire complete sets of newspapers from the Great War period, including those documenting the occupation of parts of Romania by the Germans. Today, these newspapers—the only cataloged copies available in the United States—are housed in the Hoover Institution Library.

Active collecting by Hoover archivists in Romania continued until 1947. During the communist period, however, collection depended heavily on the émigré population, who placed valuable documents in the Hoover Archives for safekeeping. These materials include an original holograph memoir of Romania in World War I by Prime Minister Ion Duca and a plea to Romanians abroad from Iuliu Maniu in 1946 to preserve the memory of a precommunist Romania. Following the collapse of communism, Hoover archivists have been traveling to the region often, interviewing key political figures and eyewitnesses to the turbulent events of the period and searching for, collecting, and protecting unique artifacts, services for which the Hoover Archives are well known.

The Bossy family pursued the principles of a free Romania throughout the period of communist rule. We hope the words of Raoul Bossy will be appropriately noted in history. The translation by George H. Bossy and Michel-André Bossy, as well as the scholarly introduction by Professor Fischer-Galati, merit our appreciation.

In addition to the Bossy family, the Hoover Institution acknowledges the efforts of Patricia Baker, Elena Danielson, and Charles Palm, all representing the Hoover Institution, for their significant efforts in the accomplishment of this project.

John Raisian
Director
Hoover Institution

Foreword

At a time when the interpretation of the history of the interwar years, of the Second World War, and of the Cold War is being revised according to various prejudices and interests, when the rehabilitation or denigration of political leaders and other participants in the shaping of the history of their times and of the contemporary world has become de rigueur, the *Recollections of a Romanian Diplomat* provides an invaluable *mise à point.*

Raoul V. Bossy was first and foremost a diplomat of the old school. A member of the Romanian aristocracy, having the entrée into European aristocratic circles, he enjoyed the privileges reserved for the elite. At an early age, he chose a diplomatic career, for which he was well qualified by virtue of his exceptionally successful studies, political intelligence, and social standing. It is noteworthy that even though he occasionally held such important political posts in Romania as Political Director of the Presidency of the Council of Ministers (1923–1926), Secretary-General of the Regency (1927–1930), and Cabinet Director of the Ministry of Foreign Affairs (1931), he was never an elected official, nor, for that matter, did he ever serve as a member of the Council of Ministers of any Romanian government. He was, however, Romania's leading diplomatic representative in Italy, Austria, Finland, Hungary, Switzerland, and Germany, at one time or another during his long foreign service career that started in 1918 and ended, with the advent of communism, in 1946.

It is fair to say that the primary historic importance of the book lies in Raoul Bossy's recollections of his years in Budapest (1936–1939), in Rome (1921–1923, 1926–1927, and, especially, 1939–1940), and Berlin

(1941–1943). However, his comments on Romanian politics, politicians, and above all the monarchy are interesting and significant, as are those made on various international developments during his years in exile after 1947.

His evolution as a diplomat reflects the societal, cultural, and political changes of his times. As an elitist remote from but aware of the realities of the transition from aristocratic monarchic Europe to what were to become the "proletarian states," he followed the modus operandi of traditional diplomacy. By the same token he was committed to the Romanian monarchic traditions, identified with the Hohenzollern dynasty, which he believed were compromised by King Carol II. Nevertheless, for the sake of preserving the territorial integrity and political independence of Greater Romania, he was able to make the necessary adjustments required by the policies and actions of the Axis powers and the Soviet Union related to Central and Eastern Europe.

The memoirs related to Italy, and both its domestic and foreign policies, are most revealing. As his first diplomatic post, where he became chargé d'affaires at the age of twenty-seven, Bossy witnessed the Fascists' assumption of power without realizing, at first, the incompatibility between Mussolini's aims and those of the monarchy. Although uncomfortable with fascist practices, he, like most fellow diplomats, entertained cordial relations with the Italian foreign office still manned by the upper classes of society. Galeazzo Ciano was a cordial interlocutor in those days, in contrast to the arrogant and vulgar partner of Joachim von Ribbentrop in the resolution of the Transylvanian question in Vienna he became some twenty years later. It is true that Bossy became increasingly skeptical of Italian policies in Central and Southeastern Europe during his diplomatic missions in Budapest and Rome, both preceding and following Italy's entry into the war in June 1940. But he considered the Vienna Diktat a painful double cross because he had reason to believe that Italian support of Hungarian revisionism would be limited to resolution of minority questions not involving changes in the territorial status of Transylvania.

Indeed, during his mission to Hungary, Bossy, while cognizant of Hungary's determination to seek revision of the Treaty of Trianon, chiefly but not only with respect to Transylvania, sought to find a diplomatic solution to all, except territorial, questions affecting the Hungarian minority in Romania. However, as in the case of his original mission to Italy, he underestimated the virulence and tenacity of the revisionists because of the conciliatory and civilized attitudes of the aristocratically dominated foreign office and, above all, of Regent Nicholas Horthy. But once more civility only masked the ever present goal of nullifying the Treaty of Trianon at a propitious moment.

Whatever hopes Bossy may have entertained in 1936 became illusory in 1940. In the course of protracted discussions and negotiations with Hungarian officials, it became more and more evident that equivocal commitments made by the Hungarian side were strictly opportunistic and that after the Anschluss, and certainly after Munich, Budapest as a partner of the Axis was determined to secure as much territory as possible at the expense of its neighbors. Bossy's memoirs are an indispensable source of information on the gradual shifting of Hungary's reliance on Italy toward dependency on German support for the realization of its revisionist goals. They also shed much light on the gradual decline of Italian influence, and the corollary corresponding German aim of domination of Southeastern Europe by Hitler.

The realities of the relationship between Hitler and Mussolini with respect to the future of Central and Eastern Europe were readily grasped by Raoul Bossy upon his return to Rome as Romania's envoy to Italy in late 1939. The Nazi-Soviet pact of August 1939, the ensuing partition of Poland between Germany and the Soviet Union, and the Soviet annexation of Bessarabia and northern Bukovina persuaded the Hungarian government to raise the ante of its demands. Whatever reluctance to satisfy Hungary's revisionist goals Germany may have shown previously was to be set aside in deference to Hitler's war aims. Germany's dependence on Romanian oil for its war with Britain, the fragility of the *mariage de convenance* with the Soviet Union, the need, at least temporarily, to support Mussolini's belated entry into the war, all led to the extension of German control over Eastern Europe. The greatest beneficiary of the German strategy was Hungary; the greatest loser in 1940 was Romania.

The dismemberment of Greater Romania, completed with the cession of southern Dobrudja to Bulgaria, was shattering for Raoul Bossy. The ensuing forced abdication of King Carol in favor of his son Michael, who became nominal ruler of the National Legionary Romanian state headed by Field Marshal Ion Antonescu, affected the scope of Romanian diplomacy particularly after Romania joined Nazi Germany in the war against the Soviet Union in June 1941. Bossy, who had been relegated by the Iron Guard to the post of envoy to Switzerland for a few months in late 1940 and early 1941, was brought back by Antonescu to assume reluctantly the same post in Berlin in March 1941. Under the then prevailing international situation, his primary concern turned to the future of Romania.

Bossy was fully aware of the obstacles he faced as he found himself truly between a rock and a hard place. He was unable to secure German support from preventing Hungarian violations of the terms of the Vienna Diktat by what, in contemporary parlance, would be known as "ethnic cleansing" in Transylvania. After the start of the Russian campaign he was alarmed by Hitler's plan to compensate Romania, in the event of a German victory, for the loss of northern Transylvania by territorial adjustments in the east at the expense of a defeated Soviet Union. He was also skeptical about the wisdom of Field Marshal Antonescu's decision to pursue the war against Russia after the recovery of Bessarabia. And even after he became convinced that Germany would lose the war, he had few illusions about Romania's future after Germany's defeat on the Russian front.

Although persevering steadfastly in what had become a hopeless diplomatic mission, Raoul Bossy, while fully aware of Romania's unenviable international position and uncertain future, did not envisage the total abandonment of Romania by the Western allies or the brutality of the Communist takeover at the end of the war. Surely he knew that the position of the Romanian monarchy had been weakened by Carol and, after his abdication, by the advent of the Antonescu-Legionary regime. King Michael was young, inexperienced and, de facto, a figurehead. But the royal entourage was more decent than that of King Carol's camarilla. Granted, Antonescu was a military dictator and the rank and file of the Legionnaries was by and large a brutal, unruly, and uncouth mob. Yet Antonescu destroyed the Iron Guard in early 1941 and ruled as best he could in those exceptional times. Bossy's idols King Ferdinand and Ion I.C. Brătianu were men of their times. King Michael, unlike his father, was a worthy successor to the dynastic values and spirit of his grandfather, and Dinu Brătianu, of wartime Romania, was a worthy successor to Ionel Brătianu. Moreover, Antonescu consulted with many old-time diplomats and distinguished specialists in matters of national interest and even condoned, if not encouraged, unofficial negotiations with the United States and Great Britain for an honorable exit from the war in late 1943.

In fact, Raoul Bossy, in his unofficial capacity as Romania's representative to the International Red Cross Committee in Switzerland, negotiated possible terms for Romania's exiting the war with Allen Dulles—then OSS representative in Switzerland—albeit unsuccessfully. Antonescu, in extremis, would have agreed to "unconditional surrender" as demanded by the United States had it not been for the American and British insistence that the Soviet Union should be an integral member of the victorious alliance.

The rest is history! The entrance of Russian troops into Romania, the overthrow of Antonescu after the so-called royal coup of August 23, 1944, and then Romania's joining the Allies in the war against Germany in no way forestalled the ultimate Communist takeover. Raoul Bossy resisted all entreaties by all governments that antedated the forced abdication of King Michael and the formal establishment of the Romanian People's Republic in 1947. From his vantage point in Switzerland Bossy was hoping against hope that American pressure on the Soviet Union would at least permit limited participation of non-communists in the governance of Romania. By 1946, however, when he refused the last request to return to Romania to assume a governmental position, he fully realized the hopelessness of the situation. This time, however, he had few illusions about Romania's future.

Although actively engaged in the American-initiated "Crusade for Freedom" aimed at Eastern Europe's liberation from communism, his participation in the activities of the Romanian National Committee, the Assembly of European Captive Nations, the Voice of America, and Radio Free Europe was limited because of his reluctance to become engaged in émigré politics and by his shying away from the uncompromising nationalism and anti-communism manifested by most of the political emigration. In time, his participation in the "Crusade" became restricted to political commentaries, lectures, and writings on contemporary and historic developments in Eastern Europe and, of course, Romania.

In 1965 Raoul Bossy returned to Europe from the United States, partly because of his appointment as commentator in the Paris studio of Radio Free Europe but also because of his seeking "whatever whiff of pre–World War I atmosphere."

Raoul Bossy died in 1975. As a distinguished and dignified diplomatic representative of his nation during long chaotic years of drastically changing values, philosophies, and governmental structures, he had devoted his life to preserving and promoting Romania's independence and traditional cultural and spiritual values. He died as he had lived, an *homme du monde* albeit *d'un monde passé.*

Stephen Fischer-Galati

Preface

Throughout his active life my father kept a diary, which he used as a basis for writing his memoirs, covering the period from 1918 to 1940 (until the end of his mission to Rome). These memoirs were published in Romania in 1993 by the publishing house Humanitas in two volumes (340 and 327 pages, respectively, with an introductory study by Stelian Neagoe), under the title *Amintiri din viaţa diplomatică* (Recollections from a Diplomatic Life).

In the late 1960s, again with his diary as a guide, my father drafted two monographs in French, with an eye to possible publication in French historical journals. One of them dealt with his mission to Rome, the other with his assignment to Berlin. These monographs, which were never printed, were translated into English by my brother Michel-André, professor of comparative literature and French studies at Brown University.

The Hoover Institution had endeavored in the early 1990s to have my father's memoirs and diaries edited and translated into English. However, owing to various mishaps, the work had fallen into abeyance by 1998, when I undertook to revive the project and bring it to completion. The timing was propitious for me, since I had just finished a three-year overseas assignment as economic adviser to the Central Bank of Madagascar, after retiring from the Federal Reserve Bank of New York.

In preparing these volumes I first translated the memoirs up to the Rome mission, but in a somewhat shortened version. (In order to keep the translated text lucid and flowing for the reader, such excisions are not indicated.) Following that, I included my brother's translations for the Rome and Berlin missions, which contain my father's most analytical overview of these assignments. These I then rounded off with sections from the memoirs (e.g., the Vienna arbitrage in the case of Rome) or from the unpublished diaries (e.g., the mission to Copenhagen in the case of Berlin). Finally, I incorporated selected entries from the diaries, in order to fashion the chapters "Berne," "The End of a Career," and, in summarized fashion, "Exile."

As for the Romanian text of the diaries, the publishing house Editura Enciclopedică, in Bucharest, published in 2001 the final portions (from late 1940 to their end in mid-1969, but with many deletions for the later years) under the title *Jurnal* (Diary). That volume includes a foreword by Florin Constantiniu.

✧ ✧ ✧

I have retained the geographical names that were used by my father and that were common usage at that time, rather than substituting more modern names: Jassy rather than Iaşi; Constantinople rather than Istanbul; Helsingfors rather than Helsinki; St. Petersburg, Petrograd, or Leningrad, as the case may be.

Until World War II, heads of diplomatic missions were titled either Ambassador Plenipotentiary and Envoy Extraordinary or Minister Plenipotentiary and Envoy Extraordinary—Ambassador and Minister, for short. Ambassadors (representing heads of state) were exchanged only among the great powers; the smaller powers were restricted to the use of ministers (representing governments). Since the title of minister can lead to confusion (minister plenipotentiary or government minister?), I decided to use the title "envoy" for diplomatic corps ministers.

✧ ✧ ✧

My brother and I would like to thank our wives, Kathleen and Sanda, for their patience and support while we were immersed in the task of translation. I am also especially indebted to Sanda for her many helpful suggestions as she ploughed twice through the entire manuscript. At the Hoover Institution Press, my thanks go particularly to Shirley Taylor, editor, who beautifully succeeded in making the manuscript more readable, and to Ann Wood, senior editor, for her highly appreciated advice on many matters.

New York, N.Y. George H. Bossy
November 2001

1

First Steps in Diplomacy (1918–1921)

I was led to a diplomatic career more by fate, it would seem, than by will. My parents told me that on my first birthday, following an old Romanian custom, they placed in front of me a silver tray with items representing various occupations, the idea being that the first object I picked up would foretell the activity to which I would devote my life. On the tray were a handful of wheat grains, representing agriculture, a writer's pen, a few gold coins for finance, a book for the legal profession, and, among others, a miniature sword meant to represent the harmless weapon attached to the diplomatic uniform. The story is that I immediately grabbed the sword—no doubt the shiniest. Or perhaps it was an atavistic impulse inherited from my forefather Neculai Bossy, whom Prince Ioniţă Sturdza, after ascending to the throne of Moldavia, appointed in 1822 "Kapukehaia to Tsarigrad," or, as one would have said in Western Europe, Envoy of Moldavia to Constantinople, elevating him simultaneously to the rank of Aga-Paè. These envoys of our rulers had diplomatic status since the Treaty of Kutchuk-Kainardji (1774), and when my ancestor left Constantinople in 1828, at the end of Ioniţă Sturdza's reign, he was presented by the Porte with various gifts, among which was a mother-of-pearl chess set that has remained in the family to this day. Nevertheless, I am not prepared to affirm that it is Aga Neculai's blood in my veins that made me choose, at the age of one, the diplomatic sword, or, later, to enter by marriage into a family that has given the country many outstanding diplomats.

STUDENT IN PARIS

What seems more significant, however, is that on my own and without giving much thought to a future profession, I chose International Law as my major at the Paris Law School and, having been accepted at the School of Political Sciences (the famous "Sciences-Po" on the rue Saint-Guillaume, headed at that time by Eugène d'Eichtal), I chose the diplomatic section so as to attend the International Law course of the great jurist Louis Renault and the Diplomatic History courses of Emile Bourgeois and Christian Scheffer, true feasts for the mind of a youth.

I have, naturally, kept indelible memories of that period of studies in Paris. Nothing can be more favorable to the development of the mind and soul in the years of intellectual shaping than the incomparable atmosphere of the City of Light. The splendid setting, with which I was acquainted from my most tender childhood, since my parents took us each year to Paris, where my father had spent his own childhood and adolescence; the incomparable sources of culture, among which plays, concerts, and conferences must be put on a par with museums and historic monuments, thus intertwining past and present; the electricity in the air that seems to stir even the most sluggish beings, sharpening their intelligence and wit: together, all these elements formed a most propitious stimulus, the most fruitful of goads for one fortunate enough to begin blossoming out on the banks of the Seine. In the mornings, I took the medieval rue St. Jacques to get to the Law School, personified for us, first-year students (*bizuts*), by the famous usher (*tangente*) nicknamed "Canrobert" because of his likeness to the glorious field marshal. "Canrobert" stood guard at the entrance of our large lecture hall, in tail-coat and with a gilded chain reminiscent of the Golden Fleece collar around his neck. In the afternoons, I followed the "Boul' Mich" and the boulevard St. Germain to reach the "Sciences Po," at that time a veritable club and the training ground of future French diplomats and political figures. I met there Maurice Petsche, future finance minister; Jacques Truelle, future Envoy of France to Bucharest; Pierre de Polignac, future Prince of Monaco; Bonichon de Castellane (son of the famous Marquis Boni de Castellane), who died young; and so many others.

Examinations at the Law School were very solemn and intimidating, being taken in front of three professors in red robes bordered with ermine, with red caps on their heads, seated around the "operating table." At the School of Political Sciences, by contrast, exams were less frightening, more informal, more *en famille*. I still remember, as if it had happened yesterday, my Comparative Constitutional Law examination by the witty and charming Charles Benoist, a fiery royalist and deputy of the Fifth arrondissement of Paris (the Latin Quarter). He was questioning me on the constitution of the Austro-Hungarian monarchy. At that time the problem of the Banat was being discussed in chancelleries, and since he knew I was Romanian, he asked in order to tease me: "What can you tell me, Mr. First Candidate, about the Banat? Admit that you had never heard of it before Iorga invented it!" His eyes twinkled mischievously while, with youthful enthusiasm and patriotic eloquence, I retraced the Banat's history and refuted with ethnic and economic arguments the Serbian thesis. "Yes, yes, I know all that," Professor Benoist interrupted me, "what I was saying was only to rile you."

During World War I, it was, of course, very difficult to reach France, since it was necessary to cross the borders of two countries at war with each other: Austro-Hungary and France.[1] To make things easier for me, my father got the Ministry of Foreign Affairs to entrust me with the diplomatic pouches for our legations in Vienna, Berne, and Paris. I was thus provided with various and impressive credentials as Romanian diplomatic courier and given laissez-passers of the respective countries, none of which mentioned my somewhat more modest standing as a student at the University of Paris. In 1915 I crossed the "front line" without a hitch, returning to Paris after delivering the pouches to our envoys in the three capitals and being warmly received by them. These were my first contacts with my future bosses: Edgar Mavrocordat, Romanian envoy to Vienna and my father's schoolmate in Jassy and Strasbourg; Mihail M. Păcleanu, envoy to Berne; and Alexander Em. Lahovary, envoy to Paris (whose mother was my mother's godmother and who was going to be my first chief abroad).

JOINING THE DIPLOMATIC SERVICE

My career in diplomacy really began as the result of an unanticipated event. Times were bleak in January 1918, under General Averescu's administration in Jassy.[2] The armistice concluded with the enemy powers (Austro-Hungary, Germany, Turkey, and Bulgaria), to which Romania had been compelled to agree after the Russian desertion of Brest-Litovsk,

---

[1]Romania was neutral until August 1916.

[2]After some initial successes, the Romanian army was forced to retreat from the western part of the country, including Bucharest, and the government withdrew to Jassy.

seemed to be leading us to the humiliating and grievous peace of Buftea. Like all young men of my age, I was then quite demoralized and disoriented: there no longer was war—and yet there was—so I could not return to Paris, the Romanian borders being closed and the country split in two by the armistice line. Our house in Bucharest was occupied by German officers, and our estates in Wallachia were under forced administration (*Zwangsverwaltung*). Suddenly, an advertisement appeared in the press that the Ministry of Foreign Affairs, which had been moved to the Copou district of Jassy, would hold within a few days a competitive examination to select diplomatic attachés. My mother, worried about my predicament, urged me to enter the competition. Though I resisted the idea, pleading too little time to prepare, my mother continued to insist, and the secretary-general of the Ministry—through my father—also urged me to go ahead. And so, prodded from all sides, I took the exam. In order not to hurt any feelings, the examination board accepted us all outright, without ranking, but it did place my name at the head of the list. On February 16, 1918, I thus entered the Romanian diplomatic corps as attaché.

I was at once assigned to the Political Department, as I had hoped. But I found out in very short order that, in fact, the department was more of a legal office, rather than the "laboratory of our foreign policy," whose mysteries were known only to the minister's office and to the coding section. I had the feared Nicolae Docan as director, a historian and jurist of great merit (the codification of our maritime legislation was his work), member of the Romanian Academy, but incredibly cantankerous. For some reason—I'm not quite sure why—he instilled a holy terror in the Ministry's staff, so I was surprised to find him pleasant and courteous in his relations with me. He visibly liked me and valued my work, approbations that, as a rule, he did not willingly bestow. He even wanted to make me "chief" of all the other attachés who had entered the Ministry along with me and to have me assign them work as I saw fit. I had to point out the impossibility of such an arrangement, which would have made me the most unpopular person among my peers and which could not even be justified by, say, a longer experience. I shall always keep a grateful memory of Docan for what I learned from him (and how few are the chiefs in one's career from whom one can learn something!), namely, the juridical bases of our profession and the great importance of style in writing: conciseness, clarity, elimination of unnecessary information, avoidance of neologisms and of florid sentences.

After the government of Alexander Marghiloman took the helm of our poor divided country and after the conclusion of the grievous peace treaty of Buftea, in the spring of 1918, our Ministry decided to open a "branch" in Bucharest to establish a contact between the government in Jassy and the command of the occupation armies in Wallachia. The seat of what could have been called "the Romanian Legation in Bucharest" was right in front of the Sturdza Palace, where the offices of the Ministry of Foreign Affairs had been transformed into a Turkish military hospital. From our windows, we could see the Turkish flag that flew on the roof of the multicolored palace. The head of the chancellery was Ion P. Carp and the assistant head N.D. Germani. They had been appointed because of their fluency in German and the many years spent at our legation in Vienna, not to mention the high regard in which the Germans and Austrians held Petre P. Carp, the father of our counselor. I had also been included in the "Bucharest team" by Foreign Minister C.C. Arion, an old friend of the family (he had been married to a cousin of my mother and had served as witness at my parents' civil marriage), so that I might help my parents disentangle their affairs. They had succeeded in evicting the German occupants from our house and had settled down again in Bucharest, where they were taking an inventory of all that the "uninvited guests" had taken when they left (silverware, linen, icons, and a superb old surplice of purple brocade that had belonged to my great-grandfather). They were also endeavoring to get rid of the administrator of their property who had been imposed in their absence by the "civilian administration of the occupation armies."

My particular assignment was relations with foreigners. I was thus in frequent communication with Freddy Horstmann, the political chief of the German military headquarters, a career diplomat (afterward envoy to Portugal) whom I was to see very often many years later, when I was envoy to Berlin. At the Austrian headquarters, that position was also held by a career diplomat, Count Demblin, whom I was likewise to meet much later, when I was counselor in Vienna. I also remember the new envoy of Greece, Psychas, and his attractive wife, for whom I had to facilitate the passage to Jassy for the remittal of his credentials. But I shall never forget the heartache I felt when, on my way home, I would see Field Marshal Mackensen, supreme commander of the German occupation army, riding past with his military escort, in a brilliant hussar's uniform, with a skull and crossed bones on his cap (*Totenhussaren*), on his way back from his daily ride on the Şoseaua Kisselef.

There are regiments where the most important person is the quartermaster. At the Ministry of Foreign Affairs, especially in those times of defeat, of general shortages and turmoil, everything turned around

"Mr. Franz," the superintendent, whose full name was Franz Ştefănescu (odd pairing of names!). It was said that he was a Saxon from Transylvania, and no one could remember when he joined the Ministry. He was head of the porters, ruler of the furniture, and the person with the most "precedents" at hand to defend his points of view. At each change of government, he reportedly presented himself to the new foreign minister saying, "Welcome, your excellency, it is a good thing that those others have left!" Of course, "those others" were, by turn, either the Conservatives or the Liberals. It was also said of him that, during the German occupation, he had been "more Franz than Ştefănescu." But these nasty comments were at bottom more akin to jokes, for all diplomats, whether Romanian or foreign, were fond of the perdurable "Mr. Franz," full of dignity in his uniform with two rows of gilded buttons. At any rate, it is to him that we all owe a moment of intense emotion. In November 1918 the end of the war was rapidly approaching. Germany's defeat was as if achieved. The occupation troops were set to evacuate but had not yet left. At one point, looking out of my window, I saw an historic scene and hastened to call my colleagues so that they might witness it too: the Turkish flag was slowly being lowered from the roof of the Sturdza Palace, and in its stead our national banner was being raised. It was like the confirmation of victory and of the reunification of the Romanian people! Shortly thereafter I found out who was the author of this prophetic, yet still daring deed: it was Franz who, without consulting anybody and on his own responsibility, had climbed into the attic of the Sturdza Palace, each and every nook of which he had been familiar with for a few decades, and had proceeded with the patriotic substitution of flags.

From these windows, too, I watched the glorious reentry of our victorious troops into the capital, led by King Ferdinand, with General Berthelot to his right and Queen Marie to his left, all three on horseback. The columns of soldiers marched through the thunderously cheering population, bearing aloft large signs with the names of all the reunited Romanian provinces: Moldavia, Wallachia, Transylvania, Bessarabia, Bukovina, Northern and Southern Dobrudja, Oltenia, the Banat, Crişana, Maramureş. Each one of them was greeted with even louder cheers and also with tears of joy in everyone's eyes.

Months of readjustment followed. The government returned to Bucharest, the Ministry of Foreign Affairs went back to the Sturdza Palace, following a thorough disinfection and reconditioning. After a succession of governments, a new Averescu government came to power.

The new foreign minister, the writer Duiliu Zamfirescu, asked Docan (by now the Ministry's secretary-general) to recommend one of the attachés—other than his own son—to serve as his cabinet chief. Docan, foreseeably, chose me, because I was, in his words, "at the head of the list." My relations with this new boss, a former career diplomat, could not have been more pleasant. And I assume he was not too dissatisfied with the performance of his son's friend and colleague; when shortly thereafter he became president of the Chamber of Deputies, he insisted on my being seconded to serve as his cabinet chief. However, since there was no reason why a diplomat should be needed in Parliament, the Ministry took me back within its ranks.

During Duiliu Zamfirescu's short tenure our group of second-year attachés took the examination for promotion to the rank of third secretary. The written test assigned us the subject "The Eastern Question." Sturdza, Plessia, and I were the only ones to whom the topic had not been discreetly imparted ahead of time, but this was such a "classic" subject that we were all well prepared, and I placed first. A most enjoyable episode marked this "old style" examination. At lunchtime, we the candidates said we needed a few more hours to finish. What could be done? All of us—examiners and examinees—were famished. Duiliu Zamfirescu found the solution: he called Franz and had him order a delicious luncheon from Capşa.[3] A table was set in the examination room, presided over by the old minister C.G. Nanu, the head of the examination board. After coffee, liqueurs, and cigars, we went back to our papers, which we completed in "the communicative warmth of banquets." Yes, "those were the times!"

CHIEF OF TAKE IONESCU'S CABINET

Soon after that the Averescu government was reshuffled, and Take Ionescu[4] came in as minister of foreign affairs. This is not the place to describe the appearance or personality of Take Ionescu, who entered history while still alive, and about whom so much has already been written. He was a friend of my father's ever since they had attended together the University of Paris, and I knew him from my earliest childhood. As a teenager, I often had lunch at his home in Sinaia[5] and was commandeered after the meals to take part in the famous and huge puzzle games

[3]The premier restaurant of Bucharest at that time.

[4]Conservative statesman. Occasionally referred to simply as Take (pronounced TAH-keh).

[5]Mountain resort north of Bucharest.

organized by Bessy, his first wife, British by birth. She was a very intelligent woman and was reputed to have been a beauty in her youth. Thanks to horseback riding, she had kept a slender, youthful figure. I saw her often riding through the forests of the Peleş Castle, followed by a superb collie. She died in 1918 in London after a riding accident on Rotten Row, in Hyde Park.

Take Ionescu took me on as cabinet chief, and I was privileged to spend the entire summer of 1921 in his beautiful English-style villa in Sinaia. What a contrast between his somewhat grandiloquent and superior demeanor in Parliament and his simplicity and amiability in domestic surroundings! There were always guests, some of whom spent entire weeks with him and his wife in their villa, the most steadfast being Grigore and Margareta Ghika, with whom I had been very close for years. In the evenings we played parlor games, and I think I must be one of the few people who ever saw Take Ionescu doing equilibristics: he would place an empty bottle on the nape of his neck and, without holding it, could lie down on the floor and then stand up again, the bottle still balanced on his neck. We would all laugh, and I can still hear Margareta Ghika telling him, "What would Ionel Brătianu[6] say if he saw you now!"

It goes without saying that the conversation of a statesman with so much experience in foreign policy was of invaluable benefit to a beginner in diplomatic matters, and I listened insatiably to Take Ionescu's reminiscences about Bülow, Kiderlen-Wächter, and other influential personalities whom he had befriended. He peppered his conversation with anecdotes that were full of wit, and he related them most amusingly.

I was posted in Rome when Take Ionescu died there, on June 22, 1922, and I was among the last to see him on the eve of his death. He fell ill after eating spoiled oysters in Naples, and in spite of all the care given to him for several weeks in a Roman clinic, the poison that had entered his blood brought his end through a heart attack.

Ionel Brătianu was almost the only politician for whom Take Ionescu expressed respect. He called the others "stupid" and gave rather good imitations of their voices and gestures; but when somebody asked him about Ionel Brătianu, he answered laconically, without hesitation: "Yes, that one is intelligent." (Ionel Brătianu was to give him the satisfaction of being made prime minister, though for only four weeks.)

Take Ionescu gave our foreign policy a new slant, directing it definitively toward an alliance (backed by France) with the neighboring states.

---

[6]Ion I.C. Brătianu, head of the Liberal party and political adversary of Take Ionescu.

Already during the war, while he was in Paris, he developed, along with Masaryk and Pašić, a close understanding with Czechoslovakia and Serbia (which was to become the Kingdom of Serbs, Croats, and Slovenes), and named it the Little Entente, to distinguish it from the Triple Entente between the great powers.

One thing Brătianu could never forgive: in order to seal the alliance with Serbia, Take Ionescu had agreed even before the conclusion of the peace to the principle of a partition of the Banat between our two neighboring countries, even though the Banat in its entirety had been solemnly promised to us in the secret Convention concluded with the Allies in 1916. Ionel Brătianu complained to me more than once of the difficulties he had to face in his fight for the Banat because of Take Ionescu's yielding attitude. For instance, while passing through Belgrade on his way to Paris, Brătianu tried to convince Prince-Regent Alexander (the future King Alexander I) to forgo raising claims on our Banat, so as not to open a gulf between two nations bound by a traditional friendship; the Prince answered: "I do not believe that the Romanian people are unanimously behind you. Look, Mr. Take Ionescu was here and told me that he as well as his party are favorable to a partition of the Banat between your country and mine." Likewise, in Paris, when he explained to Clemenceau and Lloyd George that he could not take the responsibility toward the Romanian people of acquiescing to the dismembering of a Romanian land, they retorted that all he had to do was to pass the hand to Take Ionescu, since the latter was prepared to assume such a responsibility. This was the reason, according to Brătianu, that he did not include Take Ionescu in our delegation to the 1919 Peace Conference, even though Take Ionescu was in Paris at that time.

Take Ionescu was convinced that the Great Powers had long since decided to follow the example of Solomon and to divide the Banat between Romania and Serbia. This being so, it was preferable that the operation be carried out with our assent rather than against our will, since such a sacrifice accepted readily would make possible the conclusion of a lasting and sincere alliance with the Belgrade authorities, on whose friendship we could rely in the so much more serious disputes with our Hungarian and Bulgarian neighbors. My chief in Rome, Alexander Em. Lahovary, told me later that, according to his information, Take Ionescu would have secured far more favorable terms through direct negotiations with Belgrade than those that were imposed in absentia by the Great Powers after Brătianu's withdrawal from the Peace Conference.

But Brătianu felt that he had served the country well because he had "preserved the future"; in support of his view he invoked his father's precedent at the Congress of Berlin in 1878. Just like him, his father had felt duty-bound to oppose and protest the seizure of Bessarabia,[7] even though a border improvement in Dobrudja was held out "if he proved tractable"; by so doing, he had preserved our right to claim Bessarabia in 1918. Be that as it may, we must let history and future generations settle this issue, which separated two patriots equally convinced that they were serving their country, each one the way his mind and conscience dictated.

In 1920 and 1921, through the alliances concluded between Romania, Czechoslovakia, and Yugoslavia, the Little Entente was set up on the lines envisioned during the war by Take Ionescu, Masaryk, and Pašić. Support was thus acquired for the preservation of the peace and international order established by the peace treaties signed in the outskirts of Paris. What was still needed was to raise a peace bulwark in the East to check Russian expansion. Take Ionescu went to Warsaw, and in 1921 the first alliance treaty was signed with Poland.

This treaty was of course the occasion for the exchange of official visits. Later in 1921, Poland's minister of foreign affairs, Prince Eustace Sapieha, came to Bucharest with his wife to return Take Ionescu's visit to Warsaw. The three days the Sapiehas spent in our country were filled with luncheons, dinners, and brilliant receptions, all of which I remember with pleasure. The Polish envoy to Bucharest, Count Alexander Skrzynski, future minister of foreign affairs and prime minister, knew how to temper the official character of the program by including social gatherings. Sapieha was a historian, and the Romanian Academy elected him honorary member at a solemn session I attended. In an address evoking the long-standing relations between Romania and Poland, Nicolae Iorga strove to prove Prince Sapieha's descent from Stephen the Great (I believe through the Radziwill family) and hailed him as a true scion of the great Moldavian ruler. Catching the ball on the rebound, the Polish foreign minister stood up—he was very handsome and stately—and in impeccable French (which contrasted with Iorga's homespun accent) improvised a remarkable reply in which he inserted with panache the sentence, "I am proud of the blood of your great hero that flows in my veins." That evening, at a dinner party at Skrzynski's, I approached Princess Sapieha while coffee was being served and told her how much I

[7] By the Russians.

had admired her husband's words a few hours earlier at the Romanian Academy. I added that I had been particularly moved to see that Prince Sapieha was aware of and valued the fact that he was a descendant of Stephen the Great. "Frankly," the graceful princess admitted, "he hadn't the slightest idea, but now that he knows, he is mightily proud of it."

Another important area of our foreign policy in which Take Ionescu took a new—and intransigent—stance was that of our relations with Soviet Russia. The Vaida-Voevod government was seeking a way to respond to the proposal broadcast by Chicherin, the Soviet commissar for foreign affairs, aiming at a rapprochement between the two countries. Following the civil war and the economic crisis in Russia, the government in Moscow was eager to reestablish relations with the civilized world, and in view of the Great Powers' hostility, it would have been satisfied to be recognized by a smaller country such as ours. The Romanian government therefore considered it appropriate to find out whether, in these circumstances, it would be possible to obtain from the Soviets the recognition of the reattachment of Bessarabia to the Old Kingdom. An emissary, Dimitrie Ciotori, was sent to Copenhagen to make contact with an unofficial representative of Moscow who in future years was to play a prominent role: Maxim Litvinov. Litvinov told our emissary on February 19, 1920, on the basis of instructions received from the Kremlin, that "within the framework of the principle of autodetermination and on the occasion of a formal conference, it will be possible to recognize the reattachment of Bessarabia."

When the Averescu government came to power, it remained on the course taken by Vaida-Voevod and accepted the idea of unofficial Romano-Soviet negotiations meant to prepare such a conference. A Romanian minister plenipotentiary, George Filality, was consequently sent to Vienna in August 1921 to begin preliminary talks with a Soviet delegation, headed by Karahan. The talks lingered through October, when, as was to be expected, the Russians raised the question of Bessarabia and we that of the Romanian Treasure deposited in Moscow. In 1917, in anticipation of a new German offensive that could have led to the occupation of Moldavia, the government in Jassy had decided to evacuate the State Treasure and the deposits with the National Bank to neighboring, and then allied, Russia. The Imperial Russian government undertook to safeguard these national assets of Romania at the Kremlin and to return them at the end of the hostilities. In the meantime, however, revolution had broken out in Russia, and the Bolsheviks who had become masters over that huge empire declared that they did not feel bound by any of the obligations undertaken by the tsarist regime. They therefore refused to return the Romanian Treasure—which included the country's gold reserves, the famous *Cloşca cu Pui*[8], Queen Marie's jewelry, and many private deposits. Even my mother, following the advice of many, had placed all her jewelry in a safe at the Jassy branch of the National Bank, through fear of the Russian soldiers' plundering. Overnight, and without consulting the depositors, all these assets took off for Russia, never to come back. This material loss was of course overshadowed by joy at the attainment of the national dream, the reunification of all the Romanian provinces. But it was nevertheless appropriate for the issue to be raised in Romano-Russian negotiations, the more so since, in Copenhagen, Litvinov had promised our emissary that the State Treasure would be restored to us.

During the above-mentioned Filality-Karahan talks, the head of the Soviet delegation requested to have a private meeting with our representative, at which he showed himself particularly conciliatory, no doubt because of the critical situation of the Soviet army pursued by Wrangel's troops. He admitted to Filality that for the Soviets, Bessarabia was, frankly speaking, just a bargaining chip: they were willing to give up their claim to it if the Romanian government desisted from making financial claims—that is, if it gave up the State Treasure. To satisfy public opinion in the two countries, there would be a neutrality treaty, which, in exchange for Bessarabia, would give the Soviets the assurance that Romania would not aid Wrangel, and an agreement declaring that the Romanian financial claims were offset by the value of Russian military equipment left in Romania after the armistice of Brest-Litovsk. Karahan's reasoning can be summed up as follows: "Why are we quarreling? Let's be realistic. You have Bessarabia, which we are in no position to take back. We have the Romanian Treasure, which you cannot recover for the good reason that it no longer exists; it was plundered in the first days of the revolution. If by chance there remain a few of your cases in the Kremlin, we promise to give them back to you, but there won't be many. Why don't we recognize this reality by an exchange of signatures?" Filality recorded this conversation in a note he sent to Bucharest, which I read. Averescu penned an approving comment, authorizing Filality, as I recall, to pursue the talks on the lines indicated

[8]The Hen with Chicks is the collective name given, from one of its components, to a trove of gold objects and jewelry unearthed in 1837 and believed to have been part of the treasure of the fourth-century Visigoth king Athanaric.

by Karahan. Of course, if we could have secured a Russian recognition of the reattachment of Bessarabia in exchange for a Treasure that no longer existed, the deal would not have been a bad one. To be sure, the Bolsheviks would not have kept their word, and as soon as the danger of a Wrangel offensive had passed they would have resumed their claim on our land. But since Romania had then neither the intention nor the possibility of helping Wrangel, the loss would not have been great (the shadow of a missing State Treasure!). Russian recognition of the reattachment of Bessarabia, even if subsequently withdrawn, would have been an important exhibit in this century-old suit. This is also how General Averescu saw things.

At that point, however, Take Ionescu took over as minister of foreign affairs. He was returning from a trip to Western Europe. He had been told in Paris that neither France nor Great Britain would admit that Romania—for whom they had done so much—might break ranks with them by extending recognition to the new regime in Russia. For Romania to tie itself to the Bolsheviks by a neutrality pact would contravene the obligations undertaken through both the Covenant of the League of Nations and our alliance treaty with Poland. Moreover, the Allied Great Powers—France, Great Britain, Italy, and Japan—had recognized our sovereignty over Bessarabia by signing the Treaty of Paris on October 28, 1920. We were therefore morally committed toward the Western powers precisely in this area of relations with Russia. And it should be remembered that London, and Paris too, were supporting Wrangel both morally and materially. Because of these obstacles, and also because of Take Ionescu's deep aversion to the Asiatic totalitarianism that had supplanted the imperial government, the new minister of foreign affairs insisted that Karahan's suggestions be rejected. "An understanding with the Soviets," Take Ionescu pointed out, "would jeopardize our position in relation to the future Russian government, while the proposed agreement would be tantamount to an alliance, which would be beneath Romania's dignity." General Averescu, on the other hand, was of the opinion that, however fragile and short-lived, a Russian recognition of the reattachment of Bessarabia could be of eventual use. The advice of Ion I.C. Brătianu was sought on this divergence of views, and he sided with Take Ionescu, since the acceptance of Karahan's proposal would have threatened to weaken our ties of alliance with France and Poland. Filality was therefore instructed to turn down Karahan's suggestion.

Of our Treasure held at the Kremlin, only a few cases with old documents and a platinum-meter from the National Bank were returned, and that much later, in the time of Titulescu's government. We were, however, given the mortal remains of the Moldavian ruler Dimitrie Cantemir, exhumed from a church in Moscow (let's hope that they are truly his!), which found their last resting place where it behooved: in the Trei Ierarhi church of his capital, Jassy. As for France and Britain, they later abandoned Wrangel's cause and, in 1927, recognized the Soviet Union—forgetting of course to safeguard Romania's interests, that Romania which they had prevented from coming to an agreement directly with Moscow.

ALLIANCES AND ROYAL WEDDINGS

The year 1921 turned out to be a very important one, from both a diplomatic and a dynastic point of view.

On March 26, as mentioned above, Take Ionescu concluded our first treaty of alliance, with Poland, followed that same spring by similar treaties with Czechoslovakia and Yugoslavia. Romania could thus rely on an alliance with Poland for defense against a possible Russian aggression and on the system of bilateral agreements with Czechoslovakia and Yugoslavia, called the Little Entente, for protection against Hungarian revisionism. Take Ionescu did not succeed in blending the two alliance systems into a single one. On the one hand, the government in Warsaw, recalling Poland's historical ties with Hungary, did not want to be drawn into disputes with that country, nor did it wish to become allied to Czechoslovakia, with which it was at odds over the Teschen territory; on the other, the governments in Prague and Belgrade had Pan-Slavic reminiscences that made them hesitate at an alliance that might oppose them to Russia.

With Greece, ties were being strengthened not by treaties of alliance but by matrimonial alliances. On February 27, 1921, Princess Elizabeth of Romania was married to Crown Prince George of Greece (the future King George II), and on March 10 Prince Carol married Princess Helen of Greece, the daughter of King Constantine and Queen Sophie.

I was present at the first of these weddings, which was celebrated in Bucharest, and I remember the gala that followed at the Royal Palace. The bridegroom's family was represented by Prince Nicholas of Greece, the king's brother, a man of distinguished appearance and great culture. He had an extensive knowledge of archaeology, for which the Romanian Academy elected him honorary member at a solemn session I attended. The Greek prince was accompanied by his wife, Princess Helen, born grand duchess of Russia, a woman of rare distinction and beauty, traits inherited by her daughters: Princess Olga of Yugoslavia, Countess Elizabeth of Törring, and Duchess Marina of Kent.

The ball at the Royal Palace reminds me of two amusing occurrences, both featuring the eccentric Dutch envoy Dr. Moeller van Werendyke, one of the most entertaining characters in international diplomacy at that time. He was a Boer, a native of Transvaal, the owner of many oil wells, and had rendered signal services to the Netherlands during World War I. Queen Wilhelmina could therefore not refuse his request to be named minister plenipotentiary. And since he was an oil magnate, it seemed logical to appoint him to an oil-rich country, namely, the unfortunate Romania. Many anecdotes made the rounds about this man—plump, bearded, fierce-looking, and, Lord bless him, completely ridiculous. His presence at the head of the legation of the Netherlands was a cruel torment for his colleagues, since no diplomatic corps is more reserved, more punctilious, more full of dignity and elegance than the Dutch one. At the Royal Ball, we were all in diplomatic uniforms. Moeller van Werendyke, in accordance with Dutch usage, was wearing white breeches with a gold stripe and a gold-embroidered coat. At one point, clearly weary of the proceedings, he approached my friend Alexandrina Kretzulescu and said: "It's terribly boring here. Let's go to a nightclub where we could at least have some fun." Alexandrina quite properly replied, "You know, in our country girls don't usually go out alone in the evenings with gentlemen." Moeller van Werendyke's reply became a classic in diplomatic annals: "I would have you know, young lady, that when I wear these white breeches, my name is Wilhelmina."

Moeller van Werendyke then tackled me: "I say, old boy, one gets bored to death here. Come with me to the bar of the Athénée Palace; we'll meet friends and have drinks together." I told him I could not leave before the sovereigns did, and then I had some protocol duties to perform for the Ministry of Foreign Affairs, but that done, I would be delighted to accept his kind invitation. I told my parents not to wait for me and not to send the car back since I expected to be able to use the Dutch legation's vehicle. When I was at last able to leave, I beckoned to my Dutchman and we went down the staircase. To my astonishment, he had no car waiting. Instead, he took me by the arm and made me march with him along the Calea Victoriei, both of us in diplomatic uniforms and he in his famous white breeches. It must have been quite a sight for the passers-by. In front of the Athénée Palace I met a friend who was getting into his car, and I asked him to give me a lift home. I made my excuses to Moeller van Werendyke, pleading weariness, and thus escaped the risk of having to go, possibly on foot, all the way home in full diplomatic uniform in the middle of the night. The poor Moeller van Werendyke was later transferred to Prague, where he was said to travel by streetcar but to refuse to pay the fare under the pretext that he was the representative of Queen Wilhelmina!

Prince Carol's wedding with the enchanting Princess Helen of Greece took place in Athens, but I do remember their official arrival in Bucharest. The royal procession followed the Calea Victoriei from the railway station to the Metropolitan Church. The city's inhabitants lining the route were won over by the loveliness of the shy young princess in the first carriage—their future queen. Next to her sat Carol, sullen and withdrawn, ill at ease facing all those people who, no doubt, were astonished at how quickly he had forgotten his first reckless marriage and the son he had fathered.[9] In the second carriage were King Ferdinand and Queen Marie, beaming and smiling to the crowd. One could read on their faces their joy at having successfully escaped from the predicament in which their son's matrimonial adventure in Odessa had placed them. Their joy, however, was not going to last for long.

On October 25, 1921, Prince Michael was born. His name was seen as a symbol of the unification of the nation[10] and was therefore particularly dear to all Romanians; it seemed to bestow on the young royal scion an aura of glory and felicity. But a cruel fate decreed that Michael I would instead twice lose his throne: first snatched from him by his own father, and then a second time by the mortal enemy of the country, communism. But in due course, Divine Providence will undoubtedly seat him once more on the Throne of Michael the Brave and of Ferdinand I.

---

[9]For details, see "Carol's Renouncement of the Throne," pp. 55–59.

[10]He was named after Michael the Brave, the Romanian national hero who, in the early 1600s, briefly united under his rule Wallachia, Moldavia, and Transylvania.

2

Rome (1921–1923)

On November 15, 1921, I was appointed second secretary of our legation in Rome. It was with understandable excitement and eagerness that the apprentice in diplomacy that I was received his first posting abroad. And what a dream to begin one's career in Italy! As a child, I had traveled with my parents in this wonderful country, and I had been brought up in the celebration of Florence and Rome. My first stop, Venice, seemed to open the doors to an enchanted kingdom. I broke with the family tradition and, instead of the Bauer-Grünwald Hotel, I stayed at the Danieli to spend a few hours at least in the remembrance of Musset and George Sand. I wished that I could spend days seeking out the treasures of "proud Venice," and it took all my sense of duty to tear myself from the Queen of the Adriatic and continue on to the Eternal City, even though I knew what delights were also awaiting me there.

THE ROMANIAN LEGATION IN ROME

I had left Bucharest in the midst of winter: icy north wind, snow, furs, hoods, fur hats. In Rome, I was met by spring: blue sky, sun, flowers everywhere, and that subdued joy of the Romans, that *dolcezza* that floats in the warm air and seems to be a blending of youthful enchantment and nostalgia for bygone times. And then, the matchless wonder of daily living and moving among the vestiges of three successive civilizations.

The legation was located on the second floor of the Palazzo Santa Croce on Piazza Cairoli, at equal distances from the Tiber and the Palazzo Farnese, a few steps from the Fontana delle Tartarughe, the most enchanting of Roman fountains, and from the Sant'Andrea dela Valle church (the scene of act 2 of *La Traviata*). The route from my hotel on the Via Veneto to the legation took me past the Pantheon, that ancient temple untouched by the ages, the medieval Palazzo Venezia, and the charming Fontana del Tritone, the baroque jewel by Bernini. The sixteenth-century Palazzo Santa Croce, containing small frescoes by Claude Lorrain above the doors, inside had been built by Cardinal Santa Croce and after his death had passed from hand to hand down to the present owners, the Counts Pasolini. One of the brothers was married to a Borghese, the other to an Altieri, both women equally attractive; they lived on the upper floors and often came down to attend receptions at our legation. In former times, the notorious Countess Mirafiore, the mistress of King Victor Emmanuel II, had lived in the palace. After her death, her furniture was sold at one of those renowned Roman *vendite*. A nice Chinese lacquer cabinet of hers came into my parents' possession, and I inherited it.

The legation was headed by Alexander Em. Lahovary, the dean of the Romanian diplomatic corps. He had been brought up in Paris, where he attended the Lycée Condorcet along with future statesmen such as Raymond Poincaré, and earned a doctorate in law cum laude. Lahovary entered the diplomatic service at a very young age and always kept away from the swirl of party politics, to the point of refusing the position of minister of foreign affairs offered to him by Take Ionescu. He was an exceptionally cultivated person, a man of great distinction, endowed with a penetrating intelligence and a renowned tactfulness. His career was as brilliant as it was deserved: Envoy to Rome in 1893 (at the age of thirty-eight), then to Constantinople (where he obtained from the sultan the historic *iradé* in favor of the Aromâni,[1] to Vienna, to Paris (where he concluded in 1916 the alliance with France), and a second time to Rome, where he ended, at an advanced age, his long diplomatic career.

Alexander Lahovary was the ideal chief for a young diplomat, and I was grateful for the opportunity to be trained by him. He always showed me kindness and courtesy, and even invited me to stay for some time in his apartment at the legation when his family was away. What interesting and instructive conversations I had at that time with my chief, whose only collaborator I was during most of my stay in Rome! Whether we

[1]Also known as Macedo-Romanians, the Aromâni speak a Romanian dialect and are spread throughout the Balkans, where they mainly used to be shepherds practicing transhumance.

had lunch together at the Circollo della Caccia, the club of the diplomats accredited to the Quirinal, or whether we made an excursion by car in the environs of Rome, I had the opportunity to learn much from a man with such varied experience. He had attended, in 1883, the coronation of Tsar Alexander III, he had known Abdul-Hamid II and Emperor Franz Joseph, and he had negotiated with Aristide Briand the treaty that was to lead to the war for Romania's unification.

In those days, political reports of chiefs of mission to the Ministry of Foreign Affairs, as well as coded telegrams, were all written in French. It was the general practice in most European chancelleries, including those of prewar Austria and Russia, explainable by the fact that it is more accurate to record a diplomatic conversation in the French language in which it had been held, rather than translating it (*traduttore, traditore*) into a national language. Lahovary's reports were models of style, and the impeccable French he used proved his deep knowledge of all the subtleties and nuances of that admirable instrument for conveying thought.

A central, picturesque, and long-serving member of the legation in Rome was the aged steward and factotum Paolo Ionescu. In a way, he was the counterpart of Franz Ştefănescu at the Ministry in Bucharest, in part because he was more Paolo[2] than Ionescu. He was completely deaf, but he knew and arranged everything. It was said that he had been brought to the legation by Nicolae Fleva[3] when he was the envoy, and no one believed that he was Romanian by birth. His origins seemed mysterious, his appearance was alien, and it was said that Fleva gave him a Romanian passport, baptizing him Ionescu.[4] Legation secretaries changed, envoys succeeded each other, but Paolo, just like Amedeo the driver, remained in place, irremovable.

THE ITALIAN GOVERNMENT AND ROYAL COURT

When I arrived in Italy, the Facta government was in power. The prime minister, a likable but rather colorless old man whose main feature was an impressive moustache, white and bushy, played no significant role in his country's politics. The foreign minister was Schanzer, a taciturn and bearded man, whose appearance was no more Italian than his name, but who did not lack subtlety or ability. The Ministry of Foreign Affairs was

---

[2]*Paolo* is Italian for "Paul"; in Romanian it would be *Pavel* or *Paul*.

[3]Romanian politician, 1840–1913.

[4]One of the most common Romanian surnames.

still in the Palazzo della Consulta, on the Piazza del Quirinale, across from the Royal Palace. I often had to go there to deliver a note or to make a démarche in the name of the Romanian envoy. I had to deal mostly with Secretary-General Contarini, with Marquess Cavriani, the head of Protocol (*capo ceremoniale*), and with Schanzer's chief of cabinet, Giacomo Barone Russo, with whom I became friends.

It was in the first months of my sojourn in Rome that the Conference of the Successor States of the Austro-Hungarian Empire met, with Lahovary representing Romania. I was appointed to the Conference's secretariat, whose secretary-general was Gabriele Preziosi, councillor of the Italian embassy in London. I had the opportunity of maintaining cordial relations with Preziosi and his family during my career, for he was named envoy to Bucharest and later to Vienna, when I was also posted there. The Conference of the Successor States dealt with the most inextricable financial issues, because inheritances are hard to untangle, be they between individuals or states, and it was no easy matter to divide the assets of some countries that had formed a single administrative unit for so many centuries.

For New Year's, the diplomatic corps went *in corpore* to present its wishes to the sovereigns. The foreign missions were led into the throne room according to the seniority in post of the ambassadors or ministers. I was accompanying Lahovary and was thus introduced to King Victor Emmanuel III and Queen Helena. They had a very happy family life in Villa Savoia and did not feel quite at ease when they had to take part in official functions at the Quirinal Palace. Though most gracious and friendly, they both seemed to suffer from a certain timidity, a condition that is widespread among the members of most ruling houses. The king's shyness was perhaps intensified by a complex resulting from his diminutive size, betrayed by the tic of constantly moving his lower jaw. He was, however, a refined and cultivated man, full of wisdom—and with a good sense of humor, as I discovered when, in my turn as Romanian envoy to Italy, I had the opportunity of several lengthy conversations with him.

Much taller than her husband, Queen Helena had the charm and simplicity of a good housewife. She had grown up in the informal and patriarchal setting of Cettigne, at the unpretentious court of her parents, Prince (later King) Nikita and Princess (later Queen) Milena of Montenegro. Nikita of Montenegro—"my only true friend," used to say the tsar—was the most picturesque figure among the gallery of European monarchs. Thanks to skillful political tightrope walking between Vienna and Petersburg, he was able to maintain the independence of his small country until, after World War I, it was swallowed up by the new Yugoslav kingdom of his son-in-law, Peter I Karageorgević. Nikita had studied in Paris and had been a fixture of Latin Quarter cafés. It was said that when his daughter, Queen Helena of Italy, made her first official visit with her husband to Paris, she asked to be taken to La Source, the famous café on the "Boul' Mich," where her father had told her he had spent so many pleasant hours. The protocol chief of the Quai d'Orsay was given the task of explaining to the queen that such a filial pilgrimage could not be easily fitted into an official royal visit.

Among the courtiers surrounding the sovereigns at official receptions, I shall never forget the grand master of the court, the nonagenarian Duke Borea d'Olmo, stiff in the armchair from which he no longer rose and with one eye bandaged (probably a cataract), an image in the style of El Greco; nor the almost royal distinction of Princess di Viggiano, lady-in-waiting of the queen, née Bauffremont, whose mother was wed in a second marriage with a Romanian, *Beizadea*[5] George Bibescu.

After calling on King Victor Emmanuel and Queen Helena, the diplomatic corps removed itself to the Palazzo Margheritta on the Via Veneto (now the United States embassy) to offer its New Year's wishes to Queen Mother Margheritta. Being born a princess of the House of Savoy, Umberto I's widow was also his first cousin. She was quite old when I met her and her hair was completely white, but she held herself straight and always had a smile on her lips. She had a special charm, a happy amiability, the gift of creating a warm atmosphere around whomever she was receiving. The contrast between her and her daughter-in-law was striking; one could have said of her what had been said about Empress Eugénie of France: "She's more than a queen, she's a lady."

If the reception at the Quirinal was a duty for the diplomats, the one at the Palazzo Margheritta was truly a pleasure. In the course of her conversation with us, the queen mother recalled that our ruler, Carol I, had asked her in marriage. She was on the point of taking him for husband when a weightier suitor came on the scene: the heir to the throne of Italy. "As you see," she concluded, "I almost became your queen." "But it is the cousin who won," observed Lahovary. "Well," the queen answered, "it is so seldom that a princess can get married in her own country, without exiling herself from her family!" (I should add that in each of our subsequent audiences with Queen Margheritta, she reminded us of this

[5]Title given to the sons of Romanian reigning princes.

episode from her youth.) Of course, being queen of Italy was a much more attractive proposition, in the middle of the nineteenth century, than being the princess of a vassal principality at the mouth of the Danube. On the other hand, she would have had in Carol I a more faithful, if not more entertaining, husband than the philanderer Umberto I, and she would have been spared the tragedy of Monza (where Umberto was assassinated).

Queen Margheritta was well known for her wit and quick repartee. At another New Year reception, the minister of war was congratulating her very warmly for the promotion of her grandson Umberto, then aged sixteen, to the rank of second lieutenant. "Yes," answered the queen mother, "I too believe that he has some future in the army" ("*farà cariera*"). When Queen Margheritta died and was buried next to her husband in the cold vastness of the Pantheon, it seemed that, along with her nice smile, it was also the guiding light of the House of Savoy that had vanished, and indeed of Italy itself, fated to so much turmoil and so many defeats.

THE DIPLOMATIC CORPS ACCREDITED TO THE QUIRINAL

The diplomatic corps was numerous in Rome, since part of it was accredited to the king of Italy and part to the pope. As secretary of our legation to the Quirinal, most of my relations were of course with the former.

Our legation, as was traditional, had the closest relations with the French embassy, whose seat is in the most magnificent of Roman palazzi, the neighboring Palazzo Farnese. The ambassador was one of the most brilliant figures in French diplomacy, Camille Barrère. He had been in post in Rome for some twenty years and was the dean of the diplomatic corps. It was said that in 1870, when he was very young, he had been a member of the Paris Commune and had even actively taken part in the setting on fire of the Tuileries and the Hôtel de Ville. This rumor circulating in Rome was partly a malicious exaggeration, but it is a fact that he had to spend many years in exile. The famous Juliette Adam, née Lambert, who had influence in French government circles, obtained for him an amnesty and permission to return to France. At the first reception to which Madame Adam invited Barrère, General de Gallifet, who had been largely responsible for putting down the revolution started by the Commune of 1870, was also present. Madame Adam introduced Barrère, saying, "General, may I introduce to you a Communard you failed to have shot." General de Gallifet looked Barrère straight in the eyes and said, "I regret it, sir." It was also said that once Barrère had become ambassador to Italy, he was explaining to a Roman lady that he had been given such a short leave that he hadn't even had time to stop in Paris, saying, "Imagine, I had to *brûler*[6] Paris." The lady is said to have answered back, "What, once again, Mr. Ambassador?"

Grown more moderate and entering political life, Barrère held various public positions, among which was that of France's delegate to the European Danube Commission. During his stays in Galaţi he drafted a scheme to resolve the Danube question, a scheme known in the history of that river as "the Barrère plan." Then he was appointed envoy extraordinary and minister plenipotentiary to King Oscar II of Sweden and Norway. It was said that the Scandinavian ruler was somewhat astonished that the French Republic had deemed it appropriate to accredit a former revolutionary and Communard to a royal court, and that at the remittal of the credentials of the new envoy he had made an ironical allusion to the latter's "red" past. Without losing his poise in the least, Barrère replied, "Sire, who is not a revolutionary at twenty has no heart, who is not a conservative at thirty has no brains." A fine rejoinder, worthy of the witty and caustic Barrère.

His appearance was imposing, slightly disdainful, and although of modest origins, he had the profile and bearing of a prince of the Italian Renaissance. Yet another of his witticisms comes to mind. I was chargé d'affaires in the absence of my chief, and I went to see Barrère to confirm certain information. Our talk turned to life in Rome, and I mentioned that many ambassadors must envy his luck of having been for more than two decades ambassador of France in Italy, with residence in the Palazzo Farnese—the proudest and most sumptuous one in the Eternal City. He wrinkled his nose and said: "Oh, you know, I would have liked a change. My dream was to be ambassador to London, but the Quai d'Orsay has always been opposed to the idea. There is, indeed, a great handicap against me: I am the only ambassador of France who speaks English."

The French embassy's counselor, François Charles-Roux, another distinguished figure of French diplomacy, was most obliging toward younger colleagues, and more than once I profitably had recourse to his advice and knowledge. I was already acquainted with his valuable historical writings, several of which I had consulted for my own works on diplomatic history. He, too, had a nice career: envoy to Prague, ambassador to the Vatican,

[6] *Brûler* in French means both "to burn" and "to skip."

secretary-general at the Quai d'Orsay, member of the Academy of Moral and Political Sciences, and finally president of the Compagnie de Suez. Later on, when I was envoy to Rome, I often met again his attractive daughter Cyprienne, who had married Marcellino del Drago, Ciano's chief of cabinet. Following a short period in disgrace after the collapse of the Mussolini regime, del Drago became envoy to Stockholm and then ambassador to Tokyo; on their way to Japan, they came to see my wife and me in New York.

The Belgian ambassador was the old Count van den Steen de Jehay, a friend of many Romanians and very hospitable. But I have to admit that his house's main attraction was his daughter, the exceptionally beautiful Ghislaine, whose blond hair and blue eyes were wreaking ravages in the ranks of the young embassy and legation attachés.

The German ambassador was Baron Konstantin von Neurath, former head of mission in Copenhagen and then in Constantinople. His situation was somewhat awkward so soon after the end of the war. His embassy—Palazzo Caffarelli, on the Capitoline hill—had been confiscated and work on the restoration of the Villa Wolkonsky alle Rose (near San Giovanni Laterano), the future German embassy, was still under way, so the ambassador was staying at the Albergo Palazzo, where I too was staying. We ran into each other all the time, in the elevator, in the dining room, in the sitting rooms. Many years later, when he was minister of foreign affairs, he came to Budapest on an official visit. I was the Romanian envoy at the time, and at one of the receptions we reminisced about our stay at the Albergo Palazzo and our after-dinner conversations. Baroness von Neurath looked like a worthy housewife whose only interest was her children, a son (who also became a diplomat, I believe) and a pretty and demure daughter, the fair Winnifred, who was to become later the wife of Hans-Georg Mackensen. This quiet and decent family was destined to a tragic fate. Minister of foreign affairs of the Third Reich, then "Protector of Bohemia" under Hitler, Neurath was sentenced in Nuremberg to life imprisonment. After ten years, having reached a very old age, he was amnestied, mainly thanks to the efforts of his devoted daughter, Winnifred von Mackensen.

The German embassy's counselor was von Prittwitz und Gaffron, future ambassador to Washington, an intelligent and pleasant man, assisted by the charm of a most attractive wife. The first secretary was the above-mentioned future son-in-law of von Neurath, Field Marshal von Mackensen's son. I remember that I was seated next to him at a dinner Lahovary gave and, wishing to be friendly, he talked with more warmth than tact of the beauties of Sinaia, which he had had the opportunity of appreciating when he had stayed with his father at Peleş Castle during the German occupation of Wallachia. "Do their majesties still spend the summers at Peleş Castle?" he asked me. I took my revenge by answering, "After our victory and the union with Transylvania, their majesties spend a good part of the summer in Predeal." [7] I was going to meet Hans-Georg Mackensen again in Budapest, where we were both envoys and had the best of relations, and later in Rome, where he was ambassador of the Reich and I envoy of Romania.

The Spanish embassy to the Quirinal was then in the famous Palazzo Barberini, on Via delle Quattro Fontane, around the corner from Piazza del Tritone. At my arrival in Rome, the ambassador was the witty Marquess de Villa-Urrutia, a man of letters and of excellent taste, with a permanent smile that revealed his buckteeth.

It was at his home that, accompanying my chief, I attended my first Roman party. It was on the occasion of the marriage of the ambassador's daughter to the young Count Mazzarino. Following a Spanish custom, the wedding took place at precisely midnight in Palazzo Barberini's superb ballroom, under a ceiling painted by Piero della Cortona. At the far end stood the royal throne under a canopy, turned to face the wall, as is customary when the Spanish king is not present. It was one of the most magnificent soirées that I was ever to see: sparkling chandeliers, the glitter of the diadems and jewelry worn by the great ladies of the Roman aristocracy, old tapestries on the walls, whole rooms filled with museum pieces on which the gifts to the bride were exhibited—all this the background against which strolled statesmen, ambassadors, wearers of illustrious Italian or Spanish names, and, last but not least, a constellation of young women and girls who seemed, perhaps because I was very young, to come straight out of fairy tales. During my stay in Rome, I was often to meet the fashionable debutantes among them, for they missed no party at which young people danced.

Among the men to whom Alexander Lahovary introduced me that evening, Marquess Imperiali, former Italian ambassador to London, made a particular impression on me. He had an ancien régime distinction and elegance, perhaps a bit distant and cold but with a friendly look behind his monocle. He graciously asked me what had struck me the most in this first contact with Roman high society. I replied that it was the number of blondes, whereas I had expected to find in Italy only

[7] Transylvanian resort just north of Sinaia.

brunettes with black eyes. "Let me explain this anomaly to you," the old ambassador said, peering through his monocle at the dancing couples. "Some of the lovely women you are looking at are foreign, some are Italians with English or American mothers, and others simply bleach their hair."

Diplomats accredited to the Quirinal usually belonged to the club Circolo della Caccia (those accredited to the Vatican were members of the Circolo degli Scacchi), so my chief took the necessary steps for my admittance to the Caccia. There were in those days two successive ballots. First, one had to be admitted as temporary member, having been sponsored by two full members (my sponsors were Don Urbano del Drago and Marquess Patrizi). Then, after going to the club for several weeks and trying to meet as many members as possible, one had to be proposed as permanent member by another set of sponsors (mine were the likable and always cheerful Count Giulio Macchi di Cellere and Colonel Magistrati, an old friend of Lahovary's). For foreign diplomats these ballots were mere formalities, since it was unthinkable to reject a member of a mission accredited to the king of Italy, the club's honorary president.

When I was admitted to the Caccia, the club was still in the Palazzo Marignoli, on the Corso, across from the Palazzo Chigi and a few steps from the Piazza Colonna. The sitting rooms had that slightly worn charm and that trace of cigar smoke typical of all clubs. And when I went into the reading room, where only the rustling of newspapers broke a religious silence, it was as if I found myself in the warm and friendly ambience of our old Jockey Club in Bucharest when it was still on Calea Victoriei, across from the Royal Palace. Later, the Caccia moved to the Palazzo Borghese, one of Rome's wonders. Here, however, one no longer had the impression of being in a club but rather of being the guest of a haughty Cardinal Borghese, perhaps of the one who, after becoming Pope Paul V, had his name arrogantly carved on the frontispiece of Saint Peter ("Paulus V Borghesius Romanus"). Huge rooms with marvelous frescoes, an extravagance of Renaissance treasures but, inevitably, less of a club atmosphere and a lack of intimacy. Yet, as the French say, no one complains that the bride is too beautiful, and it was a delight for the eye to feast on this royal setting, in which uncaring players were engrossed in their bridge games and solitary members swallowed, indifferent, their helpings of *mozzarella in carozza*.

Since Mrs. Lahovary was absent from Rome and I was still a bachelor, my chief and I regularly lunched at the club. Our most frequent table companions were August Zaleski, Poland's envoy, future minister of foreign affairs and president of the Polish republic, as well as old Prince Felix Yussupoff, the father of Rasputin's murderer. Zaleski was an unsurpassed raconteur, with an endless store of anecdotes, which he never repeated. Old Yussupoff reeled off recollections from his former years of splendor, when he received crowned heads in his castle at Arkhangelsk, near Moscow. Prince Ferdinand, at that time still heir to the Romanian throne, and Princess Marie had been among his guests when they came for the coronation of the last tsar, Nicholas II (1894). The young princely couple so enjoyed themselves that, according to Yussupoff, they asked him to send a telegram to King Carol I requesting permission to extend their stay in Arkhangelsk. The permission was granted, but so stingily that Ferdinand and Marie had to leave just a few days later, when the partying was still in full swing. Yussupoff claimed that in those days Princess Marie kept in her bedroom a human skull from which she refused to part. Since I never heard, from anybody, this story of a skull, I strongly suspect that in this instance the old Russian nobleman mistook Princess Marie for one of the eccentric grand duchesses from the Russian court.

I often met, at the Caccia as well as elsewhere, two former ambassadors of the tsar, who now lived in exile in Rome: the brothers Anatole and Basil Krupenski, belonging to the Bessarabian branch, by now completely russified, of the old Moldavian boyar family of that name. The former had been ambassador to the Quirinal, the latter to Tokyo, and both had the typical demeanor of Russians of the ancien régime. Since my paternal grandmother was born Krupenski (of the Moldavian branch) and one of my father's sisters had married a Krupenski from Jassy, they considered me almost a cousin, and I was often invited by Anatole Krupenski and his German wife. Basil Krupenski came frequently to see me at the legation's chancellery, not so much out of love of family but to ask for an extension of his Romanian passport. Indeed, with the reattachment of Bessarabia to Romania he had become, to his great chagrin, a Romanian citizen. I imagine, however, that since he could no longer be the tsar's subject, he preferred to be the subject of the king of Romania than of Lenin. This gave him the security of his livelihood, as well as a passport!

THE FIRST MONTHS OF MY ASSIGNMENT

During my first months in Rome I had the advantage of getting better acquainted with our two great historians: Nicolae Iorga and Vasile

Pârvan. Iorga had come to give a series of lectures, and I attended all of them. He was very highly thought of by his learned audience, though some felt that he made too many long digressions, laced with too many jokes and anecdotes. And then there were rather many mistakes in his Italian. Nevertheless, the warmth of his presentations and his profound knowledge of Italian culture made a strong impression on his listeners.

Pârvan was to stay much longer in Rome. Apart from giving lectures, he was setting up the future Romanian Academy in Rome, whose first director he became. I had the good fortune to spend many pleasant and interesting moments in his company. I would go pick him up at the Albergo Quirinale on Via Nazionale, where he was staying, and then we would wander in ancient Rome for hours at a time. To roam along the Via Appia with Pârvan and hear him bring the past back to life, to examine the stones of the Forum or of the imperial Palatine on sun-bathed mornings, and to remain under the spell of his words on summer nights in front of the Colosseum—these are unforgettable memories. Thanks to this invaluable guide, the youth that I then was succeeded in learning and understanding the many aspects of Roman grandeur and Latin civilization. Along with an enlightened mind, Pârvan had a generous and understanding heart. I have always viewed his untimely death[8] as a grievous loss not only for Romanian scholarship but also for our public life, in which he would have played a leading role.

Another interesting personage I had the good fortune of getting close to during my first months in Rome was Tommaso Tittoni, president of the Italian senate, former minister of foreign affairs, former ambassador to Paris (where he and our then envoy to France, Alexander Lahovary, became close friends), and future president of the Italian Academy. At that time, our legation's foremost goal was to obtain Italy's ratification of the 1920 treaty that recognized the reattachment of Bessarabia to Romania, a treaty ratified by France and Great Britain, but not by Italy or Japan. My chief therefore asked his famous and influential friend, who had always shown himself favorable to Romania, to raise his voice in support of our cause. Tittoni immediately agreed and offered to publish an article in the journal *Nuova Antologia* reminding the Italian public of Romania's rights to that old Moldavian region. At the same time, however, he admitted frankly that he was a bit hazy about the details of the Bessarabian question. Lahovary then proposed that I be placed at Tittoni's disposal to supply him with the required data, recommending

[8]At the age of forty-four, in 1927.

me as a young diplomat whose hobby was historical studies. (I had just published in the journal *Romania*—issued by friends of our country in Rome with the help of our government—a historic study of the long relationship between Italy and the Romanian Principalities, a study that I was later to expand in *Convorbiri Literare*.) Tittoni was delighted with the suggestion, which would spare him the *grattatesta*[9] of doing research in dusty books and records.

We consequently decided that I would spend two or three mornings a week at his residence to assist him with the projected study. Exempt those days from duties at the chancellery, I would show up at the palace in the narrow Via Rasella where, guarded by a host of picturesque carabinieri, President Tittoni lived. The hours spent with him in a room full of books and, if I recall correctly, appointed with green eighteenth-century Venetian furniture decorated with chinoiseries, were of course most pleasant. After I had given him the papers I had prepared and answered his questions while he took notes, he would retell stories from his political and diplomatic life around a decanter of Cinzano. I was sorry when he completed the study, which we revised together as to historical and ethnographical accuracy, since this brought to an end meetings with a prominent statesman whom a legation secretary would not under normal circumstances have met one-on-one. I was flattered to see that the published text of the study mentioned our collaboration. At Tittoni's death, I wrote an article in *Convorbiri Literare* entitled "Tittoni and the Romanians," in which I related the various occasions on which the old politician had given a helping hand to our country, be it as ambassador or as foreign minister.

THE GENOA CONFERENCE (APRIL 10–MAY 19, 1922)

A few months after my arrival in Rome, maybe in February, it was announced that a big international economic conference would be held in Genoa. The participants would include not only the European Allied countries and those of the vanquished Triple Alliance but also, for the first time, Soviet Russia. This initial contact with the representatives of the bloodthirsty and merciless Russian revolution was anticipated everywhere with apprehension. We received at the legation the official notice that the prime minister, Ion I.C. ("Ionel") Brătianu, would head the Romanian delegation. The notice added that I was to be attached as

[9]Trouble.

secretary to the delegation and that I would have to be in Genoa on the eve of our delegation's arrival.

I established myself in Genoa on April 8. Two days later the delegation arrived from Bucharest, headed by Ionel Brătianu and Constantin Diamandy. Its secretariat consisted, apart from myself, of my colleagues Ionel Plessia and Atta Constantinescu and also the young Ştefan Pleşoianu, the prime minister's chief of cabinet. Fluttering around us, Dr. Luigi Tomellini, the likable honorary consul of Romania, outdid himself with kind and helpful services on our behalf; he was married to Zoe Gârbea, the daughter of the well-known writer and lecturer Smara Gârbea.

From the first day I was deeply impressed by the powerful personality of Ion I.C. Brătianu. His imposing appearance, the dignity of his conduct and bearing, his unfailing politeness toward the lowly as well as the great, and finally his renowned charm, which he was reputed to have inherited from his father and with which he conquered so many political adversaries—as well as a few enchanting women—could not fail to win over a very young diplomat called to work directly under the "Vizier," as he was nicknamed. His brilliant intelligence and the tenacity with which he defended the country's rights were to become evident to me in the very first days of the Conference. But now I was making the acquaintance of the *man*, of the *moşnean*[10] of the Bratia valley in Argeş, as he liked to call himself. He seemed to me an oak with roots thrust deep into the Romanian soil. There wasn't a landscape that he would not compare with some corner of our country and, to make us smile, he would say again and again at the sight of the splendors of the Italian Riviera, "Whatever you may say, Florica is more beautiful." In his mind, he could not tear himself away from the ancestral estate. Yet he had a deep knowledge and appreciation of Western art, he had visited all of Italy's cities, and in our frequent strolls around Genoa I realized that I was with a diligent and sharp scholar of European history. The long hours he spent throughout his life reading in the solitude of Florica were seen by those not in the know as idleness. But the hours of work and political meditation in his library were certainly more valuable than conversations in the hallways of the Chamber or audiences liberally granted to one and all.

One anecdote that was told illustrates Ionel Brătianu's charm: an influential Liberal comes to him with a request; after some twenty minutes, he leaves the prime minister's office beaming. "So, he granted what you were asking for?" asked a friend who was there. "No, not at all," answers the first man, "but there is no doubt, he really is a good-hearted fellow!" A few days

[10]Yeoman.

later the same petitioner presents the same request to the minister of finance, Vintilă Brătianu, the "Vizier's" brother, who hid a heart of gold under a stern, even somewhat forbidding, appearance. After a few moments, our man leaves the minister's office downcast and scowling. "Say, did Vintilă turn you down?" asks an acquaintance. "No, not at all," is the answer, "he gave me full satisfaction, but he lectured me, he upbraided me—what a crabby fellow!" There was a saying among Liberals: "It is more pleasant to be turned down by Ionel than to have one's request granted by Vintilă." But the common talk was mistaken. Vintilă Brătianu had both high principles and a soft heart. But he did not admit favoritism or special deals, and was particularly adamant in this respect when members of his own party were concerned. Ionel Brătianu was equally uncompromising but preferred to clothe his refusals in mantles of friendliness and smiles. Neither of the Brătianus—each in his own way—made concessions or strayed from the path he deemed to be the right one. Elise Brătianu, Ionel Brătianu's wife, had a nice comment, which she repeated to me many times: "In this country where everybody hastens to say *yes*, the Brătianus know how to say *no*."

Constantin Diamandy, a career diplomat, was one of our most intelligent and energetic heads of mission. He was considered difficult and irritable, and yet I always had the best of relations with him; I liked his wit, and he was always very friendly. I also had good relations with the other members of the delegation and with my colleagues at the secretariat.

Ionel Brătianu had particular recourse to Atta Constantinescu and to me—he jokingly named us "Max und Moritz," Max being Atta and I Moritz, because he always summoned us together—and he would dictate to us his confidential notes, which we would then rework into formal reports that he would send to the king and to the government. In the first days, however, Brătianu had not sent any information to Bucharest, to the exasperation of the young Foreign Minister Duca. Not daring to criticize the prime minister directly, Duca cabled Diamandy (with whom he had never got along) in a rather unpleasant tone that "the king and government are left completely in the dark about what is happening in Genoa," and asking him to report immediately. Brătianu, quite understanding that the telegraphic admonition was meant for him, answered Duca in an ironic and somewhat mocking way that "in the three months that he (Duca) had been foreign minister he lost the patience that he (Brătianu) had been able to keep during the long years in which he was not only foreign minister, but also prime minister."

The purpose of the Conference was the resumption of relations between Europe and Russia, first of all in economic matters. Twenty-nine

European countries were represented, almost all by their prime minister or minister of foreign affairs. Attending were Barthou, Barrère, and Colrat, for France; Lloyd George for Great Britain; Facta and Schanzer for Italy; Gounaris and Theotokis for Greece; Stambolisky for Bulgaria; Chicherin for Russia; Rathenau for Germany.

The Conference was doomed to failure from the start, and that for two reasons. The first was the signing, on April 16, 1922, of the Rapallo Treaty between Germany and Russia, which enabled Chicherin, the Soviet commissar of foreign affairs, to take an intransigent attitude. The second reason was that the conciliatory Briand, who was seeking to find some understanding with Moscow, had been replaced as the head of the French government by Poincaré, an unbending man opposed to any concession to the Bolshevik regime. Caught between Barthou and Barrère on the one side and Chicherin on the other—all equally unyielding—Lloyd George's project of a nonaggression pact, submitted to the Conference on April 25, led to nothing. Ostensibly, the Conference's failure resulted from the Belgian government's insistence on the full restitution of its nationals' assets seized by the Bolshevik regime, to which Chicherin was opposed. In fact, however, the Conference failed because of the split that had occurred between London and Paris. Britain was willing to make concessions in order to reopen the Russian market (where British products could have filled the void left after the war by German exports), while France remained faithful to its old alliance with tsarist Russia and unflinchingly insisted on the respect of the principles of international law, which Lenin's government had violated. So as not to reveal the extent of the failure, it was decided that a new conference of technical experts would be held in The Hague.

In one of the first sessions, Chicherin had raised the Bessarabian question. Brătianu immediately asked for the floor. In a short but firm statement he explained that this ancient Moldavian land had been torn away and annexed by the Russian empire, that it had declared its independence and then later, of its own free will, had asked to be reattached to Romania. After the session, Diamandy engaged Chicherin in conversation and asked whether an understanding could not be reached between our two countries, the recognition by the Soviet government of the fait accompli across the river Prut forming the basis of good neighborly relations. Diamandy told me that Chicherin listened to him, but without answering, bowed and left.

Chicherin was a somewhat curious figure in the gallery of Bolshevik leaders. He was the descendant of a family of small Russian nobility, a family of diplomats; he may have been the son or a close relative of the Chicherin who, as chargé d'affaires of Tsar Alexander II in Paris, signed the 1866 agreement recognizing Carol I as ruler of Romania. He was a highly cultivated man, who knew several foreign languages well and could express himself in them with ease and elegance, albeit in a squeaky voice. He had entered the tsarist diplomatic service, but had had to leave it because of some unpleasant business. Thereafter, embittered by his failure in life, he had drawn close to the Communists. After the revolution, Lenin (who came from the same class of small Russian nobility) chose him to direct Russian foreign policy. His hair and beard were reddish, and he had shifty eyes that never looked at one directly. I always told myself that, had he lived in the Florence of the Middle Ages, Masaccio or some other of the Quattrocento painters would have used him as a model for the portrayal of Judas. In other respects, he was carefully attired and, in contrast to today's Soviet leaders, he wore a tailcoat in the evenings—but with a red flower in the buttonhole. In daytime he wore a dark suit with a red tie. People were curious about him, and he had become Genoa's "celebrity." He also had lunch with the king of Italy, to the great indignation of Empress Mother Maria Feodorovna, who had taken refuge in Copenhagen. It was even said later that she had refused to receive the Italian royal couple during its visit to the Danish court, saying she could not meet with someone who shook hands with the representative of her son's murderers.

Another interesting personage was Walter Rathenau, he too a man of great culture, later assassinated by the Nazis. He had a skull-like face and a pronounced Semitic type. A great financier, he was also a connoisseur of the art and literature of all of Europe. He ended his first speech with Dante's line: *adesso gridiamo: pace, pace, pace!*[11] On hearing these words spoken in Italian, the spectators in the hall burst into thunderous applause, despite the prohibition of any kind of demonstration during the Conference. Rathenau's greatest diplomatic success was the signing of the Germano-Russian agreement at Rapallo. I met many Germans who believed that, had his life not been so tragically and prematurely cut off, this *realpolitiker* would have had the ability required to integrate his country into the European family, instead of its setting itself against it.

Lloyd George, Europe's darling, the cheerful Welsh head of the Liberal party and of the British government, who by his dynamism and

[11]And now we cry: peace, peace, peace!

fiery eloquence had contributed so much to the victory of 1918, was likewise a center of attraction for all. With his buffoon's face crowned by a white mane, his piercing eyes full of humor and irony, and his jokes purposefully chosen to defuse tense situations, Lloyd George was, if not the most representative embodiment of the British character, then certainly the most Celtic personality, and therefore the closest to his Continental colleagues. He was undoubtedly the most likable, and the best liked, of the Conference's delegates, and this despite the fact that he sought a rapprochement, at least economic, with the Bolsheviks. Whenever he spoke, we all pricked our ears because we knew some jokes might follow. At one session, Chicherin complained that no Soviet delegate had been included in the Economic Commission. The commission's president, the Frenchman Colrat, answered, quite rightfully, "We did not have recourse to a representative of Soviet Russia, since in our opinion that country, in its present situation, is perhaps not qualified to give economic advice to others." The audience seemed to gasp, but Lloyd George, quickly stepping in, said smilingly: "Mr. Chicherin, when you don't yet know someone well, you at first invite him only for an outing on a rowboat. If he proves a pleasant companion, you then invite him for a longer trip on your yacht. It is the same with you. We are now on a rowboat outing. It depends on you if we shall want a closer collaboration." The general laughter broke the tension.

The only really ferocious appearance was that of the Bulgarian prime minister, Alexander Stambolisky, head of the Agrarian party and deemed to be a dyed-in-the-wool revolutionary. He, too, was fated to a tragic end. His nature was perhaps not quite as terrifying as his mien: huge head, dishevelled hair, bloodshot eyes, massive fists clenched on the table. He spoke only Bulgarian, in a thunderous voice, and the audience fancied that he was making who knows what wild statements, but his graceful interpreter, Nadejda Stancioff (the daughter of Bulgaria's envoy to Paris and later to London, who by marriage was to become Lady Kay-Muir) would immediately stand up and, in flawless French, pour forth in her melodious voice a stream of sweet and reassuring words: "Bulgaria, gentlemen, wishes only peace and good relations. . . ." A French colleague leaned over and whispered in my ear: "Come on! I bet he never said that, with his gruff voice and fist-blows on the table! It is that charming girl who fixes things up and voices all those sweet sentiments!" In any case, if it is true that *traduttore, traditore*, there couldn't have been for the audience a more charming treason!

CHARGÉ D'AFFAIRES AT THE AGE OF 27; THE FASCISTS COME TO POWER

From the end of summer and into fall my chief was on vacation in Romania, leaving me as chargé d'affaires to replace him. For the first time, if only temporarily, I assumed the responsibilities of a head of mission. For the first time I sent, signed by me, reports and coded telegrams to the Ministry of Foreign Affairs in Bucharest. For the first time I made official representations to the Palazzo della Consulta and was received by Foreign Minister Schanzer in my new capacity as *capomissione*. This was a stirring moment in my life as a diplomatic apprentice, akin to that of a young second lieutenant finding himself for the first time in command of a unit that is awaiting his orders.

During this brief period when I was in charge of the legation, I had to organize a major reception on the occasion of the coronation of King Ferdinand and Queen Marie in Alba Iulia. The members of the Italian government and the diplomatic corps were of course present, so that the reception rooms of the Palazzo Santa Croce were packed with guests. Only Count Nemes de Hidweg, Hungary's envoy, was absent. He had sent me a letter apologizing for not being able to attend on account of illness. The counselor of the Hungarian legation, with whom I had good personal relations, lunching with him almost daily at the Caccia, confessed that had the crowning of King Ferdinand not taken place in the very heart of Transylvania, at Alba Iulia, it is quite possible that his chief would have felt less ailing that day.

But by far the most important event during my stewardship of the legation was the coming to power in Italy of the Fascist party. From my first days in Rome, I had been aware of the growing strength of this still undefined and little understood movement. In the superficial opinion of Roman society, the Fascists were looked upon as a band of very theatrical loudmouths; some people even considered them rather ridiculous, with their black shirts (so they didn't have to be changed so often, wisecrackers said) and thick cudgels. Their main activity seemed to be to beat up their opponents or force them to swallow copious potions of castor oil. Under the fatherly and somewhat irresponsible governance of the patriarchal Facta, the cabinet took no measures against the movement, and the authorities intervened only rarely, in individual cases, to come to the rescue of victims of too energetic a bastinado or an excessive purging. The powers to be were no more frightened by the antiparliamentary theories of the Fascists than by the party's pseudomilitary structure.

"How could fascism catch on among us?" I often heard said around me. "The Italian is, by nature, skeptical, unaggressive, and too much 'of the left' to let himself be seduced by young windbags aping military formations and opposed to the political parties that encompass all the country's citizens. *Niente pericolo!*"

It was known that the chief of the Fascists was a certain Benito Mussolini, a deputy with socialistic leanings, but his name was far from familiar, and it evoked no particular emotional appeal in the public at large. At that time, the Fascist movement outshone Mussolini—as, later on, his personality was going to outshine fascism. But, day after day, the Fascists increasingly imposed themselves as a political force in the provinces. They were taking hold of town halls, prefectures, and people's minds, at first by force, later by the force of conviction that springs from enthusiastic young people who are determined to change the world.

The weakness of the Facta government, the "immobilism" or lack of decisiveness of the traditional political parties, the economic stagnation, and the king's difficulty in piecing together a new government created an atmosphere of depression and discouragement favorable to the march on Rome threatened by the Fascists. To avoid such a *marcia sù Roma*—with the possibility of bloody clashes between the army and the Fascist units—and in the absence of any other solution, Victor Emmanuel III resigned himself to calling the chief of the Fascists, Benito Mussolini, and entrusting him with the formation of a government.

Although now installed in the Palazzo Viminale, Mussolini still wanted to give himself the satisfaction of a *marcia sù Roma,* which he had announced so many times. And so he gave his troops the order to "occupy Rome." But now the march was without danger, and even protected by the police against possible hostile reactions from the public. In order to make this peaceful and theatrical procession of the Fascist formations through the streets of Rome last longer, the "black shirts" marched only three abreast. The king, with his new prime minister next to him, was compelled to stay on the Quirinal's balcony until late in the evening to watch, even by torchlight, the Fascist detachments march past. I remember that, after watching the marching for over two hours, I went to the legation's chancellery to send a telegraphic report of the events to Bucharest. I stayed late to code, alone, the telegram. When I finally left, night had fallen but the march was still continuing. Obviously, the Duce's intention was to impress the Romans if not with the bravery, at least with the number and discipline of his followers.

Two days later, Prime Minister Mussolini appeared in front of the Chamber of Deputies, at Monte-Citorio. I attended that memorable session from the diplomatic gallery, and like everyone in the galleries and obviously on the floor, I was dumbfounded by the arrogant and contemptuous speech of the new head of government. "I could have made this Chamber an encampment for my Fascist troops," Mussolini declared, "but I want to leave you the possibility of raising yourselves to the demands of the present times." Detachments of black shirts marched through the streets, and the public stood aside. When *Giovinezza,* the Fascist hymn, was struck up in a theater or movie house, the spectators had to rise. Those who, not yet knowing the tune or not ascribing to it the same official character as to the royal anthem (*Marcia Reale*), did not stand up, were seized, hit, and thrown out.

As time went on, orderly conditions returned, and normal life resumed for the most peaceful, tolerant, and tractable people in the world. The low- and even mid-level officials were the same as before, while the leading Fascists began to acquire "fine manners" and even, like the field marshals of Napoleon I, tended to mix with high society. The new regime was still acting with kid gloves, the gloves of the "demo-liberal" governments of the past.

It was around that time that Romania signed a commercial agreement with Italy. According to custom, the occasion was used for an exchange of decorations between the two countries. Being prime minister and minister of foreign affairs, Mussolini was awarded by King Ferdinand the Grand Cross of the Star of Romania (*Steaua României*). My chief, Alexander Lahovary, was charged with handing the Romanian sash to the new dictator, whom he was meeting for the first time. Lahovary later told me that he left the Palazzo Chigi with the impression that Mussolini wanted a rapprochement with France, which also suited our policy.

To celebrate the awarding of the Romanian decoration and to give the head of the Italian government the opportunity to wear it for the first time, my chief invited him to a formal dinner at our legation in the Palazzo Santa Croce. I remember that party as if it had taken place yesterday. Mrs. Lahovary being absent from Rome, our envoy asked a lady-in-waiting of Queen Helena, the beautiful and charming Duchess Vittoria di Sermoneta, to act as hostess. Conforming to a somewhat antiquated custom, Lahovary chose not to use those small cards that, at the entrance, indicated to each male guest which lady he was to offer his arm to and lead to the dining room, preferring this function to be carried out orally by one of the legation's young secretaries. I was therefore instructed to inform the head of the Italian government that he was requested to offer his arm to Mme Barrère, the French ambassador's wife, who was also the doyenne of the diplomatic corps accredited to the Quirinal. A few moments before the doors to the dining room were to be opened, I therefore approached Mussolini who, a glass of vermouth in hand, was talking with Lady Sybil Graham, the charming wife of the British ambassador, and asked him to escort Mme Barrère to the table. Whether Mussolini attached little importance to this point of etiquette or because, between two ambassadresses, he preferred to take the arm of the younger and more attractive woman, he seized Lady Sybil's arm and led her to the dining room. Lahovary, flabbergasted, had to hastily push a lonely general toward the offended wife of the French ambassador. During the whole dinner, Mussolini's fiery eyes were riveted on the Duchess di Sermoneta, next to whom he was sitting. At the end of the meal I succeeded, with the help of Barone Russo, Schanzer's chief of cabinet, in directing the Duce toward Mme Barrère. This was Mussolini's debut in the diplomatic world. With time, he learned all the diplomatic niceties, and he proved to be a witty and very pleasant table companion, highly appreciated by the ladies to whom it was given to sit next to him.

OTHER RECOLLECTIONS FROM MY FIRST POSTING ABROAD

The Greek military catastrophe in Asia Minor set off toward the end of September 1922 the revolt of the Greek army and navy. King Constantine abdicated and took refuge with his family in Palermo. Soon thereafter the crown princess of Romania arrived in Rome, on the way to her parents in Sicily. Lahovary and I went to meet her at the railway station. The old Metaxas, the Greek envoy to Italy, soon to be recalled, and his wife were also there. Princess Helen seemed very depressed. Her brother, George II, nominally still king of the Hellenes, was very shaky on his throne (he was driven out in October 1923). But the most terrible tragedy occurred on December 2, 1922, when the revolutionary committee in Athens, after a sham trial, had almost the entire preceding government shot, holding it responsible for the defeat of the Greek army by Turkey and for the dramatic exodus from Smyrna and Asia Minor. And it was thus that perished, with courage and unjustly, former Prime Minister Gounaris (whom I had met at the Genoa Conference), Foreign Minister Baltazzi (who decorated me with the George I order, and who died with his monocle in place, merely advising his sons not to go into politics), Theotokis, Stratos, Protopapadakis, and General Hadjanesti.

The Greek royal family, in deep sorrow, went into mourning in Palermo. Princess Helen asked us to transmit to her husband and to the Romanian government a plea to intercede in Athens to save her uncle, Prince Andrew, who had been arrested and indicted by the revolutionaries. Thanks to these interventions, and especially to the energetic intercession of the British government, Prince Andrew of Greece was saved and taken aboard a British ship. His attractive wife, Princess Alice (née Battenberg and unfortunately hard of hearing), as well as her sweet little daughters and her year-old son (the future Duke of Edinburgh), arrived in Rome, and I had the pleasant duty, as chargé d'affaires, of giving her the good news of her husband's rescue. Prince Carol also passed through Rome on his way to Palermo, to join his wife and parents-in-law.

✧ ✧ ✧

A farcical event took place while I was secretary of the legation in Rome: its "seizure" by the Romanian students from Turin. In those days, our students abroad received from the state what amounted to a scholarship in the currency of their country of study, meant to compensate for the sharp drop in the exchange rate of the *leu*.[12] Owing to financial difficulties, these scholarships were paid with some irregularity, and one month they did not arrive at all. To force the government's hand, the Romanian students in Paris had occupied the premises of the legation there, holding as hostage the unfortunate Vladimir Mavrocordat, the financial counselor, who had of course nothing to do with the delay. The example being catching, our students in Turin, who were attending the Polytechnic School and were the largest group of Romanian students in Italy, thought that by occupying the Palazzo Santa Croce, the seat of our legation, they would force the government to loosen its purse strings. And so one day, at around one o'clock, while I was finishing a piece of work before going to lunch, I found myself with some twenty young men—quite proper and polite—who declared that they would occupy the legation and hold the envoy and me hostage until they received their scholarships. Unfortunately for them, Lahovary had gone to lunch at his Greek colleague Metaxas's, so that I was the only one who could be taken hostage. The hostage taking amounted, in fact, to the seizure of my hat, which they kept in custody, for in those days it was inconceivable that anyone, and especially a diplomat, would go into the street without a hat.

[12]The Romanian currency. Plural, *lei*.

The young invaders seemed highly embarrassed, and they kept on apologizing for having "inconvenienced" me, who had nothing to do with the problem, but they said this seemed to be the only way they could get the money they needed for their room and board. The most embarrassed of them all seemed to be the young Mircea Iorga, the son of the professor, dragged by his comrades into this childish adventure but unwilling to dissociate himself from them; he was visibly terrified of "what will Dad say when he finds out, if he finds out. . . ." But what about my lunch, since it was now well past one-thirty and I was getting hungry? I felt sorry for the boys and made two friendly observations: first, instead of spending all that money for the Turin-Rome fare, wouldn't they have done better to use it for their sustenance and to have continued attending their courses? At most, they could have sent a telegraphic SOS to the legation. Also, since the delay in sending the money was no doubt due to compelling circumstances, neither the king, nor the government, nor the Romanian people would be seized with horror or galvanized into action because the secretary of the legation in Rome was prevented from having lunch at his usual hour or obliged—*oh horror!*—to go bareheaded on Via Veneto. The arguments seemed to convince them—but what were they to do? Return to Turin as they had come, losing face? Paolo, the steward, was proposing to call the carabinieri to evict them, but I was utterly opposed to such a solution, which would have been humiliating for these decent and diligent students, and somewhat ridiculous for the legation.

I went up the back stairs to my chief's residence, and from there I phoned him at the Greek legation—he had just risen from table—to ask for instructions. Lahovary, half amused, half annoyed, said he would take care of the matter. About fifteen minutes later he arrived at the legation accompanied by Commodore Gavrilescu, who had come to Italy on an arms-purchasing mission and was acting as temporary military attaché. The commodore, in uniform decked with medals, bellowed, "You are all called up and are being sent back to Romania; each of you, give me your name and the military unit you belong to." The poor boys, completely shaken, capitulated. On our side, we felt bad about their situation and, in petto, blamed our government for its negligence. In the end, Lahovary advanced the students, from the legation's funds and his own, not only the fares for their immediate return to Turin but also a first installment on what they were owed. Then, in their presence, he dictated a telegram to Bucharest requesting that the scholarships be remitted without delay, but not mentioning the planned hostage taking. The young men left delighted (the money arrived from Bucharest a few days later), and I was able to go to the Circolo della Caccia for a belated lunch.

✧ ✧ ✧

In early 1922, Pope Benedict XV died. I had still been able to see him celebrate a pontifical mass (on the anniversary of his enthronement) in the Sistine Chapel, where I had been snuck in, in my diplomatic uniform, as if I had been a member of our legation to the Vatican. Although he had an unsightly face and appeared somewhat deformed, he was a man of great distinction. Contrary to his predecessor, the saintly and rustic Pius X, one could see that he came from an aristocratic family. Born in Genoa as Marquess della Chiesa, he had been elevated to cardinal and archbishop of Bologna by 1914, when the pontifical throne became vacant. He was elected pope, in a way, as posthumous amends to the famous Cardinal Rampolla, whose secretary he had been, and who could not attain the highest Catholic ecclesiastical office because of the veto of the emperor of Austria.

I next saw him after his death, yellow as wax, laid out in one of St. Peter's chapels. I was not entitled to attend the burial service. I complained to my colleagues at the club of the frustration of being in Rome and yet of not being able to see this ceremony, unchanged for centuries. Alexander Lissakowski, former counselor of the Imperial Russian legation in Bucharest and the Russian envoy to the Vatican—where he continued to be recognized as such in spite of the overthrow of the tsarist regime—then proposed to take me with him. And so, in diplomatic uniform and passing myself as secretary of the tsarist legation, I was able to watch the ceremony of the burial of a sovereign pontiff in all the traditional splendor of its unfolding. "See that stout cardinal in the second row of pews?" whispered Lissakowski. "That is Cardinal Ratti, Archbishop of Milan, who undoubtedly will be elected pope." And so he was.

It is also thanks to a diplomatic subterfuge that I, a diplomat of the "white world" of the Quirinal, was able to watch the dazzling ceremony of Pope Pius XI's coronation, worthy of a Renaissance fresco and rather remote from the austere poverty of Him whose vicar the bishop of Rome claims to be. According to a joke that was making the rounds in Rome, a foreigner would have told the new pope: "What a pity that coronations take place so seldom!"

3

Political Director of the Presidency of the Council of Ministers (1923–1926)

In mid-January 1923 I returned to Romania on leave, to attend my brother's wedding. Ion I.C. Brătianu invited me to lunch in his beautiful house on Lascar Catargi street and, when coffee was served, asked me if I would be willing to give up my posting in Rome in order to work for him as political director of the Presidency of the Council of Ministers. The proposal was flattering, although I realized that it might also have been due in part to the entreaties of the prime minister's wife, who wished to have a newlywed nephew of hers appointed to my job in Rome. Leaving Rome, especially so soon, would be heartbreaking, but my admiration and affection for the great statesman urged me not to forgo the opportunity—in all likelihood the only one I would have in my career—of being for a time in close contact with him, enjoying his brilliant intelligence and benefiting from his vast political experience. I therefore accepted without hesitation. It was a decision I never regretted, and it led to three of the most interesting years of my youth, years rich in political lessons and learning. My new position enabled me, indeed, not only to get to know Romania's entire diplomatic activity at first hand and from the center of things, but also to familiarize myself with the workings of our domestic politics, an area totally unfamiliar to me.

My family had kept itself aloof from the turmoil of national politics. My father had been a Junimist member of Parliament, and then secretary-general of the Ministry of Justice, but when he married my mother he was appointed to the bench and thereafter had nothing to do with partisan struggles. In any case, his personal inclination and friendships from early life brought him in relation exclusively with Conservative circles.

Likewise, on my mother's side there were only Conservatives: my grandfather, Ştefan Borănescu, a big landowner in the Buzău district, was an ardent follower of Lascar Catargi, and was repeatedly elected Conservative senator from the first electoral district of Buzău. He kept Lascar Catargi's picture on his desk, and I clearly remember when my brother and I, as very small children, were brought to the sitting room to be introduced to the venerable head of the Conservative party, who, on the eve of taking over the government in 1899, had come to call on my old grandfather. Unfortunately, Lascar Catargi died a few days later, before being sworn in as prime minister. I remember my grandfather's deep grief and that of his son, also an ardent Conservative, when they heard the distressing news. I relate all this to show that, whereas I had an approximate and fragmentary knowledge of the workings of the Conservative party and of our domestic politics in general, I was totally ignorant about the organization of the other great party, the Liberal party.

My assignment was to act as a link between the prime minister and the minister of foreign affairs, to read and sort out our legations' cables, copies of which were forwarded to the head of government, and to transmit any of his instructions. More generally, I was to screen the reports and cables so as to submit to Brătianu only those presenting a special interest, since it was hardly possible for him to read all of them. Each day I summarized for him the contents of the other reports and cables, often while we were being driven together by car. In time, however, my duties broadened beyond the limits of strictly defined foreign policy. I was spending my entire days in the home of the prime minister, where he did all his work, receiving members of the government and the heads of foreign missions. I was thus able to follow closely the activities of this statesman who was also a seasoned expert in the area of domestic policy.

I was often invited to stay for lunch, and on numerous occasions I accompanied Mr. and Mrs. Brătianu to Florica, so that I can say that I was quite immersed in their family. Besides, my mother and her brothers were childhood friends of the Brătianus, and the Brătianu sisters remained close lifelong friends of my mother's, especially Sabina. Vintilă Brătianu had known me since I was a child. I had founded along with several other boys of my age an athletic club and, for I know not what reason—perhaps because his wife had us often over for tea and showered us with kindnesses—we proclaimed Vintilă Brătianu honorary president. This unexpected distinction must have greatly amused the then mayor of the capital. He sent us word that he accepted, since he believed that the honorary presidency of an athletic club established by high-school boys would give him fewer headaches than the mayoralty of Bucharest. As for the prime minister's wife, Elise Brătianu, née Ştirbey, she knew me, if I may put it so, from before my birth. Indeed, when she was still married to Alexander Marghiloman, they had acted as sponsors at my parents' wedding (my father was at that time secretary-general of the Ministry of Justice, which was headed by Marghiloman). Since this had taken place during her first marriage, she refrained from mentioning to me the role she had played at my parents' wedding, except to say to me once: "Your parents were married, I believe, on December 5, 1893, at the Domniţa Bălaşa church and, although it was winter, they had the good fortune that it turned out to be a perfect springlike day." I admired her memory, after so many years. She maintained good relations with my parents even after her divorce, and they all set up together the association Cercul Nostru,[1] where writers such as Octavian Goga and Radu Rosetti-Răducanu read their literary works and amateurs put on plays. The meetings were held either at my parents' place (I sometimes was given small roles in the comedies being played) or at the homes of other members of the association.

Elise Brătianu was a handsome and elegant woman, with an enchanting smile that would all of a sudden light up her entire face, which most of the time remained serious. But she was, in particular, a woman with a really superior and brilliant intellect, perhaps more masculine than feminine in character: she had a keen political mind and an unfailing judgment about men and events. No doubt her two husbands, both outstanding statesmen, as well as the political environment in which she had lived, surrounded by Conservative and then Liberal leaders, contributed to the shaping and perfecting of her judgments and insights in all matters political. She told me she was more in her element talking with men than with women, who, in her days, limited themselves to conversations about literature or the arts, although she was very fond of Romanian popular art and had an outstanding collection of peasant costumes and embroideries. It was said in her family that she had a difficult disposition, perhaps because she was somewhat authoritarian and not always patient with persons of lesser intelligence, but I always found her most agreeable. She could be full of fun, and she had a warm heart and was ready to jump to anyone's assistance.

[1]"Our Circle."

A large number of nephews and nieces swarmed around the Brătianu couple. Ionel Brătianu's son from his first marriage, Gheorghe, a future historian of great merit, a highly cultivated man and not much inclined toward political battles, was an infrequent visitor. He had spent his childhood in Jassy with his mother, and because he married young, he did not have much opportunity to stay in his father's house. He conducted himself with dignity under Communist rule and died in jail with a patriotism worthy of the Brătianus. The real son of the household seemed, rather, to be Constantin Brătianu, called Bébé even into his old age, the son of a first cousin of the prime minister's. Intelligent, completely devoted to his uncle,[2] who entrusted him with his political archives. Bébé was an extremely sincere, friendly, and likeable man. I had full confidence in him and a real affection for him. My respect for the integrity of his character grew even further when I heard of his bravery and patriotism under the Communist regime, in whose jails he died, as did his uncle Dinu and his aforementioned cousin Gheorghe.

DOMESTIC POLITICAL FIGHTS

From the first days in my new position I found myself immersed, willy-nilly, in the billows of domestic politics. The Presidency of the Council of Ministers, as well as the government and, I dare say, the entire political world and public opinion in general, were much more engrossed in the enacting of a new constitution than in the external situation, which was more or less stable at that time. A new basic charter was absolutely necessary after the reattachment of the new provinces. The old constitutional provisions set down in 1866, at the arrival of Carol I, and amended for the first time only in 1917 to enact land reform and universal suffrage, could not be automatically applied to Transylvania, Bukovina, or Bessarabia. Moreover, the act of union with Transylvania and Bessarabia itself called for the convening of a Constituent Assembly. It would obviously have been desirable, at the time of the vote on the new constitution, for the government to include representatives of Transylvania's National party. But all attempts to put together a Brătianu-Maniu government in January 1922 failed because of a disagreement over the number of ministries and parliamentary mandates to be allotted to each of the two parties, Liberal and National. The March 1922 elections yielded a large Liberal majority, but this was contested by the opposition, which did not recognize the new Parliament's right to draw up a new constitution, or even to legislate.

[2] In Romanian usage, the terms *uncle* or *aunt* are used for any relative belonging to the parents' generation.

The relations between government and opposition had become so strained that the members of Transylvania's National party refused to attend the king's coronation at Alba Iulia. This gesture saddened and greatly surprised both the sovereign and the population at large. It was rightfully acknowledged that it would have been appropriate for a government comprising all parties to be in power, at least for that historic day. Nevertheless, the facts that the government was that of a single party and that political warfare was in full swing were not sufficient reasons for the Transylvanians, of all people, to absent themselves from the religious and national ceremonies dedicated to consecrate, in Transylvania's historic stronghold, their emancipation. From a political point of view, this attitude was simply self-defeating, since the Liberals remained in power for the next four years and wrote the new constitution in whichever way they wanted.

The debates on the constitution were taking place in the Chamber of Deputies in an overheated and impassioned atmosphere; both sides engaged in violent and aggressive attacks that exceeded almost all bounds. I attended the session in March 1923 at which the Constitution was enacted. Brătianu was there. He faced the uproar raised by the opposition with Olympian serenity and a slightly disdainful smile. When Iorga passionately declared that the opposition parties would never accept the new basic charter and would repeal it when they came to power, Brătianu answered calmly, "Mr. Iorga, even you yourself will apply this Constitution, and you as well as the other heads of the opposition who are today fighting it, will one day defend it with your last energies." Prophetic words! Indeed, Iorga was prime minister under that Constitution and did not make the slightest move to set it aside, nor did Maniu and Vaida-Voevod in their turn. From then and until the national catastrophe of 1944, the National-Peasant party,[3] with Iuliu Maniu at its head, repeatedly called for the respect of that Constitution of 1923 which it had sworn to abolish. As its author had foreseen, common sense prevailed.

OFFICIAL VISITS

I had been political director of the Presidency of the Council for one year when I accompanied my chief on the official visit by King Ferdinand and

[3]Formed by the fusion of Maniu's National party from Transylvania with various parties from the Old Kingdom, and in particular with Ion Mihalache's Peasant party.

Queen Marie to Warsaw in June 1924. The royal suite comprised, in addition to the prime minister, Foreign Minister I.G. Duca, Minister of the Royal Court Nicolae Mişu, Grand Master of the Royal Court's Ceremonies Baron Ion Stîrcea, Grand Master of the Royal Hunts Anton Mocsonyi, the queen's lady-in-waiting Elena Mavrodi, the military houses of the two sovereigns, and Chief of Cabinet of the Foreign Minister Atta Constantinescu. We all left in the royal train, in high spirits: it was the sovereigns' first official visit since the coronation and, moreover, a visit to an allied country! We all took our meals in the royal dining car. The queen sat at the head of the table, with the king to her right and Ionel Brătianu to her left, and the others followed according to rank, with us the youngest ones at the end of the table, where jokes flew from all sides. When the laughter intensified, the "grown-ups" would ask for the reason and the joke had to be repeated, whereupon everyone joined in the laughter. The king and queen seemed to be delighted by the trip, which was a sort of holiday for them.

It was interesting to get to know them at close quarters, as people rather than only as symbols. I remembered how I had attended, on that gloomy morning of September 1914, King Ferdinand's swearing in, the day after the death of Carol I. I was in the Chamber of Deputies' gallery reserved for the High Court of Appeal,[4] where my father usually took me to see the opening sessions of Parliament. A group of women in black veils were in the area normally reserved for the government. The new queen, the princesses, the ladies-in-waiting, were advancing slowly like a procession of black shadows. Under one of the veils I caught a glimpse of the sash of the Crown of Romania order; it was Queen Marie. At that instant one of the Chamber's quaestors ascended to the dais and announced: "His Majesty the King!" Instead of the figure we had grown so used to, that of old King Carol I starting to read the Royal Message with a pronounced German accent ("Chentlemen Zenadors, Chentlemen Tebudies . . ."), it was the delicate, shy, distinguished figure of his nephew, our new king, that appeared. All those present burst into endless acclamations of "Long live the King!" Ferdinand, who was then forty-nine years old, seemed sad, tired, overcome by emotion. Nevertheless, he recited the Oath in a firm voice, although with a strong foreign accent. He then began reading his Proclamation to the Romanian people. When he came to his promise to be "a good Romanian and king," he was inter-

[4]Înalta Curte de Casaţie, Romania's equivalent of the Supreme Court.

rupted by an unending round of applause, for everyone understood that he was pledging to the Romanian people that he would forget his German birth when the time came to enter the war for the unification of the nation. He had to repeat the sentence, the end of which had been drowned out by the ovation of the members of Parliament.

Now, after nearly nine years, I was seeing the king again, crowned with victory and at the height of his popularity. His hair was a bit whiter and his waistline was not quite as slender, but his eyes were cheerful, and he was talkative and amusing. The queen, too, seemed happy, and her conversation, in a French tinged with a slight English accent, was very witty.

The morning of our arrival in Warsaw we were all waiting for the royal train to get to the station, spruced up in our uniforms (diplomatic or military; Mocsonyi, as grand master of the hunts, wore a green one that was a great success) or in ministerial tailcoats adorned with multicolored sashes. All of a sudden we heard our national anthem, played, it is true, with a rather unusual beat: we were entering the station. As they alighted from their railway car, the sovereigns were met by the president of the Polish Republic, Stanislaw Wojciechowski and his wife. Brătianu was cordially greeted by Polish Prime Minister Witos, head of the Agrarian party, who was wearing peasant attire (somewhat improved esthetically for the occasion, we were to learn later). The procession of carriages moved from the railway station toward the Lazenki Palace, built in the Adam de Stanislas Poniatowsi style, where the royal couple was to be housed. The king and the president were in the first carriage, in the second the queen and Mrs. Wojciechowska. The third carriage was a landau seating four—Brătianu and Witos, and facing them Count Michael Potulicki (Witos' chief of cabinet, attached to Brătianu during our stay) and I. The city was decked with our flag, and the crowd along the route cheered warmly. Brătianu and the rest of us were then taken to our lodgings in various Branicki palaces situated in a park in the center of Warsaw.

I cannot recall all the details of the festivities, but I do remember a big official dinner given by the president of the republic at which we were served a vintage Tokay, and a gala at the Opera. There was an endless series of lunches and dinners. One of the dinners, at our legation, was attended by Field Marshal Pilsudski, who was not yet at the helm of his country. At another dinner I was seated next to a high ecclesiastical dignitary who spoke no living language except Polish and addressed me in Latin—surely the only time in my life that I had to converse in my ancestors' tongue.

Since high-school Latin was fading from my memory and I kept confusing it with the more recently learned Italian, our conversation was rather halting. I know he asked me, "*Ecclesia catholica persecutata est in Romania?*" To which I answered emphatically: "*Ecclesia catholica non est persecutata in Romania!*" I don't believe we told each other much else. A garden party in the castle of Wilanow, near Warsaw, also comes to mind.

After visiting Cracow, we all spent a delightful weekend at Zanćut, the Potocki family's castle—a huge place in a bizarre variety of styles, but set in a superb park and containing furniture and art objects of great value, among which the furniture of Marie Antoinette's sitting room at Trianon and a series of large Chinese vases given by a Chinese emperor to the Polish king Sobieski. Luxury reached even into the numerous thoroughbred stables, which had big red carpets in the center. Each stable contained leather armchairs along with a table with glasses and a cabinet containing bottles, so that gentlemen might sit down comfortably with a drink while admiring the horses. The coachhouses were packed with all kinds of rare carriages and vehicles of all periods, and we were driven in them throughout the estate. The mistress of the castle was the famous and still beautiful Countess Betka Potocka, née Radziwill, who did the honors with her son, Count Alfred Potocki, the head of the family. I had occasion to meet them often in Switzerland during our common exile after World War II. They always seemed pleased to meet with someone who had known Zanćut in its time of splendor and with whom they could reminisce about their past wealth and happiness. They told me that they had had at least the good fortune of saving the works of art and the valuable pieces of furniture, which they had entrusted to the Reigning Prince of Liechtenstein, whose subjects they subsequently became in order to acquire a nationality. Alfred Potocki married at the age of seventy-two, after his mother's death, Mrs. Sidney, a likable and rich Polish woman, the widow of an American.

The castle had escaped untouched during World War I, even though battles had been fought nearby. It had been protected, Betka Potocka explained, by Russian grand dukes and Austrian archdukes alike, all of them recalling with warm feelings the famous hunting parties and the brilliant balls they had attended as guests of the Potocki family. And indeed, looking through the castle's guest book, I came upon the signatures of the sovereigns and army commanders who later waged war against each other.

It was said that the Potockis could take each meal in a different room for an entire month, so large was their castle. In any event, I never ate twice in the same room during the few days I stayed there. I shall never forget the formal dinner they gave in a huge hall in which Sobieski's renowned Chinese vases were aligned on their pedestals. The table glittered with silverware, the flower arrangement was all in one hue of pink, the glasses bore the monogram of King Stanislas Poniatowsky, to whom they had belonged. Around the table, set for perhaps sixty people, were the most beautiful women of Poland, sparkling with diadems and jewelry. Officialdom was absent, it was exclusively a social dinner, and I had the impression that King Ferdinand and Queen Marie were delighted and felt in their milieu. As a diplomat, I obviously attended over the years many formal dinners, in many courts and embassies, as is required by our profession, but I can't remember having ever been at a party that was more splendidly arranged in all aspects: the setting, the menu, the wines, the powdered footmen behind each chair, and, above all, the beauty and elegance of the women who were there. And all this overflow of luxury and brilliance offered by mere private citizens, persons to whom fate was to reserve such a sorrowful end of their lives.

✧ ✧ ✧

In August 1924 I was temporarily attached to the illustrious British admiral Lord Beatty, who was coming on a quasi-official visit to our country. Admiral David Beatty, elevated to an earldom by George V, had won the renowned naval victories of Helgoland, Dogger Bank, and Jutland, and was now seen as one of the great figures of the British navy. Our government, wanting him to be received with all due honors, had prepared a detailed program to impress him and his companions with the beauty and riches of our country. I was sent to Constanţa to greet them on their arrival in the yacht *Sheila.*

The yacht, flying the admiral's colors, was magnificent—big and luxuriously appointed. When I went aboard to greet the First Sea Lord on behalf of the government, I found a typical Englishman, cordial, likable, and looking much younger than his fifty-two years. After the usual exchange of civilities he invited me to a drink in one of the yacht's staterooms, where I met the passengers who were accompanying him: Lady Beatty (a quite sophisticated American), their son David, the Duke and Duchess of Sutherland (she, a British beauty full of Irish charm), Viscount and Viscountess Ednam (he, the future Earl Ednam, a close friend of Edward VIII; she, Sutherland's sister), as well as another young Englishman whose name escapes me. After some time, the local authorities (prefect, mayor, commander of the naval base, admirals, and other high-ranking officers of our navy) boarded the yacht to greet Lord Beatty, while I acted as interpreter. Then came Constanţa's British colony, with the vice-consul at its head; to my astonishment, they were completely ignored by their fellow countrymen from the yacht.

Then we all left by special train for Bucharest and the official welcome. This began as soon as the guests had been quartered at the Athénée Palace—with the usual series of official visits, luncheons, and dinner parties, including a dancing party at the Ministry of Foreign Affairs. The young diplomats had received formal instructions from Duca to dance continuously with the Englishwomen, without letting them catch their breath. We carried out the instructions to the letter and with pleasure, because all three were very attractive and two of them were even young. The parquets of the Sturdza Palace creaked under the dancing to the tunes of jazz and waltzes, as they hadn't since the times of *Beizadea* Grigore and Princess Raluca Sturdza.

The most pleasant part of the visit was, however, a journey down the Danube on the fine yacht of our Fluvial Service. The meals on board were excellent—caviar and Odobeşti wine, to the sound of Grigoraş Dinicu and his folk music band, all perfectly organized by Atta Constantinescu. Ionel Brătianu and his colleagues in the government were full of zest. The beautiful Duchess of Sutherland rendered them lyrical. One of them addressed compliments to her in an imperfect French, which she seemed not quite to understand. Brătianu was in excellent form and won over his guests with his unpretentiousness and kindness.

On the way back to Bucharest, when stopping in Ploeşti, we went to the famous restaurant at the railway station (one of the best in Romania, until recently managed, surprisingly, by the well-known critic and Socialist leader Dobrogeanu-Gherea) to taste the famous pâtés with *ţuică*.[5] On the table there was a plate of hot red peppers. The beautiful Eileen Sutherland reached for one. I stopped her, telling her that they were extremely hot and that she had better keep away from them. But she did not believe me and put an entire pepper in her mouth. Everybody can imagine what followed: tears, moans, glassfuls of water. We did not know how to comfort her; we nearly called a physician! I met the duchess again some years later at the British embassy in Rome, and as we both recalled the wayward red pepper from Ploeşti, she jokingly told

[5]Romanian plum brandy.

me that henceforth she would follow whatever advice I gave her. We never met again.

A few days later we left for Sinaia, where Lord and Lady Beatty had been invited by the king and queen to stay with them at Peleş Castle. At an informal dancing party at the castle the admiral proved himself an indefatigable dancer. From Sinaia we went into Transylvania, where Bébé Brătianu had organized, not without difficulty in view of the lack of adequate accommodations in the countryside, an outstanding excursion, with stops at Câmpeni and Mount Găina. In those days our highways were mediocre, and one was engulfed in the dust raised by cars and carts. Lady Beatty, her son, and the young Englishman preferred to await our return at the Athénée Palace where the stifling heat could be fought by taking showers and refreshing oneself at the bar, amenities that were unknown in Câmpeni or on Mount Găina. The other guests, however, joined by Grand Duchesses Masha and Kira (the queen's nieces), manly confronted the dust and the heat and seemed much taken by the splendid views and the picturesque costumes of the peasant women.

A few weeks after our British guests left Romania, I received through the British legation a parcel containing Lord Beatty's dedicated photograph, a silver cigarette case with his signature engraved inside, and a letter of thanks. The Duchess of Sutherland had also added a snapshot of herself, a silver Dunhill lighter, and some very kind lines.

✧ ✧ ✧

Among the numerous official visits on which I accompanied Ionel Brătianu, the ones I remember with the most pleasure are those to the new provinces attached to our country.

The visit King Ferdinand, Queen Marie, and the government paid to the Banat was undertaken by royal train and with the same high spirits as the one to Poland. We were all enraptured by the landscape of the Banat, quite unknown to most of us, and by the diversity of the villages and of the peasant costumes. We stayed in the larger urban centers, from where we would drive along country back roads in search of villages and hamlets inhabited by Romanians, Swabians, Serbs, and others. At the primary school of a small Bulgarian village, we heard a child, dressed in his nation's costume, reciting with much conviction Neniţescu's lines: "From the union of Dacia and Rome, forever lion cubs shall be born!" The diversity of the Banat is owing to Maria Theresa, who garrisoned the border province with inhabitants from the farthest reaches of the

Holy Empire, so that to this day there are villages where German, Hungarian, Serbo-Croatian, and even French are spoken.

In larger cities, such as Timişoara, Caransebeş, and Lugoj, our stay would be more prolonged. The king and queen, accompanied by the entourage, would attend Te Deums in the Orthodox church, the Uniate church, the Roman Catholic church, a Protestant church or other, and even at times a synagogue, to give satisfaction to all their subjects, whatever their creed. I remember a slight problem at the Timişoara synagogue, I think it was, when the choir began to sing the royal anthem. The king and the officers saluted militarily, while we civilians instinctively took off our hats. The synagogue's elders came hurriedly to ask us to cover ourselves again, in accordance with the rules of the Jewish religion. I do not know who took the initiative of putting his hat back on and saluting militarily; we all followed that example, from Brătianu down.

Another official visit took us with royal pomp to Oradea Mare for the inauguration of Ferdinand's statue. Out of discretion and modesty, the king himself did not attend, and it was up to Prince Carol to give the required speech. He delivered it with much ardor, almost theatrically. On the way back, after a stop in Cluj, while we were all in the dining car, Carol remarked to Brătianu: "I am glad not to suffer from my father's difficulty in public speaking. Fortunately, words come so easily to me." Brătianu, only half jokingly, retorted: "Your Highness, you'd better watch that. There is nothing more dangerous for a sovereign than to have words come to him too easily."

✧ ✧ ✧

A journey that was particularly stirring for me was the one to Bessarabia, with which my family has had so many close ties. A forebear of mine, chief magistrate of Orhei, founded in the seventeenth century a monastery on the banks of the Răut river, and following the marriage of the *Căminar*[6] Iordaki Bossy with Anastasia Şendrea, my family inherited two of the seven estates given by Stephen the Great to his brother-in-law Şendrea, chief magistrate of Suceava. Both estates were on the bank of the Dniester, and it was with emotion that I approached that river, in the waters of which, following Brătianu's example, we all waded. The Hotin Fortress and Cetatea Albă,[7] glorious reminders of Moldavian valor, were equally moving; we felt proud,

[6]High-ranking boyar in charge of levying liquor taxes.
[7]White Fortress.

and grateful, that our country had been reunited "from the Dniester to the Tisza," in the words of the poet. At Ismail, Ionel Brătianu's eyes seemed to fill with tears when he was presented with the city's golden book, in which he found his father's signature, "I.C. Brătianu, 1876." Under it his son, also prime minister, added his signature: "Ion I.C. Brătianu, 1924." As I write this, an exile on foreign soil, Divine Providence has once again subjected the Romanian nation to a cruel trial: the Fortress of Hotin, Cetatea Albă, Ismail, the Dniester have again fallen under the domination of the same old and implacable foe. But unwavering faith remains in my heart that the wheel shall turn once again, that right shall prevail, that poor truncated Moldavia shall recover its unity and its ancestral borders.

✧ ✧ ✧

It was around this time that the government was reshuffled, and Ionel Brătianu, hoping to put an end to rivalries between his political friends, took over as minister of the interior, in addition to his position as prime minister. He told us, his closer collaborators: "If someone comes looking for me at the Presidency of the Council of Ministers and does not find me there, you will know that I am at the Ministry of the Interior. But if someone looks for me at the Ministry of the Interior and does not find me, then you'll know that I am at the Presidency of the Council." In fact, however, the prime minister never went to either the Presidency of the Council or the Ministry of the Interior: he still continued to work from his home at No. 5 Lascar Catargi Street, where he as well as his collaborators had offices, and where he saw those who wanted to meet with him—members of the government, foreign diplomats, party leaders (not just his own), and, when time permitted, fellow historians.

CAROL'S RENOUNCEMENT OF THE THRONE

In the fall of 1925, insistent rumors began to circulate about problems in the heir apparent's private life. Carol had always been capricious and rather flighty. He was endowed with undeniable intellectual gifts, fairly cultured, and he had considerable personal charm when he was willing to make the effort, but he could be surly, even impolite, to those whom he disliked. Certainly he was a big question mark for the future. His upbringing had been neglected and his education had been entrusted to a Swiss tutor, Moehrlen, whom many strongly criticized. This was in crying contrast to the grooming generally given to royal offspring. When the

Kronprinz came to Romania to deliver to King Carol I the baton of field marshal in the German army, people had been impressed by the good manners of the heir to the imperial throne and his politeness toward the ladies—he kissed their hands respectfully, he stepped aside to let them pass first—a natural behavior, to be sure, but one that was not usual among his Hohenzollern cousins from Romania. At a reception around that time, for instance, the young Prince Carol, in greeting the venerable doyenne of Bucharest society, Mrs. Anastasia Filipescu, vigorously shook her hand. The old lady could not keep back a slight moan of pain. The prince excused himself, laughing: "Did I shake your hand too strongly?" She replied calmly, "It's nothing, it's my fault. For many years I have no longer been used to having young men shake my hand; they usually kiss it." Unfortunately, Carol had greater faults than his lack of courtesy.

Toward the end of the war, in 1918, the heir to the Romanian throne had run off from the military front to Odessa to marry Ioana Lambrino, nicknamed Zizi, knowing full well that a marriage with the daughter of a Moldavian boyar, however distinguished and honorable the family, would meet the same "this ain't possible" with which Lascar Catargi had opposed, a quarter century earlier, the proposed marriage of Prince Ferdinand with Elena Văcărescu, who, though the descendant of one of the oldest and most illustrious Romanian families, was not of royal blood. Carol's idyll was short-lived. The newlyweds soon gave in and were brought back to Romania, Carol receiving, apart from a severe paternal reprimand, several weeks of arrest for abandonment of post. The marriage was then quickly annulled, even though both religious and civil ceremonies had been performed in Odessa. Carol seems to have had little trouble getting over his attachment to his Zizi and the son he had given her, a son he had the unheard-of heartlessness of refusing to see, even once, during his entire life.

After a voyage around the world, Carol met in Switzerland the beautiful Princess Helen of Greece and easily let himself be persuaded to become engaged. The wedding took place in Athens on March 10, 1921. There is no doubt that this marriage had more to do with dynastic considerations than with real love—at most, it was the sequel to a physical attraction. There was an abyss between the two personalities—the hot-tempered Carol and the sensitive and refined Helen—as well as between their sense of personal and moral obligation. Nothing can excuse Carol's indelicacy and cynicism toward the future queen and the mother of his son Michael. She overlooked with royal elegance her husband's unfaithfulness and adultery—which he made no effort to hide.

Indeed, there was no point in Carol's running away with Elena Lupescu after his trip to London to attend Queen Alexandra's funeral, not even from a purely selfish point of view. The liaison could have continued, with the resigned and tacit assent of his legitimate spouse. Public opinion therefore obviously asked itself, why this theatrical and useless gesture? Persons in the know about the private life of the reigning family made allusions, more or less transparent, to some long-standing situations that Carol's pride could no longer endure. Indignant, sickened, after a few painful scenes, he would have decided to call it quits, to break relations with his family, to renounce once more the throne, and to decamp with his paramour. If this is how things stood, Carol's reaction would evidently have had some extenuating reasons. Even so, that does not exactly explain why he was so determined to leave his wife and child. His actions were paradoxical: to escape what he regarded as an intolerable situation, he himself was producing a situation that was far worse—for many people. In the name of "offended morality," he adopted an attitude incomparably more immoral and cynical than that which, rightly or wrongly, he so harshly denounced. The fact is that he wrote to his father from Milan, from the Albergo della Città, that he had taken the decision not to return.

Constantin Hiott, minister of the royal household, described to me later the morning when King Ferdinand told him with grief: "I am greatly saddened: I received from Carol a letter in which he informs me that he is renouncing his rights to the throne, and this time I will accept his renunciation!" The last part of the sentence had been uttered with particular resolution. The sovereigns and the government hurriedly sent the minister of the royal household to Milan, to beseech Carol to reconsider and not to betray once more his duties toward his country and family. Hiott had with him the original of the instructions received from King Ferdinand, written in French and entitled *Instructions pour Hiott* (part of which he later read to me). One of the conditions the king set for Carol's return was a change in his private life. I was asked by the prime minister to accompany Hiott to the railway station and to transmit to him some last-minute instructions. The minister of the royal household seemed pessimistic about what could result from his journey, knowing how obstinate and proud Carol was. To go back on the dramatic decision he had taken would obviously have been a loss of face. Only if the king and government's last appeal failed was Hiott authorized to submit to the prince the text of the legally drafted renunciation to the throne.

From the very first cables sent by Hiott from Milan, it became clear that nothing more could be expected from Carol's side. I had the opportunity of talking again with Hiott when he came back from Italy. He told me that the prince had been calm and polite, but adamant in his decision. Hiott was a good friend of my parents and trusted me fully, and he read to me excerpts from the report he submitted to King Ferdinand on his return from Milan. In that report (written in French so as to be better understood by the sovereigns) he said that, as instructed, he had asked Carol to choose between two alternatives: either to part from Elena Lupescu, return to Romania, and report to the king, who would initially designate his place of residence; or to renounce all his rights and prerogatives as crown prince. According to the report, Hiott pleaded, almost with tears in his eyes, for the first alternative, but Carol was resolved in his decision, and without hesitation signed the text prepared by the king. Hiott, unwilling to take the renunciation deed on the spot, gave him twenty-four hours to change his mind. The next day, in the face of Carol's resoluteness, Hiott had to accept the renunciation instrument and bring it back to Bucharest. As they were parting, Carol made a point of emphasizing that his irrevocable decision had no political motive, only a private one. In a letter to Princess Helen he wrote, "Hiott behaved like a gentleman." Later he was to say that, had he known that his father had only a year and a half to live, he would not have renounced the throne.

Once Hiott had handed the renunciation deed to the king, only constitutional formalities remained to change the succession to the throne. Carol's renunciation deed was submitted to Parliament for approval on January 4, 1926, and, notwithstanding the noisy protests of the opposition, led by Maniu and Iorga, it became law. The former Prince Carol became the citizen Carol Caraiman.[8] At the same time, the young Michael, aged four, was proclaimed heir to the throne and a Regency was established for the eventuality that he might become king before coming of age. There had been many discussions in Brătianu's house about the composition of the Regency, and a number of names had been mentioned, among which those of Queen Marie, of Princess Helen, and of former President of the High Court of Appeal Corneliu Manolescu-Râmniceanu. In the end, the decision was that the three regents would be Prince Nicholas,[9] as representative of the royal family; Patriarch Miron Cristea, as head of the Church; and the highest magistrate in office, Gheorghe V. Buzdugan, president of the High Court of Appeal.

---

[8]Caraiman is a mountain not far from Sinaia.

[9]Ferdinand's second son, born 1903.

The opposition parties and a substantial part of public opinion, whether from ignorance of the facts or hostility toward the Liberals in power, seemed convinced that Carol's removal had been plotted by Brătianu and his brother-in-law Barbu Ştirbey in order to get rid of the only member of the royal family who opposed the "all-powerful Vizier," as Ionel Brătianu was named in the ranks of the opposition. The former heir apparent's amorous escapades, his flight with Elena Lupescu, the abandonment of his home, of an enchanting young bride, of a charming little son—all these were either overlooked or were viewed as the desperate acts of a man who was thwarted in his efforts to develop aviation, and who, moreover, suffered from certain irregularities in the reigning family that had repercussions on public life. The simplistic summary of the dynastic drama went as follows: in view of the more than cool relations between Carol and the prime minister, the latter realized that his predominant role in the country's political life would come to an end at the same time as Ferdinand's reign; it was for this reason that he conspired with Ştirbey to get the heir to the throne in a situation from which he could escape only by once more renouncing the crown, thereby securing Brătianu's own future.

This charge was entirely unfounded and unfair. I recall how one afternoon, as I was strolling with Brătianu, our conversation drifted to this scenario that was spreading, disseminated in good part by the National-Peasant party. He shrugged his shoulders: "As if kings chose their prime ministers according to their personal sympathies! Does anybody believe that King Ferdinand has kept me in power for so many years because I was dear to him? Come on! It is only for the reason that, during his reign, it is the Liberal party that has been the strongest political force in the country, and that he therefore felt safer leaning on that force. And it is for this same reason that I would have remained in government even had Prince Carol become king, regardless of his personal feelings toward me."

But it was Brătianu's opinion—the facts being as they were, shaped by the will of that rash and mercurial individual who had twice placed his family and country in such dramatic situations—that Romania had been lucky (a "blessing in disguise"), to be saved forever, as he believed, from the danger of having such a man at the helm of the state.

BRĂTIANU GOES, AVERESCU COMES

Toward the end of March 1926, the Liberal party having been in power for four years and new elections being due, Ionel Brătianu tendered to King

Ferdinand the resignation of his government. The resignation was in no way called for by the current situation, but the "Vizier" considered it useful for his party to "rest," to draw up a new political program, a new electoral platform, and to reappraise all its officials, knowing full well that the time spent in opposition would not be overly long. Besides, it was good for the country for other political forces to taste the bittersweet fruits of power, to, in effect, associate themselves with the constitutional system set up after Carol's renunciation of his rights to the throne.

It was obvious that the most appropriate party to take over, owing to its size and political authority, was the National party, whose chief, Iuliu Maniu, symbolized the reunification of the nation and the fulfillment of the secular dream of the Romanians. The party had not yet merged with Mihalache's Peasant party, however, and it deliberately remained ambiguous with regard to the "constitutional question"—that is, to Carol's renunciation of the throne. Furthermore, the National party, in its political fight against the Liberals, had gone to the extreme of not attending King Ferdinand's coronation, and in other ways it attacked the crown for keeping the Brătianu government in power. Grigore Filipescu, in his father's *Epoca,* led a campaign against the "camarilla" with all the passion and violence inherited from his father and grandfather. Daily there appeared a cartoon with Barbu Ştirbey's caricature, but the attacks were directed above his head, toward the government accused of leaving the reins of the state exclusively in the hands of Brătianu, Ştirbey's brother-in-law.

This antidynastic sentiment, which if not building up steam in the background was at least clearly apparent, had turned by 1926 into "carlism." The National party was almost openly betting on Carol, whom it was to bring back to Romania in 1930, to its grief and that of the country. In these circumstances, collaboration between Ferdinand and the Transylvanians of the National party was almost impossible. There remained only an Averescu solution. The news of the formation of a government headed by General Alexandru Averescu came as a great surprise to several groups that had even been predicting the composition of a Maniu-Mihalache government, with Vaida-Voevod at Foreign Affairs and Carol A. Davila as his undersecretary of state.

I recall the customary courtesy visit paid by Averescu to his predecessor, in which he informed him of the composition of his government. Included were also some former Conservatives, such as Constantin Garoflid at Agriculture and Ion M. Mitilineu at Foreign Affairs, and Transylvanians, such as Octavian Goga at Internal Affairs and Vasile Goldiş at the Ministry of Religious Affairs (not to mention the infamous Petru Groza!).

Mitilineu, son and brother of diplomats, was one of the most likable Bucharest figures. Although he had served as chief commissioner of police, deputy, the capital's mayor, and minister of justice, he had been less involved in political fights than his predecessor, Duca. His arrival at the Sturdza Palace had been greeted with joy not only by our diplomatic corps but also by the foreign diplomatic corps accredited to Bucharest. Very intelligent, cultured, distinguished, a gentleman, everybody found him more flexible, more polite, and with much more personal appeal than his predecessors in that position.

With the withdrawal of Ionel Brătianu, my position as his political director came to an end. Mitilineu proposed that I return to my former post in Rome, this time as first secretary. I had left Rome with some regret and only to be able to work closely with the greatest Romanian statesman of his time. In the meantime, happy events had also occurred in my personal life. I had got married, and our first child had been born. It would be a joy for my young wife and for me to spend our first years of marriage in lovely Italy. I therefore accepted the proposal with the greatest satisfaction, glad to find again in Rome my former boss, Alexander Lahovary, for whom I had so much respect and affection. Another happy piece of news for us: we would be accompanied to Italy by my brother and sister-in-law, for my brother, by then a captain, had been named assistant military attaché of our legation in Rome.

4

Second Tour in Rome (1926–1927)

After a lapse of three years I was returning to Rome, happy to find myself again in that marvelous city and to resume my old duties and habits. The same office in the Palazzo Santa Croce, the same pilgrimages to Rome's monuments, churches, and museums, the same hours of respite at nightfall at the Circolo della Caccia. My wife and I had had the luck of finding an exquisitely furnished apartment, packed with art objects, in the neighborhood of the Villa Borghese. Walking to the legation, I passed by the pines of Piazza di Siena, toward the Fontana dei Cavalli Marini, then on to the Pincio, in front of the Villa Medici, to Trinità dei Monti, from where I descended the famous steps of Piazza di Spagna.

At the legation, the work was enjoyable because, under the leadership of Averescu and Mitilineu, Romania's foreign policy was going through a phase of unusual euphoria after the signing, on June 10, 1926, of the treaty of alliance with France, which guaranteed our borders. We could put aside the doubts and worries awakened the year before when France began talking of returning to the Soviet Union the Russian Black Sea fleet, interned in Bizerta after Wrangel's defeat. Concurrently, on the instructions of Averescu—a great Italophile, who in his youth had attended Turin's War School and who was married to an Italian—Mitilineu had been working through the intermediary of my chief, Alexander Lahovary, for a rapprochement with the government in Rome. There has always been an abiding sense of rivalry between the Italians and the French, especially with regard to political and cultural penetration in Central and Southeastern Europe. France's predominant influence in this region and the establishment under its aegis of the Little Entente and of Poland's system of alliances were among the many reasons for the Fascist government's "jealousy." It was therefore a true tour de force to succeed in concluding, almost concomitantly, similar alliances with the two rival powers.

To sign the Italo-Romanian alliance treaty, the prime minister himself decided to come to Rome in September 1926. Lahovary and I went to receive him at the Termini station where an official welcoming party had been organized, Mussolini being represented by his undersecretary of state from the Palazzo Chigi, Dino Grandi. It was my first contact with our great national hero of Mărăşti,[1] General (later Field Marshal) Alexandru Averescu. Tall, thin, very reserved and dignified, he did not strike one as a first-rate political mind, and he occasionally made blunders when he did not follow the advice of his much more experienced and skilled foreign minister, Ion Mitilineu.

The day before the official luncheon Mussolini was to give in his honor, and knowing I was a student of the history of Italo-Romanian diplomatic relations (a topic on which I had published several articles), Averescu asked me to jot down the most significant points of these relations. I prepared a brief note mentioning the diplomatic help we received from Sardinia, and later from Italy, at the time of the Congress of Paris in 1856, of the proclamation of the union of the Principalities, of the proclamation of independence, and so on. Either because his aide did not realize that these were merely a few points to assist in the drafting of his remarks, or because he himself, not being used to such diplomatic exchanges, thought I had prepared the actual text of his address, the fact is that Averescu had my note translated and, to my astonishment, read it word for word the next day at the official luncheon. His toast was becoming a sort of lecture on diplomatic history, with a dry stringing of facts. Volpi di Misurata, the Italian finance minister, who was sitting across the table from me, raised his eyebrows in surprise. The Duce's reply was very cordial and encouraging with regard to Bessarabia.

I remember well the stately background of the Empire-style Villa Torlonia where Mussolini lived, and the huge round dining room with a large marble table of the same shape around which we all sat in an atmosphere of

[1]In the fierce battle of Mărăşti (July 22–August 1, 1917), the Romanian First Army under General Averescu succeeded in breaching the German lines on a length of 30 km and a depth of 20 km, but it was unable to follow up because of the defection of the Russian troops on its flank.

restored friendship. I was seated between the owner of the house, the auburn-haired Prince Torlonia, and the subsecretary of state for foreign affairs, Dino Grandi. At one point in our conversation Grandi told me: "Do you know why we, the Fascist officials, work with so much zeal? It is because we were nobodies, lost in the humble mass of the population from which the Duce raised us to the positions of leadership we now hold. We are therefore fully aware that we are totally dependent on the Duce, and that the day he feels we are no longer performing our tasks satisfactorily, he will let us fall back into the anonymity of the mass of the population." It is apparent, however, that Grandi knew for many years how to live up to the dictator's expectations, since he became minister of foreign affairs and was raised by the Duce to the rank of count. And when he fell into relative disfavor, he was appointed ambassador to London—a rather pleasant disfavor. Nevertheless, Grandi was one of Mussolini's collaborators who unseated him in the Council of the Fascist Hierarchy of August 1943.

The Mussolini-Averescu talks led to the conclusion of a Treaty of Friendship and Cordial Collaboration, with the implicit pledge to recognize Bessarabia as an integral part of Romania—a recognition that was to follow shortly. In the signing of the treaty, each of the two heads of government had to impress his seal on wax melted onto the document. General Averescu was unable to perform this formality, either because he had forgotten to bring his seal along or because he did not have one. My chief, Alexander Lahovary, had the happy thought of rummaging through the drawers in which he kept family souvenirs. He found among them the seal of his maternal grandfather, Dr. Apostol Arsaki, who had been appointed prime minister of Romania on June 8, 1862, following the murder of Barbu Catargi. Since the initials were the same, Averescu could use the seal. And so, sixty-four years later, the poor Arsaki once more endorsed an official Romanian document! On that occasion Mussolini distributed among us his photograph with a dedication; I still have the one the Duce gave me two decades before his dramatic downfall.

After the Italian parliament had ratified the treaty concerning Bessarabia, General Badoglio, chief of Italy's general staff, paid in turn an official visit to Romania. He was made an honorary citizen of Romania and was given in Bessarabia, which he also visited, a piece of farmland of the same size as those that were given to landless veterans after the land reform. Each time I met him thereafter, he would talk to me about his "small estate" in Bessarabia.

Returning to Romania on vacation in early summer 1927, I learned of the fatal cancer that had stricken King Ferdinand. In spite of all the rather belated surgical interventions he underwent, the king was living his last days. Brătianu decided to take again the reins of the country, being afraid of leaving it in the weak hands of the Averescu government, which would not have commanded the strength necessary to oppose a possible Carlist agitation. The transition was to take place in two steps: first, the famous "sandbagging," as Averescu himself was to describe his abrupt replacement (Hiott gave him to countersign the decree naming his successor); and then the parody of a government presided over by Barbu Ştirbey, which lasted but two weeks. I think Ştirbey may have deluded himself into believing he could maintain himself in power by obtaining the opposition's support, but the National-Peasants spurned him and he had to resign. On his deathbed, the king asked Brătianu to form the next government, and the latter asked me to stand by him as political director of the Presidency of the Council of Ministers. It is thus, and for the same reason as before, that my second stay in Italy came to an end.

5

Secretary-General of the Regency (1927–1930)

General elections were being held, but the fatal outcome of King Ferdinand's cancer seemed so imminent that a rather ticklish constitutional issue arose. The new Parliament could not be deemed constituted until half of the mandates of the deputies and senators had been validated. Unless this occurred, it would be the old Parliament that would have to be called into session to receive the oath of the new sovereign or, in this case, of the regents. The king's agony dragged on until after the end of the elections. The deliberations over the validation of the mandates began, and the Liberal majorities in both houses tried to hasten the process. The very day that half the mandates had been validated, news came from Sinaia that the king had only a few more hours to live.

THE DEATH OF KING FERDINAND AND THE SETTING UP OF THE REGENCY

I accompanied the prime minister to Sinaia. On the way, he told me that he had given much thought in the past few days to the most appropriate way of organizing the functioning of the future Regency; its task would not be easy, both because of the lack of political experience of its members and because there would be three people to convince or to bring into agreement. They would need a competent and capable secretary-general, serious, discreet, tactful—qualities that Ionel Brătianu seemed to think I had, and he asked me whether I would be willing to accept this position, since he did not want to propose my name to the future regents without having first secured my agreement. But I should not think he would be in the least displeased were I to give him a negative answer, Brătianu added; on the contrary, from a purely selfish point of view, he would be happy to have me continue my direct collaboration with him at the Presidency of the Council of Ministers. The decision was entirely up to me, he said, but he asked me not to lose sight of the fact that, the king's death being imminent, the organization of the Regency must not be delayed. I felt that Brătianu hoped that I would accept—otherwise he would not have made the proposal—and he pointed out the importance of the mission and of the role I would play. I answered that when I entered the diplomatic career I was preparing to serve abroad. But since the statesman on whose shoulders lay, in these grave moments, responsibilities of historic significance seemed to think that I would be of greater use in Romania, I asked him to decide where I could best serve the country. It therefore remained that the prime minister would propose to the regents that I be appointed secretary-general of the Regency. Later on, Hiott was to disclose to me that already in April 1926, when King Ferdinand was ill with pneumonia, Averescu, who was then prime minister, and Brătianu had agreed that, in the event of a fatal outcome, I would be recalled from Rome to take up the position of secretary-general of the Regency.

We arrived in Sinaia, on July 19, 1927, under pouring rain—a true deluge, quite unusual for midsummer. Day after day bad weather had pounded the region of the country where Romania's second king was dying. Brătianu spent the night in Braşov, at his brother-in-law Ştirbey's, while I stayed in Sinaia at my father-in-law's Villa Cantacuzino, from which I could be called at a moment's notice to Pelişor Castle.

I was aroused in the middle of the night by the telephone. The aide-de-camp on duty, Colonel Zwiedenek, informed me with emotion, "At 2:15 A.M., his majesty gave up the soul." A car was sent for me and drove me to Pelişor, from where I called Brătianu, who left immediately for Sinaia. A heavy rain, uninterrupted and penetrating, shrouded Sinaia, the Bucegi Mountains, and the entire Prahova Valley like a funeral veil on that gloomy morning of July 20, 1927. It had been known that the king had fallen prey to an unforgiving disease, and that he was in such terrible agony that his death would be a deliverance for his tortured and exhausted body. And yet, in this sorrowful moment, an undefinable feeling of anxiety, of fear of what lay ahead, was interspersed in everyone's breast with the natural grief for the loss of the man, honest and pure at heart, whose name had been inscribed at the head of the most glorious page of Romanian history.

The king's bedroom was on the ground floor of Pelişor Castle. In his narrow cot, his face furrowed by suffering, the monarch had finally reached the shores of peacefulness. The paleness of his emaciated face seemed to accentuate the aristocratic delicacy of his features. *Un grand seigneur au repos*. In front of the bed, his unsheathed sword held in the prescribed position, Lieutenant Colonel Manolescu, Prince Nicholas's aide-de-camp, stood guard, motionless. After a while, the Catholic priest Carol Fischer arrived. He had been my German-language teacher, and now was substituting as vicar of the Catholic chapel in Sinaia. After so many years, we met again with emotion near the bed of the dead king. Father Fischer knelt and, in a low voice, began to recite the ritual prayers.

In the presence of the lifeless body of my king, in that atmosphere of silent and reverent recollection, I was contemplating the life of he who had been Ferdinand von Hohenzollern.[1] Reflections on the past and worries about the future were interrupted by the arrival of the prime minister, who was instantly received in their living quarters, by the dowager queen and those of her children who were in Romania.

Then, in a ground-floor drawing room, we—hastily assembled members of the government, court officials, and high-level civil servants—immediately set to the task of making the necessary arrangements for the succession. First of all, the Romanian people had to be informed of the death of their king. Ion Duca, the minister of internal affairs, proposed that the official communiqué state that King Ferdinand had died in the arms of Queen Marie, although, in fact, when he passed away in the middle of the night he was being looked after only by a nurse, the royal family, after so many exhausting and anxious hours, resting at that time on the second floor. The proposal was adopted, because "it will make a good impression on the public." History must sometimes "improve" on reality! We then discussed the attire in which Ferdinand should be buried and with what decorations. It was decided that he would wear the uniform of an officer of mountain troops, because that was the first uniform he wore on his arrival in Romania. On my suggestion, it was decided that, along with the Romanian decorations, the plaque of the Hohenzollern Order and the Golden Fleece chain, which he prized so much, should also be included.

Another discussion then arose: under what name should the new king be proclaimed? Brătianu told us that General Averescu had favored

[1]These reminiscences are set forth in Appendix A.

"Michael IV" (the first three being obviously Michael the Brave, Michael Racoviţă, and Michael Suţu),[2] or at least Michael II. I proposed the following title: "Michael II, Prince of Wallachia, of Moldavia, and of Transylvania, King of Romania." Brătianu disagreed, saying that the young Michael was the first of our kings with that name and, besides, Michael the Brave had not been prince of Transylvania but only its imperial lieutenant. It was therefore settled that the new king would be called "Michael I." Stelian Popescu, minister of justice, was entrusted with issuing Ferdinand I's death certificate.

Telegrams were being sent all over. Queen Elizabeth of Greece cabled her brother Carol in Paris. There were debates concerning the letter King Ferdinand had left for his son Carol. Titulescu and Argetoianu were opposed to its publication, while Brătianu favored it: "This is the last will of King Ferdinand, and it is natural that he would speak to his son with some affection. Besides, I drafted the letter myself!"

That same morning, around noon, we left with young King Michael—just five years old—his mother, Helen, the regents, the government, and the court, by a royal train that was taking us to Bucharest for the swearing-in ceremony. The Chamber of Deputies was packed. A wave of tenderness swept members of Parliament and the public alike when, as soon as the Chamber's director had solemnly announced: "His Majesty the King," a small fair-haired child appeared, dressed all in white and holding the hand of his mother, who was in deep mourning. The little boy lifted his right hand to his forehead in a military salute. As the three regents took their oath of allegiance in front of the boy who would bear the steel crown of Carol I, the same tormenting question could be read on all faces: what will the nation's future be in the new phase that was opening after the dynastic turmoils that shook the country's institutions to their foundations?

It was as if we had had the premonition that the only bulwark that remained, the great counselor who had stood next to the king during his entire reign, was destined to follow him soon to the grave. The course of events was to show that these worries were unfortunately fully justified. The apogee that was, in the history of our people, the reign of Ferdinand I was followed after a short period by a merciless cascade of disasters of internal and external origin that within two decades of senseless dictatorships, territorial losses, and pressures from the conflict between two major neighboring powers, would culminate in Communist rule.

[2]All of them having reigned in both Moldavia and Wallachia.

In the afternoon of that July 20, Ionel Brătianu informed me that the regents had approved my appointment as secretary-general of the Regency. I would assume the office on my return from Rome, where I had to take care of moving out of our apartment and make the customary farewell visits.

The Orthodox funeral service was held on a hot July 24, in the Byzantine hall of the Cotroceni Palace. Around the coffin, watch was kept by King Alexander of Serbia (in the uniform of a Romanian colonel of mountain troops), Prince Nicholas of Romania, Prince Friedrich von Hohenzollern (in the uniform of a knight of the Order of Malta), and Prince Gottfried von Hohenlohe-Langenburg, the queen dowager's nephew (in the uniform of a German uhlan, not quite appropriate at the funeral of a king who had fought the German army). The procession threaded its way toward the Gara de Nord railway station. The train journey to Curtea de Argeş[3] was a real torture because of the tropical heat. In the Curtea de Argeş church, where a short burial service was held, I noticed that the dead king was wearing the uniform of a cavalry officer. It was explained to me that, in his will, Ferdinand had asked to be buried in his uniform of cavalry general, even though he was not much of a horseman. (Ştirbey whispered, "At least he didn't ask to be dressed in his admiral's uniform, of which he was very fond, but which would have been quite out of place in view of our insignificant navy!")

✧ ✧ ✧

My wife and I returned to Rome by sea, a beautiful trip that took us to Constantinople, Athens, Corinth, and Brindisi. After completing all the required rituals of departure, we revisited favorite places such as Siena, San Gimignano, Empoli, and Pisa. Then, after a short stay in Paris, the Orient-Express took us to Bucharest. I assumed my new position at the Regency on October 3. I was to use as office the so-called "Japanese room" on the second floor of the left wing of the old Royal Palace, exactly under the great clock. I began by officially introducing myself to my new bosses.

Prince Nicholas was then a carefree youth of twenty-three, who showed more interest in automobiles and automobile engines than in politics. He had in no way been prepared for the position of responsibility he was assuming and for which he felt no attraction. He was good looking, with refined features, and he more than Carol resembled

[3]Site of a fourteenth-century church that served as the burial place of princes of Wallachia and where King Carol I and Queen Elisabeta were also buried.

his father, in appearance, in gait, and even in his fits of rage (a characteristic of timid persons). He was likable and unpretentious, but, like Carol, lacked a royal upbringing. In company he behaved neither as a *grand seigneur* nor as a man-about-town, and his parents had not trained him in the sort of small talk that is so necessary to members of ruling houses. I recall how at a luncheon at the Jockey Club, where he was seated between the wives of the club's two vice presidents, he failed to address them a single word during the entire meal but sat looking bored and sulky. It would seem to have been a sign of ill breeding, but in fact his behavior was the result of a total lack of breeding, of social ease, of savoir-faire. What a contrast with someone like Alphonso XIII, for instance, who won over all men—and women!—by the charm of his conversation and the politeness of a great lord. Although my business meetings with Prince Nicholas were pleasant enough, they occurred seldom and were always brief, for I realized how little interest he had in diplomatic developments or the reports of our envoys abroad. I could discuss the more important questions only with the other two regents.

Patriarch Miron Cristea, the son of peasants from Topliţa Română in the Mureş district, was about sixty years old when he became regent of the country. He was the most striking and impressive of the regents, in spite of his modest origin—handsome, intelligent, with sparkling eyes. He seemed more a statesman than a high-ranking prelate. After an audience with Patriarch Miron, who was wearing a Transylvanian-style cassock with red frogs, Constantin Stere exclaimed, "A bright man, but he looks more like a cavalry colonel than a patriarch!" I had known him for some time. When he was still metropolitan primate, he had celebrated in 1923 the religious marriage of my brother Robert with Alexandra ("Ala") Ghica. I saw him often again when I was political director of the Presidency of the Council of Ministers. And now I was presenting myself to him as his future closest political collaborator. Patriarch Miron spoke to me at length about King Ferdinand and his scruples as a Catholic. Spiritual son of the Roman Church, denied its sacraments because his children had been baptized in the Orthodox faith, Ferdinand was seeking the pope's forgiveness and reconciliation with the Vatican. In pursuance of this goal, he would have wished to avoid at his coronation a religious service in the Orthodox church at Alba Iulia, or at least that the participation of the Orthodox clergy be minimal. Patriarch Miron confided to me: "The king finally gave in to my insistence, but he sent word that he did not want to be met at the church door by the clergy carrying icons, and that he would not make the

Orthodox sign of the cross.[4] I asked Brătianu to explain to him that this would be an insult to Romania's predominant religion, and that he absolutely must cross himself when entering the church. I had Brătianu tell him that if he did not make the sign of the cross in front of the icons, I and all the clergy would not perform the religious service. Faced with this peremptory declaration and after many arguments, even on the church steps (people thought he was chatting with his prime minister about trivial matters), the king yielded. I met him at the door with the icons, in front of which he bowed but without crossing himself, while the queen was ostentatiously making big Orthodox signs of the cross. During the service, however, he did make Orthodox signs of the cross. I was duty-bound to be firm, since I am the head of my Church by divine right, and I could not submit to the will of a temporal king. I answer to God, not to the people or to the king. The king kissed my hand, but I did not kiss his."

I had met the third regent, Gheorghe V. Buzdugan, a career magistrate, through my father when they both served on the High Court of Appeal, and through his sons who had been schoolmates of my brother and me. He was a man of integrity and, among the regents, the one who was the most active and the most able, and also the one who showed the most interest in his high office. He greeted me with much affection, expressing his satisfaction at having as close associate a "son of gentlefolk," a favorite expression of his, which he pronounced with a strong Moldavian accent. He told me that I had been recommended to him most warmly by the prime minister, adding: "Brătianu is very fond of you and appreciates you as well. He had many good things to say about you, among which, 'he was brought up by a remarkable mother, a superior woman I have known from childhood.'" The regent then asked news of my father, whom he had not seen for quite some time, "I am most fond of him, a Moldavian boyar, refined and witty."

In my new position, I also had to introduce myself officially to Queen Dowager Marie, who of course had known me for a long time. At Cotroceni Palace, in her long mourning dress, one would never have given her the age that, in its brutal frankness, the *Almanach de Gotha* reported.[5] She was enchanting, full of charm, and had an easy and informal friendliness. The conversation, in English, touched at first on the subject

[4] That is, from right to left, rather than from left to right as the Catholics do.

[5] She was fifty-two.

of travel: Constantinople, where she would like to go in the spring, Amalfi, Ravello . . . and places that were closest to her heart: Balcic and Bran (the places where her heart was to be successively buried). "At Balcic," she told me, "Brătianu found that we were spending too much. But it was from my own money, and later he himself conceded that I had been right in building such a beautiful house." We then talked about Brătianu and the obstacles the opposition was placing in his way, just at a time when the new order of succession to the throne would have required stability and the union of all. I am copying here the queen's words from the notes I made at that time in my diary: "Maniu and his friends come to see me often. They think I am against them. It is not so, but can we, as long as these hard moments last, venture to have a new government, which we would not be sure of? And can one have faith in these men, full of good will I am sure, who seem so reasonable when they talk to me but who, as soon as they leave me, begin to 'aufhetzen'[6] the people? Romanians are very kind hearted, but if they keep being told lies about everybody, they can get as indignant as any other people. If we had quiet times now, I would tell Brătianu: let those people come and see *qu'ils ne sont pas des aigles.*"[7]

Turning to the possibility of piecing together a coalition government, I explained to the queen that this would be extremely difficult. Since the National-Peasants were now, after the disintegration of Averescu's party, the only possible successors to the Liberals, they were emboldened to harden their uncompromising attitude and demanded power without conditions. The queen asked me whether I thought a rapprochement between the followers of Averescu and the Liberals was possible. I did not hide my skepticism: as far as I knew, the Liberals no longer had any confidence in General Averescu. The queen shared my view, although in her opinion the "dear old fellow" was more a fool than a rascal ("*plus bête que fourbe; tout ce qu'il fait est par bêtise*"[8]). She then gave me several examples to prove her point. "Personally, however, I have always got along very well with him," she concluded, "and we were even good friends, for I never want to quarrel with my prime ministers."

Talking with the patriarch about the political role Queen Marie wanted to play, I asked him whether the rumor that she had converted to Orthodoxy was true. He replied at length: "Formally, *no*; essentially, *yes*.

[6]Stir up.
[7]That they are no geniuses.
[8]More stupid than treacherous; everything he does is out of stupidity.

This is how things stand: She asked me a few years ago to hear her confession and to give her Holy Communion. I explained that an Orthodox priest is not allowed to give Holy Communion to a Protestant. She replied that, settled in Romania for a number of years, she identified with our nation and wanted from now on to live in its religion, which was also that of her children. I did not conceal my joy at her statement, which I consider to be a solemn conversion to the Orthodox faith. I told her that she did well to want to live in the ambience of the Orthodox faith, which, in spite of the temporary weaknesses of its clergy owing to poverty and lack of education, was the only true church, as proved by the Anglican church's opening toward closer relations. I then had her kneel; I placed the stole over her head and let her confess all her sins. After that, I gave her Holy Communion and, from that instant, I have considered her to be truly Orthodox, even though she prefers not to declare this officially so as not to upset Anglican quarters."

✧ ✧ ✧

The Regency made its first official appearance on October 15, 1927, for the opening of Parliament. The Message was read by Prince Nicholas, who kept stumbling over his words. A few days later, on October 24, the Regency took its first political decision. Returning from Paris, Mihail Manoilescu, an ardent supporter of the former prince Carol, was arrested on the route between the border and Bucharest and was taken off the train in Braşov to be searched. He was carrying letters from Carol to Ionel Brătianu, to General Averescu, and to Iuliu Maniu, as well as clippings from French newspapers reporting an interview Carol had given in Dinard to the Havas Agency. Ion Duca, the minister of internal affairs, asked Buzdugan, in his capacity as magistrate, to examine the case and, after consulting his colleagues, to give the Regency's view as to the advisability of bringing Mihail Manoilescu to trial by the Military Court. I was directed by Buzdugan to give Duca the Regency's reply, which was as follows: "We believe that until the contents of the discovered documents are known, the severe measure in question cannot be justified, the more so since one of the letters is addressed to the highest guardian of public order himself." Duca assured me that Manoilescu would not be charged until the contents of the documents were known. That evening the government, having taken cognizance of those contents, ordered the imprisonment of Manoilescu in the Jilava jail and his indictment in front of the Military Court.

THE DEATH OF ION I.C. BRĂTIANU

One of my last lengthy conversations with Ionel Brătianu took place in the garden of his house, on November 4, 1927. We talked for almost an hour and a half, sometimes sitting, occasionally strolling along the garden paths. With his far-ranging conversation, moving from one topic to another, untwining the threads of the past, the great statesman showed himself more than ever to be a fascinating conversationalist. He talked to me of his father, to whom he had been greatly attached, of the string of political battles his father led, and of his "radical" or "red" party established in 1848. He revealed details of the past political life of our country unknown to me and perhaps to all in these later generations. He told me, for instance, that Ion Ghica, the former bey of Samos, would have liked to become ruler of Romania. He had a following among the youths of the nobility, who constituted a more modern party than that of I.C. Brătianu. In 1870, after the incident of the Slătineanu Hall[9] and the resignation, demanded by Prince Carol himself, of Ion Ghica's government, relations between the former prime minister and the sovereign became very strained. Realizing this, Ion Ghica's adherents distanced themselves from him in order to follow I.C. Brătianu.

✧ ✧ ✧

On November 18 the members of the government and a delegation of deputies went to the Royal Palace to give the Regency their reply to the Message read at the opening of Parliament. It was the first such ceremony under the new regime. Prince Nicholas then read (with less difficulty this time) the Regency's reply (a reply to the reply!) drafted by Buzdugan, in which the word "justice" came up a number of times—quite naturally, in view of the author's career. I then had a chance to chat alone with the prime minister. I told him that talks with the regents had given me the impression that they would like to see a government of national unity formed under his leadership, in order to ease their first steps. Since the new Regency was still a bit frail, it should not be shaken by fights between government and opposition. Ionel Brătianu confirmed that my impression was correct and said the regents had spoken to him in the same vein. But he had explained to them that the time did not seem right to undertake talks for the forming of a national unity government, since

[9]An anti-German riot.

the opposition had not yet definitively given up raising the constitutional question of the succession to the throne: it was still looking toward Carol. "I told the regents," Brătianu concluded, "that such negotiations would lead to nought since the National-Peasants would not accept such a government now, when *I* know they are licked, but only when *they* realize that they are licked."

The next day, November 19, the same ceremony took place for the Senate's reply to the Message. This time, the Regency's address was written by Patriarch Miron, and the emphasis, not surprisingly, was on the Church. (I was wondering how such a speech would turn out if Prince Nicholas penned one in turn: would there be repeated mentions of automobile engines?) Ionel Brătianu took me aside in a corner of the library to tell me an anecdote he had recently heard: Edmond de Goncourt was seated at a restaurant next to the table of an old man. The waiter asked the old man if he wished anything else. "I wish nothing more," was the reply. "He wishes nothing more?" exclaimed Goncourt. "But then it's not an old man—it's old age itself!" I looked at Brătianu: was he thinking of himself as he told the story? He seemed so vigorous, ramrod straight, like a mighty oak. But this brief conversation was to be the last that I had with him. Behind him, unseen, merciless fate was approaching, scythe in hand.

Only four days later I received a phone call at the Royal Palace telling me that, because of attacks of suffocation caused by a tonsillitis Brătianu had contracted a couple of days earlier, Dr. Constantin Angelescu, minister of education and surgeon by profession, had performed a tracheotomy on him. A few seconds later Duca arrived at the Palace and, taking me aside, advised me that the prime minister's condition was extremely serious: "It may be a question of only a few hours." I hastened to Ionel Brătianu's home. Dr. Angelescu told me that if the infection spread, the case would be hopeless. I returned after lunch and found Drs. Danielopol, Burileanu, and Lupu, who seemed no longer to hold any hope. The house was full of people: family, close friends, members of government, Queen Marie, the regents, all were calling on Elise Brătianu. The poor woman was devastated. In the hope of finding pus in the tonsils (which would indicate that the infection was localized), a further surgical procedure was undertaken at six in the evening. No pus was found, only suppurating ganglions. The last hope melted away.

At four o'clock the next morning, as November 24, 1927, was dawning, the death struggle of Ionel Brătianu began. I went into his room. He saw me, but I don't know that he recognized me. At six o'clock he went into a coma. Elise Brătianu took him into her arms; his son Gheorghe, who had arrived from Jassy during the night, held his right hand. A priest was kneeling near the bed. The family (the Brătianus, the Ştirbeys, the Balşes) and all of us remained in the room. Through the door, which was ajar, I could see Ionel's brother Vintilă collapsed in an armchair, crying. After a terrible agony—for his sturdy organism was locked in a last struggle with the infection—Ion I.C. Brătianu gave up the soul at 6:45 A.M.

It was decided on the spot to hold two cabinet meetings: one, immediately, at the Ministry of the Interior so that the members of the cabinet could appoint a new prime minister, who turned out to be Vintilă I.C. Brătianu; and a second meeting at the Royal Palace, at 7:30 A.M., for the new prime minister to take the required oath in front of the Regency. I then went to the Palace, where the regents, whom I had informed by telephone, were arriving. The members of the cabinet were also arriving. I called the priest of the small church behind the Palace and went with him into the library, where I witnessed the swearing in of Vintilă Brătianu and the other ministers. A national funeral was proposed, but Vintilă Brătianu pleaded for an ordinary burial: "This was my brother's wish, and it is our family's tradition."

After the cabinet members had left, the regents instructed me to meet with the heads of the opposition parties—Averescu, Maniu, and Iorga—and invite them to come to the palace for talks aiming at the constitution of a coalition government. The regents had pursued this goal from the very beginning of their appointment, and they felt it was now more necessary than ever in order to avoid the turmoil that could follow the demise of the man on whose shoulders the country's polity had in fact rested.

I went first to see General Averescu. He inquired about the nature of the former prime minister's illness and declared himself willing to come to the Palace at the appointed time (10:30 A.M.), but he seemed to think it rather odd that we should be putting together a government of national unity so quickly.

Maniu greeted me saying: "What calamity for our country! Even though we were strongly opposed to each other, I do recognize that the loss of Ion I.C. Brătianu is a terrible blow for Romania." He added that he was at the Regency's disposal and would come to the Palace at the appointed time (11:30 A.M.). As I was leaving, I encountered a visibly beaming Mihalache. When he saw Maniu, who was accompanying me to the door with a saddened expression, he remarked ironically, without realizing I was there, "I see you are highly afflicted, Mr. Maniu!" I had the impression that Maniu, a civilized person, was hurt by this ill-bred remark. Buzdugan, too, when I related the incident to him, was astonished by this cynical lack of humaneness from a man generally admired for the decency and thoughtfulness characteristic of the Romanian peasant, which he had never shed even in ferocious political fights, as neither had he shed his peasant dress.

Iorga being out of town, at Vălenii de Munte, I asked his son to inform him of the Regency's summons.

At the end of the meetings with the heads of the opposition, the regents apprised me of the talks and asked that, in turn, I pass this information on to Vintilă Brătianu. Averescu had apparently been frank: he considered it neither advisable nor possible to form a government of national unity. However, if it were possible to constitute such a government, he would give it all his assistance.

As for Maniu, the regents told me he had "beaten around the bush for two hours." What could best be deduced from what he had said was that he demanded the prime ministership, the dissolution of Parliament, and new elections in three or four months. He said that he was willing to guarantee the maintenance of the present dynastic situation and to take full responsibility for the preservation of constitutional order; indeed, he readily admitted that he was using Carol Caraiman "as a scarecrow" only while he remained in opposition. In light of the events of June 1930, under Maniu's government, one can judge now how much weight should have been given to those guarantees and promises and to what extent Carol Caraiman was only a weapon in opposition.

That same afternoon I briefed the new prime minister, as requested by the Regency, on the views expressed by the heads of the opposition. He told me that he had also asked to see them. Averescu, a kindhearted man, came himself to Vintilă, presented his condolences, and told him the same things he had told the regents. Maniu, however, demanded that Vintilă Brătianu, in spite of his mourning and exhaustion after a night of sorrow at his brother's deathbed, should come to him. Vintilă Brătianu's comment was, "Well, it's all a matter of upbringing and sensibility." Maniu further told him, as he had told the regents, that he wanted to head the government, and he wanted Parliament to be dissolved and free elections with separate lists, followed by collaboration based on the electoral results.

Next day (November 25) Iorga returned to Bucharest and recommended to the regents a government headed by Maniu. He did not directly address the dynastic issue, because "it is not pertinent now." The regents again asked me to keep the prime minister abreast, and Vintilă Brătianu then told me that Iorga had spoken to him in the same vein, but that he had also insisted on the necessity of recalling Carol to Romania: "Why don't you all want to bring him back? He is so easily influenced that you will wrap him, too, around your little finger." Iorga had gone on to assail the dead and the living—especially Ferdinand among the dead, and Duca and Titulescu among the living. Trying to part on a friendlier note, Vintilă Brătianu told him: "I have two qualities that I believe even you will acknowledge: I am frank and I am tenacious. I won't leave you alone until you too have convinced yourself of the impossibility of bringing back such a man as Carol, and until I get you to put yourself at the country's service, collaborating with us. And I will win the battle!" Iorga seemed flattered.

Ion I.C. Brătianu's burial took place on November 27, at Florica, after a funeral service in the rotunda of the Romanian Atheneum, with the Regency, the government, the diplomatic corps, and, in spirit, the entire country in attendance. When I approached Elise Brătianu to lead her to the railway station, she took me apart and burst into tears. The poor woman was beginning her long widowhood, which would last no less than thirty years. Placing her arm on my shoulder, she said: "I thank you from the bottom of my heart for the affection you had for my husband all these years, which he reciprocated. He was very fond of you. Don't forget it, for I also have much affection for you." And she gave me the last photograph of Ionel Brătianu. At Florica, the casket, covered with the Romanian flag, was buried in the crypt of the ancestral estate's church, next to the tomb of I.C. Brătianu, his father.

On the way to Florica and back, I traveled in the same railway car as General Prezan. We spoke about Ionel Brătianu, and Prezan's association with him during the war years: "When the bolshevized Russian troops gathered at Socola, I gave the order that our soldiers disarm them. But at one o'clock in the morning, Ionel Brătianu phoned telling me to postpone the action. I then managed to have General Tcherbatcheff request me in writing to disarm the bolshevized Russian soldiers. The envoys of France, Britain, and Italy backed this request: 'the last sacrifice demanded of Romania.' At the cabinet meeting that followed, Take Ionescu opposed the measure, proposing instead that the king abdicate and go abroad. Ionel Brătianu held his head in his hands for a couple of minutes, then said: 'We cannot let the king go into the wide world, he who by sacrificing his family ties has identified completely with our country. As for the bolshevized Russian soldiers, we must accept General Prezan's decision.' All the cabinet members agreeing with Brătianu, Take Ionescu, in spite of Titulescu's entreaties, felt he had to tender his resignation. The king, however, summoned him to the Palace and bawled him out as if he were a mere corporal, reminding him that he had loudly called for Romania's entry into the war, but now was trying to evade responsibility. It is only this way that Take Ionescu withdrew his resignation."

✧ ✧ ✧

Nearly two months went by before I could bring myself to cross once more the threshold of Ionel Brătianu's house, where I had spent so many unforgettable years, but when Elise Brătianu, back from Florica, phoned me to come see her, I did so, on January 17, 1928. It was strange entering that house, so full of life two months ago and now so empty. Nothing had changed in Brătianu's study, but his smile—full of charm, benevolence, and irony—was missing, and a veil of funereal silence spread over the entire room. Elise Brătianu told me that Saint-Aulaire (the French envoy to Romania during World War I) had written asking her for some details on her husband, which would be useful for a study that he was soon to publish. She had drafted a reply and wanted my opinion on it. The letter was beautiful and moving, and the style outstanding.

After that, we of course talked about *him!* The widow quoted to me two of his characteristic statements. After the war, he told Duca: "You must judge a man by his intentions, not by what seems to you to be the immediate results of his actions. When I reflect on my life, on all my actions, I absolve myself of everything I did." And another time, when Elise asked him why he had shown himself so well disposed toward a man he did not think much of, he answered: "It is not what I think of him that matters, it is what he believes I think of him. Because he believes now that I suppose him to be a better man than he really is, I am certain that, in leaving me, he felt that he was better." I repeated to her one of her husband's sentences that had made a deep impression on me, for if we made it our own, it could bestow peace of mind to all of us. The conversation had turned to the fierce attacks Ionel Brătianu's political adversaries were launching against him. With philosophical calm, he only said: "I am not afraid of the stones that are cast at me during my lifetime, I only worry about the headstone that will be placed on my grave."

CHANGE OF GOVERNMENT AND CHANGE IN THE REGENCY

With Ionel Brătianu gone, Buzdugan set about the task of bringing the National-Peasants to power. It was widely whispered that he had been induced to do so by his family, and especially by his eldest son, to whom the National-Peasant party was said to have made certain promises. The rumor seemed to be confirmed later, after the advent of the Maniu government, because the young man in question was appointed a director of the National Bank, then minister plenipotentiary, and finally was decorated with the order of the Star of Romania at the grand officer level, a distinction usually reserved for aging high officials; the other two regents felt obliged in the end to assent to the granting of this decoration so as not to hurt their colleague's feelings. Nevertheless, to imagine that such petty and self-serving considerations would induce a man of Gheorghe Buzdugan's integrity and moral value to take a historic responsibility with such widespread repercussions for the country's fate, would be an injustice and insult to the memory of this decent man, of this "son of gentlefolk," to use his expression. No: I believe that Buzdugan shared the view of a large part of public opinion, which held that there was no ground for excluding forever from the helm of the country a major party such as the National-Peasants. And this all the more so since that party had as president a great son of the nation, Iuliu Maniu, who had become the symbol of the reunification of the Romanian people and almost the living representation of Transylvania.

Ionel Brătianu's opposition was in large part due to his wish for a merger of Transylvania's National party with his Liberal party, which lacked roots in the electorate on the other side of the mountains. It stemmed as well from his belief that the Transylvanian politicians would not be content with being the trans-Carpathian branch of the great and all-powerful political organization from the Old Kingdom until they convinced themselves that, alone, they would never taste the sweetness of power. Indeed, a rather nasty saying was making the rounds: "We, the Transylvanians, have developed a millenary hunger."

With the "Vizier" gone and with his brother—less hostile to the National-Peasants—coming to power (if only to let the public see their incompetence in governing), it was easier for Buzdugan to convince his colleagues of the necessity of calling Maniu to power. The only doubt that remained was whether or not Maniu could resist an attempted restoration of Carol to the throne. In this instance, Buzdugan's unfounded optimism and extraordinary illusions can be explained only up to a point by his lack of political experience. Knowing Maniu's principles of moral integrity, and being himself a highly principled man of law, Buzdugan could not conceive that the politician brought up in the clerical ambiance of Blaj could agree to accept such a cynical and amoral man as Carol Caraiman as head of the country. The regent was evidently not aware of the pressures on Maniu from party stalwarts who believed that once Carol was put on the throne by the National-Peasants, he would be so grateful that he would keep them in power forever. In their reckoning, Carol II was to be for the National-Peasants what Ferdinand I had been for the Liberals. That their reasoning was wrong was to be proved in short order: Carol was soon to drive from power those who had helped him dethrone his son, entrusting the government to his sworn enemies, the Liberals, and namely to the most rabid of them, Duca. The maxim about the ingratitude of rulers is as old as the world.

On October 28, 1928, during the Jubilee festivities celebrating in Constanţa the fiftieth anniversary of the reattachment of Dobrudja (and when, for the last time, the veterans of the war of 1877 marched past with their old banners), the regents broached again with Vintilă Brătianu the need for a change in government. That they were determined on such a change was also confirmed by Titulescu's recent resignation. Having certainly been informed by Buzdugan, he judged it wiser to make a strategic withdrawal so as not to be completely associated with the Liberals, and thus to make it possible for him eventually to join a future National-Peasant government as a foreign affairs expert. Ionel Brătianu had foreseen such an eventuality when he assembled his cabinet in June 1927. When he received Titulescu's cable from London accepting the appointment of minister of foreign affairs, Brătianu told us, his intimates: "Should you congratulate or pity me?" Seeing our bewilderment, he added: "He, as well as Dr. Lupu, will be the first to abandon me when they feel that my ship is sinking."

On the way back from Constanţa, in his railway car, Buzdugan related to me the unfolding of his decisive conversations with the patriarch, and then with the prime minister. With the assent of his colleague, Buzdugan conveyed to the prime minister the Regency's opinion that, since the internal situation was now calmer, it would be appropriate for the Liberal party to withdraw from power after signing the financial agreements with the group of bankers extending a loan to Romania, and to make way for the National-Peasant party after it gave its guarantee of staying the course. Vintilă Brătianu reportedly recognized the necessity of letting the National-Peasants take the helm, but on condition that their guarantee of continuity consist in participation in a government of all the parties; if they refused, the Liberal party would continue its rule. Faced with this alternative, the National-Peasants might well accept collaboration so as not to lose their position as a possible governing party.

Buzdugan clearly thought that it would be impossible to present such a proposal to Maniu, so he suggested another solution: if Maniu was not persuaded by the Regency's arguments and instead continued to oppose the idea of a government of national unity, he could at least guarantee a continuation of the Liberals' financial policy by having an official statement to that effect read in the Chamber of Deputies. Vintilă Brătianu did not like this attempt at getting out of the impasse, for he didn't think Buzdugan was sufficiently convinced of the necessity of a government of national unity to compel Maniu to accept it. And this was indeed the case: Buzdugan was in favor of the creation of a National-Peasant government, and his suggestion was merely intended to avoid cutting all ties with the Liberals. The parting of Vintilă Brătianu and Buzdugan was reportedly rather cool.

The Liberal prime minister drew his conclusions from this conversation. Rather than being formally asked by the regents to resign at a time convenient to them and to the National-Peasants, he preferred to choose his own time. Besides, he realized that the regents would not let him carry out to the end his economic stabilization efforts.

Surprised and somewhat unprepared for the sudden resignation of the Liberal government (on November 3, 1928), the regents began their consultations according to the provisions of the constitution. The presidents of the Senate and of the Chamber of Deputies, as well as the heads of the political parties and groups (Averescu, Maniu, Iorga, Dr. Lupu) followed each other at the Palace. But a solution still had to be found to resolve the crisis. Holding to his earlier view, Buzdugan was in favor of bringing the National-Peasants to power immediately. The patriarch and Prince Nicholas (the latter, no doubt, on the advice of his mother) felt, however, that the formation of a national unity government had to be tried first, even if only as a formality. Buzdugan in the end rallied to his colleagues' view, and the names of all the men "above the fray" who could be entrusted with sounding out the various parties were passed in review. Titulescu seemed the best suited for this mission: he had resumed his position as envoy to London and therefore had not been mixed up in the recent political strife, and he was a personal friend of both Vintilă Brătianu (in whose government he had served) and of Iuliu Maniu (in whose government he did not exclude the possibility of serving).

Recalled by cable, Titulescu arrived in Bucharest on November 9. He was immediately received by the regents, who charged him with the formation of a government of national unity. After the audience, he came to my office and told me he thought he had little chance of succeeding. My belief, however, is that he had reached an agreement with Maniu some time earlier, that he had probably strongly advised the regents, and Buzdugan in particular, to bring the National-Peasants to power: in other words, the formal consultations he was to undertake were all part of a previously drawn-up plan. Certainly the gain for Titulescu was an enhanced stature in domestic politics that might, at some future time, lead to a prime ministership, as well as the possibility of being given a free hand in foreign affairs by Maniu, whom he would have helped come into power.

Two days later, as was to be expected, Titulescu gave up, having been unable to get the parties to agree. Queen Marie then invited Buzdugan to Cotroceni Palace. According to Buzdugan, she strongly insisted that the reins of government be entrusted to Barbu Ştirbey, but he showed her the impossibility of such a solution, "which would lead to a general indignation that would be to no one's advantage." Besides, such a solution would only be temporary; the elections were going to be won by the National-Peasants, and the Regency would then be forced to replace Ştirbey with Maniu. By immediately calling on Maniu, the Regency would have appointed him, rather than having him imposed on them. And so Buzdugan managed to have Iuliu Maniu summoned to the Palace immediately, where he was given the mission of putting together a government.

An incontestable sentiment of relief swept the country when the great Transylvanian patriot took up the reins of government. It seemed to be the dawn of an era of moral resurgence and achievements. In this state of euphoria, the public forgot that the Transylvanians, as well as the members of the Peasant party, totally lacked governing experience. As for moral renewal and the raising of the level of political ethics, one can only recall Cicio-Pop's famous words directed at the time of unification to those from the Old Kingdom: "Neither are we as upstanding as you believe, nor are you as wicked as you pretend." But there is no doubt that the experiment made by bringing Maniu to power was absolutely necessary in that phase of our political life and that Buzdugan's initiative, obviously dangerous in its consequences, corresponded to the public's wishes.

Iuliu Maniu was a great historical figure of our nation, a man of character and integrity, severe, austere, molded by the Uniate church's schooling.

He will forever be remembered as a patriot and martyr, if not as a statesman. In Central and Danubian Europe, his name has remained linked to all the struggles to unfetter oppressed nationalities and safeguard democratic regimes. Already as a young man he had established, along with other Romanian, Slovak, and Serb students at the University of Budapest, an association—to whose presidency he was soon to be elected—for the defense of the rights of the minorities subjected to the crown of St. Stephen. When he entered the Hungarian Parliament in 1906, he joined his Romanian colleagues from Transylvania and the Serb and Slovak deputies, as well as the Croat delegates, to form a group of forty Parliamentarians from minority nationalities that was to lead a fierce battle against the reactionary and chauvinistic policy of the Budapest government of that time. In addition, this group unceasingly demanded, in stormy sessions in which the young Maniu earned an ever growing reputation, the enactment of advanced social reforms and equal treatment for all the nationalities of the Dual Monarchy. This daring position, however, was seen on the hill of Buda as having as its real goal the destruction of the already badly undermined old Habsburg empire, and as being almost a crime of lèse majesté.

It thus required much civic courage for Iuliu Maniu to promote with such steadfastness and energy equal rights for all the nationalities subject to the two-headed eagle and respect for individual freedoms. Many personal dangers threatened him in a country where freedom of thought and speech, even though not as suppressed as under Nazi or Communist regimes, was nevertheless strictly limited in the area of politics. But on the harsh road he had chosen, he could draw support from the spiritual strength of his Graeco-Catholic church as well as from the tradition of regional heroism that stretched back to the revolt of Horia, Cloşca, and Crişan, memories that he inherited from his direct forebears, the brave companions of Avram Iancu in 1848 and the "memorandists" of 1892. Along with Milan Hodža, the future Czechoslovak prime minister, he helped to lay the foundations of the alliance that Take Ionescu, Beneš, and Pasić were to call the Little Entente. The efforts of these fighters were equally directed toward the freedom of nationalities and individual freedoms. Their cooperation with the Austro-Hungarian leftist parties—with Karl Renner and Otto Bauer in Austria, with the Socialists in Hungary—was therefore natural.

The years went by, and in middle age Maniu had the satisfaction of seeing his youthful dreams realized, which Vauvenargues considered to be life's supreme reward. After World War I, when the antiquated

Habsburg empire was crumbling away, Iuliu Maniu became, at the head of a few thousand Romanian soldiers from his native province, the almost absolute master of Vienna. From the palace of the Dual Monarchy's former war ministry, he issued the orders that were to allow the free determination not only of the nationality he represented and guided but also of all the nations that were under the scepter of Emperor-King Charles. Upon returning home, Maniu became president of the Directing Council of Transylvania after the Great National Assembly of Alba Iulia voted for unification with Romania.

Between 1921 and 1923, Maniu, Hodža, and Stephen Radić, faithful to the ideals of their youth, decided on a close cooperation of the agrarian parties they headed. It was the seed of the future "Green International," headquartered in Prague, to which the Poles and the Bulgarians would later adhere. The endeavors of Maniu, Hodža, Svehla, Witos, and Radić to establish a close friendship between the agricultural workers of this part of Europe were to be brought to an end only by the Nazi aggression.

The end of Maniu's life darkened with a veil of Greek tragedy the political career of a great Romanian. Faithful to himself and to the principles to which he devoted his entire life, he steadfastly opposed all internal dictatorships and external oppressions, becoming a martyr to his beliefs. Dragged in front of a mimicry of popular justice, he was sentenced, imprisoned, and left to die without medical attention in a Communist jail.

This unyielding fighter, this dissident during much of his life, did not, however, play a constructive part during more serene periods. And neither could one find anyone who had held a position of responsibility among his political friends (almost all of whom were proved patriots), for in Hungary minority members had to be content with modest jobs to support themselves. The most capable of Maniu's followers, the future prime minister Alexandru Vaida-Voevod, had been house physician of the Karlsbad spa.

Maniu's government of 1928 contained some noted Transylvanian personalities, such as Vaida-Voevod, Mihai Popovici, and a few Peasant leaders, such as Mihalache, Iunian, Mirto, and Madgearu. To everybody's surprise, the Ministry of Foreign Affairs was entrusted to Gheorghe Mironescu, a colorless man lacking personality, character, and intelligence; his son said of him that "he is neither as kindhearted nor as stupid as people believe" (the first part of the statement being more accurate than the second). Mironescu's only merit was the substantial contributions he had made to the opposition party from the profits of the

Bragadiru brewery, of which he was co-owner. A former member and deputy of the People's party, he switched to Take Ionescu when Ionescu was forming his one-month government in December 1921, so as to obtain an ephemeral ministerial portfolio, that of public education. (The pro-Averescu paper *Indreptarea* printed for days on end the picture of the two "renegades," Mironescu and Dumitrescu-Brăila, with the captions "Toady No. 1" and "Toady No. 2.") When the residue of Take Ionescu's grouping joined the National-Peasant party, Mironescu followed suit. And now he was Titulescu's successor at the Sturdza Palace! Fortunately, he was soon given as secretary-general a young man of exceptional culture, refinement, and intelligence, Grigore Gafencu. But jealous of his collaborator's superior intellect and reputation, Mironescu was instrumental in having him transferred to the Ministry of the Interior—the deplorable "Uncle Ghiţă," as Mironescu was nicknamed, being left to his fate. He scraped by only thanks to his servility toward Titulescu, who saved him from drowning.

The National-Peasant ministers, for the most part decent men but (with the exception of Mihalache, Iunian, and Madgearu) lacking competence and governmental experience, tended to stir up problems rather than to solve them. Because the regents had not imposed conditions or demanded guarantees, they had a free rein and at times concocted rather strange laws such as the one on administrative reforms, with all its political fantasies. The Liberal opposition withdrew from Parliament. The pro-Carlist press was in no way restrained, and *Cuvântul* and *Curentul,* for which talented people wrote, were seeking to generate a current in favor of bringing the former prince Carol to the throne. Though Maniu was a popular figure, his indecisiveness and lack of energy prevented the government from taking command and ensuring constitutional order. Meanwhile, the National-Peasants continued to enjoy Titulescu's support and Buzdugan's open protection.

The patriarch accused them of an anti-Orthodox policy due to the influence of Maniu and his Uniate followers. He complained to me several times of the government's persecution of the Orthodox in all sorts of matters: only Uniates were appointed to public positions, even in Braşov, one of Transylvania's most important Orthodox centers, and Uniate opposition party members were favored over Orthodox supporters of the government. "To be sure, the deceased[10] had also tried to introduce a somewhat pro-Catholic policy in order to obtain the pope's forgiveness

[10]King Ferdinand.

[for the baptism of his children in the Orthodox faith], but now this government wants to do it openly!"

Returning on August 26, 1929, from Iachimov, where he had gone for treatment, Buzdugan spoke to me highly of the government, "which does its duty." He considered the withdrawal of the Liberals from Parliament "a political error and a dangerous precedent." He admitted that the administrative reform law drawn up by the government included many errors: "I modified the draft as much as I could. But had I stretched things further, Maniu would have resigned. And whom could I have replaced him with? The Liberals have scarcely left!"

He told me that Queen Marie was highly displeased with the unobtrusive role she was obliged to play in the country's current political life. She had said to Buzdugan, "What I have done for the country gives me the right to have a say in the country's affairs." Telling me this, Buzdugan added with a smile, "It is said that she would like to take my place in the Regency." He also mentioned the family difficulties encountered by Princess-Mother Helen. Not even Prince Nicholas liked her. He had reportedly cried out one day, "If only all these Greeks would go away!"—referring also, of course, to the presence in Bucharest of the exiled King George II of Greece, married to his sister Elizabeth, and to other members of the former Hellenic ruling house.

At the end of the conversation Buzdugan said, with a certain sadness in his eyes: "All I am asking is to stay alive until the coming of age of little King Michael, so that I may place the crown on his head." Fate did not fulfill his wish, and this was my last conversation with Regent Gheorghe V. Buzdugan.

✧ ✧ ✧

At the end of September 1929 Buzdugan fell seriously ill as a local infection became generalized. I spoke with his physicians on October 5, and they disclosed the sad truth that the regent's septicemia would very soon lead to his death. Unfortunately for the country, which in recent years had lost some of its best sons, the fatal end could not be avoided in view of the patient's age and his weakness following two weeks of high temperature. The two other regents asked me to pass several times a day by Buzdugan's home, so as to keep them informed of the results of the medical consultations. I could but bring them the distressing news that the poor man was struggling with death. Even before he died, however, discussions had begun as to who would replace him as regent.

On his return from Balcic, where he had gone with Ştirbey to keep Queen Marie abreast of developments, Hiott told me that the possibility of her being chosen as regent had been discussed. The queen reportedly declared: "I'm not even thinking of it, first because I know my name would be dragged in the mud, and second because it would mean giving up my freedom. And between the two, I must say that it is the loss of my freedom that matters the most to me." After a few seconds of silence, she added: "No, I'm not thinking of it, but that the Romanian people don't think about it, that is what I cannot understand." Nevertheless, Queen Marie was urging through third parties that she be appointed to the Regency. Apart from General Averescu, none of the party heads was in favor of the queen's candidacy, which was warmly backed by Ştirbey and Stere. Even among the Liberals, opinion was divided; I learned from Constantin ("Bébé") Brătianu that Vintilă Brătianu was categorically opposed to Queen Marie's inclusion in the Regency, believing that it would contravene the spirit of the Constitution, which did not provide for women holding official positions, and also for wishes expressed by Ferdinand I and Ionel Brătianu. As for the patriarch, he told me he wished another jurist to replace Buzdugan.

Maniu came to see the patriarch and Prince Nicholas on October 6 and asked them to agree with the government's interpretation of the constitutional provisions regarding the Regency: that it was not up to the regents to co-opt (subject to Parliamentary confirmation) a replacement to fill a vacancy, rather, it was the duty of the Parliament to elect the new regent. The regents agreed, but on condition that they be consulted regarding the person the government nominated. Maniu fully reassured them in this respect. He also secured their agreement that, until the election of the new regent, the royal prerogatives would be transferred to the Council of Ministers. The regents thus yielded on a rather delicate issue, even though their attention had been drawn to the dangers inherent in such a concession.

Gheorghe V. Buzdugan died at 7:00 A.M. on October 7, 1929. Thus disappeared a pure and just soul, a clear and enlightened mind, a deeply Romanian heart, a brave and proud member of the Moldavian country gentry. In the afternoon, the regents received Maniu and suggested Queen Marie as the third member of the Regency. The prime minister answered that he would be guided in his choice by the spirit of the Constitution and the country's wishes, while at the same time he would try not to jeopardize his party's interests. This reply, however diplomatic, was clearly negative; the Constitution's spirit did not allow the election of a woman to the country's leadership, the wish of the country, as expressed by all party heads except Averescu, was not to have Queen Marie as a regent, and the interests of the National-Peasant party would have seemed somewhat threatened if Queen Marie, whose influence in the past had been applied in favor of the Liberals, were to have a deciding voice in the Regency, since she could count on her son's vote.

Now public opinion was aroused. Political circles, in general, did not appear favorable to Queen Marie's candidacy, for all Ştirbey and Stere's work, and if anything seemed to want General Prezan or a high-ranking magistrate elected to replace Buzdugan. After endless negotiations in which Stere played the major role, Maniu faced the following situation: the members of the Peasant party stated that they would break with the National party if two members of the royal house were to be included in the Regency, where they could at any time form the majority. Mihalache unwaveringly held to that position, to which Madgearu subscribed by cable. The prime minister then proposed to the queen that she replace her son in the Regency, the royal house being thus represented by a single member at the helm of the country. Obviously, Queen Marie could not accept that alternative. To save the queen's face, Maniu asked her to authorize him to state from the Chamber of Deputies' rostrum that she did not wish to be part of the Regency. (Diamandy told me that the prime minister, believing he could thus lessen the bitterness of the pill, would have hinted to an increase in Prince Nicholas's civil list.) Indignant, Queen Marie refused the authorization requested by Maniu. "The queen of Romania," she is said to have exclaimed, "cannot lie, nor can she be mercenary!" Hiott's silence when I repeated this to him served only to confirm the truth of the story. He said he attended only the end of the meeting when, coming back to the question of her candidacy, Queen Marie told Maniu: "No one can hold the scales as evenly as I. The proof: regents named by the ones have been attracted by the others," an allusion to Buzdugan, "while I, who supported your coming to power, am, like the dynasty I represent, above the parties."

The election of a new regent took place in the Chamber of Deputies in the afternoon of October 9. The members of the Council of Ministers were very late in arriving, having no doubt pondered until the last minute whom to propose. Buzdugan's eulogy was delivered. Iorga insisted vigorously that Queen Marie be elected regent. The members of the government spread through the halls, asking their followers to vote for Constantin Sărăţeanu, counselor of the High Court of Appeal—a by-and-large unknown name, which no one at all had mentioned for this high office. This was a true coup de théâtre, and he was of course elected with a strong majority of the votes and proclaimed regent. Iorga, who had perhaps hoped to be elected himself, whispered in my ear, "The man they elected is honest, but he will trip on his mantle."

I left immediately by court car for Sărăţeanu's home in order to take him to the Royal Palace, from where the official procession was to go to the Chamber of Deputies for the swearing in. Sărăţeanu received me with great affection. Like his predecessor, he was a former colleague of my father's at the High Court of Appeal, and was even a personal friend. (I remember how, when I was about eight years old, my father sent me to Sărăţeanu, at that time secretary-general of the Ministry of Justice, with a letter—probably a request for a leave of absence. In those long-gone-by days, there were not too many people in the waiting rooms of the ministry, and I was very proud to have been immediately received by the secretary-general, with all the courtesies usually given to adults, and even offered a *dulceaţă.*[11]) Sărăţeanu was particularly close to my uncle, Costel Borănescu, for they were of the same age. Being from Buzău, he knew well my Borănescu grandparents, who had estates in that county, and I believe also my great-grandparents Sibiceanu. My relations with him during the few months the regency was still to last were excellent, and in spite of the difference in our ages, we became friends. Admittedly, we talked more about genealogy than about politics, Sărăţeanu being one of the best genealogists of the aristocratic families of Wallachia. I was surprised when, in one of our first meetings in the Palace, he gave me copies of the genealogical trees of the Borănescus and of the Sibiceanus he had especially drawn up for me; they are still in my possession. Many a time he described to me the old links between the boyars from Sărata, from whom he descended, and the boyars from Sibiciu, my ancestors.

As officer in the reserves, he had been attached during the war, in spite of his advanced age, to the general staff of General Averescu, and a close friendship developed between them. When Averescu was forming his first government, after the armistice of 1918, he proposed Sărăţeanu as minister of justice and Argetoianu as minister of the interior. After King Ferdinand raised some objections to the appointment of Argetoianu as minister of the interior (possibly at the urging of Brătianu, for Argetoianu, until then a member of the Conservative party, had virulently assailed the Liberals), the general shifted Argetoianu to the Ministry of Justice and named Sărăţeanu minister of the interior, a position he held for

[11] A thick, very sweet jam served in a spoon and accompanied by a glass of water.

some two months, until the arrival to power of the Marghiloman government. A man of great culture, especially in the area of Romanian history, Sărăţeanu highly valued his membership in the Geographical Society, although I doubt he ever was active in it. He haunted me so much about it that I finally gave in and joined that society, even though my geographic grounding was as rudimentary as his.

Bucharesters did not extend to the new regent the consideration this honorable man deserved. The newspapers accused him of not returning with sufficient politeness (no doubt through shyness) the greetings of passers-by, merely raising his hand to his hat rather than uncovering himself. Poor Sărăţeanu, a very well-bred man, was particularly hurt by this accusation, which he considered unfair and unfounded.

Sărăţeanu owed his rise to the Regency only to the fact that his wife was the sister of Mihai Popovici and the niece of Vaida-Voevod. The National-Peasants therefore believed, correctly, that he would toe their line. The new regent did not have the authority, or perhaps the intention, of opposing the movement that was afoot to bring Carol back, though as yet he probably had no knowledge of it. After Buzdugan's death, the Regency had indeed lost its hold on the country's helm.

✧ ✧ ✧

It must be conceded that, because of the weakness of the Regency and of the government, as well as because the royal family lacked a head, a feeling of uncertainty had spread through the country. Romania was like a rudderless boat, tossed hither and thither by the wind. Contributing in no small part to this feeling of wavering and vacillation within the country's top layer was the irresponsible handling of the engagement of Princess Ileana, Queen Marie's youngest daughter, to a young German, Count Alexander von Hochberg, the son of the Prince von Pless, an enormously rich Silesian. Queen Marie, a friend of Princess Daisy Pless, née Cornwallis-West, had consented to the engagement; I believe that the young princess was genuinely attracted to the blond and tall Hochberg. Nevertheless, both the mother and the government were duty-bound to seek information about the young man before making an official announcement, so they would have found out what all Germany knew: that he was notorious for his depraved behavior and that he had been implicated in scandals that had had judicial consequences. When this distressing news reached the queen, she preferred to ignore it. But when Mutius, the German envoy to Bucharest, paid an official visit to the Ministry of

Foreign Affairs to draw attention to the fiancé's reputation—the German government feeling morally obliged to open the eyes of those concerned—Maniu had no choice but to transmit to Queen Marie the government's insistent advice that she give up the proposed marriage. And at this junction, too, matters were handled in an inexcusable manner. Instead of simply breaking off the engagement, the old prince Pless—who, as a gentleman, had attempted to prevent the marriage, justifying his opposition by the fact that his was not a royal family—was invited to Bucharest and had to attend a large dinner party, a "breaking off" party, as the people in the know were fully aware. Then, after the departure of the unfortunate father, it was announced in the *Monitorul Oficial* that, by common consent, the young fiancés were calling off their marriage. An odd way of doing things! Hochberg pursued Ileana to Egypt, but he was threatened with expulsion by King Fuad and had to leave.

CAROL'S RETURN

Toward the middle of April 1930, Iorga received a letter from the former heir to the throne informing him that Carol Caraiman had broken off with Elena Lupescu and requesting Iorga to present again the former prince's case to the appropriate authorities so that it could be examined in a broad and Christian spirit. The letter, drafted with great skill, implied that Carol had come to realize his errors. He stated that he would place himself at the country's disposal were the Regency and Parliament to call on him. The letter was signed "Carol, Prince of Romania," a title to which he no longer had any right. Iorga turned the letter over to Maniu, who, in turn, apprised the Regency of it. The Regency took no action. Prince Nicholas, influenced by his military entourage, was becoming increasingly favorable to his brother's return to Romania. Sărăţeanu was in no position to take any initiative, but followed the instructions of his relatives, Mihai Popovici and Alexandru Vaida-Voevod. As for the patriarch, cautious and foreseeing, he preferred not to commit himself on this constitutional issue.

The reason for Prince Nicholas's about-face was essentially a personal one. He had been uninterested, from the very beginning, in the management of affairs of state, and now that he had a sentimental attachment with a young divorcée from the Romanian lower middle class, he wished more than ever to be rid of his duties as regent. And what more elegant way of accomplishing that than by handing the reins of government to his older brother? Rumors and idle talk were flying around. Some referred to a Masonic scheme, the two brothers being said to have become very close to the Freemason movement to which some of Prince Nicholas's aides-de-camp would have belonged. I myself see no need to look for a mysterious or melodramatic explanation. There was a Carlist undercurrent in Romania, the Maniu government—not yet knowing Carol's nature—did not oppose him and was actually even smoothing his way, the Regency lacked authority, and Prince Nicholas was bored beyond measure with the unwanted burdens of ruling. Nicholas's words to Buzdugan seemed long in the past: "Carol's supporters don't realize the royal family's position. Were Carol to return, we would have to leave Romania, all of us." I consider it was Prince Nicholas who was most responsible for his brother's return, for all his denials, many years later when I told him so at the Hôtel Beau-Rivage in Ouchy, that he had ever wanted to see Carol ("that scoundrel") climb the steps of the throne.

A first hint of Prince Nicholas's Carlism came to light when he insisted that his brother's donation for the victims of the Costineşti conflagration (in which more than one hundred faithful were burned to death in the village church on Good Friday night) be entered under the name of "Prince Carol." The second hint, a much more significant one, was the prince's continuous efforts to have effective military commands entrusted to generals who were considered Carlists, displacing those who were seen as loyal to King Michael. Finally, the "prince regent" no longer refrained, in private conversation with his colleagues from the Regency, from saying that he saw no other way out for the country than the return of his brother. This viewpoint led to a serious disagreement between him and his mother. An indication of the crisis in the ruling family was that Prince Nicholas gave an audience to Grigore N. Filipescu, an implacable opponent of Queen Marie, who ceaselessly attacked her in *Epoca,* as for years on end he had attacked Ştirbey in the pages of that same newspaper. The queen was particularly offended that Filipescu always referred to her as "the *former* sovereign," wanting to underscore that she no longer had any right to interfere in affairs of state.

In view of the passivity of the governmental bodies, the Liberal party—whose Congress of May 4, 1930, had revealed its true strength—decided to issue a new *Green Book,* containing all the Romanian and foreign official documents concerning Carol's activities before and after his renunciation of the throne. Vintilă Brătianu, as the party's head, instructed Constantin ("Bébé") Brătianu to provide the Regency with copies of the work, so that the royal family and those at the head of the state might become acquainted with it before the public at large. Hiott, the minister of the royal household, gave Prince Nicholas's reply directly to Vintilă Brătianu: the prince was of the opinion that the booklet should not be put into circulation (a third indication of his Carlism) and requested, as an exception, to present his views in a one-on-one meeting with the head of the Liberal party.

Vintilă Brătianu therefore went to see Prince Nicholas, not at the Royal Palace but at Cotroceni. Speaking first, he urged the prince to take the helm of the country in his hands when issues arose that directly concerned the kingdom and the dynasty. Nicholas demurred on the grounds that, being young and inexperienced, he felt obliged to make decisions in agreement with the two other regents. Vintilă Brătianu retorted that experience was not necessary in momentous and vital issues, only heart and mind. Vintilă Brătianu then broached the topic of the *Green Book*. He promised that, in view of the wishes expressed by the prince, he would postpone distribution of the booklet by three days, in the hope that the Regency would use this respite to issue an explanatory communiqué that would categorically declare that the question of the succession to the throne had been definitively resolved and that the issue was therefore closed. If the heads of state took such a position, he said, the booklet would no longer be needed. Prince Nicholas seemed attracted by the idea, but asked for time to think it over and to consult his colleagues. Twenty-four hours passed without a reply.

What was happening inside the Regency? Egged on by his military aides, the prince regent was categorically opposed to the idea of a communiqué. The Maniu government was obviously of the same opinion, for Sărăţeanu, who always faithfully expressed its views, seconded his royal colleague's position. As for the patriarch, he was not opposed to the issuance of a communiqué on the lines wanted by the Liberals, but being outnumbered in the three-member council, he felt it wiser to stay prudently noncommittal. Result: the proposal of issuing a communiqué was rejected. Bébé Brătianu was asked on May 9 to tell his cousin Vintilă that "the Regency considers Mr. Vintilă Brătianu's request insulting, since it appears to put in doubt the Regency's good faith in keeping its sworn oath." The events that followed were to prove that the "good faith" of the three regents and their willingness to keep their "sworn oath" were to hold for a mere three weeks after this declaration.

Bébé Brătianu told me that Vintilă and the Liberal party were obviously displeased by this reaction of the regents. What had been wished, and had been expected, was a public statement from the Regency that would put an end to the Carlist agitation. Since that had not occurred, the booklet prepared by the Liberals was put in circulation. At the

Palace, we all received it on May 13. It was also officially delivered to the regents. Then we learned that the Maniu government, which by now was openly supporting the Carlist movement, had ordered the seizure of the booklet as well as of all the newspapers that mentioned that "closed issue." There was to be no public discussion of the contents of the booklet.

✧ ✧ ✧

In the first days of June 1930, a hidden agitation seemed to pervade all political groups. The ambiguous position of the Regency and of the Maniu government concerning the so-called "closed issue" worried one sector of public opinion, while another sector, full of impatience and vain hopes, placed its trust in a new leadership.

On June 5, unexpectedly, Queen Marie announced that she was going abroad. I went to see her off at the railway station, in the name of the Regency. She arrived at the last minute and in a hurry, almost as if she were worried or embarrassed, and immediately climbed aboard, without chatting as she usually did with those who were there to see her off. It was only later that I came to understand her behavior: Prince Nicholas must certainly have let her know what was being plotted, and she did not want to be present at what was going to take place against her will.

When I went to see Prince Nicholas on the morning of June 6, I heard him ask General Condeescu, the minister of the army and former head of King Michael's military entourage: "Good news?" accompanying this question with a knowing smile and gesture. There was no doubt in my mind that they were talking about Carol. Prince Nicholas, sounding slightly mysterious, asked me to inform Maniu that he would like to talk with him, alone, before he met with the entire Regency. I went to Hiott's office to tell him of my suspicions, but the minister of the royal household calmly assured me that he knew of nothing that would justify my fears. Indeed, there was no sign of unusual activity, no commotion; the day passed normally and people were all going about their business.

And yet that very evening, at seven o'clock, a plane landed at Cluj with King Michael's father aboard. The military commanders, informed in advance, received him warmly. He then left for Bucharest in another plane, landing at Băneasa at ten o'clock. From there he went straight to the Cotroceni plateau where he was awaited, in square formations, by the Second and Ninth regiments of mountain troops from the brigade of Colonel Iacobici, who was also in the plot. General Condeescu, who obviously felt that this was going a bit too fast and who would have preferred a somewhat less spectacular arrival, asked by whose orders the soldiers were being paraded. He was told that it was by Prince Nicholas's order, conveyed by our military attaché in Paris, Colonel Tătăranu, one of the officers who had hatched the plot. I know these details from General Athanasescu, Queen Marie's aide-de-camp, who witnessed from a distance Carol's arrival at Cotroceni. Entering Cotroceni Palace, Carol was warmly greeted by his brother and the two embraced.

Political talks began that very night. Maniu pointed out to Carol the impossibility for the government and the armed forces of breaking their loyalty oaths to King Michael. Carol seemed somewhat understanding and said he would be satisfied with a seat in the Regency but, to be sure, with the stipulation that he would proclaim himself king in at most six months. At the crack of dawn next day (June 7), he received in audience at Cotroceni General Prezan, who in all likelihood assured him of his popularity in the armed forces. In any case, it is to Prezan that political circles attributed Carol's about-face. Carol, indeed, summoned Maniu and told him bluntly that he had changed his mind and that, with the armed forces and Parliament behind him, he demanded the repeal of the law of January 4, 1926, and his immediate proclamation as king. The prime minister, an honest and upright man, a man of his word, came out from this audience upset and indignant. He asked for time to think things over and to consult with the members of his government. At the Palace, the two four-horse royal carriages (one for Carol and Nicholas, the other for the patriarch and Sărăţeanu), which were ready to drive them to Parliament for Carol's swearing-in as regent, were immediately countermanded.

The dismay at the Palace was universal. Stîrcea, grand master of the royal court's ceremonies, went from office to office declaring that it was unthinkable to break one's oath of allegiance to King Michael. The sovereign's father could at most be regent during his son's minority. (Baron Stîrcea was soon to change, becoming highly devoted to Carol II.)

General Condeescu came to report to the regents. While waiting for them to arrive at the Palace, he stepped into my office and said ingenuously: "How about it? I hadn't the slightest idea. Prince Nicholas said to me: 'Do you know that Carol has arrived in Romania?' I answered, 'That is not possible, Your Highness!' And actually, at the time he announced the news to me, it had not yet occurred." However, the fact that the army was in the know and that it had awaited Carol's arrival at night on the barrack grounds does not quite mesh, in my view, with the statement of the minister of the army that he was completely in the dark. It was by now clear that the return of the former prince had been prepared thoroughly and for some time.

The regents arrived, one by one, on that morning of June 7. Patriarch Miron took me by the arm and said: "Well, what can be done if the army wants him? Frankly, I'm fed up!" Sărăţeanu also came in, and, as he saw me, he uttered more or less the same words as his ecclesiastical colleague: "Reversal of direction! If the army wants him, what can we do?" Finally, Prince Nicholas made his appearance. Faithful to his newly fashioned formula, Sărăţeanu also greeted him: "Reversal of direction, Your Highness!"

With great dignity, Hiott personally handed the regents his written resignation as minister of the royal household. The regents refused to accept it, but it goes without saying that Hiott gave up his functions, unwilling to have anything to do, even indirectly, with the negotiations under way to place on the throne the man who, in Milan, had solemnly declared to him that he was definitively renouncing the crown.

The entire day was devoted to political meetings, discussions, and deals between Maniu and the regents, between Maniu and the other members of his cabinet, between Maniu and Carol. Overly eager politicians queued up at Cotroceni Palace. Even Gheorghe I. Brătianu, Ion I.C. Brătianu's son, was among the first and keenest of those going to see the "man of the day," the "rising star"—to the great astonishment and indignation of his family and of the Liberal party. The patriarch, too, took the road to Cotroceni, where he had a heated discussion with Carol and Nicholas, which he related to me upon his return. He told me he had appealed to the king's father, saying: "Don't force us to break the oath we swore to Your Highness's son. Accept instead to become regent." Carol replied that were he to take the oath as regent and later proclaim himself king, he would be breaking his oath. He concluded, the patriarch said, "in a rather uncalled for way" by saying: "Better if you gentlemen, rather than I, break the oath."

In view of Carol's determination to be proclaimed king, the following procedure was finally agreed upon: the Maniu government, which had sworn allegiance to King Michael and the Regency, would resign and would propose that a new government be formed under the presidency of Mihalache, of Vaida-Voevod, or, as a last resort, of Mironescu. Mihalache and Vaida refused to perjure themselves. Endowed with a less prickly sense of honor, Mironescu hastened to accept the offer of heading a government, even at the cost of being stigmatized as a perjurer. With his perpetual smile, he took me by the arm in my office and whispered in my ear: "What unexpected events! I must be prime minister for twenty-four hours, as a favor to them. I would have preferred Mihalache to undertake the task, but he refused because of this oath business—a mere formality—and then they called on me, who am better known abroad." At nine o'clock that evening Mironescu and his colleagues swore, in front of the Regency, allegiance to King Michael, only to break that oath the next day by swearing allegiance to Carol II.

The Regency itself was now breaking up: Patriarch Miron and Sărăţeanu, likewise not wanting to be remembered in history as perjurers, tendered their resignations. This way, neither the two regents nor the prime minister would formally break their oath, since, in fact . . . Oh holy Ignatius of Loyola!

Prince Nicholas, being less fastidious about the oath, was the only one not to resign. And since the Constitution required that the regency be composed of three members, this institution, intended to last for twelve years, ceased to exist after only three. The Mironescu government consequently assumed the Regency's constitutional powers and prerogatives, which it was to use to dethrone King Michael I. When the members of that government were swearing by all that is sacred allegiance to King Michael, they had already decided, up to the smallest detail, the procedure for driving him off the throne.

The following day, June 8, the shameful deed was consummated. A father drove away his son in order to take his place, and Michael's guardians helped deprive a minor of his inheritance. While Carol, accompanied by his brother Nicholas, was headed in a horse-driven carriage toward Metropolitan Hill to be enthroned as king, I went to the residence of King Michael and signed his register-book and that of his mother, identifying myself as "former secretary general of the Regency." Another chapter—a sad one—of my career had come to an end.

I handed over the archives of the secretariat-general of the Regency to the Palace's librarian and to the chancery of the Ministry of the Royal Household. Hiott did the same. I then took leave from the staff and asked to say my farewells to the former regents. Prince Nicholas was away at Curtea de Argeş and let me know that he would see me upon his return. So the first of the former regents to receive me was Patriarch Miron, in the Patriarchate's garden. We passed together in review the almost three years of the Regency. He said to me: "I could not have prevented what happened, when even King Michael's uncle, Prince Nicholas, hatched the removal of his nephew, whose guardian he was. But at least I did not perjure myself! It is only after Carol was proclaimed king that I crossed the threshold of the legislative assemblies in my capacity as senator ex officio. Although I was asked to swear in Carol, I had my vicar do it instead of me, so as not to be party to the last step of King Michael's dethroning."

The patriarch foresaw an era of persecutions unleashed by a vengeful Carol. Added to the raging economic crisis, it would soon lessen Bucharesters' apparent enthusiasm. When I stood up to take my leave, Patriarch Miron thanked me with warmth and affection for my services. I detected a bit of emotion in his voice when he told me, "You surrounded me with loyalty and love, more so it seems than you did the other two." I replied that, apart from the special respect I obviously had for the head of my Church, I felt that I had carried out my duties with the same conscientiousness and correctness for all the regents. I thanked him, in turn, for the kindness he had shown me.

I then went to see Sărăţeanu, who likewise thanked me for my cooperation and, very friendly, said: "I leave without any bitterness. My only regret is that we shall no longer see each other daily." After I also expressed my thanks, we talked about the dramatic recent events. He told me of Maniu's stupefaction and aching disappointment at Carol's behavior, who at 2:00 A.M. assured him that he would be satisfied with a place in the Regency, but in the morning demanded the crown. Maniu's amazement was all the greater because during his exile Carol had repeatedly declared that he did not covet his son's position but wished only to return to his country in whatever position. I asked Sărăţeanu if the government had told him ahead of time the date of Carol's arrival. He assured me that he had found out about it only after the fact. "In my opinion," I said, "this secretiveness of the government toward one of the heads of the state was, not to use stronger terms, somewhat excessive." And I did not conceal my belief that the entire blame for what had happened fell on the government, which had encouraged that which it was duty-bound, and able, to prevent. Let us hope, I concluded, that the country will not suffer too much from this coup d'état. Sărăţeanu remained silent—it was, after all, this government that had raised him to the Regency—but he nodded approvingly. The poor man took comfort then in the hope, which he shared with me, that some way would be found to make him ex officio senator (like his two colleagues of the Regency) and that he would be given certain perquisites and honors. We parted cordially and with all the friendliness stemming from his ties to my family.

Upon his return to Bucharest, Prince Nicholas received me in his wing of the Cotroceni Palace. He was very cordial and cheerful, visibly relieved at being rid of the burdens of the Regency, even though these had never weighed very heavily on his shoulders. He shook my hand in a friendly fashion and thanked me for my assistance: "I know your assignment was often tough and ticklish, since it is not easy to conciliate three people." Turning to the assignment his brother had given him—commander-in-chief of the armed forces—he told me he was sorry he hadn't been given only the command of the air force, as he had requested, since he would now "have to work with three chiefs of staff." Sighing, he added: "It is again three; I cannot escape the Regency!"

6

Cabinet Director of the Ministry of Foreign Affairs (1931)

Donec eris felix, multos numerabis amicos,
Tempora cum fuerint nubila, solus eris![1]
—Ovid, *Tristes 1.1.39*

These verses, which Ovid wrote from exile in Tomis, our Constanţa of today, state a truth as old as the world. I, too, had occasion to become aware of it when, brought down from the heights of my position at the Regency by Carol's return, I resumed my place alongside my colleagues at the Ministry of Foreign Affairs.

CAROL SETTLES ACCOUNTS

In their haste to curry the favors of the "new lord," many were those who preferred not to "compromise" themselves with anyone connected with the Regency or the "Brătianu tyranny," and to discover for themselves an imaginary Carlist past. The watchword was to keep us in the background: in the first place me, as former political director of Ionel Brătianu and as secretary-general of the Regency; Alexander Cretzianu, as relative by marriage of Brătianu and especially of Barbu Ştirbey; and Dinu Hiott, as son-in-law of the same Ştirbey. In my case, the directive came from above, since the deplorable Mironescu, who had a most supple backbone, opposed any responsible mandate proposed for me by the Ministry's secretary-general, Gheorghe Filality, a straightforward man uncontaminated by the prevailing servility.

There was great commotion at the Ministry. Dinu Hiott was going from office to office to let off steam and express his revulsion at seeing a

[1]So long as you are happy, you shall have many friends, / But when times grow cloudy, you shall be alone.

man of Carol's stamp at the head of the country. Alexander Cretzianu asked his aunt Elise Brătianu for advice as to how to react to his colleagues' ostracism. The widow of the great statesman replied: "When they are talking about the new king, tell them: 'My uncle Ion I.C. Brătianu was seldom mistaken in his judgment of people; let's hope that in Carol's case he was mistaken.'" Even an in-law of the Brătianus and former cabinet chief of Ionel Brătianu, Aurel Vasiliu, was advising us to claim association only with Brătianu's foreign policy, not with his domestic policy. I retorted: "Brătianu's memory does not need my defense, history will bear witness for him. But if my humble opinion happens to be sought, I will say that I admire him as much for the courage and foresight he showed on the succession issue as for his actions in the other political areas." Shamed, Vasiliu changed the subject. A childhood friend, Georgel Mavrocordat, Mironescu's cabinet chief, faulted me for not having gone to Parliament to witness Carol's swearing in. "It was the most beautiful day of my life," he uttered lyrically. "It may have been," I answered, "but it wasn't for me; besides, what business did I have to be in the Chamber, since I no longer have an official position at the court, the Regency no longer existing?"

I must admit, however, that there were honorable exceptions to the lines from *Tristes*. I should mention the praiseworthy and chivalrous behavior of Mihail A. Arion, the Ministry's political director, toward the blacklisted, if I may so refer to us. A principled man as well as a diplomat of real ability, he insistently demanded that Alexander Cretzianu and I be assigned to his directorate, and he succeeded in having his way in spite of Mironescu's anger. I was at first assigned to head the Balkan section, then the Russian one. In the latter capacity, I was an ex officio member of a national security commission attached to the Ministry of War. Although the commission in fact never met, the minister of foreign affairs had nevertheless to inform the minister of war that I, as head of the Russian section, would henceforth represent our Political Directorate in that phantom commission. Horrified, Mironescu refused to place his signature on the required letter. "What would the king say," he bemoaned, "were he to find out that I signed an order concerning the former secretary-general of the Regency!" The wretch was forgetting that he had been the Regency's foreign minister and, for a few hours, even its prime minister! He therefore asked that "any other of the gentlemen of the Political Directorate" be entrusted with the weighty duty of representing the Ministry of Foreign Affairs in a commission that was never convened. Here again, Mihail Arion gave proof of his high character. Rallying the entire staff to his point of view, he had them tell Mironescu that they considered insulting his refusal to name a particular one of them as the Ministry's representative, and that in consequence none of them would accept to replace me. Mironescu, reportedly dumbfounded, gave in. But he had my appointment signed by a protocol officer.

Another "enemy of the regime"—and one hit particularly hard—was Constantin Diamandy, former envoy to Sofia, Rome, Petersburg, and Paris, as well as former high commissioner in Budapest during the Romanian army's occupation. We had frequent conversations, and he did not hide his bitterness at the brutal manner in which Mironescu had treated him, obviously on orders from above. The very day Carol proclaimed himself king, Diamandy was not only recalled from his posting as envoy to Paris but also was pensioned off, without even receiving a letter of thanks for the services he had rendered the country over several decades. And all this because he had been the loyal collaborator of Ionel Brătianu and King Michael's representative in Paris at a time when Carol Caraiman hung around that city. Diamandy complained to me about the pettiness and especially the stupidity of the day's rulers, who wanted at all cost to present him to public opinion as an "enemy of the king," as they had done to Ştirbey and to so many others. "Why enemy?" he asked. "Because I did my duty? Because I didn't betray King Michael and the Regency? When King Ferdinand accepted his son's renunciation of the throne, should I have shown myself more king than the king and more father than the father?" To say that he had persecuted or spied on Carol in Paris was more than infamous, it was idiotic, Diamandy declared. He assured me he had had no dealings with Rădoi, the Romanian security services' agent in Paris, whom he never saw. And how was he to spy on Carol himself? "I had better things to do and, besides, we obviously did not move in the same circles."

A PARENTHESIS: DIAMANDY'S MISSION TO PARIS (1926–1930)

All that was now left for poor Diamandy was to write his memoirs. Knowing that I had written books on diplomatic history, he asked me to pen an account of his mission to Paris, but this only later, when he was no longer alive. For that purpose he was going to tell his children to hand over to me, at his death, his entire personal archive pertaining to his assignment to Paris. I later reminded his heirs of their father's wish, but although they were aware of it, they did not carry it out. Diamandy's mission to Paris thus remains untold, which is a pity. I did, however, take some notes on what he disclosed to me during the course of our conversations, and feel duty-bound to make them public so that I, at least, comply in part with his last wishes.

Diamandy described to me the difficulties he had to struggle against when he arrived in Paris in 1926. The pacifist and internationalist Herriot government had replaced the government of Raymond Poincaré, a staunch friend of Romania since the war years. Diamandy therefore had to stay in close touch with left-of-center milieus. In his time, one could thus encounter in the legation's reception rooms the whole gamut of French politicians, from Rohan-Chabot and Luynes to Paul Boncour and Léon Blum. Even Cachin came once.

The most difficult problems he had to deal with as envoy to Paris were the question of the Soviet fleet at Bizerta and the negotiations leading to the Franco-Romanian treaty of alliance. Herriot had decided to hand over to the Soviets the Russian warships interned at Bizerta, basing his decision on an earlier promise by Poincaré that the return of the fleet would take place after France's official recognition of the Soviet Union. Diamandy told both Herriot and Painlevé, the minister of the navy, that were the French government to carry out the decision, it would constitute an unfriendly act toward Romania. The French cabinet, meeting at the Elysée, then gave us satisfaction. Subsequently, however, Painlevé suggested to Diamandy a compromise solution: the French government, as a symbolic gesture, would return to the Soviet Union two of the seized vessels. But our envoy explained to him that even a single Russian warship arriving in the Black Sea from Bizerta would be seen by the Romanian people as meaning that its enemies were being rearmed by France. In conclusion, Diamandy told him: "Keep them at Bizerta, and preferably under the water than on it—as at Scapa Flow."[2]

As for the treaty of alliance, it had first been proposed by France during its military occupation of the Ruhr, when it feared Germany, but it had by now become more important to Romania, which was seeking to safeguard Bessarabia. That was the reason that the negotiations had lasted no fewer than two years. The French government was trying to exclude Bessarabia from the treaty's provisions. Diamandy pointed out the impossibility of establishing two types of Romanian territory, the one defended under the treaty, the other not. When a governmental crisis arose in 1926, Diamandy pointed out to Briand, the resigning foreign

---

[2]Sea basin in the Orkneys where the German fleet was interned at the end of World War I, and where most of the ships were scuttled by their German crews in June 1919.

minister, that he could be accused by his opponents of having made a serious mistake by not having secured more tightly the links between France and its former allies in the east, in case its policy of rapprochement with Germany did not bear fruit. "There must be two to reach an agreement. If Germany does not want a rapprochement, what will you do?" In the end Briand let himself be persuaded, in order to prevent future attacks on his policy, and he signed the treaty.

CAROL SEEKS A NEW GOVERNMENT

Nicolae Titulescu had too overwhelming a personality to pay attention to Carol's whims and to his discrimination between those who enjoyed his favor and those who were in disgrace. Each time he came from London to Bucharest, he received me with great friendliness and offered me an hour of interesting and pleasant conversation. Titulescu was called back by the king in March 1931 to explore the possibility of a government of national unity. As usual, I asked to see Titulescu, for his stays were almost always of short duration. He received me on March 21. He seemed doubtful about the success of the mission entrusted to him by Carol and inveighed harshly against the French loan obtained by the National-Peasant government. "There was no need for a loan," he told me, "and if it was nevertheless contracted, it was only because of the petty personal interests of some members of the government."

He returned to London a few days later, but was back again on April 9, charged this time by the king with forming a government of national unity following the fall of the government headed by the inadequate Mironescu. Titulescu's attempt did not succeed, because the smaller political parties refused to join such a government. In this connection, there was a quite heated discussion between Titulescu and Gheorghe Brătianu, the head of the dissident Liberals. Titulescu apparently became exasperated with Brătianu's obstinate refusal and lost his temper. To avoid the repetition of such a scene, Carol insisted on attending the meeting between Titulescu and Dr. N. Lupu.[3] The royal presence, however, did not prevent a violent confrontation between the two politicians. This time, Lupu was the one who lost his cool, vehemently denouncing Titulescu, who claimed to be "a newcomer," hence impartial. "You, a newcomer?" shouted Lupu. "You, a former follower of Take Ionescu, who was leading us to disaster with your fiscal policy,

[3]Vice president of the National-Peasant party.

you who abandoned Take Ionescu, who abandoned Vintilă Brătianu when you foresaw his fall?" The scene was said to have been awful.

A collaboration of the two main parties was not possible without the participation of the smaller ones, since the Liberals did not want to assume sole responsibility for the National-Peasant's bungling. Carol then considered the possibility of a government of technicians, still headed by Titulescu and with Demetrius I. Ghika at Foreign Affairs, which would work with the National-Peasant party. Carol wanted also to include Argetoianu and Manoilescu in the government, but Maniu did not accept this, refusing the cooperation of the Parliament elected under his administration. The next step could have been to dissolve Parliament and hold new elections, but Titulescu, impregnated by the ideals of Western democracy, rejected this solution, which would have been seen abroad, correctly, as dictatorial in nature. He gave up the assignment of forming a government and returned to London.

Carol then turned to his old teacher—and staunch friend even in the darkest days—Nicolae Iorga, who had long desired to become prime minister. Iorga was a great historic figure on account of his brilliant intelligence, enormous industry, and profound patriotism, as well as of his gift for expressing the true thoughts and aspirations of the Romanian people, especially in times of crisis. But perhaps precisely because of his idealism, of a certain contempt for the petty realities of day-to-day politics, and, perhaps, of some measure of personal vanity, as well as of his explosive temper and lack of flexibility, he was not endowed with the traits required for a head of government—traits often found in men plainly inferior to him in moral qualities and even in intelligence. His government therefore was unlikely to last, and besides, I believe the king had from the beginning looked on Iorga only as a temporary solution.

And so, on April 18, 1931, the Iorga government was formed. Its mainstay and real leader, however, was Constantin Argetoianu, a man of great intelligence and energy, witty and cynical, and with knowledge of all the shady deals of our political world. A former career diplomat and large landowner, he had at one time or another joined most of the political parties. He once told me: "It is not I who change, it is the political parties, and when one of them adopts my ideas, I cooperate with it, but I always remain the same." A conversation with him was always a delight. Argetoianu began by being minister of finance in Iorga's government, but in time he became the real prime minister, whom the king consulted on all major issues, to the old professor's chagrin.

Carol had asked that Dr. Ion Cantacuzino and Demetrius I. Ghika, our envoy to Rome, be included in the new government, the first as minister of health, the second as minister of foreign affairs. Ghika accepted, but without much enthusiasm. An outstanding diplomat of brilliant intelligence, he too a most witty man, he did not feel that he was made for the political arena, where he was also somewhat handicapped by his at times awkward handling of the Romanian language and his French accent (he had been brought up in France), but especially by his nature of perfect gentleman, which permitted no compromise or promiscuity. Upon his arrival from Rome on April 27, while still in the railway station, he took me aside and, confessing his uneasiness about the new responsibilities he was shouldering, he asked me to work with him as his cabinet director. "I would not venture to address such a request to the former secretary of the Regency, but I dare to address it to my nephew."[4] I accepted the proposal with alacrity, glad to be able to work closely with one of our foremost diplomats, whom I valued for the vivacity of his mind and to whom I was tied by real affection.

The first issue facing the new government was that of economic ties with Germany, an issue that was obviously political in nature. With the aim of incorporating Romania into the Austro-German customs union, the Berlin government asked that negotiations toward the conclusion of an economic agreement be resumed without delay; preliminary discussions had been suspended because of the governmental crisis. France and Czechoslovakia entreated us not to negotiate before the League of Nations, which was to meet for that purpose on May 18, had pronounced itself on the recently concluded Austro-German customs union. In view of Germany's insistence, the government decided that economic negotiations with Berlin should nevertheless start in Bucharest immediately after the Conference of the Little Entente, which was to begin on May 3. I passed on this information to Kirchholtes, the German chargé d'affaires, who promised to cable his government to that effect. Whether there had been some mix-up in Berlin or, as Ghika thought, Kirchholtes had advised the German delegation to come immediately, or the delegation was already on its way, in any case, the imminent arrival of the German economic experts was announced. Ghika, in despair and indignation, was certain that this was a "piece of Boche skullduggery" to sabotage the Bucharest Conference of the Little Entente: "Czechoslovakia asks us to postpone the negotiations with Germany, and yet we will have

[4]Ghika's wife was the aunt of Bossy's wife.

to begin them in the presence of the Czechoslovak minister of foreign affairs, and this even during the Conference of the Little Entente." As an old friend of France, Ghika was also worrying about the reaction in Paris. On May 2, he phoned Kirchholtes and asked him to do his utmost to delay the arrival of the delegation until after the Conference of the Little Entente. If not, he would issue a communiqué to put the mess in its proper perspective. In fact, the whole affair had an undisclosed aspect that Ghika had at first not suspected: the king, Argetoianu, and Manoilescu were the ones who wanted to rush an agreement with Berlin. They eventually told him so. He tried to convince them, and especially the king, that it would be better to put off the discussions with the Germans, since the French government was also offering Romania preferential rights (not by means of duty reductions but through refunds), and this without demanding in exchange the placing of industrial orders.

BUCHAREST CONFERENCE OF THE LITTLE ENTENTE

The Conference took place from May 3 to May 5. I served as its secretary, and was thus able to make various observations. I noted from Beneš's attitude, for instance, that there had been a certain détente between Czechoslovakia and Poland. From Marinković, Yugoslavia's foreign minister, one could infer his country's disapproval of the recent meeting of the Ambassadors' Conference, which gave Italy a sort of mandate over Albania. Marinković stated frankly that Belgrade could not agree to any Italian interference in Albania, and he did not hide his country's wish to draw closer to Britain. (Was this because he saw in Britain, a maritime power, the only means of reining in Italy's ambition to be master of the Adriatic?)

However, it was of course the German-Austrian tariff agreement that dominated the Conference. Beneš shared the view of the French government that this customs union was the first step toward the Anschluss. The future was to prove him right. Beneš and Marinković declared it was necessary to go shoulder to shoulder with the Allies. Ghika asked for a more precise definition of what this meant; for instance, what would we do if France mobilized? Beneš replied that it would be appropriate to join a customs war against Germany. Agreeing with Marinković, Ghika said an industrialized country such as Czechoslovakia could more easily take this position than agricultural countries such as Romania or Yugoslavia, for whom it would not be possible to go that far, and which would only be able to look with approval at the measures taken by the Allies. The three foreign ministers decided that, in any case, their governments would stick together on this issue, at least until the May session of the Council of the League of Nations and of the Study Commission for European Union. If nothing was achieved in Geneva, Ghika said, we would reclaim our freedom of action, because Romania had to find outlets for its agricultural products; at the moment, the Romanian people were dying of hunger while their silos were full. Beneš then expounded the French solution for easing the truly dramatic economic crisis that was hitting all the agrarian states of Central and Eastern Europe, that is, granting preferential treatment for agricultural products, on the basis of refunds and without requiring industrial concessions.

At one of the receptions for the Little Entente, I talked with Iorga. Our government was troubled by the press campaign waged against Carol abroad, and especially in Britain. Iorga attributed it to Titulescu, an accusation based solely on presumptions.

PRINCESS ILEANA'S MARRIAGE

When Demetrius Ghika came in June 1931 to congratulate us on the birth of our daughter Ilinca, he revealed to me that serious difficulties had arisen with regard to the projected marriage of Princess Ileana and Archduke Anton of Austria-Tuscany. The princess wanted an Orthodox religious wedding, but the Habsburg family opposed this. Some ten days later Ghika told me that, at the Habsburgs's insistence, Princess Ileana had agreed to have a Catholic ceremony, but she wished this to be followed by an Orthodox wedding. He asserted that in order to obtain this, she had let it be understood that, as future mother of Catholics, she did not exclude the possibility that, at a later stage, she might also convert to that religion; knowing the young princess as well as I did, I doubted this very much—or, rather, I didn't believe it at all. However, the talks undertaken in this connection with the Vatican did not succeed, which is not surprising in view of the well-known narrow-mindedness of the Catholic clergy of that time. Ileana then proposed another concession: the wedding would be performed according to the Catholic rite, but it would be preceded by an engagement ceremony blessed by the Orthodox clergy. But the pope had become wary after the marriage in Assisi of Princess Giovanna of Italy to King Boris of Bulgaria: on their return to Sofia, they were married again, following the Orthodox rite. In order to avoid the recurrence of such a ruse—about which he had been unable to protest since she was the daughter of the king of Italy, with whom he had just concluded the Concordat—Pius XI was uncompromising: if there was to be an Orthodox ceremony, of whatever nature, he would not grant a marriage dispensation. The general impression was that the betrothed couple would have been quite happy to be married by our patriarch, but Archduke Leopold Salvator and Archduchess Bianca, the bridegroom's parents, hurriedly cabled Carol that if that were the case, they would not come to the wedding and would announce that they were not giving their consent.

The Ileana-Anton wedding finally took place on July 26, in Peleş Castle. Our foreign minister's brother, Vladimir Ghika, a Catholic priest and protonotary apostolic, celebrated it according to the Roman Catholic rite. He found it fitting, in his sermon, to trace the history of the relations between Austria and the Romanian Principalities during the reigns of Ghika princes, which highly annoyed the royal family. Princess Ileana, in particular, was furious, and she later told me, "He seemed to place the Ghikas and the Habsburgs on equal footing; but for us, Ghika or Popescu, it's all the same." An odd pronouncement from Princess Ileana! "That is not quite so," I replied; "from our history's perspective, for instance, Ştirbey and Ionescu are not at all the same."[5]

TWELFTH MEETING OF THE ASSEMBLY OF THE LEAGUE OF NATIONS

On September 1, I was temporarily attached to our delegation to the League of Nations in the capacity of "expert"—that is, a sort of junior delegate. Demetrius Ghika, as minister of foreign affairs, headed the delegation, of which Titulescu, however, remained the soul. I therefore left on a six-week journey that took me to Switzerland, France, and Yugoslavia. It might be best to restrict myself here to some entries from my diary.

September 6. I arrive in Geneva, after a stay of three days in Vienna and one of two days in Lausanne. Titulescu takes me by the arm and introduces me to Joseph d'Avenol, assistant secretary-general of the League of Nations: "This is my friend Bossy. He has been political director of the Presidency of the Council of Ministers under Ionel Brătianu, secretary-general of the Regency, and is now cabinet director of his

[5]It is generally accepted that Princess Ileana was the daughter of Queen Marie and Barbu Ştirbey. Ionescu and Popescu are very common surnames in Romania, while Ghica (or Ghika) and Ştirbey are among the most aristocratic.

uncle, Prince Ghika. Which is to show you he is not a 'Titulax.' But I nevertheless like him very much because he is honest and able." ["Titulax" was a term introduced by Grigore Filipescu to denote Titulescu's friends, starting with the journalist Pertinax (Henry Guérand).] He followed this with a series of flattering comments. Remaining alone with Titulescu, I thanked him for his kind words and, jokingly, added: "Among the reservations I have about what you just said is your statement that I am not a 'Titulax.' To get that title, two are needed." Titulescu laughed and said: "You are right; I name you today a 'Titulax candidate.'"

September 7. Opening of the Twelfth Assembly of the League of Nations. Assignments to commissions are made. I will be on Commissions II, V, and VI. Aristide Aguerro y Bethancourt, Cuba's delegate, confides to me that he and the South Americans will ensure the reelection of the "great Latin" Titulescu, who is also warmly supported by Lord Robert Cecil.

September 8. Election of Titulescu as president of the League of Nations' meeting and defeat of Apponyi. Exchange of cables between Titulescu and Carol. In the first draft of his telegram, Titulescu assures his sovereign of his "affection," but then changes this word to "devotion." Smiling, he comments: "Et encore!"[6]

September 12. Tea at Mrs. Barton's, "the queen of Lake Geneva," in her marvelous residence on the lakeshore. The garden seems plucked out of a dream; the house is filled with works of art, as well as with keepsakes of Sir Robert Peel, the hostess's grandfather. In a corner of the garden, Duchess Edmée de La Rochefoucauld asked me, "So, is it true that Carol has banished his wife?" On the terrace, Elena Văcărescu tells me that she loves my mother, a childhood friend, and she recites from memory some of mother's verses. She had recited them to Paul Valéry, "who also liked them very much."

September 13. Excursion by car, with Ghika, along the shores of Lake Geneva: Ouchy, Lausanne, Montreux, Territet, Vevey. Beautiful weather, the autumn sun in a clear sky throwing silver flashes in the blue waters. Moments of complete serenity.

September 14. Meetings of Commissions II and V and of the General Assembly. At 1 P.M., press luncheon at the Hôtel des Bergues, where the Romanian delegation is also staying. Most amusingly composed menu. Very witty toasts. The most admirable of the speeches was

---

[6] "If even that!"

unmistakably that of Aristide Briand. "The cello voice," as he was called, struck up a ringing hymn to peace, which enwrapped and deeply stirred me. "Remarkable speech," whispered Mrs. Titulescu in my ear, "but we've heard it repeatedly for the past eight years."

September 15. In the morning, Commissions II and VI. Luncheon offered by my wife's aunt Alexandrina ("Didine") Cantacuzino, also a member of our delegation, in the splendid setting of the Eaux Vives. Among those present are Apponyi and his wife and Albert Mensdorff-Pouilly, former—and last—ambassador to London of Austria-Hungary. In the afternoon, meeting of Commission V, where I make my maiden speech at the League of Nations. I talk on Romania's legislation to fight the introduction and dissemination of narcotics!

September 16. Commissions II, V, and VI. Luncheon offered by Ghika at the Eaux Vives. Among the more interesting guests were Osusky, Czechoslovak envoy to Paris, and Sauerwein from *Le Matin.* In the evening, "feminist" dinner at the Cercle International, where I was taken against my will by Aunt Didine. There were hundreds of women from all the corners of the earth, while we, the men, were only four or five wretches dragged along by the distaff sides of our families. Alexandrina Cantacuzino delivered an eloquent speech, although perhaps too melodramatic. Countess Apponyi began her speech: "Ladies and gentleman!" I turned and looked around the room: indeed, I was the only remaining male. Seated at the head table, and right across from my aunt, I had been unable, contrary to my luckier brethren in misfortune, to abandon ship. Apart from that, many of the speeches were very good, and some even witty. The president in particular, an Australian woman wearing a monocle, had an excellent sense of humor. A Canadian delegate, addressing herself to her European colleagues, declared, "You've got the cathedrals, but I believe we've got the bathrooms."

September 19. The Commissions continue their work daily. I will not mention here the topics that were discussed, since the deliberations will all be published. Tea at Mrs. Claire Boas de Jouvenel's, one of the famous "Précieuses de Genève," along with Richard M. Coudenhove-Kalergi, the founder of Pan-Europa.

The Conference of the Little Entente, which was held during the League of Nations' meeting, ended today. The following decisions were taken regarding a possible attempt at the restoration of the Habsburg monarchy in Hungary, in favor of Archduke Otto. The three governments would:

1. Withdraw their diplomatic representatives from Budapest.
2. Close their borders with Hungary and suspend all communications with that country.
3. Appeal to the League of Nations and to the great powers.

The three countries would not mobilize at first. They would, however, take steps that would enable them to do so after four or five days if necessary and, at a later date, allow them to take direct coercive actions against Hungary.

September 26. I ask Titulescu why the Little Entente so tenaciously opposes a restoration of the Habsburgs. Do we fear that were a "beloved emperor" to return, the Romanians from Transylvania, the Czechs, the Slovaks, the Croats, the Slovenes would give up their freedom in order to subject themselves once again to the sway of the black and yellow banner? Titulescu fully shares my view, but tells me that Beneš is so obsessed by this alleged "peril" that Romania and Yugoslavia felt they had to fall in with his anti-Habsburg policy, wherever it may lead, so as not to irritate him unduly. For Beneš, indeed, the Anschluss is a lesser danger than Archduke Otto on the throne.

The commissions of the League of Nations have finished their work. I had the opportunity of taking the floor, along with Fierlinger (Czechoslovakia) and Fotić (Yugoslavia), to answer the Hungarian representative, who had complained that the governments of the Little Entente hindered intellectual cooperation by stopping Hungarian publications at their borders. I explained that the Romanian government made a distinction between Hungarian publications with a purely scientific or literary nature, which are allowed to enter the country, and those that, under the label of cultural, indulge in subversive propaganda. The latter are, and always will remain, prohibited.

September 30. After three days with my sister Madeleine at her convent in Langres, I arrive in Paris at the height of the Colonial Exhibition in Vincennes. Lunch with D. Ghika at the Cercle de l'Union. Frangulis notifies me that I have been elected a member of the International Diplomatic Academy.

October 8. With D. Ghika, I arrive in Belgrade from Paris on an official visit. We are warmly greeted at the station by Marinković, with whom we have lunch. In the evening, dinner at the Romanian legation with Marinković, Dard (envoy of France), Galli (envoy of Italy), Flieder (envoy of Czechoslovakia), Fotić (undersecretary of state at the Yugoslav

Ministry of Foreign Affairs), their wives, and the staff of our legation. After dinner, dancing party attended by the entire diplomatic corps. I meet again my former colleague in Rome, Schwarzburg-Günther, now Polish envoy to Belgrade.

October 9. Luncheon at King Alexander's, in his attractive castle at Dedinje. At table, I am seated next to Marinković. Also attending is the prime minister, General Jivković (who is said to have personally killed Queen Draga, whose aide-de-camp he was!). All the buildings around the castle are either guard barracks, or military clubs, or housing for officers. The king is thus well protected, the more so since there is a secret exit, which was shown to me, in the basement, an escape exit leading to an underground passage. In the evening, gala banquet hosted by Jivković at the guard's military club.

October 10. Luncheon at Dard's—the French legation has a superb building of white marble—then a stroll through Topshide and tea at the Czechoslovak legation. Dinner on board the yacht *Aleksandar.* The yacht sails after the departure of the guests, taking us to Turnul-Severin.

October 12. Return to Bucharest.

November 1. I am appointed counselor of our legation in Vienna.

END OF THE IORGA GOVERNMENT; INCREASING STRAINS WITHIN THE ROYAL FAMILY

The Iorga government lasted for only another seven months. I found out from Demetrius Ghika how it had ended. Its fate had been sealed for some time because of budgetary difficulties it had been unable to cope with. There was growing agitation among officers in Bessarabian garrisons who, having failed to receive their pay for months on end, threatened the king. At the last Council of Ministers meeting, Iorga requested a reconfirmation of the king's confidence, so that he might *govern* from now on (meaning that he, not Argetoianu, would govern). Carol, however, merely smiled enigmatically and asked Iorga to present in a week's time a plan for coming up with the soldiers' pay and the civil servants' salaries. After that the ministers left, leaving Iorga alone with the king.

Easy in mind, Ghika went to see a movie. When he came out of the movie house, he found out from the newspapers' special editions that he along with the rest of the government had resigned. He went immediately to see Iorga, who described his private conversation with the king after the end of the Council of Ministers meeting. Iorga had begun by asking the king why he had given him a deadline of one week to come up with a plan, when he well knew that there were no solutions to the problem. "Others do have solutions," Carol replied. "Who, Titulescu?" asked Iorga. "Yes," said Carol. "Then," retorted Iorga, "there remains only one more service I can render the crown: to resign. Do you have a pen?" "Here's one." Iorga said that after he had written his government's resignation, Carol placed hands on both his shoulders and, "with tears in his eyes"(?), told him: "Forgive me, my dear teacher, for having placed you in this hell."

I was told that in those last months of its existence, in addition to the many serious problems it had had to face, the Iorga government had been afflicted with another bane: growing feuds within the royal family. To be sure, this was a relatively minor aspect of governance and had no effect on the conduct of state affairs; yet the continuous decline in the dynasty's prestige created a threat of future problems and was to some extent shaking the monarchy's foundations.

One of the problems was the increasingly strained relations between Queen Marie and her eldest son, who wanted to eliminate his mother's political influence altogether and to reduce her public appearances to a minimum. Craving power, loving both political maneuvering (to which she had become accustomed from the time of her husband's reign) and public ceremonies (at which her handsome bearing sparked off waves of cheering), Queen Marie could not resign herself to the inconspicuous role of "former sovereign" (to use Grigore Filipescu's expression in *Epoca*). When I joined our legation in Vienna and had the opportunity of seeing her often and in private, she more than once complained bitterly about her son's behavior toward her. Unfortunately, the queen mother tended to share her resentment and biting comments about Carol with more or less anyone she met, and some hastened to repeat them to the king in order to curry favor. This obviously poisoned even more the relations between mother and son.

Another family row had been caused by the so-called "Prince Nicholas question." The king's brother had married a Romanian commoner, a certain Mrs. Dumitrescu-Tohani, the daughter of a vintner from the region of Mizil and the divorced daughter-in-law of a former Liberal minister. Disregarding his own morganatic marriage to Zizi Lambrino in 1918, Carol ordered the annulment of that of his brother, even though—as Archduke Leopold revealed to me later—he had at first told Nicholas, "Present me with a fait accompli," which amounted to a tacit authorization. It was said that Elena Lupescu, unsuccessful at that time in having her relationship with Carol legalized, did not want another commoner to obtain the distinction of being the legitimate spouse of a member of the ruling house, and had therefore urged her royal lover to take that measure. The measure, however, was excessive and arbitrary (as had been the annulment of the Carol–Zizi Lambrino marriage), since Nicholas had been forced to renounce his rights to the throne and to take up residence abroad under the name "Nicholas Brana." Carol obviously felt no empathy from the identical fate he had experienced a few years earlier when he was wandering in foreign parts under the name "Carol Caraiman."

I was given the following account by Demetrius Ghika. Nicholas approached his brother many times asking him to rescind, as seemed logical, the annulment of the ordinary citizen Nicholas Brana's marriage. Indignant at his brother's refusal, he returned unexpectedly to Romania on a CIDNA flight, his passage through Yugoslavia being reported by our legation in Belgrade. Field Marshal Prezan and the prefect of police, Colonel Gavrilă Marinescu, were waiting for him at the Băneasa airport. Approaching Nicholas, Prezan notified him that since he had returned to Romania without the king's prior approval, the king ordered him to remove himself to Scrovişte and to remain there until further notice. At that point, aiming a handgun toward Prezan, Nicholas is said to have yelled loudly, in front of the Romanian and French passengers of the CIDNA aircraft, "There are two bullets in this gun: one is for you and the other for that swine of Carol!" And then, according to Ghika, he flung Prezan into the mud. I must confess that I find this difficult to believe. Faced with this situation, Colonel Marinescu was said to have taken Nicholas to Cotroceni, where Colonel Zwiedenek settled him in his former apartment. Accurate in all details or not, or perhaps grossly exaggerated, these rumors (as well as the one according to which Nicholas shot and wounded Carol during a violent argument) were sapping day by day the aura of prestige that still surrounded the ruling family, more and more eroding the monarchical ideal in Romania. Only the ascension to the throne of King Michael I, in 1940, would put an end to this progressive disintegration, for the young sovereign, conscientious and morally honest as was his admirable mother, drew toward the dynasty established by Carol I a new wave of confidence and love from the Romanian people.

7

Vienna (1931–1934)

Appointed at my request to the vacant position of counselor of our legation in Vienna, I took up my duties on November 17, 1931. The legation was at 6 Eugenstrasse, in the diplomatic district. In front of it was the Belvedere Palace, the lovely imperial palace built by the architect Hildebrand for Prince Eugene of Savoy. It is there that, at the beginning of the twentieth century, the secret meetings of the Transylvanian patriots with Archduke Franz Ferdinand, the heir apparent, took place.

FIRST IMPRESSIONS

The Romanian envoy at my arrival was Caius Brediceanu, the son of the well-known nationalist fighter from the Banat, Coriolan Brediceanu. He had been a student in Vienna, a member of a nation oppressed under Hungary's yoke, and he felt deeply satisfied to find himself now in the old imperial capital in the capacity of *königlich rumänischer Gesandte*—royal Romanian envoy. Of a cheerful and lively disposition, he was a sincere and honest man, a lover of music, and favorably inclined toward all. Without great ambition and not much interested in paperwork or international political affairs, he gave a free hand to the legation's counselor both in dispatching chancellery matters and in writing the mission's political reports, thereby freeing himself to enjoy unhindered and in full the charms of Viennese life. Diplomatic receptions bored him no end, and he avoided them as much as he could, but he never missed a first-rate concert or one of the brilliant performances of the Vienna Opera. I remember his astonishment when Titulescu, who was in Austria for a few days, preferred to spend evenings in his room at the Grand Hotel talking politics with us rather than attending the opera, as Brediceanu was urging. “A flower without scent,” the latter whispered in my ear. I have the best of memories of my collaboration with Caius Brediceanu, who manifested the friendliest sentiments toward me, sentiments I reciprocated.

Accompanied by him, I entered for the first time the stately Ballhausplatz—Ballplatz for short—the sanctuary of modern diplomacy, whose glory is tied in particular to the renowned chancellors Kaunitz and Metternich, as well as to the epoch-making Congress of Vienna of 1815. I was introduced to the minister of foreign affairs, Vice-Chancellor Schober (himself a former chancellor). Cordial and most congenial, he offered to look for a residence where “you and your spouse will feel right at home in Vienna.” I visited with professional reverence the splendid Empire-style room of the famous Congress; I was shown where, for that occasion, an additional door had been pierced in the wall to resolve a delicate problem of precedence, so that all envoys could enter the room at the same time, and I was also shown Metternich’s office.

A mere five weeks after my arrival I began acting as chargé d’affaires, the envoy having gone on leave. My first official act was the signing with Vice-Chancellor Schober of a trade agreement between Romania and Austria. Two days later I attended the New Year’s diplomatic reception at the Ballplatz. In dress uniforms, we all filed past President Miklas, who was watched over by a large oil painting of Emperor Franz Joseph! Some time later my wife and I were invited to Mr. and Mrs. Miklas’s private residence. They were a most likable couple, leading the simple life of lower-middle-class citizens, with none of the pomp of a head of state, and surrounded by a swarm of children. Miklas was a former high-school teacher, and one of his daughters was an elementary-school teacher in a Viennese suburb. His only shortcoming was an extreme verbosity when he was called upon to give an address.

The head of government, Chancellor Dolfuss, a political disciple of his predecessor Msgr. Ignaz Seipel, was a man of diminutive stature (he was nicknamed “the Milimetternich”), unpretentious and amiable. Who would have thought he was destined for such a tragic fate (the Nazis murdered him in 1934 in a most savage way)? To be sure, he did not have the strong personality of Seipel, a real statesman—but few are found in Austria. It was said in his days that there were only two real men in Austria, and yet both wore skirts: Msgr. Seipel and Frau Sacher. (Frau Sacher, the owner of the renowned hotel and restaurant of that name, had shown remarkable courage at the time of the 1918 revolution, driving away a band of Communists who were trying to invade her premises.) When Dolfuss received me for the first time in the huge office that had been Metternich's, he seemed to be overshadowed by the aura of his predecessor. Dolfuss had just returned from Lausanne, where he had been negotiating the Austrian loan. The negotiations had not yet been completed, and Dolfuss smiled as he told me, "For that, we are still crossing our fingers." He assured me that Austria would wish after that to strengthen its economic relations with Romania by concluding a preferential agreement for cereals.

One of the most influential members of Dolfuss's government was the minister of justice, Schuschnigg, who was to succeed him at the head of the government after the tragic events of 1934. He, too, was fated to go through terrible days. He had that dramatic 1938 meeting with Hitler, which was followed by the Anschluss and the imprisonment of the Schuschnigg couple in a Nazi concentration camp. After Germany's defeat, I met Schuschnigg's second wife (née Czernin) in Gstaad. She had forgotten the foreign languages she had spoken and seemed lost and disoriented to find herself again free. Soon thereafter Schuschnigg settled in the United States with his wife and took American citizenship.

✧ ✧ ✧

I thoroughly enjoyed the charms of Viennese life, in an artistic and historic setting so telling to the soul. Coming out of the Burg—the former imperial palace—one seemed to take in the whole past of the ancient monarchy with all its glory and tragedy. In Heldenplatz, the equestrian statues of Prince Eugene of Savoy, the victor over the Turks, and of Archduke Karl, the commander of the imperial troops in the battles against Napoleon, and in the distance, the steeples of the ancient cathedral of St. Stephen. On the left, the Parliament, the City Hall, the Votivkirche. On the right, the Minoritenplatz, which housed the Habsburg archives from the most distant days and where I spent so many peaceful hours, immersed in documents forgotten in the dust of the ages. And close by—how symbolic!—Dietrichstein Palace, which at one time harbored our Romanian chapel, the sanctuary of devotion and hope of a people that, through its fight for freedom, played such a decisive role in the dismantling of the empire. The cultural life of Vienna, its unsurpassed museums, the Opera, the Burgtheater, the Josephstädter Theater, the Akademie Theater, the Theater an der Wien, were a deep spiritual joy. And so were the incomparable concerts of the Musikverein and of the Konzerttheater, which I went to regularly with my mother whenever she was in Vienna, and which were directed in turn by Richard Strauss, by Weingartner, by Bruno Walter, or by Clemens Krauss.

Similarly, in a world of ancient and refined culture, social life was most agreeable. I recall with nostalgia Countess Charles Lančkoronska's receptions in her handsome palace in Joaquimgasse, where her husband, a vigorous man of over eighty, would show you his collection of Italian Quattrocento paintings, a superb Botticelli, a few well-known Rembrandts, and many a Flemish or French canvas. I also remember receptions at Princess Nora Fugger's, or, finally, at Pauline Metternich's daughters'.

My wife and I frequently saw Princess Ileana and her husband, Archduke Anton, who lived in a small house in Mödling, as well as the rest of their family: Archduchess Bianca (daughter of Don Carlos of Spain), of whose stinginess all her children and her daughter-in-law complained, the Archdukes Leopold, Franz Joseph, and Carlos, and the sibling who turned out best, Archduchess Margarete (who later married the Italian ambassador Taliani). The young archdukes hoped to settle in Romania and help reorganize our air force. "We lost the war," Archduke Franz Joseph told me, "and at home in Austria we can't do anything because of the republic. Rather than remain useless all our lives, we would rather place ourselves in the service of a country with whose reigning family we are related." He hoped Ileana might manage something with Carol at an opportune time!

Franz Joseph also recounted his two-day stay in the castle at Doorn, as guest of the old Emperor Wilhelm II. He told me he found the overthrown emperor incredibly "upstart" and ridiculous, theatrical and vulgar. In exile, Wilhelm II surrounded himself with the same pomp as in Potsdam. His wife used as signature "Herminie I.R.," as if nothing had happened in 1918. As for the Kaiser, he changed his uniforms and decorations all day long. His program was as follows. At eight o'clock there was a religious service at which he read from the Bible in a loud and declamatory voice, from a seat overadorned with eagles and crowns. After that, a somewhat too copious breakfast. Later, the guests were invited to saw firewood in the company of the former emperor (hunting togs and boots) until lunchtime (another suit of clothes). The Kaiser took a siesta after lunch, followed by tea, conversation, and a walk. At dinner, full-dress uniforms with medals were de rigueur. Franz Joseph told me he found it very difficult to suppress his giggles. In his honor, as son of a Spanish infanta, Wilhelm II had adorned himself with the Golden Fleece and all the Spanish decorations he had received. At first, he only spoke to him of Spain, ignoring the Habsburgs and the Austrians ever since Emperor Charles had wanted to conclude a separate peace with the Allies. On the last day, however, he could no longer contain himself and, referring to former Emperor Charles's correspondence with his brother-in-law Sixte de Bourbon, he told Franz Joseph "that Emperor Charles is the greatest liar I have ever encountered," which placed the archduke in a most awkward position. At his departure, though, the Kaiser gave him a photograph of himself in a Hungarian uniform!

QUEEN MARIE ON ROYAL FAMILY TENSIONS

Queen Marie came often to Mödling to see her daughter and to escape Carol's surveillance. She stayed for months on end in that outskirt of Vienna. I met her frequently, either at a luncheon or dinner at Princess Ileana's, or at the Krantz Hotel when she stayed there, or on outings by car to Semmering or Wienerwald, and I always enjoyed talking with such a gifted and witty woman. In my conversations with Queen Marie she always came back to her son Carol's ingratitude and lack of regard toward her, as well as to her bitterness at being totally excluded from affairs of state. I carefully recorded some of her comments to me, spoken in turn in either English or French.

From her first arrival—I was at that time acting as chargé d'affaires—she told me she would be unable to attend any official reception. "The king wants me to consult him each time I am invited to appear in public and, since I am not in daily touch with my son, I prefer to forbear doing so," she complained, her eyes flashing with suppressed anger. She was particularly incensed that the king and the Vaida-Voevod government had not allowed Ileana to give birth to her first child in her native country but had forced her to leave, pregnant as she was, for Austria. The true reason was Carol's fear that a son of his sister's, born in Romania, could opt for Romanian citizenship when coming of age and—who knows—claim at one point rights to the throne. Her face flushed, Queen Marie exclaimed: "It is pure meanness. To the Romanian throne! Fancy the absurdity of the thing! One shouldn't even give it a thought!" The king had instructed Vaida-Voevod to inform her of the harsh prohibition, which he did with a total lack of respect. The queen then asked me about the results of our elections, which she said "fortunately" appear not to have been particularly favorable to the Vaida-Voevod government. "I heard," interjected Ileana, "that the Liberals have done much better than the government; how pleased I am."

Ileana had recently received a letter from Carol in which he more or less apologized for having prevented her from giving birth in Romania. He—bravely!—placed all the blame on Vaida-Voevod, who, he said, being Transylvanian, had a phobia of the Habsburgs. Ileana answered, the queen told me, that wherever her child was to be born, she would bring him up "as the royal child we want him to be."

At a luncheon my wife and I held for her at Schloss Kobentzl, Queen Marie told us she had been invited to go to America with the young Michael "whom they are eager to see because he has been a king," but she was wondering whether Carol would not be opposed to the idea. She complained about Carol's most unsatisfactory entourage. His private secretary, Puiu Dumitrescu, in particular, had a deplorable influence on Carol. He was setting son against mother, but, the queen raised her voice with royal pride, "When one comes from where I come, one can't let oneself be suppressed by a Puiu Dumitrescu!" The topic was broached again another day, after a luncheon at Mödling, "since we are among friends." The only well brought up man in the king's entourage is Dinu Cesianu, who, she said, had once been instructed by the king to convey "something very unpleasant" to her, while she was in Paris. The poor Cesianu seemed miserable to have an assignment so unsuitable to his nature. And the queen remarked, "I would never have thought that the king would have the nerve to have such a thing told to his mother."

Ileana complained that Carol didn't allow her to play any role in Romania: "He won't even let me attend the Boy Scouts' oath taking." She could not hide her indignation at the insolent things her brother had conveyed to her through General Ilasievici, chief of the Military House, whom she called "the most stupid man I ever met."

Another time, speaking again of her relations with Carol, Queen Marie told us, with tears in her eyes: "He does not want to have a mother, he does not want to have a wife, he wants no family at all. And I would have been so happy to help him, as I helped his father and old King Carol. Should I not have loved my son, I should still have wanted to help him in my own interest, as I can't possibly work against the monarchy. As for myself personally, I have no wish at all, since I know women can't reign in Romania. Old King Carol used to say to me: 'I want you to be very kind to so-and-so, as I need him.' With my husband, I had a special role: I invited to tea the *récalcitrants,* and in popped—unexpectedly!—the king. I left the men alone, and they often agreed! Now, Averescu would like me to do the same, since he does not want to ask for an audience and make the *premier pas*. But Carol does not want to hear about it. He is afraid I might get too much political influence! I don't even dare talk to Duca, lest one should say: la reine conspire. And if I ever talked to a political man, I would certainly tell my son all about it. But life, as it is, is growing very monotonous for me. *Je m'ennuie à mourir! A mon âge, d'autres femmes sont 'kaput,' mais moi je me sens pleine d'énergie et de vitalité.*"[1]

Passing then in review the Romanian politicians, Queen Marie told me: "Maniu played me false when there was a vacancy in the Regency. Can you remember? Brătianu was the only man. But I did not get on with him as well as people think. We quarreled often, but, once we agreed, he stood firmly by me."

AUSTRIAN DOMESTIC POLITICS

Austrian domestic politics were dominated at that time by the struggle between, on the one hand, nationalist and monarchist elements supported by the Fascist-leaning *Heimatfront* movement of Prince Stachemberg, and, on the other, the pro-Anschluss movement to which the remnants of the former *Grossdeutschen* party had allied themselves and that was, in fact, a Nazi movement. On the left were the Socialists, who could claim significant economic achievements (such as massive housing developments for workers, patterned on the Karl-Marx-Hof), but who were losing ground politically and electorally. And in the middle, Dolfuss and his Christian-Democrats, inherited from Msgr. Seipel, tried to "muddle through." After 1931 and the failure of the economic *Gleichschaltung*[2] attempt, and after the collapse of the Kreditanstalt, the National-Socialist peril loomed more and more clearly on the horizon.

Nazi demonstrations were becoming increasingly frequent and violent. I was present at one of them. On June 30, 1932, invited along with some friends for dinner at the International Country Club—the golf club in Lainz, near Vienna—I witnessed a savage attack by young Nazis, under the pretext that this rather aristocratic club had accepted among its members a few Rothschilds and other wealthy Jews. The Nazis invaded the club, devastating everything, hitting men and women with cudgels, rocks, leather straps, and yelling: "Germany, awake! Croak, Judas! Go off to

---

[1]I am bored to death. Other women at my age are finished, but I feel full of energy and vitality.

[2]Alignment.

Palestine!" Women of whatever age were struck with revolting cowardice, and I don't even believe they were Jewish, but members of Austrian high society. Chairs and bottles were thrown at peaceful club members who were finishing their dinners. In the scuffle, Brediceanu, who had just risen from table, was pushed down the staircase, fell, and hurt his hands. In the end, the attackers were put to flight by handgun shots. The police arrived only when everything had quieted down. The following day, I lodged a protest at the Ballplatz about the mistreatment of Romania's envoy, and received an apology and the assurance that the thugs would be brought to book and severely punished. I was deeply shaken by this infamous deed, of which I would never have thought the Austrians capable, they who are always so peaceful and decent. Learning later of the horrors committed under the Anschluss regime by Austrians (first of whom, as a matter of fact, was the Austrian Hitler), I had to conclude that such shameful and criminal passions could be awoken in any nation going through a wave of collective frenzy.

CONVERSATIONS WITH TITULESCU

As usual, I spent the summer vacations in Sinaia, with my wife, children, and parents. Before returning to work in mid-September 1932, I called on the Ministry of Foreign Affairs and had a long meeting with Undersecretary of State Grigore Gafencu. I had known him since we were teenagers, even though he had been brought up in Switzerland. He was handsome, intelligent, gifted in communicating orally or in writing, and had considerable personal charm. A consummate man about town, he had become a friend of the banker Ion Chrissoveloni, who helped him found the papers *Argus* and *Timpul*, in which he wrote with great talent the editorials on foreign affairs. He had joined the National-Peasant party and was very close to Maniu who, when he took over the government in 1928, imposed him on Mironescu as secretary-general of the Ministry of Foreign Affairs.

The appointment had at first been very unpopular among the members of our diplomatic corps, both because of the age (thirty-six) of the one called to be the second in command at the Ministry and because that position had until then always been filled by a career diplomat. However, as they gradually came to recognize the competence and industry of the new secretary-general, as well as to appreciate his politeness and consideration toward his colleagues at whatever level, the Ministry's staff ended by liking Gafencu quite a lot. But the more he gained the affection and respect of the diplomats, the more he was disliked by Mironescu, who envied the intellectual superiority, the training, and the personal reputation of his deputy. A conversation with Gafencu was infinitely more pleasant and interesting than one with poor "Uncle Ghiţă," as the minister was nicknamed, and that was why almost all heads of foreign missions sought out the former and avoided the latter. This wounded Mironescu's self-esteem even further, and he was not satisfied until he got Maniu to shift Gafencu to Public Works. Now Gafencu was back as secretary-general of the Ministry of Foreign Affairs, Vaida-Voevod having been appointed prime minister.

In the conversation I had with him, Gafencu brought me up to date regarding the Romano-Russian nonaggression treaty. All of Russia's neighbors had signed (in addition to the Briand-Kellogg pact) bilateral nonaggression treaties with Moscow—which, with the sole exception of Poland, they had also ratified. France had decided likewise to sign such a treaty in the near future. Since the Romanian government did not wish to find itself isolated, it had therefore decided to sign a similar treaty. If the government did not succeed in doing so, Poland, which had so far held back, would go ahead and ratify its treaty, and France would undoubtedly sign its own treaty with Russia. Gafencu told me that he and Titulescu had agreed on the attitude to take and that they had drawn up in Garstein an action program that had been adopted by the government.

Titulescu's view was that the Briand-Kellogg pact was sufficient to provide us with a legal guarantee against an attack by the Soviet Union, while in the prevailing conditions Soviet recognition of Romania's rights over Bessarabia was not to be expected. Why then conclude additional treaties that would, rather than strengthen, only weaken our position? But taking heed of Herriot's entreaties, Titulescu had nevertheless suggested a "minimal formula," which paraphrased, and in fact completed, the text of the Briand-Kellogg pact of 1929. Under the understanding reached with Titulescu, the talks were to be broken off in Moscow if that minimal formula was not accepted "without changing a single word, letter, or comma"; talks could possibly be resumed in Geneva at a later date. However, fearing Titulescu's intransigence, France and Poland had in the meantime agreed that Patek, Poland's envoy to Moscow, should lead the negotiations concerning the formula.

In Moscow, Litvinov was saying that since this was not a discussion of the Riga draft but of a different draft, he had certain reservations he wanted clarified. Like Titulescu, he saw no point in concluding a new treaty identical to the Briand-Kellogg pact. But if he did sign one, and just bilaterally with us, a formula would have to be found to protect the Soviet claim to

Bessarabia. Nevertheless, he hinted at the possibility of reaching an understanding. It was therefore decided that the negotiations would not be broken off but merely postponed, to be resumed in Geneva.

In the meantime, however, Litvinov said he would also like to speak directly with a representative of the Romanian government, since he felt that the Romanians would actually prefer not to conclude the treaty. He therefore proposed that, on the way to Geneva, he stop in Berlin where the meeting could take place. The Romanian government rejected Berlin, however, and took the opportunity to show Paris the twist the Russians wanted to give the negotiations by choosing the German capital for the talks so much desired by the Quai d'Orsay. Litvinov then proposed a meeting in Poland with the Romanian envoy to Warsaw, Cădere. In view of the urgency of the matter, the Romanian government accepted the proposal without consulting Titulescu. The meeting took place, with Cădere boarding Litvinov's train at a station in Poland. The conversation reportedly held out some promises of success.

Titulescu, however, knew nothing of the meeting, and it was obvious he would be furious if he heard about it, since he had been assured that the negotiations would be broken off if the Russians did not accept his formula in full. In the event that Titulescu nevertheless heard of the move that had been made without his assent, Gafencu asked me to explain to him that, a decision having to be taken immediately, the government was forced to approve the Cădere-Litvinov meeting without seeking his prior consent. The government would remain bound by the line of action agreed upon in Gastein. "In appeasing him with this explanation, you would do me a personal service," Gafencu concluded, appealing to our long friendship. He then wondered whom he could rope in to pursue the talks in Geneva, since Titulescu would obviously refuse to have anything to do with them. "Aren't you thinking of going yourself to Geneva to negotiate with Litvinov?" I asked. "Not me, for sure," he replied, "for in his wrath Titulescu would destroy my career."

I arrived in Vienna on September 19. The Titulescus, Brediceanu, and I went to spend the evening in a *Heuriger* (inn) in Grintzing. Titulescu told us that Alexis Léger, political director of the Quai d'Orsay, had phoned him from Paris regarding the Cădere-Litvinov meeting, and he went on to accuse Gafencu of having deviated from the plan drawn up in Garstein, and especially of having hidden this deviation from him. Since there were too many of us around the table, and especially since the surroundings were completely unsuited for a political discussion, I put off to the following day the message I had been asked to give him. Next day, I requested to meet with him alone, and Titulescu received me in his room at the Grand Hotel, where I conveyed to him Gafencu's explanations. He was considerably wrought up, and the explanations I conveyed failed to calm him down. He was indignant that the government had disregarded his formula and that, moreover, it had tried to conceal from him the meeting between Cădere and Litvinov. With his usual verbal excesses, he alternatively called the poor Gafencu "an ass" and "a knave," accusing him of being entirely responsible for this "double cross."

A day later, September 21, his wife having gone to the opera, Titulescu, alone at the Grand Hotel, sent a car for me so that the two of us might dine in tête-à-tête. After dinner, we talked until one o'clock. He was increasingly incensed at the Vaida-Voevod government and exceedingly angry with Gafencu. He read to me a note he had received from Edouard Herriot, who, not being bound to us on this issue, was informing us that if we dallied any further he would go ahead and sign alone a treaty with the USSR. The tone of the letter was not very pleasant, and—what was most odd—it suggested that we make certain concessions to the Russians that they themselves had not been asking for. Even more odd, Herriot had sent to Moscow a copy of the note addressed to us. It was Titulescu's opinion that, under the circumstances, we should tell the Quai d'Orsay: "Be our guests and sign, but we are staying with the Briand-Kellogg pact." I argued that, in my view, it would not be a bad thing if we had, in addition to the Briand-Kellogg pact, another one (as France and the European neighbors of Russia had), which would give abroad the impression that our situation had strengthened. Titulescu, of course, stuck to his opinion. I began to ask myself, in petto, whether he might not be reserving for himself the privilege of concluding at a later date a treaty with Moscow that would give us some soothing reassurances concerning Bessarabia.

Titulescu then began recounting the "vexations of my career." A plot against him had been hatched the preceding year, he insisted. Forgeries purporting to be reports from the French embassy in London to the Quai d'Orsay stated that he had slandered Carol when talking with Henderson.[3] Since then, Carol had considered him a "traitor" and had persecuted him through Argetoianu and Demetrius Ghika. I told him how badly informed he was. On the contrary, and at the risk of his own career, my uncle Ghika had defended him from others who wanted to remove him even from the Disarmament Conference, a fact Titulescu knew full well, since Ghika had

---

[3]Arthur Henderson, British foreign secretary and chairman of the World Disarmament Conference.

told him, "You can't imagine how hard I had to fight to ensure that our country was not deprived of your presence at the Disarmament Conference." At that point Titulescu read to me the letter of resignation he had handed to Carol the previous February, as well as the accompanying note that he had read himself to the king. In that note, he complained that Ghika had failed to keep him informed of anything, even (as he maintained) of the debates of the Little Entente Conference in Montreux, to which he had expected to be called. And yet Ghika was his friend, as he himself admitted. Then what was the reason for this attitude? Without any doubt, the enmity of Carol, who considered him "a betrayer of the king." What did the sovereign do to protect his accused and insulted envoy to London, Titulescu asked rhetorically? "Zilch," he answered. And he added: "It is clear that the king, who moved me out of domestic politics in April 1931, now wants to remove me from foreign politics as well." Carol had tried to reassure him, turned down his resignation, and directed in writing on a letter from Titulescu (which the latter showed me) that Titulescu be kept informed on all foreign policy issues. Since then, his relations with the king had improved somewhat, and Titulescu exclaimed, "After all, let's face it, Carol and his Lupescu woman are still preferable to Litvinov." Titulescu assured me categorically that he had not advised the king to bring to power a Vaida-Voevod government; he had suggested a Duca government, but Carol was dead-set against that.

The next day, September 22, the entire legation's staff lunched with Titulescu at the Grand Hotel. In a loud voice, he called Gafencu a liar, without heeding the fact that all his table companions were members of the Romanian diplomatic corps, and that Gafencu was at that time undersecretary of state at the Ministry of Foreign Affairs. He told us he had declined to see Cădere, who had arrived that morning to report to him on his talk with Litvinov and to seek guidance for his future negotiations in Evian. Just as dessert was being served, who pops in but the said Cădere. A real bombshell!

I was sitting next to Titulescu, and I pointed out to him that the dessert mentioned on the menu was a *bombe diplomate,* thereby provoking general hilarity and defusing to some extent the strained atmosphere. Titulescu invited Cădere to take a place at the table—"as a friend, not as envoy to Warsaw"—and offered him a helping of the *bombe diplomate*. Cădere attempted repeatedly, but unavailingly, to tell Titulescu that Litvinov agreed to the preamble of his formula and that there was only one point that still had to be negotiated. Titulescu interrupted him again and again, saying that he "didn't want to know," that he was not a "mere preamble man," and that, on national issues, he considered himself "a fourth Brătianu." The entire staffs of the legation and of our delegation to the Danube Commission witnessed this scene.

Titulescu decided to return directly to London instead of going to Geneva, since he had no wish to represent at the League of Nations a government that had "disowned" him. At the legation we received a cable from our Ministry of Foreign Affairs that we could not decipher because it used Titulescu's personal code, so I took it to him at his hotel. But he was insistent that I should say that I had not been able to find him and should give him the cable at the railway station just as he was leaving, so that he could decode it only once in London. Probably he guessed its contents and wanted to give himself time to ponder his next move. At any rate, he left on the Orient Express with the unread cable in his pocket. Before boarding, he gave an interview to the *Neue Freie Presse,* stating that he was opposed to the conclusion of the proposed nonaggression treaty, since the Briand-Kellogg pact provided sufficient guarantees to us.

Back in London, when he decoded the cable, he learned that he was being offered the position of Minister of Foreign Affairs. He accepted. Vaida-Voevod, forced to resign in order to remain consistent with his foreign policy, was replaced by Maniu. Titulescu's attitude is mainly explainable by the fact that he wanted to be "the man of reconciliation with Russia" and that he did not want others to reap the laurels of a possible recognition by Moscow of the reunion of Bessarabia with Romania. This explanation was to be subsequently confirmed by the facts.

QUEEN HELEN STANDS UP FOR HER RIGHTS

In October, I went with my wife to Stuttgart to attend her mother's funeral. On my return to Vienna, I found at the Hotel Imperial, where I was staying temporarily, *Grand Voevod*[4] Michael, who was coming from London. Over lunch he told me that he was to have spent six weeks with his mother but had been called back to Romania after only two weeks by his father, displeased that the British press had published pictures of the mother with her son! Permission to postpone the departure was granted, but only by a single

[4]This title, formerly given to the reigning princes of Moldavia and Wallachia, was bestowed to King Michael after Carol II had dethroned him.

day, because Sitta[5] and Michael had been invited for tea by the king and queen of England. Rightfully indignant, Sitta gave an interview that appeared in the *Daily Mail* of October 4, 1932, and touched off in Britain a wave of anger against Carol. The most violent of the articles appeared in the *Sunday Express* of October 9. Entitled "King Carol the Cad," it threatened to have him "kicked out of England a second time" if he ever dared set foot on British soil again. The article was reprinted throughout the world.

✧ ✧ ✧

Furious, Princess Helen decided to go to Romania to stress her inalienable rights as mother. Maniu and Titulescu phoned Brediceanu, instructing him to have the Austrian borders watched and, on her arrival, to tell her—a princess and a Romanian citizen!—that she was forbidden to enter Romania. It was later learned that she might be in Paris, and Brediceanu was told to go there and strongly "advise" her not to go to Romania now, her arrival being deemed inopportune. But during the night it was ascertained that Sitta was at her house in Fiesole. Brediceanu was now ordered to fly to Florence, where he would be informed of the contents of a cable that was in process of being encoded.

The cable was received by the legation at 5:00 A.M., and I went to decode it. It read: "The Romanian government is informed that H.M. Helen, who is in Florence, 80 via Bolognese, will come to Romania on October 25, which means that she will leave on October 22. Please go urgently to see her and ask her very respectfully, for me, not to come to Romania at this time, her presence now being contrary to the highest interests of the state. With regard to the issues raised in H.M. Helen's letter of October 7, 1932, to Prime Minister Alexandru Vaida-Voevod, the king and the government are desirous to discuss them. A delegate who enjoys the trust of H.M. Helen will arrive in Florence shortly for that purpose. Please exert all possible efforts, firmly but tactfully, to succeed in your mission. If you do not succeed, please cable me urgently whether H.M. Helen persists in her decision to arrive in Romania on October 25, so that in that event all necessary measures might be taken. [Signed:] Maniu."

What were those "necessary measures" to be? Perhaps prohibiting the mother of the former and future king to cross the border? How much it must have cost a tactful man like Maniu to take, on Carol's order, a position so opposed to his character and Christian principles!

---

[5]Nickname given to Queen Helen by her family and inner circle.

It was with considerable doubts that the unfortunate Brediceanu set forth to carry out his unpleasant mission. On October 24 he returned to Vienna, from where he cabled Bucharest: "I found the princess in such a state of aggravation that all my entreaties, for an hour and a half, were unable to lead to the desired result. She assured me that . . . from now on she would receive not a single emissary abroad, but that she was willing to discuss things in Romania, where, as mother, she had to be on her child's birthday."[6]

Brediceanu told me that Sitta used the most vehement terms in speaking of Carol. She called him a liar and accused him of having taken from her palace on Şoseaua Kisseleff even Michael's baby teeth, which she had held on to as a keepsake. She also said that she had proposed to have their divorce annulled when Carol came back in 1930, but he had refused. She was very saddened that their child knew everything about his father's affair. One day, as they drove through Bucharest, Michael had said to her, "Look, there is Papa's woman!" The king of England was furious at Carol, and she had tried in vain to calm him down. If she couldn't get justice in Romania, Helen said, she would address herself to the International Court of Justice in The Hague. In any event, she was now determined to go to Bucharest. So far as I recollect, in the end she did not go, having obtained the concession that her son would stay with her for several months a year, and having also received an improvement in her material situation.

In the meantime, Carol's relations with the rest of his family worsened day by day. Ileana told me she had had a huge row with her royal brother for having received the Boy Scouts' oath and given a short speech, "quite diplomatic, by the way." It was said that Carol had her kicked out of the scout movement as a result.

QUEEN MARIE'S RENEWED COMPLAINTS

Queen Marie returned to Vienna in January 1933, to spend several weeks with her daughter Ileana. Throughout her stay she was affable, even affectionate toward us, and we saw her constantly. While we were still at the railway station, she urged my wife to come at any time, even unannounced, to have lunch with her, "because we are always so pleased to see you." In the meantime, Ileana took me apart and warned me that the queen's aide-de-camp, Colonel Râmniceanu, was a personal friend of

[6] October 25. He would be eleven years old.

the ill-famed Puiu Dumitrescu; "Be careful when you talk with him, because he is completely on *their* side."

At a luncheon given by the Yugoslav envoy, Queen Marie told me she was worried by the way her son ruled. There was, indeed, a political crisis in Bucharest, where the Maniu government had resigned when the king overruled Interior Minister Mihalache's decision to replace Bucharest's police commissioner, Gavrilă Marinescu (the king's man) and the commander of the gendarmerie (Puiu Dumitrescu's father). The queen considered that Maniu's resignation statement amounted to a personal stand against Carol. This conversation was resumed in the evening, during an improvised dinner at Ileana and Anton's. Another time, again in the privacy of Mödling, Queen Marie told me she felt Maniu's statement that he had resigned because of the king could have serious consequences for the monarch. While she was on that subject, she complained once more of Carol's conduct toward her, which was revolting everybody: "He never wants to be seen publicly with me, as if we could not share cheers together. As my Russian sister[7] says, 'I have seen kings jealous of the future, but none jealous of the past.' I wrote to King George of England if he would mind my publishing letters of his in my memoirs. He replied asking me not to, but, talking about the life my son makes me lead, he says, 'I wonder your son's ministers don't try to influence him, for *he is a shocking example to all kings.*'"

In the tête-à-tête conversations I had at that time with Queen Marie, she confessed that she was tied by "a deep friendship to Prince Ştirbey." In the name of that friendship, she had recently sent him the manuscript of her memoirs, asking for his candid opinion. Reverting to her son Carol's conduct toward her, she was wondering why he feared her. Was it possible, she asked, that he could think "that I might be dreaming of being proclaimed reigning queen?" She had the impression that, through fear of Carol, everyone was boycotting her: "When I talk to somebody, he looks round over his shoulder to see if anybody can observe him." Wasn't it in her interest that monarchy be preserved in Romania? How could she then be working against her son, the present monarch?

She would often talk to me about her memoirs, which were to appear soon. She believed they would be of interest, "as there are not heaps of people around the world who are the granddaughters of both Queen Victoria and Tsar Alexander II." She admitted that in her memoirs she

[7]Grand Duchess Cyril.

did at times poke fun at Carmen Sylva:[8] "She was so comical!" At the beginning of World War I, when Carol I had gathered his family to expound the tragic dilemma he faced, his heart being rent between duty to his country of birth and to the country over which he reigned, the old Queen Elizabeth, romantic and lyrical as she was, suddenly proposed: "Let's all hold hands and go together to God." Exasperated, King Carol I banged the table with his fist and shouted, *"Elisabeth! Unsinn!"*[9] Of Ionel Brătianu, she wrote only favorably; named minister before he reached the age of forty, he was the only official with whom a young princess could converse: "He always was, besides, a man for ladies."

One day, in early February, we were invited to lunch by Queen Marie and her daughter Ileana, along with the British and Yugoslav envoys and the last Austro-Hungarian ambassador to London, Count Albert de Mensdorff-Pouilly-Dietrichstein. At table, the queen mentioned that her daughter-in-law Helen reproached her for the articles she had published in the British press. The queen asked me to stay on after the departure of the foreign guests. As usual, she complained about being watched by Carol's agents, and especially by our envoy to Belgrade, Gurănescu, whose past was highly questionable and whom she called *un vilain monsieur.*[10] She was convinced that he had been ordered by Carol to set King Alexander against her. "And he has the nerve to do so. As a consequence, King Alexander hates him." The queen then recounted how, when in Belgrade, Gurănescu asked to see her. Before his arrival, King Alexander advised her, "And remember each time you talk to him, that Gurănescu is a swine."

A few days later Queen Marie departed for Romania. Among those seeing her off at the railway station was her niece, Grand Duchess Masha (the daughter of Grand Duchess Cyril), with her husband, Prince Karl Leiningen. She still remembered our Transylvanian excursion organized for Admiral Beatty in 1924.

In the fall, Queen Marie returned to her daughter's house in Mödling. Both of them complained about Carol's unfeeling behavior in not allowing Michael to go to London to see his mother, who was seriously ill, and for forbidding Ileana to come to Romania. What a contrast with King Alexander of Yugoslavia, who, though only her brother-in-law, continually invited her to Belgrade! They went on to criticize the poor taste with which Carol had reconstructed Foişor, "but as long as he likes it . . .". In Mödling

[8]Nom de plume of Queen Elizabeth, Carol I's wife.
[9]"Elizabeth! Nonsense!"
[10]"Not a nice man."

we also attended the christening of the baby Archduchess Maria-Ileana, later nicknamed Minole, who married Count Jaroslaw Kottulinsky and, still very young, was to die in an airplane accident in Rio de Janeiro.

FURTHER CONVERSATIONS WITH TITULESCU

I traveled a lot in Austria during the summer of 1933, looking especially for places with Romanian historical connotations: Innsbruck, where there is a plaque at the Goldener Adler inn with the inscription "Iankula Waywoda mit Sohn, 1610";[11] Ambrass Castle, with the only authentic portrait of Vlad Ţepeş,[12] brought there with the inheritance of Petre Şchiopul;[13] and (by now in Italy) Bolzano (Bozen), with Petre Şchiopul's tomb in the Franciscan church.

I also spent a day at Bad Gastein, with Titulescu and his wife. He said he had "great plans" for me, since I was one of the three legation counselors who in his view had real ability and to whom he would soon entrust legations. He told me he now had better relations with Carol, although he did not know what the king's real feelings about him were. When he had been requested the preceding year to ask Ileana, in the name of the king and of the government, to leave the country because she had attended the Boy Scouts' oath taking, he had refused to do so. He had replied to Maniu: "Tell her yourself. You kicked out Helen, kick out this one also. I do not run such errands!" After that, Queen Marie reportedly told him, "I knew that *you* would not do such a thing." Titulescu seemed to be indignant at the campaign of slanders conducted by Carol's camarilla against Maniu, wrongfully implicated in the Seletzki case (purchase of Skoda armaments).

After the end of his treatment in Gastein, Titulescu passed through Vienna on September 28, on his way to Geneva. This gave me the opportunity of a long talk with him, in which he expounded his views about the political situation. Under the prevailing circumstances, he saw but one way to protect ourselves from the revisionist movement, namely, to establish an indissoluble bloc with the other two states of the Little Entente. "They may not be very pretty, we might like others better, but these are the ones we have as neighbors and as natural allies." Austria, in his view, was nothing but a "vast café" that had to be allowed to collapse: "The French cannot be expected to forever put money aside so as to provide the Viennese with

[11] "Prince Iancu with son, 1610." Iancu Sassu, sixteenth-century prince of Moldavia.
[12] Vlad the Impaler, fifteenth-century prince of Wallachia.
[13] Peter the Lame, sixteenth-century prince of Wallachia.

the luxury of drinking *mélanges*[14] all day long." He expected Austria to be eventually swallowed up by Germany, and so also Hungary. Then, he went on, "the Little Entente bloc would draw closer to Germany, but dealing with it on an equal footing, as between great powers."

Titulescu returned to Vienna on October 8, back from Geneva and on his way to Warsaw, Belgrade, Sofia, Ankara, and Athens. We took him to the horse races organized by Prince Ulrich Kinsky at the Polo Club, and then spent the evening with him. He brought up the same themes as in our last meeting: Austria annexed by Germany, and the Little Entente negotiating, as an indivisible bloc, the granting of zones of economic influence to Germany and Italy, but giving the preponderance to Germany since it had more interests in the Danube Basin than Italy did. Titulescu related that after the signing in London of the protocol for the definition of aggression, Litvinov had told him: "I have just given you Bessarabia. I tied myself hand and foot!" "But when," I asked, "will Moscow officially recognize Bessarabia as Romanian?" "That will also come soon," replied Titulescu, who was carrying to the Soviet envoy in Warsaw the instrument for the ratification of the protocol. Even as brilliant a mind as Titulescu's could be thrown completely off course when trying to peer into the future. Apart from the annexation of Austria by Hitler—and a temporary one at that—all his other predictions proved false. Far from dealing with a Little Entente bloc, the Nazi government dashed that bloc to pieces; Germany and Italy did not play the prominent role foreseen by Titulescu, but collapsed—at least for a good while—and it is not for them that economic zones were set aside in the Danube Basin, but for Soviet Russia, which took for itself all of Central and Eastern Europe. Finally, even if Litvinov did indeed utter those words concerning Bessarabia, they were not followed by an official recognition of Romanian sovereignty over that Moldavian region, but by two annexations of Bessarabia by Soviet Russia, in 1940 and in 1944.

In the course of their endless travels, the Titulescus made yet another stop in Vienna on November 12. We spent the entire day with them. After lunch at the legation, Titulescu led me to a small sitting room where we talked all afternoon. For the first hour, I was alone with him. He told me I would be appointed envoy to Helsingfors.[15] When he had asked the king

[14] What are known nowadays as *lattes*.

[15] Helsingfors, the Swedish name for Helsinki, was almost exclusively used in international circles in the interwar period.

for his assent to my promotion to the rank of minister plenipotentiary, the latter objected: "I believe he is close to Ştirbey?" At that time Ştirbey was anathema to Carol and had exiled himself to Switzerland to escape royal persecution. Titulescu said he had replied: "I, too, am a friend of Ştirbey's. Besides, there in the north where he is going . . .". When the name of my colleague Zamfirescu (who was also being promoted) came up, the king protested, "But that one is a friend of Kaufmann's!" Kaufmann was a Jewish banker who was an intimate of Ştirbey's. Always this obsession with Ştirbey! What a most unroyal pettiness!

Turning to foreign affairs, Titulescu showed himself to be extremely worried by the international situation. He feared that a new Franco-German war might soon break out. It might still be won by France in the near future, but if it were delayed, Germany would be the victor. Our aim must be to remain neutral, through the network of treaties and mutual guarantees that Titulescu managed to conclude, which would help neutralize moves by Hungary and Bulgaria (the Little Entente and the Balkan Entente). To prevent a Bulgaro-Yugoslav agreement that could be disastrous for us, he incited Tevfik Ruşdi Bey to obtain from Jeftić a secret written assurance that Yugoslavia would not reach an agreement with Bulgaria without Turkey's prior assent. All Balkan treaties were to have a similar clause, therefore covering us too.

During the conversation, Titulescu had the kindness of congratulating me for my political reports, and particularly for the one on "Austria between Hitlerism and monarchy." He thanked me for letting him know that Boncour intended to blame Briand, in Paris, for refusing to make any economic concessions to Austria, thereby driving it into Germany's arms.

✧ ✧ ✧

Good news for me: on December 4, 1933, the undersecretary of state at the Ministry of Foreign Affairs, Savel Rădulescu, phoned me to say that, as of December 1, I had been promoted to the rank of minister plenipotentiary. Congratulations started pouring in from colleagues, friends, relatives.

But, at the same time, bad news from Romania: martial law had been declared to curb republican and Communist agitation; Zaharia Boilă issued an anti-Carlist manifesto; a "Romanian Committee for Public Freedoms" had apparently been constituted in Vienna and had published in several languages a manifesto against "Carol Caraiman." And finally, after the interdiction of the Legionary party in Romania, the Iron

Guard's[16] vengeance: the murder by a Legionary student of the prime minister, Ion G. Duca, in the Sinaia railway station. The king imposed a Tătărescu government, which some Liberals had the weakness of accepting.

When I talked about these events with Queen Marie, she was clearly horrified by Duca's assassination, immediately after his audience with the king. "And I suppose the talk between Carol and Duca must have gone on quite pleasantly, don't you think so?" What an odd remark! The queen regretted that the Liberals didn't have the guts to support as prime minister Dinu Brătianu, their chief, and to refuse to participate in a government headed by anyone else.

✧ ✧ ✧

Titulescu passed through Vienna again on January 16, 1934, on his way to Geneva. He was deeply affected by Duca's murder and was convinced that he, too, was sentenced to death by the Legionnaires. He told me the Iron Guard was directed and financed (probably unbeknownst to most guardists) from Italy and Hungary, "but not from Germany." In a phone call to Romania just after he had heard of Duca's murder, Titulescu said "those from around the Palace killed him." The secret police stenographers who listened in on all phone calls noted his outburst and immediately reported it to the king, who made no bones about it when he repeated it to Titulescu, adding that all of the latter's phone calls were reported to him.

Carol was induced by his camarilla to present Titulescu with a fait accompli by putting together, secretly and in haste, a Tătărescu government while the minister of foreign affairs was still abroad, in St. Moritz. Titulescu, however, refused to join this cabinet, which had come to power "through the service entrance" and against the wishes of the Liberal party, which, by electing Dinu Brătianu as its head, had suggested him as prime minister and Duca's successor. Beset by insistent pleadings, Titulescu then made his entry into the government conditional on the breaking up of the camarilla—that is, on the removal of Puiu Dumitrescu (Carol's private secretary), of his father (General Dumitrescu, unlawfully commander of the gendarmerie), of General Stângaciu (director general of the Siguranţa, the secret police), of the police commissioner (Gavrilă Marinescu), and of the minister of war

[16]Romanian Fascist movement established by Cornelíu Zelea Codreanu as the Legion of Archangel Michael in 1927, and as the Iron Guard in 1930.

(General Uică, who was eventually replaced by General Antonescu). The king accepted these conditions, but after the camarilla and its friends (Franassovici, Mirto, etc.) descended on him, he changed his mind, "for he is very fickle and easy to influence."

Hearing of this about-face by Carol and the breaking of his promises, Titulescu phoned him asking for an audience. Carol answered him rudely: "Speak to the head of the government!" After a day or two, Titulescu asked again for an audience but received the same brush-off. It was only on his third try that he was granted an audience in Sinaia, where he found "the king cowering with fright, surrounded by all his keepers from Bucharest." Carol received him with hostility, didn't offer him his hand, and addressed him rudely: "I, your king, order you to join the government without conditions. I forbid you to touch Puiu Dumitrescu and the others around me! Only Ştirbey poked his nose in the Court's personnel matters. Do you understand? I am giving you an order!" Titulescu was laughing during this violent diatribe, he told me, and could not help himself from interrupting it: "Whom are you giving orders to, Your Majesty? Me? After you persecuted me since your return to Romania, after you fired me from London" (an allusion to the resignation of the summer of 1932, following the dispute with Vaida-Voevod over the treaty with the Russians), "you now order me to join a government where I will never have the assurance of speaking privately with my king since what I say will be broadcast the next day in Nae Ionescu's paper!" Then he chided him for not keeping his word: "Even if a king does not keep his word, a commoner will keep his." As Titulescu was leaving, the king again did not offer him his hand; "I thought he might hit me; I was gambling my entire career," Titulescu concluded.

Carol phoned him the next day. "*La nuit porte conseil.*[17] I accept your conditions." "But will we still be able to work together?" asked Titulescu bitterly. At Carol's insistence, a compromise was reached: Titulescu gave up on having Uică replaced, the departure of Gavrilă Marinescu was postponed by two months, while the Dumitrescus (father and son), as well as Stângaciu, were packed off immediately. "What a grudge Carol must bear me," remarked Titulescu, "but who cares, since I still am condemned to death by the Iron Guard; my motto must be 'forward without fear.'" As for the most delicate point, the Lupescu woman, Titulescu said he had told Carol: "I am not asking that Your Majesty's distaff entourage be sent away, since I am confident it is not involved in politics." (He must have had his

[17]"I slept on it."

fingers crossed behind his back when he said this.) "But the day I become convinced otherwise, I will also ask for the departure of a certain lady."

During our conversation, Titulescu informed me that the preceding day the king had signed my appointment as envoy extraordinary and minister plenipotentiary to Helsingfors, effective February 1, 1934. "It is a very sensitive location because of Finland's proximity to Russia and the forming of a Baltic union. That is why we need there a levelheaded man like you, the more so since we will soon establish official links with the Soviets."

THE END OF A PLEASANT MISSION

The date of our departure from Vienna was now approaching, and thought of the separation was painful to us. We gathered for the last time in our home friends and acquaintances, foreign colleagues and Austrian associates. Among those who gave luncheons or dinners in our honor as we were preparing to leave Vienna were the Italian envoy, Preziosi; the Italian counselor, Straneo; the French envoy, Puaux; the French counselor, Montbas; the French military attaché, Salland; the Spanish envoy, Avila, who had been envoy to Helsingfors for four years; the Polish chargé d'affaires, Gawronski, at whose luncheon Chancellor Dolfuss, champagne glass in hand, wished us a prompt return to Vienna (he was to be assassinated only a few weeks later); Princess Schwarzenberg; Princess Erbach; Princess Maritza Liechtenstein; our "aunt," as we joked, Countess Leopoldina Bossi-Fedrigotti; and Count and Countess Alexander Hoyos. Count Hoyos was the man who, as political director, had drafted the ultimatum to Serbia in 1914. He recounted to me his visit to Sinaia with Count Berchtold, at that time Austria's minister of foreign affairs, his walks in the forest with Carmen Sylva, and his reception at Zamora Castle, where he had met my wife's family and had a political discussion with her grandfather, G. Gr. Cantacuzino.

A last lunch at Mödling, at Princess Ileana's. And a last reception at our legation, during which the head of Austrian protocol, Blaas, handed me the insignia of the Grand Cross of the Austrian order of *Grosses Goldenes Ehrenkreuz für Verdienste um die Republik Oesterreich,*[18] which President Miklas had conferred on me. My colleagues from the legation and the Romanian colony gave me a silver tray that had belonged to King Louis II of Bavaria, and my foreign colleagues gave a silver tray engraved with their signatures.

---

[18]Great Golden Honor Cross for Services rendered to the Republic of Austria.

On January 30, we departed for Romania from Ostbanhof, being seen off by Legation Counselor Gruenberger, representing the Austrian government, the French envoy Puaux and his entire family, the Italian legation *in corpore,* and the heads of mission of Poland and of the Little Entente.

Thus ended a happy chapter of my career: three pleasant and interesting years in unforgettable Vienna.

8

Helsingfors (1934–1936)

I returned to Bucharest on January 31, 1934, and left for my new posting on March 28. During these two months, I had numerous meetings with political personalities, friends, and acquaintances. Queen Marie invited my wife and me to lunch at Cotroceni Palace, and since we were alone with her, she, as always, complained about the behavior of her son Carol, whom she saw as the blind instrument of Elena Lupescu. As a matter of fact, that was also the general opinion in the country: when the king decided to have the wall of the Athénée's large auditorium covered with a fresco depicting the main periods of Romanian history, the wisecrackers dubbed the future masterpiece *de la Lupoica la Lupeasca*—from the [Roman] she-wolf to the Lupescu woman.

Elise Brătianu and Bébé Brătianu related to me the details of the last governmental crisis (which I had already briefly heard from Titulescu in Vienna). After Duca's assassination, Dr. Angelescu, the oldest of the ministers, had been appointed prime minister. But scheming by Franassovici, Tătărescu, and Inculeţ led Carol to dismiss him and replace him not, as would have been normal, by the president of the ruling Liberal party, Dinu Brătianu, but by Tătărescu. Tătărescu would have liked to be named simultaneously head of the Liberal party, but no one wanted him and the cabinet positions he was offering were refused until he had concurred to the appointment of Dinu Brătianu as head of the party. Elise Brătianu acknowledged that Tătărescu's leadership qualities were superior to those of her brother-in-law: the one was "a joker, but cleverer, more supple, and without scruples," the other "a real gentleman, but too stubborn." It seems, indeed, that the forming of a Liberal government almost fell through because Dinu Brătianu refused to include in the cabinet Franassovici, for being the "camarilla's man." This would have rendered impossible any collaboration with Carol, who was completely under the thumb of the camarilla.

BRIEFINGS IN BUCHAREST

During these weeks of waiting, I had a number of meetings with Titulescu, the minister of foreign affairs. He seemed quite hurt by criticisms of his foreign policy and by accusations (probably from the extreme right) that he relied too heavily on the alliance with France and the Little Entente. He feared that were we to leave the Little Entente, Czechoslovakia and Yugoslavia could come to an agreement with Hungary behind our back and at our expense—which I felt was highly unlikely. Titulescu's idea was to protect all our borders with treaties, for his highly legalistic mind gave excessive—and unfortunately unfounded—importance to written commitments by states. That was why he wanted to reestablish diplomatic relations with Russia, since an exchange of legations between the Soviet Union and us would be equivalent to a recognition of our territorial integrity, including Bessarabia. He asserted once more that the basis of our relations with Moscow would be the London Convention of July 3, 1933, defining aggression, and he repeated that Litvinov had told him in London, "I have just given you Bessarabia." He consequently urged me to get in touch in Helsingfors with the Soviet envoy, Boris Stein, a very intelligent man he had met in Geneva at the League of Nations. Tevfik Ruşdi Bey had been instrumental in bringing about our rapprochement with the Soviets, and Titulescu therefore considered that Ankara had become pivotal to our foreign policy.

With regard to the Baltic treaty, Titulescu was not quite sure what it meant, and asked me to enlighten him from Finland, where I would undoubtedly work closely with my Polish colleague. Beck had assured him that, in the Baltic area, Poland was pursuing only economic goals. But if there was a hidden political agenda and there was thought of establishing a bloc of Russia's Baltic neighbors, that bloc should be enlarged so as to include Romania also. He asked me to probe whether Finland would be disposed to conclude with us a treaty of friendship, conciliation, and arbitration, but so far as possible without arousing Russia's touchiness.

We also talked about Carol. Titulescu was indignant at Carol's attitude and deeds; he considered him the moral perpetrator of Duca's murder.

Indeed, Titulescu believed that he himself was sentenced to death, and told me that as soon as that happened, all the Western press would publish documents proving who was really behind his murder. I asked him if the purpose of this threat was to intimidate the person he thought capable of hatching such an assassination. He answered that this was not an empty threat on his part, but the naked truth, for he had incriminating documents that he kept abroad. He expected fateful events to occur in our country: "This gentleman [Carol] irks us, he will lose his job!" As I was leaving, he wished me success, "even though I don't know what regime Romania will soon have."

FIRST DAYS IN HELSINGFORS

We arrived in Helsingfors on April 9, 1934, after sailing on the Baltic Sea for two days. To reach the wharf, we had to cross a huge ice pack, suffused in a pale, polar light. We were met by our consular staff—Consul General Gösta Salingre and Consul Prüssing—as well as by the emissary of the Ministry of Foreign Affairs, Sohlman, who took us to the hotel where we were to stay until we had set up a legation.

The following day, accompanied by Consul General Salingre, I called on the Ministry of Foreign Affairs, which was located in the former Russian governors' palace. I was met by the head of Protocol, Rafael Hakkarainen, who introduced me to Minister of Foreign Affairs Andre Hackzell. I handed Hackzell a copy of my credentials and of the remarks I was to address to the president of the republic, after which we made a *tour d'horizon.* He seemed flattered that, after so many years, Romania was again establishing a diplomatic mission in Helsingfors and that my appointment as minister plenipotentiary of Romania was increasing the number of foreign envoys accredited to his country. He interpreted my arrival in Helsingfors as proof of the growing repute in which the young Finnish state was held. Hackzell, who had been a business lawyer under the tsarist domination, was fired by an implacable hatred of Russia, whatever its regime.

I presented my credentials to President Svinhufvud on April 14. Hakkarainen, that mentor of foreign envoys, came to pick me up in the president's personal car, and took me to the Presidential Palace, the former residence of the tsars in their capacity of grand dukes of Finland. I was, of course, wearing my uniform, with sash, decorations, and medals, and the honor guard presented arms when I arrived. The officer on duty, Söderström, met me at the entrance, and we ascended the main staircase of the palace, a building in the Russian Empire style. Colonel Kekoni, the head of the military household, then led me through a number of drawing rooms, all furnished in Empire style, until we arrived in front of the president, who was flanked by the minister of foreign affairs. After the presentation of the credentials and the reading of the addresses, I was invited to sit down and we talked. The conversation was described in my report to the Ministry of Foreign Affairs. I do not have a copy of that report with me, here in exile, but it can surely be found in the ministry's archives.

Svinhufvud was tall and stocky; he looked like a resistant and fighter. The tsarist regime had exiled him for many years in Siberia, and this victim's aura contributed to the great esteem in which his fellow countrymen held him. Like Hackzell, he did not hide from me his hatred of the Russians. "We are two neighboring countries, Romania and Finland," he remarked, "since we have a common border: the border with Russia!" After some time, the president led me to his wife's quarters, where we found Mrs. Svinhufvud, Mrs. Hackzell, my wife, and the doyenne of the diplomatic corps, Baroness de Vaux. After the introductions, we all stayed for tea, in a cordial and patriarchal atmosphere.

The following days I made the usual calls on the prime minister, Kivimäki, the minister of foreign affairs, Hackzell, and his deputy, Rolf Witting. My conversations with them were also summarized in my reports to the Ministry. Later, after the failure of the sanctions in the Italo-Ethiopian conflict, Kivimäki told me that this had destroyed any illusion small countries may have had that, when in danger, they would be backed up by the League of Nations. I was going to meet Kivimäki again seven years later, as a colleague in Berlin, where we were both envoys of our respective countries.

I found in Helsingfors a widespread hostility toward Russia and a total disbelief in its purported peaceful intentions. I likewise noted that the Finnish authorities wished to stay aloof both from the Baltic Bloc (fearing a Polish hegemony) and from the Scandinavian Bloc (participation in which, I thought, would create a somewhat awkward situation for a government seeking to stress the Finnish aspects of the country at the detriment of the Swedish ones). Hackzell admitted to me that Finland had signed the London Convention for the definition of aggression only reluctantly, and this for two reasons. First, because it gave the impression that a commitment by the Soviets had some validity and that it was therefore useful to negotiate with Moscow. (Even though, like Titulescu, he was a jurist, Hackzell attached no importance to agreements signed by the Russians, who when convenient would treat them as mere scraps of paper.) Secondly, because the annex to article 3 did not exclude offenses against personal property rights from the list of cases that did not give the right to declare war; not only did this preclude the possibility of sanctions against the Soviets, it also eliminated even the threat of sanctions. These were the reasons, Hackzell told me, for the reluctance of the Scandinavian countries to sign the Convention.

In view of rumors that Titulescu was secretly negotiating with the Soviets, Hackzell asked me in December 1935, at the signing of the Romano-Finnish clearing agreement, whether they were true. I repeated to him what I had been told at our Ministry of Foreign Affairs when I had asked the same question—that no treaty was being negotiated with Moscow. "That's all to the good," Hackzell said, "for to be on good terms with the Russians is one thing, but to become bosom friends is another."

I keep a particularly pleasant memory of my visit with Field Marshal Mannerheim, former aide-de-camp of Tsar Nicholas II, former commander of a Russian division on the Dobrudja front in 1916–1917, then—after the Russian revolution of 1917—commander of the Finnish troops that drove the Bolshevik bands out of the country, and, finally, the first head of state of his native Finland. He was *grand seigneur* to the tips of his fingers and a man of refined taste; his house was full of art objects from the Far East, collected when he was traveling in those parts on a secret mission to Tibet for the tsar. He also had in his possession a key to the fortress of Hotin, and said he was thinking of giving it through me to the Romanian state; he did not carry this out, however, because (as he later confessed to me) he had qualms at seeming to participate, even if only symbolically, in the loss of one of the fortresses of the tsar he had served. (He did, however, allow me to include a reproduction of the key in a paper, *Romanian Traces in Northern Lands,* that I wrote for the Romanian Academy in 1937.) He spoke of my father-in-law, Colonel Nicholas G. Cantacuzino, who had been detached during the war to serve as Romanian liaison officer to his division. He also mentioned with affection General (later Field Marshal) Averescu. He had only words of praise for the bravery and endurance of the Romanian soldier.

By contrast, my first meeting with Boris Stein, the Soviet envoy to Finland, was bizarre and somewhat alarming. It was the first time I was stepping into a Soviet legation; when I heard the doors being bolted behind me and saw suspicious and sullen characters prowling around, I almost wondered whether I would ever be able to get away from there! The visit, however, did not turn out as gruesome as that. After following long hallways that reeked of disinfectant and old leather, I was ushered into Stein's suite, which was much friendlier. Stein was an intelligent Jew, cultured, pleasant, and with the good manners of a former bourgeois. He held a Ph.D. in economics from the prewar University of Petrograd. He led me to a typically Russian-set table, on which were placed teacups and countless plates of *kullich* and of other sweets, as well as fruit from his country. Against the subdued humming of the samovar, our conversation took on from the beginning an unconstrained and rather interesting turn. He of course spoke to me of Titulescu, whom he had met in Geneva "and who only handles major political issues"—this said with a slightly ironic smile. He then expressed the hope that, in spite of the great difficulties still standing in the way, our two countries would soon resume normal relations, "since there is goodwill on both sides." He urged me to visit Leningrad, just across the border, which I had seen in 1916 when it was still Petrograd. I replied that I would do so as soon as we had established a legation in Moscow. As early as the next day, Boris Stein returned my visit and repeated his wish that "the relations between us two become more and more cordial by the day, because the relations between our two countries are also getting closer."

I shall mention below only those of the initial conversations I had with my other diplomatic colleagues that helped me understand better the local or regional situations; other visits were merely courtesy calls. In the absence of other forms of amusement, many receptions were held in Helsingfors. Almost every evening we were either invited to dinner by one of the foreign envoys, or we organized a dinner for them and for members of government or of Finnish society (which in fact was Swedish); we had set up the legation in the attractive Villa Stockmann, located in Östra Brunnsparken, on the seashore. During these staid dinners, rendered even more formal by a strict adherence to the ceremonial of the *skål,* the atmosphere remained somewhat frozen; after dinner, however, around cups of coffee and glasses of aquavit or of *brand,* tongues loosened up.

Büsing, the German envoy, was galled by Litvinov's recent proposal to Berlin that they guarantee the independence and territorial integrity of the Baltic states. But who is threatening these states, asked Büsing heatedly, and why are they being treated as minors? The German government rejected the proposal, reportedly to Finland's great satisfaction since it does not tolerate that its fate be decided by others and without its knowledge. Viewed in the light of later events, a Russo-German agreement to guarantee the independence of the Baltic countries would have had a certain black humor, given that the Soviet Union and the Nazi Reich were equally itching to take over these unfortunate small countries, and that they did so by turn when it proved feasible.

My French colleague, Baron de Vaux, was also convinced that Finland would never tie itself to either the Scandinavians or the Balts. This attitude seemed to sadden in particular my Latvian colleague, Schumans, because the Finns were thereby hindering the formation of a Baltic union: "The Finns may want to play at maintaining a 'splendid isolation,'" he told me, "but with the Soviets breathing down one's neck, it is dangerous to pretend to be British."

By contrast, and to my great astonishment, my Polish colleague, Charwat, disapproved of the Finns' uncompromising attitude toward their powerful Russian neighbor. In spite of all the efforts he had made, he said, to bring about a détente between Helsingfors and Moscow, he had been unsuccessful because of the stubbornness of the Finns, who still hoped one day to round off their country by the addition of "Karelia irredenta." He mainly blamed Hackzell, "a businessman who knows nothing about politics." He gave me the impression of being a strong Russophile, hence quite hostile to the country to which he was accredited. He was glad that, following the exchange of letters between Titulescu and Litvinov in Geneva on June 9, 1934, Romania had resumed diplomatic relations with the Soviet Union, and he derided Finland for feeling threatened by Russia, which actually ignored it. Events were to prove Charwat's total lack of perspicacity, and it is surprising that he was entrusted with a mission as delicate as that of representing Poland in a country neighboring Russia. He even told me that Finland had "a provocative attitude toward Russia" that might call forth the anger of the Bolsheviks; and if Finland were endangered, no one would rise to its defense (in this, he was right), because its existence was of no interest to anyone, and was only a matter of "geographical esthetics" for Europe! My counterarguments had no effect on the peppery Polish diplomat.

During a luncheon given by the president of the republic, Foreign Minister Hackzell told me once more of his lack of faith in the real value of multilateral treaties (such as the Baltic Union or the Convention for the Definition of Aggression). I asked him whether he would be in favor—at the right time—of a Romano-Finnish treaty. He said he would, and added that he was deeply grateful to the Romanian government for having established a legation in Helsingfors, as a first sign of the strengthening friendship between our countries.

FINNISH COMMEMORATIONS AND ROMANIAN EXHIBITION

In the fall of 1934, the centennial of the birth of the great Finnish writer Aleksis Kivi was being celebrated in Helsingfors. I attended, as representative of the Romanian Academy, the commemorative session organized by the Finnish Literary Society and read a message of greetings. I had taken care to publish an article about Kivi in *Convorbiri Literare,* so as to show that the Finnish author was known in our country.

On my return from the commemoration I received a phone call from the Yugoslav consul general, who imparted the tragic news of the assassination in Marseilles of King Alexander and of the French minister of foreign affairs, Louis Barthou. The king had come on an official visit to France. The death of this loyal ally was a heavy blow to our country, and the death of Barthou, who had revived the cooperation among World War I's former allies and had always steadfastly backed the Little Entente, was a deep sorrow. Titulescu cabled me that, in the face of this tragedy, he had withdrawn his resignation as minister of foreign affairs, which had been prompted by his disagreements with Tătărescu, whom he suspected of wanting (along with Poland) a rapprochement with Germany. In the course of the diplomatic condolence visits, I met Boris Stein. He talked about the role Barthou had played in the Soviet Union's admission to the League of Nations. He told me, among other things, that at a luncheon given by Litvinov for the members of the League of Nations Council, he had heard Barthou relate that when the Soviet Union's admission was put to the vote, Titulescu shouted "with a thundering voice 'yes.'" The same words of admiration for our minister of foreign affairs were going to be repeated to me, after Stein's transfer to Rome, by his successor, Eric Assmus, a very Westernized young man, the son of a German minister from Latvia.

The centenary of the publication by Elias Lönnrot of the runes of the famous Finnish epic *Kalevala* fell in the spring of 1935. Official status was given to the four-day commemoration, at which I of course represented the Romanian government. At a session chaired by the head of state, I was called upon to give an address conveying Romania's greetings; by sheer luck, I had discovered that several decades earlier a translation of some of the *Kalevala* runes had been published in *Convorbiri Literare*! Shortly thereafter, there was the tribute to Sibelius, who was reaching the age of seventy.

During my mission to Finland, I took great pains to broaden people's knowledge of Romania, about which they knew very little, and that little being furthermore distorted by Hungarian propaganda. Finland was a fertile ground for that propaganda owing to the common ethnic origin of the two nations (even though their languages have in common only five words of Ugro-Finnish origin, and even these sometimes with different meanings). I remember, for instance, how a member of the Finnish government, Minister of Agriculture Jutila, in the euphoric atmosphere of the Fifth Ugro-Finnic Congress held in Reval (Tallinn), published in the summer of 1936 in the Estonian daily *Uns Esti* an article openly defending the Hungarian claims. I immediately asked to see Prime Minister Kivimäki, who was acting as foreign minister, to lodge a protest against the article written by one of his government colleagues, and to explain to him as well as I could that Hungary lost only territories that did not belong to it ethnically. I recall telling him: "England, too, lost the half of France it owned in the Middle Ages, and Spain lost Flanders. What would you say if the foreign press were to deplore the fate of unfortunate Russia, which lost Poland, Finland, and Bessarabia? It lost them because they did not belong to it. Similarly, Transylvania was not given to the Romanian people, it was restored to them. The fact that over a million Hungarians live at the far end of Transylvania, near the border with the Old Kingdom, is no reason for the entire province—where there are four million Romanians, as well as various other groups—to remain under Hungarian domination." Kivimäki seemed embarrassed and said he knew nothing about the article, which was "probably written in the magyarophile atmosphere of the congress." He promised to speak to Jutila. I took the opportunity to complain about the somewhat hostile indifference of the local press, which published only the tendentious news coming from Budapest. This attitude was in sharp contrast to the friendliness that my wife and I encountered in all Finnish circles.

Thanks to this friendliness, I succeeded in organizing various events designed to present Romania in its true light to a public that barely knew it, or knew it wrongly. The most important of these was undoubtedly the exhibition of Romanian popular art, which opened on February 23, 1935, in the presence of Mrs. Svinhufvud, the president's wife, of members of the government and of the diplomatic corps, and of a quite numerous public. In my address, I underlined the similarities between Romanian and Finnish popular art. Romanian rugs are very similar to the Finnish carpets called *ryår,* and the *bucium,* the long alpenhorn of our mountains and valleys, resembles the Finnish *tuohitorvi.* I concluded, as was fitting, with some runes from the *Kalevala.* This was followed by a concert of Romanian music and then by a visit of the stands.

The articles sent from Romania for sale were immediately sold out. It was an undeniable success for Romanian propaganda, and the first direct contact of the Finns with our distant country. That evening, radio Helsinki devoted one hour to Romanian music. Also in connection with the exhibition, the Finnish Geographic Society organized a session dedicated to Romania. A few days later, I attended the inauguration of the first Romanian-language course held at the university by Professor Tuulio. And Professor Alexandru Tzigara-Samurcaş came from Romania to give a highly appreciated conference on our national art.

DISCOVERING FINLAND AND ITS NEIGHBORS

During my mission to Helsingfors, I had the pleasant occasion of developing close relations with Finland's society—families of Swedish descent, but quite strongly influenced in their behavior and way of being by the circles around the imperial Russian court. This melding imparts to the Finns a special charm, composed of a certain Nordic formality regarding etiquette—the ritual followed at meals, for instance, with the prescribed series of *skåls*—and of a Slavic litheness and simplicity. For me, the typical exemplar was Field Marshal Mannerheim, who was, as I have mentioned, a former aide-de-camp of the tsar and, later, president of his native Finland. We were able to appreciate the courtesy and hospitality of the Finns especially in their country residences, where we often spent weekends and which reminded me so much of the *conacs*[1] of our boyars. Many aristocratic Finnish families had forebears who, as officers in the Imperial Russian army, had spent months—or even years—in the Romanian Principalities during Russian occupations, and especially in 1828. The letters they sent home from Jassy or Bucharest, describing the conditions there, were made available to me; and in 1937 I published a large number of these lively and interesting documents in a book entitled *Finnish Accounts of Romania.*

We took advantage of our years in Helsingfors to visit as many interesting places as possible in Finland and in its Scandinavian neighbors. In Finland, we traveled extensively in the southern part and in the Åland archipelago, and then undertook an "arctic expedition." We left for Lapland in July 1934, in a rather archaic train—old cars, wood-burning locomotives, tediously lengthy stops. After twenty-five hours under way we reached Rovaniemi, the end of the line. We lunched there, then left by

[1]Manors.

car for Lapland, which is inhabited less by Lapps than by reindeers and mosquitoes. We oiled our faces and hands with *Sjöbergsmyggolia,* reputedly a mosquito-repellant ointment, and covered our heads with a green netting. The mosquitoes swarmed around us and crashed against the car's windows, creating the only noise and annoyance in this region of secluded charm and absolute serenity. We reached Ivalo at ten o'clock in the evening, therefore in full daylight, and pulled up at a *maja* (roadside inn), actually an excellent hotel of the Finnish Touring Club, in which college students served as waitresses. Under the midnight sun, we visited the shores of the great Lake Inari, with its so characteristic Lapp population.

The next day, we drove along an admirably maintained road that stretched in a straight line up to the Arctic Ocean. Stark solitude, endless forests of pines and birches that were becoming progressively smaller and more shriveled as we advanced northward. We met not a single human being on the way, only, from time to time, reindeer that crossed our path with their bouncing and limber gait. We spent the night at the *maja* of Yläluostari, and the next day crossed the tundra and then barren country, entirely devoid of vegetation. Finally we reached our destination: Lünahiamari, on the Arctic Ocean, which, thanks to the Gulf Stream, never freezes over in these parts. After checking in at a tourist hotel, and in spite of our fatigue, we couldn't resist climbing up the cliffs to admire that marvel, the midnight sun. Even though it was the middle of the night, we basked in the sun as if it were high noon!

The following days we swam in the Arctic Ocean, blue as the Adriatic, but deceptively so since its temperature was 7 degrees Centigrade.[2] We also cruised on the ship *Jäämeri* (Frozen Sea). Sun, warmth in the air (but not in the water), alien landscape—polar, almost lunar. Only high cliffs and desolation. Not a living soul. We stopped at Heinasaari Island, inhabited only by birds, but in what numbers and varieties! More sensible than men, the birds of different species manage to live together peacefully on the same island. Sailing farther, we reached Vaitolahti, the northernmost point of the Finnish territory of that time, from where one could see the Soviet sentries across the border. We crossed on foot the narrow tundra peninsula to Kervanto, where we boarded the ship for the return journey. In Pummanki we ran into our friend Professor Väinö Tanner, a renowned geographer and former Finnish envoy to Bucharest. He proposed that we spend two days in the tents with which he was traveling for his scientific

[2] 45° F.

research, and we gladly accepted. Kosti, his faithful Lapp, conveyed us in a small boat with sails of unusual shapes and colors to the far end of the Pummanaki Fjord, which was out of this world. We walked for hours on end in that desolate land, bothered only by that true bane, the mosquito, from which we could protect ourselves only with the help of the *Sjöbergsmyggolia* ointment and the stifling head netting. The polar flora is a marvel of frailty and vivid colors: *alchemilla alpina, linnea borealis, empetrum nigrum* (with edible black berries), and finally *hyortron,* also known as the polar strawberry, whose yellow berries are the tastiest of Nordic fruit.

After returning to Lünahiamari, we sailed down the turbulent river Patsjoki to Kolttaköngäs, the home of the most primitive tribes of Lapps, with tiny houses perched on stilts in order to keep them safe from melting snow floods, and then on to Elvenes. From there, we drove to Norway and boarded a ship that cruised the Arctic Ocean. It was a splendid trip along the Norwegian coast, with its imposing and wild cliffs interspersed with spraying waterfalls and fjords of unsuspected and breath-taking beauty. This marvelous cruise lasted another two days, as we entered the Norwegian Sea and passed through fjords of unmatched attraction. Finally, sailing through a fjord that seemed to come straight out of a fairy tale, we arrived at Narvik. After a few hours in this small town with enchanting vistas, we boarded a train that took us through Norway and Sweden, and back to Helsingfors. We made the same trip again the following year with my brother and sister-in-law, and it again left us with the same unforgettable feelings.

Another interesting tour, in the summer of 1935, took us to eastern Finland, and especially to Karelia.[3] We started by visiting Finland's oldest city, Vyborg (Viipuri), and were immersed in the Middle Ages. Near by, Monrepos Castle, with its renowned gardens. Then Langinkoski, a former rustic residence of the tsars on an island in the midst of the impetuous Kymmene River, and close by Kirjala, where we were received by the young Nobels, Norwegian childhood friends of my wife's, in their family castle. The famous Terijoki beach, where in times past Petersburg's elegant society used to stay, seemed abandoned, a sad witness to the old imperial regime's disappearance. Our wanderings took us to Sortavala, the home of the Kalevala's bards, on the shores of Lake

[3]In March 1940, after the Finnish-Russian war, Finland ceded to the USSR its part of the Karelian Isthmus (including Vyborg) and land bordering Lake Ladoga. The treaty was confirmed after the armistice between the two countries in September 1944.

Ladoga, Europe's largest sweet water lake, a true sea, which at that time marked the border with Soviet Russia. A motorboat brought us to Valamo archipelago, the site of an imposing Orthodox monastery surrounded by a large number of churches, chapels, hermitages, and a huge inn for the pilgrims. We then went to Punkaharju, Finland's most delightful sight: a narrow rib of hill covered with silvery birch trees, rising twenty-five meters above the waters of lakes Puruvesi and Väistöselkä, which it separates over a distance of six kilometers—truly the setting for a legend. On the way back, we also visited the fifteenth-century fortified castle of Olofsborg, the oldest and most intact surviving building from Finland's past.

My vacations enabled us to travel throughout the Scandinavian cities—Stockholm, with its fine architecture and museums (in the National Museum, I saw my own bust, the work of the sculptor Anders Jönsson, whom I had befriended when we were both students in Paris!), Drottningholm, Uppsala, Göteborg, Copenhagen (where I was to be accredited six years later as Romanian envoy), Frederiksborg, Helsingør (Elsinore, with Hamlet's Kronborg castle), Klampenborg, Sorgenfri. We also visited Reval (Tallinn), Estonia being only a fifteen-minute flight from Helsingfors.

And we went three times to Russia. The first time, accompanied by our friends de la Blanchetai from the French legation, we went to Leningrad in the summer of 1935. Intourist had attached to our party "Comrade Poliakova" (probably from the GPU), the daughter of a physician and a cultured woman who had known the former way of life. She took us around Peter the Great's majestic capital, which, dethroned by Moscow, seemed to be dying in a slow agony. The streets were left untended and the façades of the palaces were allowed to become dilapidated. People in the streets were poorly dressed and downcast, with not a smile in sight to brighten things up.

St. Isaac's cathedral, in front of our hotel, had been converted into an "anticlerical museum," with rather artless and simple-minded displays. A visitor, the typical image of a Russian muzhik, studied each exhibit attentively. When he arrived in front of the big malachite icons, he crossed himself devotedly and kissed the holy images. The museum had apparently not done much to shake his faith.

At the Hermitage, I came across a copy (not mentioned in the iconographies published in Romania) of Frans Francken's famous portrait of Michael the Brave. I obtained a reproduction, which I included in my previously mentioned pamphlet, *Romanian Traces in Northern Lands.*

The Soviet authorities later gave the picture to Iorga as compensation for the loss of the chest of documents he had sent to Moscow in 1917, together with the National Bank's treasure. Iorga then presented the picture to the Romanian Academy, which hung it in its meeting hall. We returned to Leningrad for about a week in the spring of 1936, and went to Moscow and Leningrad in the fall of that same year, on our last trip back to Helsingfors before leaving that posting.

MEANWHILE, BACK AT HOME . . .

At the end of each of my leaves I would go to Bucharest to see my parents and to touch base with the government and the Ministry of Foreign Affairs. When I did so in December 1934, Titulescu invited me to lunch at his home. "Your cables are most interesting," he told me, then, addressing our table companions, he added, "Gentlemen, I proclaim Bossy a member of my party!" After the luncheon, Savel Rădulescu took me aside and disclosed that Titulescu had decided to entrust me with an important legation in the West, "more in the sunshine." In September 1935, on my way to Bucharest, I stopped in Geneva and talked for several days with our delegation at the League of Nations. Savel Rădulescu said to me: "By now, the Eastern front of our legations is in good shape: you in Helsingfors, Ciuntu in Moscow, Văllimărescu in Riga, Davidescu in Reval, Filotti in Ankara. But in my view, you head the list. Nonetheless, Titulescu will remove you from there in order to place you in a much more important posting. In a few months' time you will be moving toward the sun. I will not tell you where, so that Titulescu himself may break you the news."

The atmosphere at the League of Nations was very grim in view of the imminent armed conflict between Italy and Ethiopia. A general wave of indignation was mounting against Italy, which, by its cowardly aggression against a primitive and unarmed nation, was perhaps going to wreck the League of Nations or even provoke a widespread war. Titulescu, with whom I had lunch at Le Globe, was outraged by the attitude of the Fascist government. He considered its behavior, its disregard of the League of Nations, its will to attain its objectives by force and by a dastardly attack against a weak country, to constitute a very dangerous precedent for small nations.

Changing topics, he told me: "I would want you to be appointed to Budapest. Does that suit you? But don't announce the appointment to anybody yet, since I have not yet broached the topic with either the king or the Hungarians." At a subsequent luncheon, Titulescu told me anew that I would shortly be appointed envoy to Budapest.

Titulescu was appalled by the extent of the concessions made to Italy. The Council of the League of Nations, and in the first place France, would not be opposed to a parceling out of Abyssinia (as Ethiopia was still frequently called at that time). "If they all follow suit," exclaimed Titulescu, furious, "and go on dismembering member states, that will be truly great! I told them I would sign only if it was absolutely certain that Rome accepted, and that only to prevent a war. Otherwise, I prefer not to affix Romania's signature on a deed of spoliation perpetrated by the League of Nations."

Even though it was four years since I had last attended an Assembly meeting, I found more or less the same faces: Beneš, Herriot, Laval, Paul-Boncour, Vasoncellos, Eden (with whom I had lunch at the Finnish delegate's, Holsti), Unden, Beck, Künzl-Jizerski (former Czechoslovak envoy to Bucharest), Litvinov, Boris Stein (former Soviet envoy to Helsingfors), and many others. Only Briand's "cello voice" was missing.

In Bucharest, I rejoined my wife and children, who had come directly from Finland, and along with all other members of the family we celebrated my father's eightieth birthday. During his lifetime, he went through all the stages of the building of the united Romanian state, from the Moldavia of his forefathers to Greater Romania, and lived under six reigns: those of Grigore Ghica, Cuza, Carol I, Ferdinand I, Michael I, and Carol II.

One of my first visits was to my old friend Bébé Brătianu. He told me the gulf was continuously widening between the leadership of the Liberal party, headed by Dinu Brătianu, and the Liberal government headed by Gheorghe Tătărescu, who was becoming more and more servile toward Carol, with his whims and fancies. Bébé believed the government's days were numbered. He too confirmed that Titulescu hadn't negotiated any treaty with the Russians, for that would have amounted to turning our backs on the Poles, which would be inconceivable.

I of course also called on Titulescu, who again told me that I would be transferred to Budapest, probably in three months' time, and that the king was in full agreement. (In fact, my appointment was to occur only more than a year later, when Titulescu was no longer foreign minister.) Turning to the rumor that he was negotiating a treaty with Moscow, he denied this categorically: "I have not negotiated, nor am I now negotiating, a treaty with the Soviets; there is no reason for Gheorghe Brătianu to fret. We are, however, following France and Czechoslovakia in the evolution of their policies. We must always have good relations with the Russians. Besides, we have never been at war with them."

The following summer—the summer of 1936—while I was vacationing in St. Moritz, I heard that the Tătărescu government had been reshuffled and that Titulescu no longer held the position of minister of foreign affairs. I phoned Mihai Boerescu, our envoy to Berne, who confirmed that Titulescu had been "given the sack," adding, however, that he had asked that all of us remain at our posts. Boerescu informed me that the new foreign minister was Victor Antonescu, a second-rate man of little standing. Titulescu, the great orator who was the pride of the League of Nations, was being replaced by a man who lisped and groped for words, and who owed his career to Ionel Brătianu's benevolence.

I learned from Bébé Brătianu that Titulescu had been replaced at the urging of the king, who was displeased by his approaches to Soviet Russia and by the fact that he kept no one informed of what he was doing. Besides, the Italians stressed at every opportunity that they could never forgive him for his understandable—if unwise—berating of Italian journalists who were booing the Ethiopian negus when he ascended to the League of Nations' podium: "*Chassez donc ces sauvages!*"[4] Furthermore, even Stoiadinović, the Yugoslav prime minister, did not hide his anger at Titulescu for having issued on his own, a few months earlier in Geneva, a decidedly anti-German communiqué on behalf of the Little Entente, without consulting his country's allies beforehand. At a recent session of the Little Entente in Bratislava, Krofta, the foreign minister of Czechoslovakia, proposed that a cable of appreciation be sent to Titulescu on his departure from the government, a proposal that Victor Antonescu endorsed. But in the face of Stoiadinović's opposition, the cable was not sent.

A SERENE CHAPTER COMES TO AN END

My wife and I left for the last time for Helsingfors on November 9, in order to make our farewell visits and to clear out the house for my successor, Caius Brediceanu. We stopped on the way in Warsaw, then continued through Russia. In Moscow, my colleague Ciuntu gave us a tour of the old Russian capital. We then took the train for Leningrad. In the great confusion created on the platform by the presence of all the members of our legation, ladies with bouquets of flowers for my wife, and

[4]"Expel these savages!"

porters with our luggage, the official entrusted with obtaining the exit visas forgot to give us back our passports. I was in the grip of some anxiety during the entire trip, until the Russian police returned the precious passports to us, two days later.

Our final departure from Helsingfors was an emotional experience because of the affection with which we were surrounded but perhaps also because we knew we would never return to these parts and would never again see the Finnish friends we were leaving behind. All our foreign colleagues, according to custom, gave us farewell luncheons. So did the president of the republic, Svinhufvud, who made a most flattering toast and handed me the grand sash of the White Rose. The new foreign minister, Holsti, hosted a farewell banquet, with exchanges of toasts. The committee of the Romanian exhibition also gave a reception in our honor, attended by all the members of the former Kivimäki government and their wives, as well as by the governor of the Bank of Finland, Ryiti, a future president of the republic. The former minister of education, Mantere, gave a warm speech in German directed to me, and then read in French an address of thanks to my wife and to me for the friendship we had shown Finland. We were given a copy of the address, penned on parchment and nicely bound in leather, with the signatures of Mrs. Svinhufvud, of the members of the former government, and of the "friends of Romania." I then handed Mantera the Crown of Romania sash, which had recently been awarded to him for his support of the Romanian exhibition, and tried to express in my address our heart-felt gratitude and the wonderful memories of Finland we would cherish forever.

Among our other Finnish friends who so hospitably received us prior to our departure, I should mention Field Marshal Mannerheim, with whom I had an interesting political conversation. Clear-sighted and well informed as always—the future was to bear witness to that—he told me the Germans wanted war and that "the bomb will explode in Danzig." As we parted, he gave me his signed photograph. A few days later, Hjalmar Procopé, the former foreign minister, also organized a dinner with many of our friends.

November 28, 1936, the day of our departure. Two years and almost ten months had elapsed since our arrival on April 9, 1934. On the wharf, we found Field Marshal Mannerheim, in uniform, carrying a huge bouquet of roses for my wife. Also at hand were the members of the present and of the former government, my colleagues from the diplomatic corps, members of Finland's high society, and our faithful consul general, Gösta Salingre, with his co-workers, all bringing us flowers and gifts. My French colleague whispered to me, "This is not a sending-off party, it's an apotheosis!" We all said to each other "till we meet again," but knew full well this was an "adieu" and that we would never see each other again in this world. The ship *Velamo* began blowing its whistle, calling all passengers on board.

From the deck, we gazed for the last time on the villa Stockmann where we had lived, and then, little by little, the outline of Helsingfors faded and Finland's coast disappeared from the horizon. A chapter had come to a close. With some trepidation on my part, a new chapter was opening and, obviously, it was going to be less serene.

9

Budapest (1936–1939)

I. 1936–1937

On my way to Bucharest, where I was to be briefed before assuming my posting in Budapest, I stopped for a few days in Berlin. At the Adlon Hotel, I found a note from our envoy in Germany inviting me to lunch at the legation. I thus went to the Rauchstrasse building that would be my home in five years' time, when, in turn, I was to be appointed envoy to Berlin. The current head of the Romanian mission was a former lawyer and deputy, Nicolae Petrescu, who had added to his plebeian surname the famous one of Comnen;[1] in a country where "the ridiculous does not kill," this imperial suffix in no way hindered his political career. In Paris, he had been nicknamed "Petresco Quand Même";[2] this ruined any chance of his heading the most sought-after mission in our diplomatic service. But it must be admitted that he was an energetic and clever man, even though somewhat of a mountebank. Knowing him well, his superiors in Bucharest always took the information he supplied with a big grain of salt.

During our conversation, he said there were among German policymakers two conflicting positions toward Romania: the one—that of Hitler—favorable to Romania and opposed to Hungarian revisionism[3] regarding Transylvania, the other—that of the old hands at the Wilhelmstrasse—traditionally Magyarophile and revisionist. Hitler's opinion, he said, was clearly revealed in a *Völkischer Beobachter* article

[1]Romanian rendition of Comnenus, the surname of six Byzantine emperors.

[2]"Petrescu Nonetheless"; in French, *quand même* and *Comnène* sound very much alike.

[3]Advocacy of a revision of the treaties that brought World War I to an end, especially with a view to restoring to a vanquished country part or all of its territorial losses.

signed by Rosenberg. By and large, that was also the view of the National-Socialists. Göring would have said to our envoy: "No Müller became Müllerović in Yugoslavia, nor Müllerescu in your country, but all of them became Molnár in Hungary. Why should we therefore hand over our Saxons and Swabians[4] to the Hungarians?" The opposite view, that of the Wilhelmstrasse, was endorsed by Neurath, possibly because his son-in-law Mackensen was German envoy to Budapest, and he wanted to make things easier for him. Petrescu-Comnen asserted that Neurath went so far as to state: "I alone represent Germany's foreign policy, and I can assure you that we are revisionists by definition and that the Hungarian claims cannot leave us indifferent." But, basing himself on what Göring was telling him, Petrescu-Comnen believed that the Hitler-Göring point of view would nevertheless prevail. Göring, reportedly, had no objections to any of our alliances. He only asked that we maintain the Little Entente's defensive nature against Hungary, and that we not give it an anti-German orientation.

FIRST STEPS

Arriving in Bucharest, I called on Iorga, who said, referring to my appointment to Budapest: "What an accursed job! The Hungarians will try to poison you; don't accept any invitation to a meal; make sure you have a Romanian cook!" He asked me to have translated into Hungarian his book *The Romanians and the Hungarians,* written with objectivity. He saw no possibility of a détente. A step by us in that direction would be seen as a sign of weakness. I got more or less the same reaction from a conversation with Stelian Popescu, former minister of justice and director of the daily *Universul.* He felt that we had to be very careful, because any well-intentioned gesture could be interpreted as weakness.

With for him unusual haste, Carol received me in audience on December 11, 1936. We talked for twenty-five minutes. He had me describe the situation in Finland, and then asked me how I intended to carry out my mission in Hungary. He asked me about my former assignments. "You were also at the Regency?" I answered, "Yes." That was all.

[4]Both are German-speaking inhabitants whose ancestors were brought by the Austrians to present-day Romania (from many places other than Saxony or Swabia) and were settled in their border areas. The "Saxons" were settled in the twelfth and thirteenth centuries in Transylvania and are mainly Lutherans. The "Swabians" were brought in during the eighteenth century and settled mainly in the Banat; they are predominantly Roman Catholic.

We then reminisced about our youth and the fencing lessons we took together at the Jockey Club. He was very gracious throughout.

The next day I went to the Ministry of Foreign Affairs to meet with the current incumbent, Victor Antonescu, an amiable but second-rate man with a premature tendency to senility. He told me that he had wished to have me appointed envoy to Prague, but the king had insisted that I go to Budapest, saying: "I had agreed to that with Titulescu, who spoke highly of him. With Bossy in Budapest, we will at least not have incidents with the Hungarians." Victor Antonescu told me this was an allusion to Vasile Stoica, "who caused incident after incident in Sofia, where he was considered insufferable." I read to him the draft of the allocution I was to make at the presentation of my credentials, and he was in full agreement. He said the Italians had told him that the Hungarians were seeking at all cost a détente with us. The Romanian government was animated by a similar sentiment, he said, and would even be willing to grant Hungary parity of rights in rearmament questions if Hungary should conclude a mutual assistance treaty with Romania, or even a simple nonaggression pact—or at least subscribe to the Politis formula for the definition of aggressor.

✧ ✧ ✧

My wife and I arrived in Budapest on December 14, and we were met at the station by the staffs of the legation and of the consulate. Flowers, press photographs. Because the legation was undergoing repairs, we checked in at the Ritz Dunapalota and after lunch went to visit the legation, which was going to be our home for the next three years. It was a large and attractive house, located at 15 Horánszky-utca, in the fashionable district of Pest. It was built by Baroness Maria de Szent-Kereszty, daughter of General Ion Em. Florescu and sister of Catherine Ghica, my wife's grandmother. It then became the property of another relative, Baroness Elsa Gerliszy, née Ştirbey, who sold it to the Romanian state. Above the front door were the coats-of-arms of the families Szent-Kereszty and Florescu.

I began my duties the very next day when, accompanied by the legation's counselor, Gheorghe Căpităneanu, I went to the Ministry of Foreign Affairs, on the hill of Buda, for my first contacts. I ran into the minister's cabinet chief, the young Count Istvan Csáky (later to become foreign minister), unmarried, quite handsome, and somewhat effeminate. I had met him in his previous postings, at the Vatican and in Bucharest.

He took me to his boss, Foreign Minister Colman Kánya, who was sixty-seven but appeared much older. Single and without close family, he lived only for his job. Physically he had an old woman's head, with a cunning, penetrating, and ironical look; he was extremely intelligent, skillful, and refined, not devoid at times of personal charm and having a rather "Voltairian" skepticism, not to say cynicism. He had been trained at the Ballhausplatz and was still imbued in the traditions of Kaunitz and Metternich. He had begun his career in the consular ranks of the former Austro-Hungarian monarchy. After several years in the Balkans, he had been called back to Vienna, where he served as head of the ministry's press services; he was also said to have had a hand in the web of Balkan intrigues and political maneuverings. His last posting before the collapse of the Dual Monarchy was as envoy to Mexico. He had the reputation of detesting the Romanians. In our first meeting, since I was accompanied by Căpităneanu, the conversation remained general in nature and did not venture on the dangerous paths of international politics. We restricted ourselves to talking about my last posting, Finland, a country he had frequently visited while serving as counselor of the Austro-Hungarian embassy in Petersburg.

From Kánya, I went to see the ministry's secretary of state, Baron Gábor Apor. He was distinguished, refined, intelligent, and conciliatory. He was Transylvanian—related to our cousins Szent-Kereszty—and had spent weeks on end at Arcoş, their estate, as well as at Sinaia. He knew all of our family, including my wife's grandmother and mother. I was going to have the best of relations with him during my mission, as well as afterward.

The presentation of my credentials took place on December 21. I was received after Italy's envoy—our friend Vinci—even though he had arrived several days after me. Italy was the great favorite in Budapest, whereas Romania. . . . One of the regent's aides-de-camp came to accompany me, and I took place with him in the regent's carriage, which was followed by two other carriages transporting my legation's staff. When we arrived at the Palace, the guard of honor presented arms and the master of ceremonies stood awaiting me at the bottom of the stairs. He led me and my suite through a double row of *noble guards* (green uniforms with golden frogs, white and red mantles, tall fur caps with aigrettes) and *palatine guards* (golden helmets and halberds in hand), up to a parlor where I was greeted by the chief of the Civil Chancellery, Alexander Vértessyi. He was an elderly man, very likable and quite Austrian in his ways. He told me that, long ago, he had attended the Theresianum with our relatives, Barbu Catargi and his brother Alexis. Throughout our stay in Budapest, we maintained the most cordial relations with him and his amiable wife. As I congratulated him on the splendor of the uniforms of the noble and palatine guards, he replied, in a somewhat melancholic tone, "That's all we were left with." A few minutes later, the aide-de-camp on duty led me and Apor into a very large room at the end of which stood the imposing figure of Admiral Horthy. He approached, we shook hands, I gave him my credentials, and then read my address, in which I avoided any political allusion. Admiral Horthy paraphrased my text in his reply, but he added an allusion to "the pending issues" between our countries and failed to express any good wishes for Romania.

SKETCHES OF HUNGARIAN OFFICIALS AND FOREIGN ENVOYS

There followed a private conversation between us, in which the regent proved extremely courteous and displayed a most Austrian *gemütlichkeit.* A former aide-de-camp of Franz Joseph, whose picture was always on his desk, he spoke German with his family, a language he knew better than Hungarian, which he spoke with a foreign accent. He was a perfect gentleman, with the upbringing of a member of the Magyar gentry, and though endowed with only an average intelligence, he gave proof of enough tact and friendliness to substitute for the more brilliant gifts of the mind. After World War II, he was unjustly described as a dictator, as a totalitarian ruler on the same level as Hitler or Mussolini, and he was likened to Field Marshal Antonescu (who, however, really did want to be a dictator). In fact, Horthy had neither the required character nor the moral inclination to seek to become a dictator. He would rather have had a constitutional rule, with fewer responsibilities on his shoulders. The model he was constantly striving to emulate was that of his former sovereign, the mild and upright Franz Joseph, the faithful servant of his people, with the nature of a mid-level bureaucrat, meticulous and punctual.

Toward me, the representative of a country unanimously detested in Hungary, both he and his pleasant wife could not have had a friendlier or more considerate attitude. At a reception he gave for the king of Italy during the king's visit to Budapest, Horthy beckoned me to approach so that I might be introduced to the sovereign, and then he moved back a few steps to allow us to talk out of his hearing. Another time, when he had been "working the room," he suddenly realized that by oversight—or perhaps because of my reluctance to push through to the front row—he had failed to talk with me. He then backtracked through a number of guests to shake hands with me, and said smilingly, "Consider, Your Excellency, that we have spoken for an entire hour!" In other words, do not think I avoided you because you are the envoy of Romania. I keep the best of memories of this head of state of a country at that time openly hostile, who in a very chivalrous spirit always sought to assuage the acerbity of our official relations with an enhanced personal friendliness toward the representative of a country that Hungary was fighting tooth and nail at the diplomatic level.

On my first official visit to Prime Minister Kálman Darányi, I found him, too, a pleasant and quiet man. He was considered an expert on issues concerning minorities in Transylvania. After talking about a common acquaintance—Count Mikes, the only Transylvanian Hungarian I would meet at the Jockey Club in Bucharest—he broached the topic of the Hungarian minority in Transylvania. I explained to him that what the Budapest press branded as "terrible persecutions" were either tendentious fabrications or else the sort of administrative and bureaucratic embroilments that any of the country's other citizens could also encounter. And if at times attacks do occur in the Transylvanian press, such as the one in *Turda* that caused so much fuss, they were brought on by the provocations of the Hungarian press, which tried to exploit any small incident in order to stir up public opinion. Darányi admitted that there were very often exaggerations, and that "there are faults on both sides," but he nevertheless asked me to plead with the present government—"which I know is full of good sentiments"—to give strict orders to the local authorities to put an end to the persecutions triggered by Mussolini's revisionist speech in Milan. In turn, I appealed to him to stop the campaign of slander against Romania conducted by the press in Budapest. My relations with Darányi were always perfectly correct, and he came a number of times to lunch at the legation.

Another member of the government with whom I had very good relations was the minister of agriculture, Nicholas Kállay, whose house was across the street from our legation and who had an extremely pleasant wife, née Kállay, as well. He was later to become prime minister and ended his days as an exile in New York with his second wife, a former actress. He published at that time his memoirs, in which he had the nerve to state that the Romanian authorities had set off persecutions and killings of the Hungarian minority after the Nazi Vienna arbitrage, though it is known that it was the Hungarians who, after having taken over northern Transylvania, undertook horrifying massacres among the population that had come under their rule. Their savagery in the village of Ip remains etched in memory, where—just as the Germans did in Oradour, in France—the Hungarians killed the entire male population. I saw the photograph of the mass grave in which the victims were buried, guarded by a Hungarian gendarme. All these atrocities had taken place under his watch as prime minister; in his book, Kállay preferred to accuse the Romanian authorities of what had been perpetrated by his own people.

I, of course, made the customary calls on the other diplomatic missions. Among the colleagues with whom I maintained particularly close relations during my stay in Budapest, the first one I met was the agreeable and lively French envoy, Gaston Maugras. He was a man full of wit and philosophical skepticism, with a charming wife née d'Abzac, a family my sisters were friends with—which, needless to say, contributed to the bond between Maugras and me. Already in our first meeting he cautioned me about the difficulties of my delicate mission, given the atmosphere of hostility that surrounded all the envoys of the Little Entente. Maugras thought that the ceaseless complaints about alleged persecutions of the Hungarian minority were only a pretext—and, eyes shining with irony, my French colleague added: "Oh, if only you were willing to make a gesture that could be interpreted as your 'dropping' Czechoslovakia, you would be judged full of forbearance toward your Hungarian minority! Mind you, I am not giving you advice, far from it!" And indeed, Czechoslovakia was at that time the number one enemy in Hungary, simply for the reason that it was seen as the weakest member of the Little Entente owing to the difficulties it was having with its German minority. Maugras was later replaced by Pierre Guerlat, a more subdued man, but one with much common sense.

I obviously had the most collegial and cordial relations with the envoys of the Little Entente and of the Balkan Entente: the Czechoslovak envoy, Miloš Kobr, a sensible and perfectly well-informed man, formerly in the Austro-Hungarian consular service, which gave him a certain leeway in his conversations with Kánya; the Yugoslav envoy, Aleksandar Vukcević, later replaced by Svetosar Rašić (whom I found again in exile, in New York); the Turkish envoy, Behiş Erkin; and the Greek envoy, Panayotis Pipinelis. Of all these, it was the last one who was the most clear-sighted and interesting. A close supporter of King George II, he had a brilliant career that took him to Moscow and, during the war, to London as his king's adviser. Under the reign of Paul I, he became, in turn, minister of foreign affairs, minister of trade, and then prime minister.

I maintained with him ever after links of very cordial friendship; we would meet sometimes in Lausanne, sometimes in New York, and corresponded constantly.

I likewise keep fond memories of my collaboration with Leon Orlowski, my Polish colleague, whom I later encountered in New York as an exile, and with my American colleague, John F. Montgomery. When I arrived in Hungary, Mackensen, the son of the field marshal, was Germany's envoy. We had been colleagues in Rome, when we both were first secretaries, and I was to encounter him once more—again in Rome—when we were both our countries' envoys. In order to avoid a dry listing of names, I shall refrain from mentioning the other heads of mission, but this is in no way meant to belittle them. However, I cannot keep myself from recalling the picturesque figure of the Armenian Alexander Bekzadjan, the Soviet envoy, who was subsequently recalled and, it was said, executed.

The Romanian colony—excluding the legation's diplomatic, consular, military, and commercial services—was not large, but I relished the purely Romanian—and unofficial—atmosphere when I went on Sundays with my family to the Romanian church of the Gojdu Foundation. Some of the local parishioners, victims of the Magyarization process, had almost forgotten Romanian, yet they said their prayers in the tongue of their forebears.

Budapest being a crossroad between Central and Western Europe, I found myself frequently having to go to the railway station to greet travelers of note. Queen Marie passed through Budapest on the day I presented my credentials, and she received me in her private parlor car, reclining on a settee. She complained that the governments of the Little Entente were opposed, or so she had been informed (probably by Carol), to her daughter Ileana's coming frequently to Romania, being married to an Austrian archduke (even though of a collateral branch). This meant that she herself had to travel in order to spend Christmas with her daughter. The queen deplored that, in Spain, General Franco was not being assisted by all countries, and she seemed to be much saddened by the death of her nephew de Bourbon (the son of her sister, Infanta Beatrix) on the Nationalist battlefront. On her return, she came to see us and asked to be taken to the movies. We also put up at the legation Princess Ileana and her husband, Archduke Anton, a good and unpretentious, though unenlightened, man. The "grand voevod"—the former and future King Michael I—likewise passed through Budapest, as did several times our foreign minister. I had the opportunity of talking with

Rüştü Aras during his passage through Budapest, and of greeting at the station French Prime Minister Yvon Delbos and General Gamelin on their return from Romania.

There were the usual ceremonies. I participated, in dress uniform, at the presentation of the diplomatic corps' New Year's wishes to Regent Horthy (January 7, 1937). The nuncio made a speech in all our names, to which Horthy responded. Later, Horthy spoke to me only of home and children. On leaving, we all went to sign the registers of Mrs. Horthy, of Archduke Joseph (former palatine of Hungary) and Archduchess Augusta (Franz Joseph's granddaughter), as well as of their son, Archduke Joseph Franz (a sound but not very entertaining writer), and his wife, Archduchess Anna, princess of Saxony, a beautiful and particularly pleasant woman. Both of them said they wished for a détente with the Romanians.

A few days later I attended the big annual dinner given by the regent to mission heads accredited to Budapest. And a few days after that, Mrs. Horthy invited my wife and me for tea. The regent was also present, and both of them were very gracious. (It was then that I noticed that they spoke German to each other.) A tea at Archduke Joseph and Archduchess Augusta's, also in tête-à-tête, could also have been pleasant, for they were both very sociable, had it not been for their continuous allusions to Transylvania. "Your king hunts frequently on my former estates," the archduke told me, "and as a hunter he must enjoy it, for the most splendid stags I ever hunted were in Transylvania—in your country, now." I did not respond and tried to divert the conversation toward music, but my exalted interlocutor went on with his recriminations, as if I had been in a position to help him: "The Czechoslovaks took our castle and our goods and gave us not even a cent; they didn't even leave me a scrap." Their wounds were not going to heal quickly! Subsequently, they came to lunch with us, on which occasion Archduchess Augusta smoked a cigar with gusto.

An endless succession of receptions was held in honor of our arrival. I remember one given by Mrs. Darányi, the prime minister's wife, in the attractive palace of the Presidency of the Council, which in the past had belonged to the famous horseman Count Sándor, the father of the renowned Princess Pauline Metternich. The palace had been built in pure Empire style and was full of Gobelins and of furniture upholstered with Aubusson tapestries. I also remember a brilliant ball (as in the old days!) given by Count László Széchenyi, former envoy to Washington and London, whose wife was born Vanderbilt. Their house on Andrássy-utca was not particularly nice architecturally, but it was of vast proportions. Balls were also organized at the French and German legations, as well as at the Casino Club.

HUNGARY'S INTERNAL AND EXTERNAL SITUATIONS

Hungary's internal politics had just then entered a new phase, and its diplomacy had begun to follow new paths. General Gömbös's death two months earlier had represented a major divide. The political system he had established during the three years he ruled Hungary had been tailor-made for a personality such as his and could not be maintained unchanged by a successor. The system consisted in respect of the constitutional formalities, which was meant to conceal a political ideology imbued with dictatorial tendencies. In continuous motion, driven by the sick ambition of introducing in his country the methods of a dictatorial government drawn on the German National-Socialist model, Gömbös undoubtedly wished he could be rid of parliamentary control. But he did not dare enter into open conflict with Parliament, the guardian of the constitutional order. Rather, he deemed it more appropriate (and more prudent) to give the governing Party of National Unity such exceptional privileges, especially in terms of organization, as to be tantamount to the institution of a truly totalitarian one-party regime.

Obstructed in their political activities, the opposition parties reacted by waging a relentless campaign, supported by Catholic circles, against the prime minister. This opposition was headed by Istvan Bethlen, former prime minister and undoubtedly the most outstanding figure in Hungarian politics, with at his side, directing the sharpest arrows against Gömbös, Tibor Eckhardt, the head of the Smallholders' party, the largest opposition party. Unusually in Hungarian political feuds, Eckhardt did not resist personal attacks against the prime minister.

The conservatives led by Bethlen and the agrarians directed by Eckhardt represented an undeniable force in Hungary, particularly formidable because Gömbös's dictatorial plans were supported in his own party only by a right-wing faction of some thirty deputies led by Béla Márton, the secretary-general. The other 140 or so deputies of the majority, although followers of Gömbös, were in favor of a policy of appeasement and conciliation, and were therefore opposed to a fight without quarter against the opposition. Serious convulsions would certainly have burst out in Hungarian domestic politics had General Gömbös's unexpected illness and death not intervened. To put an end to the unrest and ensure that constitutional procedures would be respected, Kálman Darányi was brought to power. Both the parliamentary majority and the opposition could trust him, since he had been minister of agriculture in Gömbös's government and had worked closely with Bethlen when the latter had been prime minister.

Darányi had played a relatively inconspicuous role in Hungarian politics and had avoided exposing himself in the ideological fights between government and opposition. Within his own party, though he had kept aloof from the dissensions that wrenched the followers of Gömbös, he leaned toward a somewhat progressive conservatism and had no inclination toward the far right's radicalism. He was a steadfast believer in constitutional principles. When he took over the government, he was therefore received with some misgivings by Gömbös's so-called "personal guard" (sympathizers of German National-Socialist methods), with warmth by the conservative groups in the majority party, and with well-disposed anticipation by the opposition and by unaffiliated politicians.

Darányi had been in power for only a few months when I arrived in Budapest, and yet one could discern a fundamental change in Hungary's domestic politics. Totalitarian tendencies, although latent in many sections of the population, seemed to have almost disappeared from the political horizon. After Gömbös's death, Secretary-General Béla Márton had been removed from the leadership of the Party of National Unity and rendered harmless by being "kicked upstairs" with the honorary title of co-president. And the far right had been very skillfully kept in the governing party, thereby preventing it from merging with the Nazis of the Magyar National-Socialist party.

The overriding issue now was electoral reform, made inevitable by the passing of time, much debated, but still in limbo. Hungary's domestic politics were indeed dominated by the question of constitutional reform, which in turn was made necessary by the need to pass a new electoral law. For the preceding sixteen years, Hungary had succeeded in maintaining its somewhat feudal set-up based on large estates and Count Bethlen's electoral law. In order not to have to yield on the matter of large estates (there had been no land expropriations, except to the extent required to give a few acres to the so-called "heroes" holding the highest war decorations), the Hungarian political leaders were willing to make concessions on electoral legislation issues. The legislation passed by Bethlen in 1922, still under the shock of Béla Kun's Communist rule and only two years after the introduction of universal and secret suffrage, abolished secret voting in most electoral districts. All politicians, including the prime minister, now realized that the reintroduction of secret balloting was absolutely necessary and that the system of open voting could not continue. Doubts remained, however, as to the Darányi government's determination to enact electoral reforms, since no date was set for the introduction of the relevant bill and since Internal Affairs Minister Kozma had stated that certain "corrections" were needed to obviate the danger of a radicalization of future parliaments as a result of an unfettered secret vote. These "corrections," it was generally understood, would mean an enlargement of the head of state's prerogatives, a new structure of the Upper House, and in particular a limitation of voting rights. This way, a barrier to parliamentary action would be established were it to veer toward extremism.

One aspect of domestic Hungarian politics that was followed attentively by the Little Entente, and especially by Czechoslovakia, was the monarchist movement. Partisans of a restoration of the Habsburgs could be found here and there in the various political parties, but it was only the Merged Christian party that had made it part of its platform. The government, however, was not in favor of a restoration for three reasons:

1. The Protestant population was against the establishment of a Catholic dynasty, especially since there were lingering memories of Kossuth and 1848, and resentment of the suppression of the Hungarian revolution by the troops of the House of Habsburg.
2. There was no unanimity as to who should be the monarch: Archduke Otto, Archduke Frederic (who was personally liked by all), or Archduke Joseph, former palatine of Hungary.
3. The opposition of Regent Horthy, who did not wish to be removed from the country's helm.

Besides, neither Berlin nor Rome would have looked kindly upon any move to make a Habsburg king of Hungary. As for Austria, Bethlen's opinion was that Austria would not lift a finger for fear of triggering off an Anschluss.

Hungary's foreign policy was closely linked to the Berlin-Rome Axis, to which it had adhered through the Rome tripartite agreement. Under the Gömbös administration the Hungaro-German friendship had eclipsed the relations between Budapest and Rome, but as soon as the Darányi government took over, positions were reversed. With Gömbös's death, the most ardent admirer of Hitler and of his methods disappeared. Hungary's diplomatic activities were now directed, to Berlin's great disappointment, by the more moderate Foreign Minister Colman Kánya.

The consequence was that after Ciano's visit to Berlin and the further strengthening of the relations between the two powers of the Axis, Budapest was made to understand that it no longer was of primary concern to the Wilhelmstrasse. Moreover, the Austro-German agreement was seen as a real threat in Hungarian governmental circles, frightened by the thought that the strengthening of National-Socialist influence in Austria might revive the old German dream of *Drang nach Osten*. This fear was clearly apparent in a speech given by Bethlen in Milan.

German influence over Austria was viewed at the Palazzo Chigi as an unavoidable evolution, almost as a fait accompli that could no longer be prevented. All that Italian diplomacy could still strive for was to prevent the next step—that is, the extension of Hitlerian influence over Hungary. Italy had thus become Hungary's only bulwark against Nazi imperialism, hence the great esteem in which Mussolini was held in Hungarian governing circles, especially after his famous revisionist speech.

The coolness between Berlin and Budapest, which was also partly due to the ill treatment of the German minority, was revealed among other things by a series of antirevisionist articles that appeared in the German press (in particular those of Rosenberg in *Völkischer Beobachter*, supporting the Romanian position). These articles deeply wounded the sensitivity of Hungarian chauvinists. In an effort to repair relations, the Hungarian minister of internal affairs, Nicholas Kozma, was sent to Berlin under the pretext of visiting his German counterpart, Frick. Budapest, however, overlooked one detail that was highly important from a Nazi point of view: namely, that Kozma's mother was of Jewish origin. As a result, neither Göring nor Neurath organized for him the receptions to which he was entitled.

A certain coolness could also be detected in Hungary's diplomatic relations with Poland, as a consequence of Warsaw's resumption of a pro-French political orientation. Nonetheless, a covert pamphlet and press campaign advocating the establishment of a common border between Poland and Hungary was encouraged. Taking advantage of the tensions between Warsaw and Prague, a plea was made to replace the "Czechoslovak-Russian corridor" with a "Polish-Hungarian corridor."

HUNGARY AND THE LITTLE ENTENTE

Hungary's attitude toward the Little Entente was one of unwavering hostility. Any opportunity was seized to attack and disparage Romania, Czechoslovakia, and Yugoslavia. Czechoslovakia was considered the number one enemy, not so much because of the Hungarian minority in Slovakia (which Kánya himself admitted to be the one best treated), but because it was seen as the weakest of the three countries, owing to Nazi enmity. Romania came in second place, and in the third Yugoslavia, to which ceaseless overtures had been made, even in Gömbös's time. My Yugoslav colleague confessed that he was embarrassed to be treated as the "darling" of the Hungarians, who did not even eschew from speaking of a personal union between Hungary and Yugoslavia! No one in Belgrade was interested in a détente with Hungary, he said, and no one in our countries should be, because all of this was hypocrisy. However, my Austrian colleague, Baar-Baarenfels, former deputy chancellor, divulged to me that Vukicević had asked him to intercede with Kánya for a Magyaro-Yugoslav rapprochement. Vukicević told me that my predecessor, Grigorcea, placing no trust in Kánya, had nicknamed him "the old crocodile" and that, in view of their bad personal relations, he had merely left a business card when departing from Budapest. "One can't get anywhere with Budapest," concluded Vukicević, "what we need is to have strong armies to defend ourselves."

In the opinion of my German colleague Mackensen, the Hungarian revisionist campaign directed in particular against Czechoslovakia and Romania was the result of Mussolini's speech—"Eine Verrücktheit,"[5] Mackensen called it, because there are things that are done when it is possible but that are not promised, especially when one has no intention of keeping one's word. The Duce, Mackensen said, "brandishes a box of chocolates under the Hungarians' noses, as one would do with children. It is only this that enables the Hungarians to delude themselves; *from no other side are they encouraged in this regard.*" The American envoy told me, confidentially of course, that the head of the Hitlerian organizations in Hungary had admitted to him that nothing would be gained by having Transylvania's fate decided by a plebiscite, as suggested at times by Hungarian political groups, since the German minority, which played an important cultural and economic role in Transylvania, would in any event also vote against the reattachment of the province to Hungary. Moreover, he said, not even Italy was seriously considering actions aimed at revising the Treaty of Trianon. Even Kánya had reportedly told him he disapproved of this useless stirring up of passions, with potentially dangerous consequences for the Hungarian minorities; but could he rebuff the sole champion of the Magyar illusion? The Czechoslovak envoy, Kobr, went even further. He believed that his former colleague from the

[5] An imbecility.

Austro-Hungarian consular service, Kánya, was personally not that opposed to a rapprochement with the Little Entente, but that he feared Berlin and Rome, which lorded it in Budapest. Oh, the "old crocodile!" My French colleague remained highly skeptical of Kánya's alleged "personal attitude." "He's an old fox, after all," he told me. "There is no hope for you with the Hungarians . . . unless you give up the Czechoslovaks!" *Le Temps,* in an editorial of December 21, 1936, wrote: "Breaking up the Little Entente is the main objective of the opponents of peace in Central and Eastern Europe. Were this breakup to succeed, Romania and Yugoslavia would be immediately exposed to the same peril as Czechoslovakia, even though Czechoslovakia, owing to its geographical position, is more directly threatened." The Italian envoy, Vinci, told me more or less the same, pointing out that the Hungarian government was quite favorably disposed to a détente with Romania and that, in consequence, the anti-Romanian campaign of the Budapest press would soon cease and be replaced by an anti-Czechoslovak campaign. How did he know that? Was it perhaps he who was transmitting instructions to that effect, in accordance with a tactical plan elaborated by the Palazzo Chigi?

I had a strange conversation with the Soviet envoy, Bekzadjian, an Armenian with a forbidding countenance but a milder nature than his ferocious face seemed to imply (that is perhaps why he ended so tragically). We talked in German, and he summarized his impressions as follows: "The Hungarians are the Germans' lackeys, and nothing can be done with them."

Conservative spheres, however, did see some interest in a rapprochement with their non-Slav neighbor in the Danube Basin. In his Milan speech, Bethlen stressed the danger of a "Russo-Slavic" hegemony in Central Europe, which would be quite as fatal to Romania as to Hungary. In the event of a Russo-German war and a Russian victory, he emphasized—with amazing prescience—that all the nations in the Danube Basin would fall under Moscow's dominion. Bethlen was in fact addressing the government in Bucharest when he added: "The real peril for the Romanian nation is that it is surrounded on three sides by a sea of Slavs. Romania will be able to accomplish its mission in the world and safeguard its independence in the future only if it reaches an understanding with the neighboring Hungarian nation. Otherwise, it will fall under Russian rule, which in time would mean the extinction of the Romanian nation." This obviously overrated by a good deal the contribution Hungary could have brought to the defense of Romania's independence.

Bethlen's views were also conveyed to me through his brother-in-law, Count Armin Mikes, when he came to see me at the legation. I had quite a few things in common with this venerable Transylvanian grandee, distinguished, and adorned with a white beard. His estates in Transylvania neighbored those, in Wallachia, of my great-grandparents Sibiceanu, being separated only by a mountain ridge. Mikes, moreover, had been a schoolmate of our uncle Barbu Catargi at the Theresianum, and had personally known the recent generations of our families, "probably better than you yourselves," he used to tell us. He had been a guest of Carol I at Peleş Castle, and he had fairly frequent audiences with Carol II. I used to meet him from time to time at the Jockey Club. He always stressed that, although a Magyar from head to toe, he never forgot that he also was a Romanian citizen. Mikes's daughter, the beautiful Hannah (with whom I remained on friendly terms also in exile, when she was called Mrs. Van Horne), was reportedly engaged at that time to King Zog of Albania, as was confirmed to me by the Italian envoy. I believe that in the end it was she who called off the engagement, not being attracted by the prospect of settling down in Tirana with a Muslim husband.

Mikes, after the usual recriminations about the expropriation of large estates and his problems with the local authorities (I promised to intercede for their resolution), came to the point of his visit. He told me he had been empowered by Darányi and Kánya to inform me of the Hungarian government's wish to reach a détente with Romania, but for this it would be necessary that the "persecution of minorities" cease in Romania. Again the same old story! I replied that we, too, wanted a détente, but that we could not always be those who took the first step. The Hungarian press campaign against us intensified daily, and the slightest administrative problem experienced by a Hungarian was trumpeted in the whole wide world as systematic persecution. I reminded him in this connection of the miserable lot of the Transylvanian Romanians during Hungary's rule, of the infamous Apponyi law,[6] and of so many others. Besides, the German minority in Hungary also complained of the Hungarian authorities' persecution in educational and church matters. Mikes said he agreed with me: "I will mention this to Darányi and Kánya." The first person to whom he was going to report the conversation, however, was undoubtedly his brother-in-law, Bethlen.

Another "Romanian citizen" from Transylvania who spoke to me more or less in the same vein was Count Nicholas Bánffy, a likable old

[6]A series of educational acts aimed at the Magyarization of the minority populations.

man, refined and cultured. I had met him at the Genoa Conference, in the incarnation of Hungary's foreign minister. Now, he told me, he was exclusively a man of letters and a painter. He, too, advocated a rapprochement between Romania and Hungary.

I encountered the same trial balloon in a conversation with the likable envoy of the United States, Montgomery. He shared with me his impression that the Hungarians were becoming conciliatory toward Romania, saving for the time being their most venomous arrows for Czechoslovakia. Apor told him that a step forward could be made during my mission, because I was a "fine fellow." And Montgomery, amused, had replied, "I guess it is the very first time in my life I hear you saying about a Romanian that he is a fine fellow!" My American colleague gave me the friendly advice of getting in touch with the head of the opposition, Tibor Eckhardt, a promising and conciliatory man. I answered I would be interested in meeting him; I did not know then how closely I would collaborate with Eckhardt during our common exile in New York.

It was more or less the same conversation I had with my opposite number, Bárdossy, Hungary's envoy to Bucharest, who was very much liked in Romania. Later, he was going to become prime minister during the war and be executed by the Communists, after a sham treason trial. I remember my lunch with Bárdossy at the Vadaskürt Hotel, where he showed himself most courteous, despite his inevitable recriminations about the treatment of minorities and press attacks. I interrupted him, mentioning the miserable fate of the Romanian minority in Hungary and the incessant anti-Romanian campaign of the Budapest newspapers. We finally came to an agreement that each of us would strive to achieve at least a détente in the relations between our two countries. (A note from our Foreign Ministry informed me of a conversation held on February 3, 1937, between the Romanian undersecretary of state and Bárdossy: "The Hungarian envoy, Bárdossy, spoke to me in the most laudatory terms of the good impression Mr. Bossy had made in Budapest, and he mentioned anew the Hungarian government's intention of finding a way to improve relations between Budapest and Bucharest.")

In a broader context, I was impressed at that time—and I am even more impressed now because of their prophetic character—by the views of my British colleague, Sir Geoffrey Knox, the League of Nations' former High Commissioner in the Saar and a future ambassador to Brazil. He was thoroughly convinced that with Hitler's ascension to power, Germany wanted war. Its cadre of officers had not yet been brought up to full complement, Knox told me, but in two years' time, when that will have been done, Germany will state its conditions and, if they are not met, it will unleash war. This was being said in 1937, and in 1939, two years later almost to the day, the prediction of Britain's envoy to Hungary was to be fulfilled. He also foresaw that Germany would not rejoin the League of Nations, "since one constantly gives in to it." And Knox added: "If the Allied powers had faced it with a united and firm front, then, yes, it would have been in Germany's interest to come back to Geneva, but why would it do so under the present situation?"

I had my first real political talk with the Minister of Foreign Affairs, Kánya, on January 23, 1937. After a lengthy time spent on generalities, he finally decided to broach the issue: "Tell me, Excellency, will our countries have to hate each other forever? Friendship between them, I know, is impossible, or at least impossible to conceive before a century. But couldn't we at least have normal relations?" I replied, "Romania is as eager as Hungary to reach a détente." Kánya: "Hungary wants a détente, but not at any price. If this cannot be achieved, Hungary will be compelled to pursue its present policy, and even to intensify it." I listed then all the tokens of good will shown by the Romanian government, the last one being the removal from the pedestal of the Vasile Lucaciu monument, in Satu-Mare, of the Hungarian coat of arms, set on a dragon being transpierced by the lance of a Romanian soldier. This and all the other many conciliatory gestures had not been met by an equal good will from the Budapest government but, on the contrary, by an intensification of press attacks. Kánya acknowledged the good intentions of the present Romanian government, but stated that a détente between Romania and Hungary could be reached only under two conditions:

1. An improvement in the treatment of the Hungarian minority in Romania.
2. The recognition of parity of rights for Hungary in the matter of armaments.

Concerning the first condition, he complained, with an overabundance of details, about the alleged persecution of the Hungarian minority in Romania. In turn, I mentioned to him the suffering of the Romanian minority in Hungary. "But they are only fifteen thousand," he retorted. I contradicted him: "They are sixty thousand, but their number has no bearing on the matter."

Concerning the second condition, the Hungarian minister of foreign affairs asked us to make *"un beau geste,"* granting Hungary what had already been given to Germany and Austria: "Make a handsome gesture, my dear fellow, make a handsome gesture!" I told him that in this matter, too, the Little Entente could show itself conciliatory, but that until now he had not brought up the matter with either me or my colleagues. Kánya replied that he had avoided making such a request for fear that it would be met by the condition that he conclude a mutual assistance treaty, which he was not prepared to do. I asked if he would be equally opposed to a nonaggression treaty. In view of the military agreements that bound the Little Entente to other powers, he said, such a treaty would be illusive for Hungary.

However, Kánya did not leave me with the impression that he was absolutely opposed to any formula with a similar aim. And yet when I suggested, as a last recourse, a mere declaration of adherence to Politis's definition of aggression, Kánya flared up: "No way! It's a formula inspired by Litvinov!" "Then, what solution do you see?" Kánya: "It is a problem that will have to be carefully studied through diplomatic channels. Territorial issues should in any case be left aside, and one should limit oneself to a declaration of principles." Kánya wished nevertheless to know under what conditions the Romanian government believed the Little Entente would agree to recognize parity of armaments rights to Hungary, "taking into account, however, the views I have just mentioned to you." And he asked me to come see him "when you have learned something in this regard."

There were several reasons why the Hungarian government was keen to obtain this parity of rights. In the first place, it was a question of pride. Then, in the absence of such parity, it was difficult to secure internal or external credits to reequip the armed forces. And finally, training of the armed forces was hindered by the need to conceal certain types of matériel (aircraft, tanks, and so forth). Indeed, the Hungarians had violated most of the military clauses of the Trianon Treaty. Conscription had been indirectly reintroduced by the laws of physical education and air defense (1935), which provided for sanctions against draft evaders. Similarly, the total strength of the armed forces, which had been set at 35,000 by the Trianon Treaty, was in fact 60,000, and even 90,000 during the summer maneuvers. The number of officers and noncommissioned officers was five times the one authorized by the treaty. It was the same with regard to the quantity and types of arms, where the Hungarians paid no attention to the treaty's provisions. Contrary to those provisions, the Hungarians now had an air force, armored vehicles, and tanks. This equipment was bought from Germany, Italy, and Austria, and, in addition, arms and munitions were produced in great quantities in Hungary itself, thereby breaking other provisions of the treaty.

Hungary was thus rearming, and everybody knew it. The examples set by Germany and Austria, as well as the general atmosphere in Europe, were that many reasons inducing the Budapest government not to make substantial concessions in order to secure an official recognition of a state of affairs that was well known and tolerated. And this the more so since, heeding the recommendations of the Stresa Conference, even the Little Entente showed itself willing, in principle, to recognize parity of rights to Hungary in matters of armaments, but only within the framework of regional security guarantees. The Hungarian government wanted nevertheless to settle the matter through negotiations, because Germany was discouraging it from taking any rash steps that could be seen as a provocation by the Little Entente. Even Italy, in spite of its declaration at the Italo-Austro-Hungarian tripartite conference in Vienna, was not pushing for the creation of a fait accompli. I also learned at that time, through my Czechoslovak colleague, that Italy's envoy to Prague, de Facendis, was trying to find out under what conditions an understanding could be reached on this matter.

✧ ✧ ✧

One of the first things that struck me in my new mission was the effort of Hungarian diplomacy to break up the Little Entente by trying to draw close to Yugoslavia: the policy was too transparent. Forgotten were Croatia, the western Banat, and the Bačka. While Romania was vehemently denounced for the alleged treatment of its minorities and Czechoslovakia for its rapprochement with Soviet Russia, Yugoslavia had all of a sudden become the object of Budapest's praises and advances. The Belgrade government, which had been lambasted two years earlier as being the most inimical of all the Little Entente governments toward minorities, had been transformed as if by magic into the most fatherly protector of its Magyar population. All the means of seduction Hungarian diplomacy could muster were used in the hope of severing a link in the chain binding the states of the Little Entente.

It was clear that as soon as Berlin and Rome had decided to attract Yugoslavia to their side, "instructions" had been sent to the Budapest government to seek a rapprochement with Belgrade. The injunction was followed faithfully, albeit not skillfully enough and without sufficient deftness. Instead of a slow, adroit movement that would gradually prepare the two countries' public opinions for such an unexpected about-face, this diametric change in attitude toward Yugoslavia was introduced abruptly.

During his official visit to Budapest, Ciano had assured my Yugoslav colleague, Vukicević, that Hungary's revisionism was not going to threaten his country's territorial integrity, that it was aimed "in other directions." From then on, it was indeed noticeable that the formerly most Slavophobe politicians and newspapermen in Hungary fell over each other in making flattering statements about Yugoslavia. Many articles compared most favorably Yugoslavia with Romania; one even went as far as to announce the "revival of the traditional [*sic*] brotherhood between Hungarians and Serbs," while another urged the Hungarian minority to be loyal to Yugoslavia.

Vukicević told me he was literally overwhelmed by the Hungarians' wooing. But he expressed skepticism about this new enthusiasm of the Hungarians, who can control neither their pretended likes nor their hatred toward others. The Belgrade government, according to Vukicević, did not delude itself about the real meaning of this volte-face by Hungary, and Prime Minister Stoiadinović, in a February 1937 speech at the Skupština, insisted on the "untouchability of the borders" established at Trianon.

At one point, Vukicević apprised me that the Hungarian government was considering the possibility of reaching separate understandings with Yugoslavia and Romania, but not with Czechoslovakia so as not to displease Berlin. My government then authorized me to state, if such a suggestion were actually made to me (as it was several times), that the Little Entente was willing to negotiate only as a unit, not separately. Isolating Czechoslovakia was a persistent aim of the Third Reich. Kánya admitted to Maugras that Göring had strongly urged him to reach an understanding with Yugoslavia and had intimated that a rapprochement with Romania would be viewed favorably in Berlin. But a détente between Budapest and Prague would be contrary to Germany's interests. Ciano's visit to Belgrade in March 1937 was, of course, greeted with rapture by the Budapest press, and it was seen as a "historic reversal" that would have favorable consequences on the relations between Hungary and Yugoslavia. One could also detect the hope that Yugoslavia would be attracted by the Rome-Berlin Axis, thus weakening the Little Entente bond. With the Hungarian authorities' usual lack of measure, the only three foreign envoys invited to attend the reception in the Budapest railway station for the Italian sovereigns during their official visit (May 1937) were those of Austria, Germany, and Yugoslavia—as if Yugoslavia had become allied to Italy (and thus to Hungary!).

HUNGARY'S RELATIONS WITH GERMANY

The weakening of Germany's interest in Hungary and in its claims led to a weakened position of the Hungarian government not only abroad but also at home. Indeed, Hungary's foreign policy was above all a matter of domestic policy, and it was the main rostrum from which the Horthy regime presented itself to the nation. It was for that reason that the Budapest government, through spectacular gestures of all sorts, sought on the one hand to discredit to some extent the leaders of the Reich and to bypass them as allies, but, on the other, to give Hungarian public opinion the impression that there had been no change in the old bonds between the two countries and that the well-known antirevisionist articles in *Völkischer Beobachter* and *Der Angriff* were merely intemperate outbursts by people without official responsibility, such as Rosenberg. One of these gestures was the Hitler-Horthy meeting in Berchtesgaden; another was the deliberately spread rumor of the regent's official visit to Berlin. There was also the visit of Undersecretary of State Lammers, from the Reich chancellery, invited by the Hungarian government, and that of Hungary's minister of internal affairs, Nicholas Kozma, to Berlin (a not very successful visit, as noted above); and, finally, the hunting party organized by Regent Horthy on December 28 and 29 in honor of former German Chancellor von Papen (now the Reich's envoy to Vienna) and of Baron Hennett, former Austrian envoy to Budapest. This hunt elicited numerous comments because the regent, a head of state, had extended to his guests the unusual courtesy of accompanying them himself from Budapest to Gödöllo. Political significance was ascribed to this gesture, which was precisely what the Hungarian leaders sought. This interpretation, however, went too far.

It is obvious that a meeting between men of the stature of Admiral Horthy and former Chancellor von Papen was not going to be limited to hunting matters and that their conversation would also touch on current international issues. This said, however, it is difficult to believe that important decisions were taken or that crucial negotiations were held. Indeed, neither Prime Minister Darányi nor Foreign Minister Kánya was present, and in view of the latter's personality, it was out of the question that any new policy would have been mapped out in his absence. Besides, in view of the many official connections between Germany and Hungary, of the influential role played by my colleague Mackensen, as well as of the almost daily contacts between the two countries' leaders, there was no need to arrange international visits in order to draw up new agreements.

It therefore seemed to me that the truth lay elsewhere. The Hungarian government realized that the German policy—the one advocated by Göring and Rosenberg, certainly at their Führer's instigation, not the one proposed by the Wilhelmstrasse—was beginning to move away from Hungary, a static country shaped by the past, and toward the new states created after the war on the principle of nationalities, which were the dynamic forces of the future. This being the situation, and since the Reich could not be persuaded to make specific promises to Hungary, it was at least necessary to save appearances and to conceal from the country the loosening of the Germano-Hungarian bonds.

Yet the only concession to Hungary's wounded pride was a partial softening of Rosenberg's antirevisionist position. In an interview published in *Új Magyarország,* he criticized Czechoslovakia, but did not mention the other two members of the Little Entente. There is no doubt that the Hungarian government would have liked to be able to lean equally on the two powers of the Axis, but if it had to choose, it would rather have the protection of the stronger one, that is, of the Reich. The temporary preference given to Italy was only a "second-best" solution. And indeed, it was Hitler, more than Mussolini, who three years later gave Hungary the ephemeral territorial satisfaction of the Vienna arbitral award.

HUNGARIAN ADVANCES TOWARD ROMANIA

As I mentioned earlier, the political figure of greatest note in Hungary was, without any doubt, former prime minister Istvan Bethlen. Even though he was no longer in office, none of his countrymen could explain as precisely as he the political line followed by the Budapest government. It was therefore with obvious interest that I learned that he wanted to meet me and that he was inviting me for a confidential conversation at his house. When I got there, on February 17, I came face to face with a distinguished, refined, and polite man. We began by chatting about friends we had in common, and especially about Toncsi and Genny Mocsonyi, relatives of my wife. Then we moved on to political topics. Count Bethlen believed the time had come for a détente between our two countries. If Romania were willing to conclude with Hungary an agreement concerning the Hungarian minority's schools and churches, along the lines of the similar Romano-Yugoslav agreement, the Budapest government might undertake to silence the revisionist campaign, giving this problem a purely theoretical character of a distant national goal. Bethlen drew my attention to the fact that under his administrations, as well as under the present government, the word "revision" had never been officially uttered. The only remaining serious dispute with Romania was therefore the treatment of the Hungarian minority in Transylvania. It was not advisable, according to him, to avoid the issue because it was an internal one; rather, one should seek to eradicate this sore point. And in order to resolve the dispute, moving it from the plane of generalities to a concrete plane, the former prime minister argued for an agreement on schools and churches.

I answered that the agreement with Yugoslavia to which he referred was the outcome of an old and tried friendship. Prior to marriage, I said, comes the engagement: let's begin with a détente before broaching such ticklish issues. Why not establish, for the time being, normal relations bereft of belligerence, and postpone until later the discussion of the thornier issues. It would therefore be necessary to prepare as soon as possible a general atmosphere of détente between Hungary and the Little Entente.

Count Bethlen seemed to be in agreement with my views, and he even suggested the possibility of concluding a ten-year nonaggression treaty. I replied that, in my opinion, such a proposal could form the basis of discussions, provided it was made simultaneously to all three governments of the Little Entente. Bethlen objected that Hungary could not negotiate with the Little Entente as a political unit, but that it might perhaps be possible for it to conclude simultaneously three identical nonaggression treaties, one with each of the three states. I said it might not be impossible to find a satisfactory formula, but that so far none of my colleagues from the Little Entente had been approached in this sense by the Hungarian government. Bethlen asked whether I thought such a step could lead to results. I answered as follows: "Personally, I believe that if Mr. Kánya approached me and my colleagues of the Little Entente with an offer of negotiations based on a proposed nonaggression treaty, this offer might be accepted as a basis for negotiations by our governments, which also desire improved relations with Hungary."

We parted most cordially. I asked him when he would return to power. "Oh, by-and-by I will certainly come back to power" (a prediction that was not to be fulfilled). "Meanwhile, as I am on excellent terms with Mr. Darányi [his former undersecretary of state] and with Mr. Kánya [which was not true], I am at your disposal to talk to them on your behalf when you judge this necessary. Just get in touch with me." A few days later, Bethlen had a similar meeting with Vukicević, who told me that he, too, had explained that Belgrade could not conceive of a détente with Hungary without simultaneous détentes between Budapest and the other two members of the Little Entente. In view of the line adopted, Bethlen, of course, did not seek a meeting with Kobr: the objective was, after all, to create a breach between, on the one hand, Romania and Yugoslavia and, on the other, Czechoslovakia, foredoomed to extinction by Hitler.

Count Bethlen's views—which he also set forth in the Christmas and March 28 issues of *Pesti Napló*—were beginning to spread, at least in the press. *Pesti Napló,* the government's paper, was advocating the conclusion of a nonaggression pact between Romania and Hungary as the only way of ensuring the welfare of the Hungarian minority in Transylvania. The opposition's paper, *Magyarország,* characterized Bethlen's proposal for direct Romano-Hungarian negotiations as an "event of historic significance." It added that when the Hungarians realized that "the Romanian government will not admit foreign interference in the resolution of the Hungarian minority problem," they would be able to benefit from the same advantages as the German minority in Romania. The article ended with the untypical statement that in Bucharest "there is a desire to reach an understanding between Hungary and Romania." What was much more striking, however, was that even the minister of foreign affairs, Colman Kánya, wrote in a *Pester Lloyd* editorial of February 23, 1937: "all states confronting each other over disputes ought to strive to eliminate those difficulties by face-to-face discussions in an atmosphere of mutual trust." Mentioning then the conclusion of the Polono-German nonaggression treaty (of such an ephemeral value!) and the Yugoslavo-Bulgarian friendship pact, Kánya expressed the wish "that states in other parts of Europe as well follow these examples, seeking despite all the difficulties of the past the road to mutual concessions and the establishment of an atmosphere allowing agreements suited to present conditions."

This was the first time the Hungarian foreign minister had openly favored direct negotiations with neighboring states. It might be assumed that his new position was somewhat influenced by the publicly known views of Count Bethlen. Sensing that Bethlen coveted, if not the prime ministership, then at least the Ministry of Foreign Affairs, Kánya wanted to make it plain that he, too, could be instrumental in getting under way direct negotiations with the neighboring states. Bethlen's immediate inclusion in the government was thus not necessary, since he, Kánya, would also be able to carry out such a policy.

As if following instructions from the government, there was at that time a gradual stepping up of press criticism of Budapest's old stubbornness and intransigence in situations that could not be altered. Even in the case of Romania, there were quite frequent demands for the abandonment of the futile attitude of denial and for the espousal of a realistic and useful policy course.

I took advantage of a meeting with Kánya to steer the conversation to this new trend and to his article in *Pester Lloyd*. Unprompted, he told me that the passage referring to direct negotiations with neighboring countries was addressed to Romania. In answer to my question of whether it was also addressed to the other two governments of the Little Entente, Kánya replied that Hungary could not deal with the Little Entente as a political entity, but that he might possibly talk separately with each of the three component countries. He hastened to add, however, that even this solution did not seem possible, since each of the governments would have a different position. He cited as an example the fact that Czechoslovakia—and in particular Prime Minister Hodža—wanted ultimately to forge a Danubian federation, while Romania and Yugoslavia did not. I replied that I did not know whether my government had taken a position on a plan the implementation of which still seemed so far off, but that it seemed more realistic to me to examine the possibility of an immediate détente than to engage in theoretical and academic discussions. My Polish colleague, Leon Orlowski, told me that Kánya had confided to him that "relations with Romania have improved perceptively, thanks to the new Romanian envoy, with whose presence in Budapest I am delighted." To the French envoy, Maugras, Kánya admitted similarly that he found good will on the part of the Romanian government, but that for Hungary a détente could only be the prelude to a subsequent agreement on the issue of minorities.

Kánya made a speech to the same effect on March 1, at a banquet given in his honor by the Association of Newspaper Correspondents. "The objectives of Hungary's foreign policy," he stated, "are loyalty toward friends, the rejection of any thought of adventure, and the establishment of correct relations with the states from which we are still alienated by fairly numerous disputes." For that purpose, he emphasized, "the only path we must follow is that of efforts to resolve pending problems through mutual understanding and to reestablish trust; for it is only through deepening trust that we shall be able to see our efforts crowned by a successful move toward a true peace." He showed himself similarly conciliatory regarding Hungary's relations with the Little Entente when, on May 26, he addressed Parliament during the budget debate. He was in favor of an "honest understanding," following "serious negotiations," an attitude due, in all likelihood, to advice from London, and even from Rome. As for the leader of the opposition, Tibor Eckhardt, he was advocating, also during the budget debate, the conclusion of nonaggression treaties between Hungary and the Little Entente.

DOMESTIC TURBULENCE AND NAZI THREAT IN HUNGARY

Even as the Budapest government was endeavoring to give the impression that it was pursuing détente abroad, a series of internal perturbations seemed to rock the established order. Quite serious clashes were reported at Miskolc between the followers of Count Alexander Festetics's Arrow Cross and the Social-Democrats. Although Count Festetics's movement had originated among the ranks of the government party, it was adopting a Hitlerian ideology and was drifting further and further away from the program of the National Unity party. The directing spirit of the National-Socialist party was not its president, Alexander Festetics, but Zoltán Meskö. There was also a so-called "independent" National-Socialist party, in fact a splinter of the first one, led by Deputy Bálogh, whose adherents were mainly in Debrecen and in Hajdú county. Although not yet represented in Parliament, there was as well the National-Socialist faction of the Smallholders' party, the so-called Scythe and Skull movement headed by a certain Böszörmenyi, who propagated Hitlerian ideas with a marked agrarian slant, so as to make them more acceptable to farmers, and whose electoral fief was Békéscsaba and Hodmezövásárhely. The Nazi groups in Hungary were financed by Germany through the cooperative society Hangya, which specialized in commerce between Germany and Hungary. This was a well-known fact, and even the cautious *Pester Lloyd* hinted at it, expressing its indignation that a great power would interfere, by monetary means, in the internal affairs of a weaker country. There were also rumors—perhaps exaggerated—of a projected Nazi coup d'état, which disquieted many people and, obviously, especially those on the left.

The Darányi government thus had its hands full with the so-called "invisible front" of the far-right organizations, the most active of which were Count Festetics's Arrow Cross, the Blue Cross of Csillery, and Rajniss's National-Socialist party. Their demonstrations followed each other in quick succession. At the end of a meeting in Miskolc, the Socialists set upon the Hungarian Nazis, and the police had to intervene to bring the fray under control. It was asserted that the government had discovered an attempt by right-wing organizations to bring about a change in the country's regime, although this was officially denied. In Pecs, there were anti-Semitic demonstrations, also of Nazi origin. Jewish students, who were coming to receive their M.D. degrees, were gravely mistreated by teeming groups of anti-Semitic students, who occupied the university building and thus prevented the ceremony from being held. Family members who had come to attend the commencement became likewise victims of the Nazis' abuses. The Pecs University had to be temporarily closed.

Another serious disturbance was meanwhile occurring at the coal mines near Pecs, which were operated by the Austrian company Donaudampfschiffahrtgesellschaft. The inadequately paid miners demanded wage increases. The company not only turned them down but also threatened to lock them out. The miners then occupied the mines, refused to leave, and began a hunger strike. Their comrades above ground, along with their families, undertook a noisy demonstration against the company's management. The gendarmes failed to stop them and, after the statutory warnings, opened fire on the crowd, killing three workers and wounding many others. It took several days before order was reestablished and the strikers were ejected from the mines. Faced by these serious disturbances, Prime Minister Darányi announced drastic measures against troublemakers, whether of the right or the left, to maintain peace and order in the country.

The immediate reaction to these events was a perceptible intensification of anti-Nazi sentiment in Hungary's political life. The Merged Christian party, through the voice of Deputy Makay, declared that the Hungarians had "no wish for a 'hooked cross,' but only for Christ's cross, which shines on the crown of St. Stephen." In a public conference, Deputy Homonnay drew attention to "the immeasurable danger for Hungary of the penetration of Nazism in all of the German-speaking populations outside the Reich's borders." He even went so far as to declare that, from the standpoint of the Magyar nation's survival, "the German dream of annexing the Pannonic plain up to Lake Balaton," on the pretext that it was partially inhabited by Saxons, was at least as grave a peril as "the proximity of the Little Entente." The speaker saw the restoration of monarchy in Hungary as the only way of checking the spread of pan-Germanism, pan-Slavism, and communism in the heart of Europe.

Nevertheless, the daily *8 Órai Ujság,* which along with *Pesti Napló* and *Magyarsag* belonged to a concern chaired by Bethlen and reflected his views, while recognizing the advantages for Hungary of the restoration of the House of Habsburg, underscored that "such a move is made only when it is feasible," and that "the monarchic question being important but not vital for Hungary;" it should be postponed to an auspicious historic moment. It was precisely the view Bethlen outlined to me during a conversation. "The return of Archduke Otto to Austria," he added, "would not prevent an Anschluss; on the contrary, it would precipitate it, and the Hungarian government will do all it can to spare the country such an outcome." Bethlen's opposition to a restoration of the Habsburgs was also reflected in Kánya's speech to newspaper correspondents on March 1, when he said, "Hungary is against any adventure"—a hint to the legitimists that, while in principle it was not opposed to the monarchist idea, the Darányi government had a sufficient sense of reality to know that this was not an opportune time to raise the question. Besides, even Italy was reticent in this regard. Needing to strengthen the Berlin-Rome Axis, following the urgings of Hitler who was preparing his takeover of Austria, Mussolini was indeed muting the legitimist groups in Vienna and Budapest.

AUSTRIA AND HUNGARY'S RELATIONS WITH ITALY

During an official visit to Budapest in March 1937, Austrian Chancellor Schuschnigg disclosed to the Hungarian leaders his apprehension at Hitler's progressively more transparent menaces toward Austria. Schuschnigg felt very isolated, sensing that he had been abandoned by Mussolini, who was now almost openly supporting Germany's hand. No longer deeming the Rome-Berlin Axis to be a reliable support, Schuschnigg is said to have shown with great insistence to the Hungarian government the necessity for Austria to draw closer to the Little Entente, and particularly to Czechoslovakia. As a matter of fact, a passage in the communiqué issued at the end of the Austrian chancellor's visit included, at his request, an overture toward the Little Entente. On his side, Eckhardt gave an interview to *Le Petit Journal* in which he advocated the formation of an Austrian-Hungarian-Czechoslovak bloc, as a result of which he was invited by Hodža to Prague. The meeting, however, apparently led to naught, since the head of the Hungarian Smallholders' party did not see the possibility of a Danubian agreement unless the influence of all major powers was rejected, and especially unless the Czechoslovak-Soviet treaty was abrogated, which was unacceptable to Hodža. Besides, Kánya made it clear that the Hungarian government was not prepared to draw closer to Prague for fear of alienating Berlin. "I cannot discard the German card from my hand," he used to say, "no matter how detrimental Hitlerian propaganda may prove to be to the current regimes in Budapest and Vienna."

Nevertheless, a restoration of the past close relations between Austria and Italy was sought, and for that purpose a meeting between Schuschnigg and Mussolini was arranged. The results of that meeting in Venice were ambiguous. The Italian press—especially Gaida in *Giornale d'Italia*—proclaimed the indestructibility of the Rome Protocols and stated that, in Venice, the Austrian movement in favor of a Vienna-Budapest-Prague triangle had been stopped forever. In Austrian circles, by contrast, there was bitterness as they began to realize that "Italy has given Austria to Germany" as a price for the Reich's friendship. In his wish for Italian policy to make headway primarily in the Mediterranean area, the Duce had interest in conclusively consolidating the Berlin-Rome Axis, giving up for that purpose his aspiration for hegemony in the Danube Basin and the Balkans. Nevertheless, the Italian dictator intended to keep in this zone now ceded to Germany a few "defensive positions," such as his ties with Hungary, the agreements with Yugoslavia, the friendship with Poland, and an eventual rapprochement with Romania. But the predominant political role and economic penetration would be Berlin's. Austria was to be the first victim of this new course of Mussolini's.

As for the Hungarian government, it voiced through Kánya its satisfaction at the "reconfirmation of the indissolubility of the Rome Protocols," which, according to the final communiqué from Venice, were to remain open "also to the other Danube states, under conditions to be determined case by case." This calmed to some extent fears that Italy, which had sacrificed Hungarian revisionism toward Yugoslavia, might be tempted to enter into agreement with another Little Entente state, thereby fencing in Hungarian irredentism in still another direction. The pledge that specific conditions would be set for each Danube state seeking a rapprochement with Italy opened wide the door to Hungarian hopes, since such conditions could be the parity of rights in armaments and guarantees for minorities. Since sustaining an illusion was equated, in Budapest, to a political victory, Kánya was able to boast of his accomplishments at the Palazzo Chigi. The legitimist circles, however, as well as the leftist ones, did not show the same satisfaction. Austria's fall into the German zone of influence meant that strong Nazi pressures were being exerted on Hungary, dashing the hopes of restoration for the ones, for the others suggesting the danger of a dictatorship.

The official visit to Budapest of President Miklas, accompanied by Chancellor Schuschnigg (May 3, 1937), was undoubtedly a demonstration of Austro-Hungarian solidarity. In their toasts at the state dinner, which I attended along with all the other heads of mission, Horthy and

Miklas stressed their countries' close links with Italy and their friendship toward Germany. It may be assumed, however, that Schuschnigg and Guido Schmidt on the one hand, and their opposite numbers, Darányi and Kánya on the other, must have complained among themselves of both Germany, which was intensifying its pressure in the Danube Basin, and Italy, which subordinated the wishes of its satellites to the interest of its own policy. Schuschnigg, reportedly, took this opportunity to advocate once more a rapprochement with the Little Entente, and especially with Czechoslovakia—a view supported by the British government. But Kánya, in contrast to Tibor Eckhardt, considered a rapprochement with Prague just not feasible.

The most ostentatious display of Italo-Hungarian friendship, intended to put to rest the persistent rumors about Italy's indifference to Hungary's interests, was the official visit to Budapest, from May 19 to 22, of King Victor Emmanuel III, accompanied by Queen Helena and their daughter Maria, as well as by Foreign Affairs Minister Ciano. Sumptuous and theatrical reception: coaches drawn by five white horses harnessed Hungarian style, palace guards in glittering brand-new uniforms, Hungarian officials in their rich *diszmágyar* dress, military parade on Köröند tér, and, in the evening, a gala dinner at the regent's, which we, heads of mission, and our wives attended. The toasts offered by the heads of state were rather banal, stressing only the solidarity of the states bound to Germany by the Rome Protocols.

After dinner the king of Italy—whom I found to have aged quite a bit in the ten years since I last saw him—approached and greeted me most cordially. After expressing amazement that I had reached so young such a high position ("You are at least thirty years younger than I"), he inquired, as demanded by protocol, about my sovereign, toward whom it was known he had a deep antipathy. He also expressed his appreciation of the activities of my compatriots at the Romanian Academy in Rome. In other words, nothing of interest.

Of more substance was my conversation with Ciano. He spoke with me on two occasions and at length, perhaps longer than my hosts would have wished. He asked me whether a passage in his last speech, in which he mentioned the possibility of tightening the relations between Italy and Romania, had been noticed in my country. I answered that the passage had been fully appreciated, and that there was no one in Romania who did not sincerely wish the most cordial relations with Italy. Ciano added that he had been unable to say more in his speech, but that a détente between Romania and Hungary would considerably facilitate an agreement between Rome and

Bucharest. I replied that Romania had always been animated by peaceful and conciliatory sentiments and that, at the present moment, the general atmosphere seemed favorable to a détente.

Meanwhile, the queen of Italy had invited my wife to sit on a sofa next to her, and conversed with her very amiably. The Italians' intention was obviously to show the Hungarians that they would look favorably upon a rapprochement between Hungary and Romania. We met the distinguished Italian guests again at a garden party at the Royal Palace and at a ball given in the marble hall of the same palace, where the overflow of riches and luxuries gave positively the lie to the image of a "mutilated and impoverished Hungary" that the Hungarian government was seeking to propagate.

Vukicević related to me a significant conversation he had had with Ciano. The Italian foreign minister stated to him that of the three countries of the Little Entente, only Yugoslavia was of particular interest to his country, being a neighbor. He would be willing to tighten relations with Romania, provided it made a gesture to appease the Hungarians.

ENDEAVORS TO IMPROVE RELATIONS BETWEEN HUNGARY AND THE LITTLE ENTENTE

The issue of a détente in the relations between Hungary and the Little Entente was also the object of conversations, in Geneva, between the three allied foreign ministers. On his way back from the League of Nations, Victor Antonescu asked me to meet him in Vienna on June 2 and travel back with him to Budapest, so that he might brief me on the situation. In order to normalize relations, it was decided to propose to the Hungarians:

1. The recognition of the parity of their rights in the matter of armaments.
2. The conclusion of a nonaggression treaty—this having been suggested by the government in Budapest.
3. A possible gesture on our part in favor of the minorities.

If these proposals were rejected and Hungary unilaterally denounced the military clauses, it would face serious reprisals, such as the denunciation of the clause concerning the Bratislava bridgehead, the suspension of some bond payments, or even the suspension of cooperation in the execution of the Minorities' Treaty in respect to the Hungarian minorities.

In order to contribute to the improvement in atmosphere, I agreed to visit the pavilion of the Hungarian Transylvanian writers at the "Day of the Book" exhibition. I had been invited by the president of the Hungarian Transylvanian writers, Count Nicholas Bánffy, who told me that "the Hungarian writers from Transylvania, being Romanian citizens, want to affirm that connection." This being so, I went to their pavilion on Szervitá tér and even bought a number of their books, to the great joy of Count Bánffy, of Baroness Bornemisza, and of the other writers who all inscribed the books I had bought. I then invited Bánffy and Mrs. Bornemisza to lunch at the legation.

On June 5, I had a meeting with Kánya, to whom I explained the views of the Little Entente governments as they had been told to me by Victor Antonescu. Kánya tried to temporize. He said that Hungary could not pay for the recognition of its parity of rights in the matter of arms with a nonaggression pact, because public opinion would accept the conclusion of such a pact only after gestures in favor of the Hungarian minorities in the three countries. I then asked him why in his public statements he always demanded a rapprochement with the Little Entente, and what did he really want. Kánya then let loose a long explanation of why a conciliatory gesture toward the minorities was necessary, after which Hungary would be in a position to sign with each of the Little Entente's governments—not a treaty, but a declaration of nonaggression that would include a recognition of Hungary's parity of rights in rearming as well as a paraphrase of the Briand-Kellogg treaty. But Kánya added that we shouldn't hurry, the question being of sufficient importance to warrant a careful and leisurely study, taking into account the delicate situations faced by our two governments with regard to their respective public opinions. We had all the time for discussions, since the Hungarian government did not intend at this time to denounce unilaterally the military clauses of the Trianon Treaty. Darányi's June 6 speech to Parliament had more or less the same content. Kánya sent me word through Italy's envoy that I should not consider what he had told me as a rejection of the suggestions I had transmitted to him.

Turkey's foreign minister, Rüstü Aras, who was visiting Budapest and with whom I lunched at my Turkish colleague's, told me that the question of Hungary's relations with the Little Entente had not been broached in his conversation with Kánya, but Kánya had suggested that Turkey seek a direct understanding with Bulgaria, possibly at Greece's expense—a proposal Rüstü Aras rejected indignantly.

Around that time (June 11–14) Baron Konstantin von Neurath, German minister of foreign affairs, paid an official, but not necessarily political visit to Budapest. I knew him well from way back, from the time we had lodged in the same hotel in Rome, and then later, when I was first secretary of our legation in Italy. The mission entrusted to Neurath by Hitler was apparently to try to settle the existing disputes between the countries that Berlin hoped to rely on in its future diplomatic actions in Central Europe and the Balkans. The Bulgaro-Yugoslav reconciliation was seen as of little immediate use, being based on nothing concrete, but the German government did hope to accelerate the process of Magyaro-Yugoslav rapprochement. For that purpose, Belgrade was pressured to recognize unilaterally Hungary's right to rearm, but Stoiadinović categorically refused to do so, being willing to settle the issue only in unison with his allies. Though Neurath avoided mentioning the other members of the Little Entente, it is significant that in neither speeches, toasts, nor press releases did he ever associate himself with the Hungarian claims, limiting himself to expressions of amity for that old friend, Hungary. Moreover, in his official toast he referred to the German minority in Hungary as a "hyphen between our two peoples"—for the Hungarians a most unpleasant allusion to the issue of the German minority, the main apple of discord between the two countries and a problem Neurath was said to have discussed with the rulers of Hungary. Neurath's visit thus appears to have had no object other than to assert German presence and interests in a country overwhelmed by Italian visits and presentations.

In the series of dinners we gave at the legation, Prime Minister Darányi told me that our proposals could be the basis of discussions for the normalization of Hungary's relations with the Little Entente. While we had coffee, Kánya said that "it might be possible to chat" and that he would even agree that during the Council of the Little Entente, which was to be held in Sinaia on August 28, Bárdossy be authorized to negotiate, but that he would "pay nothing for the recognition of parity of rights for Hungary." He asked me to call on him the next day to help him "develop [his] thoughts." At that time, he reiterated to me that Bárdossy would present no new proposal, but would remain on the established position. I did not hesitate to tell him that such an unrealistic position was unlikely to be conducive to the establishment of a détente. With regard to the "important gesture toward the Hungarian minority" demanded as a precondition to a declaration of nonaggression, I had described to him the attitude my government intended to adopt toward its minority citizens, be it before or after agreeing to such a declaration or treaty. I also drew his attention to the fact that he told different things to each of the three envoys of the Little Entente, and that he raised his demands at each meeting.

RELATIONS BETWEEN HUNGARY AND NAZI GERMANY

Despite the close links that bound it to the other signatories of the Rome Protocols, despite all its overtures toward Britain, in this spring of 1937 Hungary's real hope of eventually having some of its claims met was still the German Reich. Tactical necessities of the moment might lead to temporary friendships with other states, but Germany kept in the Hungarians' eyes the providential character of permanent guardian of the revisionist nations. "I play the German card," Kánya would state not infrequently. And as Germany's power and importance grew, so did Hungary's illusions and aspirations.

What the Hungarian political circles did not sufficiently understand was that their feelings and hopes were not entirely shared in Berlin. As long as Germany had been "the great discontented one" and had frittered away its strengths within the walls erected around it by the solidarity of the Allies, it had been in its interest to centralize all the bitterness of the vanquished and all their revisionist tendencies. Now the situation was different: Hitler had succeeded in breaching the front of Germany's former enemies by winning Italy to its side. It was therefore no longer necessary for the Reich to assert itself as "head of the opposition," as leader and guardian of the small defeated countries, the fate of which no longer had much in common with its own. Germany wanted from now on to play the international game on a footing of equality with the other great powers. To continue supporting the unrealizable aspirations of others would have encumbered it with a totally unnecessary millstone, hampering it at every step and preventing it from having a free hand in Central Europe. The frequency of official visits between Germany and Hungary had no other purpose than to conceal this shift. Besides, when during these meetings the Hungarians spoke of their plans for the future, the Germans answered by recalling their recent wartime bonds. When the Hungarians asked for a recognition of the "rightfulness" of their cause, the Germans offered to sell them military equipment. Political conversations thus got bogged down in sentimental reminiscences or commercial discussions, both equally depressing for Budapest's incurable illusions.

In the hope of giving new life to the political facet of the Magyaro-German friendship, the Hungarian government spared no effort to eliminate the disputes that stood in the way of a perfect harmony between the two countries. However, the disputes were deep-rooted and more easily papered over than settled. There were two issues: Nazi propaganda, and the problem of the German minority in Hungary. The attempted Nazi putsch in Hungary had clearly shown Berlin's political and material support of Hungary's far-right organizations, to which some leading members of the governing party also belonged. Talks ensued between the rulers of the two countries, with reproaches from one side and soothing reassurances from the other. The governing circles in Budapest apparently became convinced that, in the future, Germany would no longer interfere in Hungary's internal affairs, as promised by the Reich's highest political players. Darányi had thereby been able to stifle the rebellion in his own party as well as the totalitarian impulses of the extremist factions. "Nevertheless," wrote the liberal *Esti Kurir* on July 15, "the fact is that we have two political movements that are under direct German control, the 'Arrow Cross' and the 'Hooked Cross.'"

Equally difficult to resolve was the problem of the German minority in Hungary, a minority that numbered over half a million, or some 5 percent of the country's total population. The members of this minority were well aware of the lenient treatment of the Saxons and Swabians in the successor states, and they compared it with their difficult lives in Hungary. This was one of the main reasons they did not back Hungarian revisionism. Rudolf Hess, Hitler's second deputy, demanded with firmness in a published statement that the German minority in Hungary be allowed to enjoy, in addition to political freedom and economic equality, the right to promote its own culture. In other words, in spite of all Hungarian efforts to give the impression that no disputes were outstanding between them and the Germans, it was impossible to conceal that they were worried by Nazi propaganda, and that the Germans resented the treatment of the German minority in Hungary.

GOGA'S VIEWS ON HUNGARY

While on vacation in Switzerland that summer, I met Octavian Goga and had a long meeting with him in Berne on August 2. He told me he was going to make no move to come to power, but expected to be asked to do so in the fall. With regard to the Hungarian question, he showed himself very conciliatory. Precisely because he was Transylvanian—and had himself belonged to a minority—he understood that something had to be done for our citizens of Hungarian extraction. That was the reason why he had earlier concluded the agreement of Ciucea. It was also he who, in fact, broke the law in order to give Romanian citizenship to Count Nicholas Bánffy, former foreign minister of Hungary, who was requesting it in order to be able to inherit the family estate near Cluj. Goga told me he had said: "The law requires a residence of ten years in Romania to acquire its citizenship, but I will nevertheless grant it to you because you are a Hungarian and a Bánffy [the nephew of the one who had persecuted the Romanians] so as to give you a proof of our generosity and chivalrousness." Goga explained that when he was minister of religious affairs, he had had good relations with Bishop Mailath: Goga had granted none of Mailath's requests but had always received him with all due respect. The way you conduct yourself plays a major role with the Hungarians: "Form is everything for them, and that is why it was a good decision to appoint an aristocrat as envoy to Budapest. Since they are snobs, they will have been flattered that we sent them a person from the elite. I would advise you to maintain the best of relations with Hungarian high society, and try to bowl them over with your French, which Hungarians tend to speak poorly." Goga was pleased I had seen Bethlen, whom he held in high regard.

NEGOTIATIONS BETWEEN THE LITTLE ENTENTE AND HUNGARY

Asked by the government to attend the meeting of the Permanent Council of the Little Entente in Sinaia, I arrived by the Orient Express on August 20. Victor Antonescu asked me to come and see him at the Palace Hôtel, so that he might brief me on the position the Romanian government would take at the Conference: unshakable loyalty to France, to the Little Entente, and to the Balkan Entente; revival of the alliance with Poland; détente and even friendliness with Germany and Italy; good relations with Soviet Russia; rapprochement to the extent possible with Bulgaria and Hungary. He stressed that in no way did we want to give up our alliances, but neither did we intend to be dragged automatically into armed conflicts. It is for that reason that we had not consented to a broadening of the obligations contained in the treaties of the Little Entente. Victor Antonescu believed that in the event of an armed conflict, we would please everyone were we to stay on the sidelines as long as possible. The Germans would be happy to be able to purchase part of our oil and cereals, rather than to seize our resources by occupying the country after heavy losses and expenses. The French, too, would be happy, for were we to join the fray they would be obliged to give us arms and money, which would, however, not prevent our defeat by the mechanized might of Germany's army and by its air force, the result being that the Germans would grab our entire economy, considerably increasing their military potential.

Turning to the Hungarian question, Victor Antonescu told me the government was eager to reach a détente, provided Budapest did not insist on discussing the minority problem, which was an internal matter. We could, on the other hand, get in touch with the heads of the Magyar party [in Romania] and examine with good will their grievances. Apparently Ugo Sola, Italy's envoy to Bucharest, who tended to poke his nose into everything, was suggesting a compromise in the matter of the nonaggression declaration: that Hungary, to avoid what it would consider a humiliation, make such a declaration to all of its neighbors, not only to the Little Entente. Victor Antonescu asked me to see Bárdossy, who was also in Sinaia, and to urge him not to insist on unacceptable points.

With regard to Soviet Russia, we wanted normal relations, but, Antonescu added, "I do not want to bind myself to it as Titulescu did." If Moscow wants a mutual assistance treaty with Romania, it must ipso facto recognize our borders, including the Bessarabian one. On our side, so as not to irritate them too much, we will avoid close relations with the Berlin-Rome Axis; that is why on several occasions we rejected a visit by Göring, and why Schacht would be received only after he had gone first to several other capitals.

With regard to Italy, Antonescu told me that, without seeking very close ties that would annoy France and especially Britain, we would be happy to tighten our traditionally friendly relations, but Rome conditioned this on a détente with Hungary, and this was not easy to envision—but not by any fault of ours. And he added, "It does not matter, we are in no hurry." Antonescu kept me for lunch and had me speak at length about the situation and people in Hungary. I realized that he must have been reading my reports quite thoroughly, since he even quoted some of my sentences.

Following Foreign Minister Antonescu's instructions, I sought out Bárdossy. I told him that if the Hungarian government truly wanted a détente with Romania—hence also with the Little Entente—this could be brought about in the following way: Hungary would declare its parity of rights, the Little Entente would not object, then Hungary would offer each state of the Little Entente a nonaggression agreement. Bárdossy considered this formula acceptable if to the mutual nonaggression declarations were added an undertaking by the governments of the Little Entente subsequently to take, within their national sovereignties, administrative measures to improve the minorities' lot and to "redress the wrongs inflicted to the minorities by noncompliance with the provisions of the treaties." I disputed that the relevant provisions of the treaties had not been observed, and told him that a wording such as he proposed would be unacceptable. I then went to the Palace Hôtel to brief Victor Antonescu, Stoiadinović, and Krofta on my conversation with Bárdossy.

That evening, Antonescu and Bárdossy had a long conversation. Bárdossy suggested the signing of three confidential protocols—one with each of the Little Entente countries—containing the recognition of the parity of rights, administrative measures for the improvement of the status of minorities, mutual declarations of nonaggression, and undertakings by the governments of the Little Entente to get in touch with the heads of their Hungarian minorities in order to resolve pending disputes. At the dinner offered in honor of Stoiadinović and Krofta, Antonescu whispered to me that the discussion he had held with Bárdossy might constitute a basis for negotiations. The Yugoslavs seemed optimistic, and Gavrilović, from their Ministry of Foreign Affairs, cited the precedent of their détente with the Italians.

After dinner, during the musical soirée, Bárdossy stealthily handed me the draft of a secret Romano-Hungarian protocol he had drawn up, asking me to submit it to our minister of foreign affairs. The draft was totally unacceptable[7] and Victor Antonescu refused to receive it, indignant that its proposals demonstrated both bad faith and cynicism. When ever did the Orthodox clergy proselyte, be it in Transylvania or elsewhere? Isn't it well known that proselytism is performed everywhere and on a large scale by the Catholic clergy? The forced Romanization of Hungarian names is a fable, whereas the Magyarization of Romanian given and family names had been a sad reality during the entire Hungarian rule of Transylvania. When one knows how the Hungarian government behaved toward the Romanians in Transylvania, the Bárdossy draft's assertions are the height of impudence, Antonescu added. I was instructed to inform the Hungarian envoy of the Romanian foreign minister's refusal to accept his draft (which I have kept). In these circumstances, Victor Antonescu, too, had become pessimistic, coming to believe that one could get nowhere with the Hungarians.

Bárdossy became quite upset when I informed him of all this. Being accredited to Romania, he did not expect our minister of foreign affairs to refuse to take his suggestions into account. He was dejected, and was wondering whether his very mission in our country was not coming to an end. For the time being, he was considering asking to go on leave. Would he still be able to see Victor Antonescu? Antonescu instructed me to reply that Bárdossy could go on leave, if he needed rest, but that a further meeting before the Geneva talks was no longer necessary, since there was nothing new to add. From what Antonescu related to me, the other two ministers of the Little Entente—Stoiadinović and Krofta—also found the exorbitant and almost defiant Hungarian pretensions to be extraordinary.

---

[7]Bárdossy's draft protocol is reproduced in Appendix B.

At the conclusion of its Sinaia Conference, on August 31, 1937, the Permanent Council of the Little Entente issued a press communiqué. It is symptomatic that only a year before international events were to lead to the outbreak of World War II and the collapse of the League of Nations, the three foreign ministers gathered at Sinaia discerned "symptoms of improvement in the European international situation," in which they saw "the hope of a détente, followed by a period of calm that will ensure peace in Europe." Equally illusory was their trust in the League of Nations, on which they based their belief in world "stability and peace." With regard to Hungary, however, the heads of the Little Entente gave proof of well-disposed and constructive intentions, stressing in paragraph six of the communiqué "their unanimous wish to achieve relations of trust" with all the states of the Danube valley, as well as their decision to "neglect no opportunity of showing their good will in this regard."

✧ ✧ ✧

When I returned to Budapest, Ugo Sola, Italy's envoy to Bucharest, called on me. He told me he had seen both Apor and Bárdossy, to whom he spoke "como se fossi Romeno."[8] I got the impression that he wanted to play the role of intermediary. He told me the Hungarians were willing to give up their "ridiculous" claims regarding the alleged Orthodox proselytism and the alleged forced Romanization of the Szeklers, provided we also made a conciliatory gesture.

Bárdossy also called on me to suggest that I ask to see Kánya, who was "very favorably inclined." I replied that such a visit on the eve of the Geneva talks was likely to "upset the apple cart," since I understood that while Horthy and Darányi were realists and were eager for détente, Kánya was said to have remained hidebound in his preconceived ideas. Bárdossy strongly disagreed with my view, and I finally understood why he so much wanted me to see Kánya: he was obliquely asking me to tell his boss that we would be happy if Bárdossy could attend the Geneva discussions. To indulge his wish, I went to see Kánya, who received me cordially. He said that while he recognized the good will of the Little Entente governments, he was not optimistic. Since he, too, was a member of a government, he realized the difficulties we would have to face in getting our public opinions to accept the concessions without which Hungary would not conceive of a détente. He asked me how we had got along with Bárdossy, and I replied that his

[8] "As if I were Romanian."

conduct had been appreciated. Then Kánya added, "I will take him along to Geneva." That evening, I invited Bárdossy to dinner on St. Margaret Island, and reported to him on my conversation with Kánya. He was delighted to have a role to play in Geneva. One already could see that he had strong political ambitions, which was why he liked to be center-stage.

✧ ✧ ✧

On September 15 I sent a personal letter to Victor Antonescu, suggesting that in Geneva he raise in his turn the question of the Romanian minority in Hungary, which was subjected to an intolerant and harsh treatment by the Hungarian authorities. The Romanian minority in Hungary was in a much more difficult situation than the Hungarian minority in Transylvania. I appended a list of the demands we were entitled to make at a time when the Hungarians were asking for totally unacceptable concessions. The list of our demands, drawn up with the help of the Romanian leaders in Hungary, was as follows:

1. Church autonomy and the right to establish a Romanian Orthodox diocese, depending in spiritual matters on the Metropolitan See of Sibiu, with a bishop and diocesan consistory; until the establishment of the bishopric, the right to train Romanian Orthodox clergymen in seminaries and theological departments in Romania.
2. Restoration of the right to use the Romanian language in Uniate churches in the Romanian parishes of the Hajdudorog diocese.
3. Right to teach in Romanian in the confessional schools.
4. Establishment of a Romanian language section at one of the Hungarian teachers colleges in Hungary, in order to train the required teaching staffs for the Romanian schools.
5. Right to publish textbooks for schools teaching in Romanian, or to reprint old textbooks approved by the Hungarian Education Ministry before the war.
6. Authorization to publish a Romanian language newspaper.
7. Right for members of the Romanian minority to buy farmland in the border area.
8. Provision of one course of Romanian language in those Hungarian public schools where a specified number of students belonging to the Romanian minority are enrolled.

9. Measures to prohibit all administrative methods tending to denationalize the Romanian minority in Hungary (such as Magyarization of surnames).
10. End of any administrative measure, or proselytism, aimed at inducing members of the Romanian minority to change their religion (most often, the proselytism is carried out in the Orthodox churches where the appointment of an Orthodox priest has not been authorized).
11. Elimination from Hungarian textbooks of passages offensive to the Romanian people.

✧ ✧ ✧

The Geneva talks ended with no definite results, but at least with the understanding that they would be resumed after the Romanian parliamentary elections. In my meetings with him, Kánya seemed to understand the situation and showed himself pleased with the way his talks with the Little Entente's ministers of foreign affairs had gone. When he returned from Berlin, where he had accompanied for two days Darányi who had been invited by Göring, he told me that Hitler and Neurath would view with relief a genuine détente between Hungary and the Little Entente. From what I heard, the Darányi-Kánya visit did not lead to a tightening of the bonds between the two countries: the Germans complained of the persecution of the Swabians by Hungary and of the hostile attitude of the left-wing Budapest press toward National-Socialism. Kánya told me that Italy's exit from the League of Nations would not change Hungary's attitude toward that international organization. Neurath had divulged to him that Halifax had made concrete proposals to Berlin regarding the former German colonies, but the proposals called for some sort of collective collaboration that Hitler had rejected.

II. 1938

In Romania, the Tătărescu government fell after losing the elections and was replaced by a government headed by Goga. The Ministry of Foreign Affairs was entrusted to Istrate Micescu, a noted lawyer and university professor.

In Hungary, the Darányi government introduced in the Chamber of Deputies an electoral reform bill, the main provision of which was the establishment of secret balloting. For in spite of the Hungarians' pride in having the second oldest parliament after England, voting in their elections had always been conducted in public, obviously making it easier for the authorities to interfere and exert pressure. The fate of the bill, however, appeared very doubtful as 1938 began, since it was opposed by the right wing and center—and particularly by Count Bethlen—which feared a "proletarization" of political life.

On January 8 at noon, all heads of foreign missions were at the Royal Palace to extend their New Year's wishes to Regent Horthy. In order to attend the ceremony I cut short my year-end vacation, spent with my family at Semmering. An amusing detail: while moving among us, Horthy stopped next to our Polish colleague, Orlowski, and whispered with him. Knowing that a visit by the Hungarian regent to Poland was being set up—ostensibly a hunting trip—I asked Orlowski whether that had been the topic of their whispered conversation. "Not at all," replied the Pole laughing, "he was merely asking me 'Tell me, who is the envoy standing close by? I just cannot remember who he is!'" The man in question was the Greek envoy, Pipinelis.

ROME PROTOCOL MEETING IN BUDAPEST

A couple of days later, Budapest hosted the meeting of the Council of States bound by the Rome Protocols. Italy was represented by Ciano, Austria by Schuschnigg and Guido Schmidt. At the party Darányi gave in their honor, my Austrian colleague Baar-Baarenfels introduced me anew to his superiors, whom I had come to know in Vienna, when the first was minister of justice, and the second secretary to President Miklas. During our conversation they told me that they were satisfied with the conference's progress and also pleased by the noticeable improvement in our relations with Hungary. As for Ciano, he was reportedly insisting that Austria and Hungary recognize the Franco government in Spain and that they criticize publicly the League of Nations, demands that Kánya was said to resist.

I left the party early in order to meet at the railway station our new minister of foreign affairs, Micescu, who was traveling from Prague to Geneva. I briefed him on the current status of our relations with Hungary. He would like us to reach an agreement, and would even be prepared to reconfirm our obligations in the matter of minorities, on condition that the document contain a reconfirmation by Hungary of its adherence to the Treaty of Trianon. Micescu told me he knew for a fact that Italy wished to form a bloc comprising the states of the Rome Protocols and of the Little Entente, as well as Poland, that could counterbalance, when needed, the German predominance in Central Europe. Micescu told me he would not go from Geneva to Paris so as not to get in the way of the policy of rapprochement with Germany and Italy that the present government wanted to pursue. He also did not want to run the risk of a cool reception following Goga's pro-German and pro-Italian statements. We parted after Micescu thanked me for the "prompt and precise" way in which I kept the government informed.

At the banquet in honor of Ciano and Schuschnigg, Kánya mentioned in his toast the recognition by the Austrian and Hungarian governments of the Italo-Ethiopian empire, as well as the recognition by Italy and Austria of the rightfulness of the Hungarian position regarding parity of arming rights. He wanted thus to underscore the identical positions and the cohesion of the three countries. In his reply Ciano stressed that the Rome Protocols were not a closed system that would isolate the three countries by the exclusion of other neighboring powers; on the contrary, the Rome Protocols were a scheme within which all the states of Central

Europe could cooperate. In accordance with this principle and "a sense of reality," the Rome-Berlin Axis was established as well as the friendly agreements between Italy and Yugoslavia and between Austria, Hungary, and Germany. It was clear that Italy's minister of foreign affairs wanted it known that his country might enter into separate agreements with other states, and that the Rome Protocols in no way hindered his freedom of action. Since he also stressed the necessity of good relations and stability in Central Europe, it would seem that the information that had been given to Micescu was not altogether baseless with regard to the more distant future. Guido Schmidt limited himself in his address to asserting the principle of respect for the legitimate interests of all the Danube Basin countries.

After dinner Ciano recognized me as soon as he saw me and hailed me "Caro Bossy!" Speaking in Italian, he asked me—what a detailed briefing he must have been given by the Italian legation!—whether I was still writing historical studies, etc. He was ostensibly cordial, as if to create a friendly atmosphere between us. Then, suddenly, he switched to politics. He told me that we had to settle things with the Hungarians, for until then "Italy will be unable to *officially* tighten its links with Romania." But the day a Romano-Hungarian agreement is signed—whatever it may be—"we will be able to work together in earnest." I briefed him on the status of our negotiations, on the Hungarians' demands, on our rightful and reasonable objections. "Find a formula," he replied, "whatever it may be. We will pressure the Hungarians to accept it." He mentioned he knew Goga, whom he spoke of with warmth, but he wondered whether the Iron Guard would let him govern, whether he would be able to reach an agreement with it. During the course of our unusually long conversation, various prominent people came to shake Ciano's hand (my French colleague Maugras, for instance, the Prince of Montenuovo, and so on). I tried discreetly to withdraw so as to let him talk with others, but Ciano shook their hands absentmindedly and then turned again toward me. He was plainly prolonging our conversation in order to emphasize Italy's "flirt" with Romania. The photographers had all the time to take our picture together. I wondered what Kánya's reaction would be.

The communiqué issued by the signatory states of the Rome Protocols after their conference represented a balancing of mutual concessions. Austria and Hungary recognized the Franco government, made common cause with the Anti-Comintern Pact, and criticized the League of Nations.

In exchange, Hungary obtained a new and superfluous recognition of its parity of rights. Italy's expressed interest in the improvement of Romano-Hungarian relations conformed with what Ciano had told me. Hungary emerged diminished, now relegated to the back burner in Italy's diplomatic operations; this was also to reduce its international value as a constituent part of a possible Danubian agreement. But the sensational passage of the communiqué, by all accounts, was the passage concerning Romania. It was the first time that a country not belonging to the grouping had been mentioned by name in an official communiqué, and in diplomatic circles this was seen as an undisguised invitation to Romania from the Italian government. Much insistence had reportedly been required to get Kánya to agree to the publication of the communiqué.

In a conversation a few days later (January 31) the Hungarian foreign minister gave me a few details on this last tripartite meeting. He told me that Schuschnigg had wanted the final communiqué to make special mention of Austria's independence, but that Ciano had opposed this "so as not to provoke Germany." This shows that by then Italy had already sacrificed its ally in order to maintain its ties with Hitler's Reich. Kánya seemed pleased with the actions of the Goga government, "which, on the Jewish issue, might well set a precedent that could be followed by Hungary, which is also crushed by the Semitic masses." He expressed the hope that our conversations would also make headway, "since the Hungarian government is only asking for compliance with the commitments made in the matter of minorities." I drew his attention to the fact that it was not we Romanians, but the Hungarians who were not complying with their commitments. I gave him as an example the issue of the Transylvanian archives, which they had pledged to hand back to us in the Trianon Treaty (arts. 77, 175, and 177), but had not done. Kánya seemed surprised and embarrassed by the unexpected counterattack, and did not answer. From what I heard from all sides (from Count Nicholas Bánffy, Count Dominic Festetics, and others), the coming to power of the Goga government was seen in Budapest as a promise of normalization of the relations between Romania and Hungary. With regard to the Anschluss, all of us in the diplomatic corps were of the opinion that it was approaching rapidly. Kánya kept repeating to us: "It is the business of France and Italy; we can do nothing."

At the same time, a strengthening of Hungarian-Polish relations was being sought. Horthy went "hunting" in Poland, accompanied by Kánya and a numerous suite. On his return to Budapest, Orlowski gave a large dinner party in Horthy's honor, and insisted that I attend so as to show that the regent's visit was purely a courtesy one, without any implication for our alliance. Apparently for the same reason, Horthy spoke lengthily with me after dinner, but only about the hunt he had participated in. Orlowski claimed that the regent told him as he was leaving, "A charming man, this Romanian envoy!" Be that as it may, the fact is that I was submerged in demonstrations of friendship and affection, lest I be too dispirited by this "waltz round the hall" of our Polish ally with our Hungarian foe.

FINIS AUSTRIAE AND ITS IMPACT ON HUNGARY

But the preludes of the great tragedy that was to strike Europe, and the world, no longer allowed either hope or delusion. The Hitler-Schuschnigg meeting portended the imminent end of Austria's independence and deeply shook the Hungarian political world. The presence of the German colossus at Hungary's doorstep gave everybody food for thought. (The Hungarian government's new disposition to resist German pressure could also be seen in the arrest in February 1938 of the Hungarian Nazi leader Szálasi, who was to play a major role in the establishment of a Fascist regime in Hungary ahead of the Russian advance in Central Europe.) The Budapest press reflected these worries, and expressed its bewilderment at Italy's attitude. Various people of importance spoke to me of the imperative need of settling the Romano-Hungarian dispute in order to form a bloc of Danubian states, this being the only possible way to resist the pressures exerted on Central Europe by the neighboring great powers. Only the perspicacious Kánya understood that it was all too late and that no defensive dike could still be raised in Central Europe.

At home, the Goga government was replaced by one headed by Patriarch Miron Cristea, with Tătărescu temporarily in charge of foreign affairs. At the latter's instructions, I told Kánya (on February 25) that we were prepared to resume negotiations with Hungary—in the name of all three Little Entente governments—and asked him to give Bárdossy, in Bucharest, the appropriate instructions. He agreed, although he forewarned me that the Hungarian government was not going to modify its position. Yet the grievous events that were about to break out on the international scene were pushing into the background the local disputes between Romania and Hungary.

Looking back, after so many years, on those fateful days, I am amazed by the fact that people who should have sensed what was about to happen seemed to have been completely out of the loop. At an official luncheon in honor of the foreign heads of mission, Regent Horthy told us (on February 26!) that Hitler wouldn't be able to achieve a full Anschluss even in twenty years. And my unfortunate Austrian colleague, former vice-chancellor Baar-Baarenfels, seemed to be more worried about Czechoslovakia's fate than that of his own country. When I told him that world opinion backed Austria in its fight to maintain its independence, Baar-Baarenfels answered: "I would prefer a bit less moral support and a bit more material assistance. But, in fact, no one will help us. And when the German army marches into Austria, we decided long ago that we would not defend ourselves. That was very wise of Schuschnigg, since we are unable to fight against the huge German army, and since no Austrian wants to shed brotherly blood. But the Anschluss will not take place so soon; Czechoslovakia is first in line. The poor Czechs are in a terrible predicament. It is only after that that Hitler will focus on Austria."

The unfortunate Baar did not realize that history would reverse the order of Hitler's victims, and that in only a few days' time.

I was on a short leave in Monte Carlo when, on March 11, it was announced like a bolt from Heaven that Hitler had ordered the German army to move into Austria. The haste with which the bloodthirsty tyrant took this criminal action is explainable by his wish to prevent the plebiscite called by Schuschnigg, which would have resulted in an overwhelming majority in favor of Austrian independence. Arriving in Linz the next day, Hitler proclaimed the annexation of Austria, thereby erasing his native country from the map of Europe.

Returned at once to my post, I found the political circles in Budapest, as well as Hungarian public opinion in general, dumbfounded and frightened by Austria's extinction. Fearful of its huge new neighbor, the Darányi government made the best of a bad situation and multiplied its demonstrations of cordiality toward Germany, a policy by now also advocated by Eckhardt. The rumor spread in diplomatic circles that, during the Halifax-Hitler meeting, the British government had declared that it would not oppose German preponderance in Central Europe as long as there was no aggression, which would not be viewed with indifference by Britain.

Bakách-Bessenyey, political director of the Ministry of Foreign Affairs, reminiscing about the years we spent together in Vienna, told me that he obviously regretted *finis Austriae,* but that in the present circumstances he saw no other solution for Hungary than a policy of close friendship with the Third Reich. Negotiations were under way with Italy to draw up a treaty to replace the "defunct" tripartite Rome Protocols. He foresaw an impending German action against Czechoslovakia, since circumstances were highly favorable to Hitler's plans. Indeed, he told me, Soviet Russia was paralyzed by its internal situation and by not being allowed to send its forces through either Poland or Romania; Britain was opposed to an intervention in favor of Czechoslovakia; France, not being directly attacked, was unlikely to be willing to enter the fight, and, besides, it would be unable to pierce the strong Siegfried line; as for the Little Entente, no help would be forthcoming, since the Yugoslav envoy had categorically stated that his country would move only if Czechoslovakia were attacked by Hungary. Bakách-Bessenyey's position mirrored that of his chief, Kánya. Kánya wanted to leave the impression that he was satisfied by the events in Austria, pretending that the only ground for friction between Budapest and Berlin—the Budapest-Vienna relationship—had now disappeared. From now on nothing stood in the way of Hungaro-German friendship. That is why Kánya hastened to convey his congratulations to the German government and to convert his legation in Vienna into a consulate general. A rare example of opportunism and cynicism from the ally of a country being annihilated! Kánya was also seeking a tightening of relations with Poland so as to reach a convergence of views by the time the Czechoslovak problem and the division of spoils came up.

I was deeply moved by the farewell visit of Colonel Eberle, Austria's military attaché to Budapest and Bucharest, on March 19. I didn't dare tell him what was in my heart so as not to put him in an awkward position, since he had a swastika embroidered on his Austrian uniform. But he realized I understood what he was feeling, and his eyes were brimming with tears. He merely said, "It was brilliantly staged," and then spoke of the wretched fate that was awaiting his comrades at arms: superior officers too old to identify with the German psyche who would be pushed aside and sentenced to fade away slowly on meager pensions.

On March 19 I sent the government the following report on Hungary's reactions to the Anschluss: "Even though Hungarian political circles had realized for some time that, following the formation of the Berlin-Rome Axis on the basis of Italy's renouncement of interest in Central European affairs, the unfolding of events had inevitably to lead to an Anschluss, they were nevertheless taken aback by the dizzying speed with which the annexation of Austria by the German Reich was achieved.

"After the Berchtesgaden meeting and the speeches by Hitler and Schuschnigg, Foreign Affairs Minister Kánya had voiced to me his profound conviction that the Führer, with whom he had had long conversations in Berlin, would refrain from any aggressive action against Austria, leaving to time, which was on his side, to achieve the unification of the German nation. At the dinner he hosted on February 26 for the heads of diplomatic missions, Regent Horthy did not hesitate to assure us all that the formal completion of the Anschluss could not be achieved in less than twenty years!

"The political director of the Ministry of Foreign Affairs, Baron Bakách-Bessenyey, told me that the Hungarian government had been informed of Chancellor Schuschnigg's intention of calling a plebiscite only a few days before the decree was published. The news alarmed the Hungarian government, which foresaw that the German Führer would never reconcile himself to the thought that a public expression of the will of the Austrian people could yield an impressive majority in favor of Austria's independence. But it was too late and nothing could stop the fatal concatenation of events.

" . . . Reportedly, at the end of January Mr. von Schuschnigg asked Mr. Puaux, France's envoy to Vienna, to let him know whether, in the event of a German military intervention in Austria, the Austrian government could count on effective French material support. Puaux is said to have consulted his government, which immediately got in touch with the British government, which in turn made some indirect inquiries in Rome. As a result, Puaux was reportedly instructed to tell Chancellor Schuschnigg that since the British government could make no commitment in this regard, neither could France promise Austria that it would effectively intervene to safeguard its independence. Dejected, Schuschnigg then must have resigned himself to go to Berchtesgaden. The announcement of the plebiscite is generally seen as a desperate and inexplicable act, based on a wrong assessment of the international situation and on a last and totally unfounded hope that, in the hour of the greatest peril, Austria would not be abandoned by its ally Italy.

"The collapse of Austria, that old Austria to which Hungary's destiny had been closely linked one way or the other for so many centuries, could not leave the Magyar nation indifferent. The tragic news shocked all Hungarians deeply. The older generation in particular, which had participated in the life of the Dual Monarchy, cannot accustom itself to the thought that Austria . . . now belongs to the past. A widespread rumor holds that Regent Horthy himself burst into tears on learning of the dramatic events across the Leitha River; this seems quite likely to those who know the sentimental nature of the former officer of the Austro-Hungarian navy and aide-de-camp of the emperor, who now finds himself at the helm of the Hungarian state.

"The Hungarian legitimists have been cruelly and irremediably hurt. One of their leaders confessed to me that the ultimate goal of their movement was the resurrection of the Austro-Hungarian dual monarchy. With this objective now shattered, there no longer is much sense in a Hungarian legitimism, since the Habsburg dynasty, in itself, cannot give Hungary any additional strength, not even morally. Hence the aggressivity toward the Hitlerian Reich of the legitimist press *(Magyarszág, Nemzeti Ujság)* . . .

"To the Hungarians' pain of a sentimental nature must be added the fear of the overwhelming power of Germanism, which from now on will exercise direct pressure from the country's very borders. The Hungarians realize that they have no defense against this pressure. With their neighbors of the Little Entente, they have the relations they wanted, having always fed the flame of hatred and revenge rather than seeking a détente animated by a sense of realities. The Rome Protocols have irrevocably lapsed. . . . Negotiations with Rome are under way to draw up a new text for direct Italo-Hungarian collaboration, but few people are left in Hungary who would still trust the friendship of Italy, which is accused of abandoning its allies in 1915 and now again in 1938. A Hungarian statesman did not hesitate to remind me of the cruel and well-known sentence attributed to the French ambassador Bompard: 'Italy's friendship must be left to one's enemies.' The formation of a Catholic Rome-Budapest-Warsaw bloc is still a dream; many obstacles stand in its way, and [common] hostility to Prague is inadequate to overcome them.

"Thus all political groupings as well as public opinion have logically reached the conclusion that the only possible foreign policy for Hungary is to stand beside Germany. The government therefore hastened to show its attachment to the Reich by sending to the Auswärtiges Amt's secretary of state, Mackensen (former envoy to Budapest), through Hungary's envoy to Berlin, General Sztójay, its 'warmest congratulations to the Führer on the occasion of Austria's reunion to the German Reich, which, to Hungary's happiness, was accomplished without the spilling of blood,' as well as the expression of "the most well-grounded hope that the good and friendly relations between the two countries will continue as in the past." At the same time, the Wilhelmstrasse announced that, the first of all countries to do so, Hungary had decided to transform its legation in Vienna into a consulate general. This zeal of the Hungarian government has been appreciated in Berlin, as shown . . . by Hitler's speech in which he praised 'Hungary's warm and cordial approval of Austria's union with Nazi Germany.'

"Officially, Kánya and his collaborators told the foreign mission chiefs that, 'apart from a natural feeling of melancholy,' the Hungarian government was pleased by the removal of the sole obstacle to a perfect Hungaro-German understanding—viz., the close ties between Austria and Hungary.

"This official position of the Budapest government seems to all to be so inevitable that even the left-wing opposition has approved it. The head of the Smallholders' party, Tibor Eckhardt, a personal friend of Chancellors Dollfuss and Schuschnigg who is known for his anti-Nazi sentiments and who advocated a Budapest-Vienna-Prague triangle, has stated in a public allocution: 'Germany's importance for Hungary has risen considerably, inasmuch as the Continent's main military power has become our immediate neighbor. . . . We have only one way to the West: Germany.' The leader of the Legitimists, Count Anton Sigray, said in an address that 'Even though destiny decreed that Germany reach Hegyeshalom (the border between Austria and Hungary), and we do want to remain friends and good neighbors with it, we do not want Germany to step over this border, for we do not intend to become the Germans' flunkeys.'

"Apart from the inexorable dictates of its geographical position, another motive is prodding the Hungarians toward the most cordial cooperation with their mighty neighbor: the hope that, in the event of a drive against Czechoslovakia, the Germans would allow them to take a share of the spoils. Their claims on Slovakia and Subcarpathian Russia represent therefore, in Hungarian eyes, the real nexus of the common interests of Germany and Hungary. . . .

"The fact that Germany considers itself henceforth the natural defender of German populations beyond its borders, as was made clear in Hitler and Göring's speeches . . . foreshadows the imminent danger of Berlin's interference in the internal affairs of Hungary in order to back the grievances and growing aspirations of the Swabians living in Hungary, along Germany's new borders.

" . . . The feelings with which the Hungarians are viewing their new geopolitical situation are therefore quite complex. The main element is anxiety about Germany's pressure, an anxiety that no rapprochement with Poland, aiming at constituting a counterbalance, can assuage. To comfort itself of the inexorability of its impending fate as a vassal of the Reich, Hungary lulls itself with the hope of some compensations at the expense of Czechoslovakia. . . . All depends on the method the Wilhelmstrasse will choose for its policy of penetration in Danubian and Balkan Europe."

A few days later, I added the following remarks on the effects of the Anschluss on Hungarian domestic politics: "Austria's incorporation into the German Reich could not fail to convulse Hungary's entire political life. The event, foreseen by almost all for a more distant period, occurred unexpectedly just at the time when the foundations of a new electoral system were being laid in Hungary, and when a call was being made on the assets of private individuals and banks for the reequipment of the country's armed forces and for social endowments. With regard to the foreign policy to be pursued, public opinion unanimously considers—some with regret, others with fear—that the only possible way is the one adopted by the government: an unswerving solidarity with the mighty new German neighbor, on whom the last revisionist hopes or illusions hang. Besides this, continued friendly relations with Italy (the saving of the remains of the Rome Protocols) and with Poland, which, according to Kánya, 'by its interest in the problems of the Danube Basin, confirms that the peaceful and cordial Hungaro-Polish cooperation should have favorable repercussions in the future.'

"Despite that, no one fools himself on the policy's consequences: Hungary's unconditional vassalage to Germany. Economic vassalage in the first place, political vassalage in the second, with the risk of continual interference in favor of the German minority. As a statesman from here summed up the situation: 'We have now become *'das Land Ungarn,'*[1] no better than Austria.' Even though Kánya has assured me recently that 'with the Germans, it is always possible to reach an understanding,' many politicians from the right of the spectrum (legitimists) and from the left (Jewish financiers, Socialists) can in no way reconcile themselves to this prospect. Count Gyorgy Széchenyi, a deputy from the Christian Union party, brought up in the Chamber of Deputies the question of the Anschluss, and in this connection deplored that the Hungarian government had shown neither loyalty nor chivalry. . . . Likewise, the independent deputy Payr mentioned in an open session of the Chamber 'the tragic fall of Austria,' the danger facing Czechoslovakia, the total inaction of the League of Nations, and he asked who from now on would guarantee the independence of small countries. . . .

"While only too few scattered voices raise a discordant note in the chorus singing self-seeking paeans in praise of the Hitlerian Reich, more marked divergences may be noted with regard to the future course of internal policy. In a press statement of March 19, the prime minister drew a di-

[1]The province of Hungary.

viding line between foreign and domestic policy: 'External events have for us but external significance and in no way influence our internal management, for foreign and domestic policies evolve on totally different planes.' Yet Darányi himself could not deny that 'in Hungary, as everywhere else, strong nationalist trends prevail.' Prior to the Anschluss, Hungary was split between the political currents of the right and of the left, with a clear tendency for the nationalist organizations to make headway. Hitlerism's show of force in Austria has broken this equilibrium in favor of the far-right current. The various pro-Nazi and pro-Fascist groups are seeking to assert themselves and to merge. All that is still missing is the man with the gifts necessary to take over the movement's leadership."

On March 23, Kánya spelled out for the Parliamentary Committee on Foreign Affairs Hungary's official viewpoint on the dramatic developments in Austria. In order to justify the Hungarian government's total inaction at the time of its ally's collapse, he mentioned the passive attitudes of Britain, and especially of France, "which did not even consider the possibility of trying to restore Austria, which to a large extent it had created." As for the future, he added, "Hungary will follow the same policy toward the German Reich as in the past," the more so since "the German government has left no doubt that it considers the present border between Germany and Hungary to be as inviolable as the borders with Italy, Switzerland, and Yugoslavia." It is to be noted that he did not mention the French border among those considered definitive by the Berlin government. Kánya also stated that "the good relations between Hungary and Italy will remain unchanged, in the spirit of the old Rome Protocols," and that "the interest shown by Poland in the problems of the Danube Basin fills Hungary with joy, and we hope that the peaceful relations between Hungary and Poland will develop favorably in the future." Regarding relations with the countries of the Little Entente, Kánya said he wished they were "better, that is, normalized" and that "the negotiations begun in September, and later suspended, have been resumed in Bucharest, with the Hungarian government bringing all its good will for their success."

✧ ✧ ✧

With regard to the resumption of negotiations, I found out from our Ministry of Foreign Affairs that the Romanian government was proposing to the Hungarian one the formula I had suggested to Victor Antonescu the preceding fall, namely: "On its own and within its full sovereignty, Romania has decided, contingent on reciprocity, to take, within the principles generally accepted in the state's internal legislation, all the necessary administrative measures to eliminate all the difficulties that might hinder the development of friendly relations with Hungary. It is well understood that this declaration can in no event be interpreted as infringing upon the principles of noninterference in Romania's internal matters."

But Kánya, whom I met on March 30, said he could not agree with my text because it did not contain the word "minority." I got the impression that he would prefer not to reach an agreement.

On April 1 I sent the following report on this meeting: "The quite lengthy conversation I had with the Hungarian minister of foreign affairs on March 30 dealt with three main points:

"1. *The events in Austria.* Kánya told me openly that, as former envoy of Emperor-King Franz Joseph and as a Viennese by education and predilection, he had personally been hard hit by Austria's disappearance from the map. As Hungary's minister of foreign affairs, however, he could but take note of a death—irrevocable, like all deaths—before which one pays one's respects, without arguing. And as heartless as such a statement may appear, this death removed the only obstacle to the best relations between Hungary and Germany.

"Kánya insisted that he had been absolutely sincere when he had excluded the possibility of a German aggression against Austria, since he was basing his opinion on what Hitler had personally stated to him. He is convinced that the Führer was sincere at that time, but that events unfolded with a speed that led to a sudden about-face in Berlin.

"Kánya assured me he knew exactly how things had unfolded, and he gave me the following account, which I believe deserves to be recorded even if only for its historical interest: Following the Berchtesgaden meeting, Kánya went incognito to Vienna to hear from Schuschnigg himself how his talks with Hitler had gone. After giving him a detailed report, Schuschnigg had added: 'My most trustworthy collaborators advise me to hold a plebiscite, which would give me, both in the country and abroad, the authority necessary to resist Germany firmly. But I believe such a solution to be too dangerous because of the reactions it would produce in the Reich, and I will never adopt it.' A few days later, however, Chancellor Schuschnigg, giving in to the urgings of his friends, sent Mussolini a letter asking for advice on the notion of a plebiscite in Austria. . . . Mussolini sent a long reply, saying that he could of course not interfere in Austria's internal affairs, but that he personally strongly advised giving up a project that Hitler might consider provocative. Nevertheless, Chancellor Schuschnigg decided on the plebiscite, informing the Hungarian government of his decision only at the last moment.

"When he ordered his troops to march into Austria, the Führer did not intend to cross the border himself, Kánya said. Göring, however, urged him to do so, to give several speeches, and then 'Austria will be yours.' Even as he was following this advice, Hitler would not have intended to annex Austria before holding a plebiscite. On the morning of his arrival in Linz, no decision to that effect had yet been taken. It was only in the afternoon that, deeply moved by the popular enthusiasm, the Führer, who is of an impulsive nature, suddenly phoned the Reich's justice minister in Berlin, telling him to draft immediately a law for the annexation of Austria. That is how this deed with such immense consequences for all of Europe was accomplished, according to the precise information Kánya told me he recieved from one of the main players. He added that he did not believe Schuschnigg to be seriously threatened, but was worried about the fate of Schmitz, a former mayor of Vienna, and of Hornbostel, political director of the Ballplatz.

"2. *Hungary's relations with Germany.* The minister of foreign affairs acknowledged that the close vicinity of great powers is not always advantageous for small countries, but since geography could not be altered, Hungary would make all efforts to continue its cordial and traditionally friendly relations with Germany.

"Kánya considers absurd the rumors claiming that Germany intends eventually to take possession of Hungarian districts inhabited by Swabians. Chancellor Hitler, he said, is a man with too strong a political and historic sense to try to break up centuries-old settlements. All he will want is cooperation with Hungary, which it is in the latter's interest to agree to.

"When I asked whether Germany's new position wouldn't hamper him in the policy he has been following until now, characterized by a certain freedom of action, he replied that since direct Italo-Hungarian relations are in no way weakened, Hungary still has the same possibilities as in the past.

"I asked Kánya again whether, in view of the cohesion of the Rome-Berlin Axis, this freedom of action wouldn't be somewhat illusory. Smiling, he remarked that 'cohesion does not exclude, in certain circumstances, some play on nuances, since we are talking about two allied great powers, not about a single, united country.' By that, I believe he wanted to tell me that, in the event of excessive German pressure, Italy's favorable influence might prove helpful to the Budapest government.

"3. *Romano-Hungarian negotiations.* Turning to the current negotiations in Bucharest with Bárdossy, Kánya told me that:

"a) In the Treaty of Trianon, Hungary had secured an article favor"able to its interests: art. 239 regarding the establishment of joint arbitration tribunals, which public opinion would not accept to be abolished.

"I pointed out to the foreign minister that since those tribunals are no longer active and since he knows the attitude of the Little Entente in that respect, the article in question is in effect obsolete. At a time when we are trying to clear the way in order to facilitate the future development of our relations, it would be appropriate to clarify this point also in a realistic way.

"Kánya, however, preferred not to commit himself for the future, since the possibility could not be excluded that, under certain circumstances, the arbitration tribunals might be reestablished. Besides, he added, other interests of which he was not at liberty to speak are at stake and militate against giving up art. 239. I believe my interlocutor was trying to let me understand that those interests are of a material nature and concern Hungarians with estates in Transylvania, a particular concern to Count Bethlen.

"b) With regard to our draft of the statement, Hungary's minister of foreign affairs said he could not accept it because it did not contain the word 'minority.' I explained to him that the reason I had drafted the text this way last fall was precisely to avoid mentioning a problem that could offend the justified sensitivity of our public opinion. I added that, in my view, the text, by its very lack of precision, covers all possible disputes between the two countries and offers both governments the guarantee that each of them will take, within its national sovereignty, measures intended to allow the development of future friendly relations. . . . If the relations between the majority and the minority are not what all of us would wish, this is due for the most part to the revisionist propaganda, which, ceaselessly and using all means, leads to dissensions. To the extent this propaganda will be brought to a halt, the atmosphere will also improve. . . . I concluded by appealing to the Hungarian government's 'spirit of Danubian cooperation' to accept the proposed text, which would entail a real loss of popularity for the Romanian government.

". . . Kánya answered in a most amiable tone: 'I must recognize the conciliatory spirit in which the Romanian government is endeavoring to find an acceptable formula. But this matter is perhaps not yet ripe enough to be presented to Romanian public opinion. In that case, it might be better to postpone its resolution.'"

The impression I developed—partly following a confidence made to me by my Italian colleague Vinci, who had just returned from Rome—was that the objections raised by the Hungarian government in its negotiations with us also stemmed from the apprehension of having to sign similar agreements with the other countries of the Little Entente, and thus also with Czechoslovakia, which would displease Berlin. And this was the more so since at that time the entire political world in Budapest was considering Czechoslovakia as doomed and had the expectation—or illusion—of an impending annexation of Slovakia and of Subcarpathian Russia. In a speech, Eckhardt went so far as to promise the future Slovak minority in Hungary "a broad autonomy."

On April 22, Kánya told me that the Hungarian government truly wished to reach an agreement with Romania. And if such an agreement was reached, there could be an understanding that it would come into force only after the other Little Entente governments had reached direct agreements with Hungary. Kánya assured me that this was "not in order to split the Little Entente—which I know would be impossible to do and which I wouldn't even attempt—but to have a free hand toward Prague," which, faced with the imminent danger of German aggression, seemed prepared to make astounding concessions, even up to granting autonomy to the regions inhabited by Hungarians. If we didn't find this solution acceptable, Kánya proposed a de facto détente—without a written agreement—between Bucharest and Budapest, similar to that between Belgrade and Budapest. I replied that what was needed was a common formula for the four countries, which would constitute the basis for our future relations. There is nothing to prevent, however, the conclusion of subsequent agreements. Thus, after the conclusion of the agreement between the Little Entente and Hungary, if it happened that the Czechoslovak or another government was willing to extend additional concessions to the Hungarian minority, it would be free to do so, since the text we propose would consist solely of a declaration of principles concerning all disputes between us, rather than a statute for minorities.

Kánya then confessed to me the thought that tormented him. He was afraid that by accepting a treaty for the minimum protection of minorities with the Little Entente, he might be prevented from taking advantage of Czechoslovakia's present predicament by demanding from it much larger concessions that he believed he could obtain. What he wanted, in effect, was to have a free hand in the event of a German operation against Czechoslovakia. Revisionist demonstrations were being held in Budapest, calling—in the event of a German aggression—for a Hungarian military intervention to recover Slovakia and Subcarpathian Ruthenia. My Czechoslovak colleague, Kobr, assured me on the other hand that his government had no intention of granting the Hungarian population a minority statute, and that it did not want to negotiate separately with Budapest. He held that Kánya's maneuvers had as its real object the breaking up of the Little Entente by taking advantage of Czechoslovakia's present difficulties.

After a luncheon I gave at the legation on April 27, Kánya again insisted that we, as well as the Yugoslavs, negotiate separately with Hungary while, concurrently, negotiations would go on between Budapest and Prague; the instruments would all enter into force simultaneously. I replied that this was impossible, that I had explained this to him repeatedly, and that it was high time we finally came to an agreement, without further complicating easy matters. Bánffy, who was also there, shared Kánya's view, and did not want a Romano-Hungarian détente to occur simultaneously with the granting of Romanian concessions to its Hungarian minority. He told me that Bethlen, who had met with Goga during the latter's stay in Budapest, was of the same opinion. We then shifted to lighter topics. Jokingly, I told Kánya, "You should be grateful to Romania, which will provide you with a Führer, since the papers assert that Major Szálasi, the leader of the Hungarian Nazis, descends from an Armenian family from Moldavia (Salaşian)." Kánya had a good laugh about this, and, in high spirits, he told me he had a friend, a Jewish banker, who asked at an inn in the Tyrol, where he used to go in summers, whether he could still come there, after the Anschluss. He received the following reply: "Anybody can come here, be he Christian or Jewish, as long as he is an Aryan."

I had a talk with Goga on the eve of his departure from Budapest, and he recounted his conversations with Bethlen and with Bánffy. He urged me to press Kánya to stop beating around the bush and to conclude an agreement with us, which was essential for all of us. Goga believed we should not tie our lot too closely to that of Czechoslovakia, which was condemned to extinction or, in the best of cases, to falling into the German orbit. He told me Hitler and Göring had solemnly pledged that Romania's borders would be respected. Turning to our domestic politics, he was convinced that the king would consent [*sic*] to the existence of three political parties: one Liberal under the leadership of Tătărescu, another National-Peasant under the presidency of Călinescu, and the third one, National-Christian, headed by Goga. Patriarch Miron had disclosed to him that he wanted to give up his position as prime minister. According to what he told me, it was only he, Goga, who knew how to handle Codreanu. He had told him to his face: "Either you shoot me, or I have you shot." Since then, Codreanu had quieted down and had given up his electoral agitation. Goga would have calmed him completely had he stayed in the government. "To put hundreds of people in jail is not a good method."

Kánya's chief of cabinet and his future successor at the head of the Ministry of Foreign Affairs, the Transylvanian Istvan Csáky, with whom I had quite good relations, also confirmed that the Hungarian government was not in a position to conclude an agreement with the Little Entente as an entity because of Czechoslovakia, about which it wished to keep all its options open. In the present circumstances, he added, Hungarian public opinion would not accept an understanding with Prague.

DISCUSSIONS WITH ROMANIAN STATESMEN AT THE TIME OF THE SINAIA MEETING OF THE LITTLE ENTENTE (MAY 4–5)

I was summoned by phone to Sinaia for consultations with the government. My first meeting was with the patriarch, in his capacity as prime minister. After reminiscing about the time when he was regent and I secretary-general of the Regency, the conversation shifted to politics. The patriarch, being Transylvanian, assured me that one should not talk of an alleged persecution of minorities in Romania, but, on the contrary, of the persecution of the majority. He gave as an example the fact that he, as head of the predominant denomination, disposed of a relatively much smaller budget and less numerous staff than the minority denominations. He was favorable to my idea of building a Romanian church in Budapest, although he would obviously prefer if we could recover the old Romano-Greek church founded by the Aromanian families Mocsonyi, Dumba, and Sina, which had been taken over in 1909 by the Greek community following a lawsuit that should be reopened. He likewise approved my proposal of helping the Romanians remaining in Hungary to buy a printing press and publish a newspaper.

I then went to see Foreign Minister Petrescu-Comnen, who spoke with me about a new proposal from Bárdossy, again referring to an exchange of letters in the matter of minorities. None of the three foreign ministers of the Little Entente agreed to this proposal. Even the German government did not demand from Krofta such a commitment, being satisfied for the time being with a direct understanding between Henlein, the leader of the German minority in the Sudetenland, and Czechoslovakia.

Petrescu-Comnen urged me to see the king immediately, and phoned in my presence to arrange for an audience that same afternoon.

Carol received me in an unusually cordial manner. He asked me many questions on a variety of subjects, with all of which, as a matter of fact, he seemed perfectly acquainted. He was an admirer of Bethlen, "the only Hungarian statesman," and was very desirous of a détente with Hungary. He said improvements were being planned for the Hungarian minority in Transylvania. Personally, he would like them to receive the right to petition in Romanian and Hungarian, with the Hungarian text being the one deemed authentic in case of doubt. Carol also felt that in municipalities exclusively inhabited by Hungarians, it should be permissible to transact business at city halls in Hungarian. He asked me what the reaction had been in Budapest to our setting up of the Committee for Minorities. I replied that the reaction had been most favorable, but people were waiting for the appointment of the committee's head, whose role would be preponderant. He disclosed that he had received that morning Sir Reginald Hoare, the British envoy, who had argued at some length in favor of a Romano-Hungarian détente, a démarche that had been likewise made in Budapest. I replied that what was important was what the Germans said in Budapest, and that I feared they were not advising a détente with Prague. I asked whether it would not be possible for us to accept that the agreement with Hungary be signed, or at least initialed now, with its entry into force being postponed to a later date, after the Czechoslovak government had granted minority status to the Hungarian population. The king was in full agreement with my suggestion. He then inquired as to how we were received in Hungarian high society, and seemed pleased to hear that we could not be treated any better. At leave-taking, he thanked me for the information I was conveying and for the efforts I was deploying; he also instructed me to appeal in his name to Horthy "to exert moral suasion" to bring about an understanding between the two governments.

The official communiqué issued in Sinaia on the Little Entente meeting included the following passages: "The Permanent Council examined most carefully the question of the relations between the states of the Little Entente and Hungary. It unanimously maintains its wish to continue the negotiations under way, which aim to contribute to the establishment of understanding and trust in the Danube Basin.

"The Little Entente reaffirms the loyalty of its members toward the League of Nations. It emphasizes the statement issued, in the name of the three countries, at the last meeting of the Council in January of this year. It affirms its will to contribute to the realization of the ideal of international cooperation, formulated by the authors of the Treaty."

Back in Budapest after a short stay with my family in Vienna, I heard of the death of Octavian Goga, felled by a stroke.

At a dinner party hosted by Prime Minister Darányi on May 9, I told him of the government's good intentions with regard to the negotiations with Hungary, which he said "gladden me greatly." Kánya joined us, and I requested to see him at the Ministry, so as to share with him "pleasant" news concerning the Sinaia meeting. "But you always tell me pleasant things, dear fellow!" he replied. "This time," I retorted, "it is pleasant facts that I want to report." We agreed to meet on May 12.

At that meeting I briefed him on the Romanian government's conciliatory intentions and asked him to arrange for me an audience with the regent, so that I might deliver the king's message. After that, we turned to the usual discussion about a wording acceptable to both Budapest and Bucharest. He kept vacillating and constantly raising new difficulties. I then asked him point-blank, "If we accepted your formula, would you sign on the spot?" He was reluctant to answer me. I tightened the screw on him: "Then why continue arguing about the wording instead of admitting frankly that you don't want to sign with Czechoslovakia?" Kánya then had to confess that Hungarian public opinion would not accept a détente and nonaggression declaration with Czechoslovakia, at a time when all Hungarian eyes were fixed on Slovakia. At most, it would go along with a provision that the diplomatic instrument would come into force only after the Prague government had come to an agreement with its Hungarian minority. In turn, I stressed the impossibility of my government's agreeing to an exchange of letters on minority matters; I added that it would constitute a dangerous precedent not only for us but also for Hungary, which at one point or another might also have to discuss minority issues with some "neighboring great power."

GOVERNMENT RESHUFFLE IN HUNGARY

Those days also witnessed a reshuffle of the government team, Darányi being replaced as prime minister by Béla Imrédy. Kánya, however, remained at the Ministry of Foreign Affairs. In his first speech as prime minister, Imrédy made plain the right-wing nature of his government by upholding the legislation concerning the Jews and the five-year economic plan that had been drawn up by his predecessor. With regard to foreign policy, he reaffirmed the cordiality of the ties with Germany, Italy, and Poland, while at the same time expressing the hope that the negotiations with the Little Entente might lead to a normalization of relations and even, after the resolution of some existing problems, to a friendly cooperation of the nations of the Danube Basin.

The causes of the Darányi government's fall are rather complex. Although he had to his credit a year and a half of untroubled governance, after the disappearance of Gömbös, and had seen through the much awaited enactment of political and economic reforms (for example, broadening of the regent's and of the Upper House's prerogatives, the introduction of secret voting in the elections, a five-year investment program), Darányi had ended up losing the confidence of the country's leadership by his lack of firmness in coping with the extreme right's increasing agitation. The regent blamed him for not having known how to put an end to the bold campaign led against him and his family by the followers of the Nazi leader in Hungary, Major Szálasi. Darányi, however, could defend himself by pointing out that if the nationalist extremists had been able to intensify their activities, this was due in good part to the leniency—and even protection—they enjoyed in Horthy's entourage.

Notwithstanding all this, Darányi ungrudgingly yielded his place to his colleague Imrédy, minister of national economy and governor of the National Bank. Imrédy, a leading financier with the ascetic features of a medieval monk—he looked very much like Savonarola—was in favor of an authoritarian regime, but one stemming from intellectual theories, not from ideological passions. I remember his once telling me that his ideal statesman was not Hitler, or Mussolini, but Salazar. And Salazar was undoubtedly his model, for he too was a man of wide culture, able to pluck an issue out of the bramble of details and raise it to the level of preoccupations of national importance. Imrédy's bearing and decisiveness, as well as his speeches—of an eloquence that was more British than Southern European—exerted an undeniable attraction on his fellow countrymen. Brought to power thanks to the influence of two former prime ministers, Istvan Bethlen and Gyula Károlyi, the governing stance prescribed to Imrédy consisted of the suppression of extremist disturbances and the introduction of a right-wing program including several of the nationalists' ideas that were intended to deprive Szálasi of his propaganda platform. Generally, the Imrédy government was seen as a last attempt to halt Hungary's drift toward right-wing extremism.

MEETING WITH REGENT HORTHY

On the morning of May 18 I was received by Horthy, in order to deliver to him my king's message. The regent received me very cordially, in an almost informal way. He began by recounting a recent hunting accident, then told me of his regret at having to give up Darányi as prime minister. "This is a dreadful aspect of my job. Here comes a man in whom I have confidence, who has accomplished much for his country, of whom I think very highly, and I must beat him over the head and say, 'Get out!'"

When the conversation moved to that part of Imrédy's speech in which the new prime minister expressed his wish for friendly relations with neighboring countries, I passed on the king's message. I then went on to remind Horthy of the several stages through which our negotiations had passed. The negotiations had been broken off the preceding fall because of the intransigence of the Hungarian government, which had been insisting on the inclusion in the agreement of a pledge concerning minorities; not even the German government had demanded such a thing from Czechoslovakia. When negotiations were resumed in the spring, Romania and its allies went so far in their proposed concessions as to accept, in spite of the exacerbation of nationalist sentiments, the possibility of making some reciprocal declarations that would provide as far as possible for the elimination through administrative measures of disputes that might hinder the development of good relations with Hungary; these administrative measures would be taken within the framework of national sovereignty and excluding any foreign interference. Yet not even this considerable concession, I added, seemed to have had any visible effect on Hungarian governmental circles, since the latest proposal given to us contained the same totally unacceptable condition of an exchange of letters concerning minority matters.

I explained to Horthy that, in our view, a détente with Hungary could not take the form of a legal document that would bind us all into narrow definitions, the more so since recent history has shown the doubtful value of commitments that are too specific. For us, such a détente would be a political act not requiring many clauses or provisos. It would require, on the contrary, the elasticity needed to create a propitious atmosphere in which even the thorniest problems could receive an obvious and equitable solution. I ended by expressing the hope that the regent would make use of his great moral authority to persuade his government to show a more conciliatory spirit and to appreciate the historic significance of the present times.

Regent Horthy answered that he appreciated the king's gesture and that he was personally convinced that the happiest periods in history had been those in which heads of state had effectively taken hold of the helm, thereby being able to help bring nations together without being hampered by short-term politics. In this connection, Horthy told me that he had held the real power in Hungary for the past eighteen years, Parliament being a mere façade; all the governments, acting under the direct control of the head of state, have always enjoyed overwhelming majorities. Turning to the ideas I had expressed as to the spirit in which the negotiations between Hungary and the allied countries of the Little Entente should be conducted, Horthy told me the following: "I am neither a jurist nor a diplomat, but I share your views. What use is a signed and sealed agreement to me if it is not complied with? What we need for the Hungarian minorities in neighboring countries is a conciliatory climate in which they are granted satisfactory living conditions. I have always opposed, with all my authority, excessively violent reactions in this country on minority issues, but something has also to be done in the other countries. I must acknowledge that gestures have been made in Romania that show that the atmosphere in this regard has improved. I will of course tell my minister of foreign affairs what we have discussed today."

As I was leaving, Horthy assured me that he would spare no efforts for a détente between our countries, which were faced with so many identical problems, be they of internal or external nature.

THE INTERNATIONAL EUCHARISTIC CONGRESS (MAY 22–29)

The Hungarians celebrated in 1938 the eight hundredth anniversary of St. Stephen's death, and the entire year lay for them under the sign of their first king. Concurrently, in the spring of that year, an International Eucharistic Congress was held in Budapest. The concurrence of the two events had, for the Hungarian nation, no other purpose than to revive the political principles of their first king.

No nation in the world other than Hungary has the capability of perpetually living in the past and in the realm of fairy tales and legends. Hence the phenomenon that could be noted at that time—and would have been inconceivable anywhere else—of responsible politicians and first-rate journalists making a current political reality out of an almost legendary hero who had lived a thousand years ago. Not a day passed without the founder of the Hungarian state being mentioned at least once in speeches or newspaper articles. There was no talk of other famous rulers of the country, such as Charles Robert of Anjou or, more recently, Maria Theresa or Franz Joseph; but St. Stephen was always mentioned, be it in the largest or smallest of political meetings. The English are undoubtedly the most traditional people on earth, showing the greatest love and respect for their proud past. But we would never see a member rising in the House of Commons to urge his colleagues, in a current matter, to take a leaf from Edward the Confessor (more or less Stephen's contemporary), nor would we find his name brought up in one of *The Times'* political editorials dealing with a modern problem. Yet what would be impossible in tradition-bound Britain, in France, in Italy, or in Germany, was a daily occurrence in Hungary.

This is the reason why the Hungarians assigned to the Eucharistic Congress not only a religious and historical character but also a current political one. This also explains why Hungarian denominations other than Catholics were collaborating directly or indirectly toward the apotheosis of the figure who represented in the minds of the Magyars the embodiment of their past history and future evolution, and thus also were working toward the success of the Eucharistic Congress.

Nevertheless, this thirty-fourth International Eucharistic Congress took place in rather unfavorable circumstances because of the international political situation. Hitler's growing aggressiveness toward Czechoslovakia (which he was preparing to annihilate) led to the absence of the numerous German and Austrian pilgrims that had been expected. They had been prevented from attending the Congress by the absolute prohibition decreed by the Berlin government, which made no exception, not even for Cardinal Innitzer. The number of Czechoslovak participants was obviously much reduced, worried as they were by the unfolding events. And many believers from more distant regions were not inclined to travel to a Central Europe threatened by war. The pomp and grandiose plans for the ceremonies were cut back in consequence. To cap it all, vile weather, with almost uninterrupted rain and thunderstorms, contributed to the lack of success of the Congress. Overall, the mood, instead of being festive as is usually the case at such occasions, was sobered by the approaching danger, and everyone's thoughts were directed more toward Berchtesgaden, from where the thunderbolt was expected, than toward the Vatican.

Outwardly, however, the ceremonies proceeded with the required pomp: pontifical liturgies, ecclesiastical assemblies, processions. For someone like me, accustomed to the pomp and circumstance of ceremonies in Rome, those in Budapest could not make that much of an impression. What I found imposing, however, was the ascetic figure of the papal legate, Cardinal Secretary of State Eugenio Pacelli, the future Pope Pius XII, whose eyes sparkled with intelligence. The inauguration of the Congress took place outdoors, on Hösök ter, with speeches that were too long and without interest and an unending colorless procession, which I viewed with my wife and relatives. After that, the minister of foreign affairs offered a luncheon in honor of the cardinal-legate, which was attended by all heads of mission except that of the Soviets. In the evening, the regent hosted a large reception. We were ushered into a special room where a receiving line was formed by the Horthy couple, Cardinal Pacelli, Archdukes Joseph, Joseph Francis, and Albrecht, and by Archduchesses Augusta and Anna. The cardinals dressed in red, the bishops in purple, the diplomats in full uniform, the Hungarian men in their *díszmagyar,* and the ladies in old Hungarian costumes presented a handsome view in the great hall. I had the opportunity of speaking at length with Cardinal Pacelli, whom I was to meet twice in Rome when he was pope. He seemed very well informed on the Catholic and Uniate dioceses in Romania, and he thanked me for the help given by the Romanian government to its citizens wishing to attend the Congress, in the number of some eight thousand. A few days later I gave a big reception in honor of the leaders of our pilgrims: Archbishop Cisar of Bucharest, Bishops Robu of Jassy and Hossu of Alba Iulia, and some seventy other clergymen and laymen.

THE IMRÉDY GOVERNMENT AND ITS RELATIONS WITH GERMANY

On June 8, I met with the new prime minister, Béla Imrédy, whom I knew well from the time he was governor of the National Bank. He described to me his governing plans, which leaned toward extended social reforms and an energetic suppression of extremist movements. With regard to our negotiations, he thought that only separate negotiations with each of the Little Entente governments could be fruitful, in view of the differences in conditions. With Romania, he noted a slight détente. This, however, was not the case with Czechoslovakia, where the Hungarians, along with the Germans, were demanding the establishment of a federal state.

In this connection Vukicević, the Yugoslav envoy, told me that Belgrade wished to start private talks with Budapest, under the condition that any eventual agreement be only initialed, the signature taking place only when all three governments reached an understanding with Hungary. I pointed out to him that the minutes of the recent meeting in Sinaia of the Little

Entente Council provided, in the last paragraph of point 3, for the possibility of separate agreements by the three governments with their respective minorities, but not with the Budapest government. Vukicević, however, claimed he was referring to a confidential decision taken in Sinaia, which Stoiadinović had authorized him to convey to Imrédy and Kánya. I immediately cabled Bucharest for clarification.

While Hungarian public opinion was feverishly awaiting the unfolding of the international crisis, the Imrédy government was cautiously taking the measures deemed likely to provide Hungary with a maximum of benefits at a minimum of risks. In official speeches as well as in private conversations, Kánya revealed the guiding principle of his diplomacy: to befriend the neighbors of Hungary's neighbors. Friendship with Italy was for Hungary an insurance against Yugoslavia; the long-standing friendship with Germany opened to it prospects on Czechoslovakia. Only toward Romania was Kánya unable to proceed the same way, because, and he seemed to apologize, "the Soviet Union's form of government prevents any rapprochement between Budapest and Moscow." The international situation being inauspicious to Czechoslovakia in the spring of 1938, the Budapest government set aside its other claims—in the hope that an opportune time would come for them—and devoted its revisionist efforts solely northward. It therefore sought Germany's unconditional support, Poland's eventual cooperation, and if at all possible, the neutrality of the other two states of the Little Entente.

Kánya was therefore going to endeavor synchronizing his diplomatic action with that of the Wilhelmstrasse, in the expectation that he would thus be able to share in Germany's spoils. An attendant, very close collaboration between the German and Hungarian general staffs was capped by the visit to Budapest of General Keitel, head of the German supreme military command. Poland's friendship toward Hungary was less forthcoming, perhaps because of the latent danger of its proximity to the Nazi Reich.

The greatest danger to the fulfillment of Magyar aspirations was still represented by the Little Entente, and that is why Hungary unceasingly sought to break that unity by separate negotiations with each of the component countries. The most receptive to such a bait seemed to be Yugoslavia, whose envoy to Budapest was overwhelmed by courtesy and friendliness, and was treated as if he were a member of the Berlin-Rome Axis. With Romania, too, although on a much lesser scale, there were efforts to improve relations. At the Ministry of Foreign Affairs I was told that our latest proposal was "under study," some of the points being easy to accept, others less so. Kánya told me he was growing more optimistic about our negotiations, but that it would require considerable time.

From a social point of view, Budapest's high society hastened to accept all invitations to the Romanian legation and to invite us in return. Among our guests at a series of luncheons and dinners (some in honor of Princess Margarete of Hohenzollern, the wife of the family's head) were various cabinet members and their spouses, Archduke Joseph Francis and Archduchess Anna, Count Istvan Csáky (the future foreign minister) and his sister, Count and Countess Szechenyi, Count and Countess Gyula Teleki, Countess Cecilia Teleki, Count Dominic Festetics, Count Revedin, Baroness Oer, and so many others. Hungarian high society also expressed its condolences for Queen Marie's death by attending in large numbers the requiem we held on July 24.

Concerning the ties between Hungary and the German Reich, I reported the following to my government on June 23, 1938: "Day by day the political and economic ties between Hungary and Germany seem to become knitted closer together. Continuing visits take place between the two countries' statesmen (Finance Minister Reményi-Schneller, Justice Minister Mikecz) and superior officers (Admiral Raeder, General Keitel). Commercial negotiations are further strengthening Hungary's economic subjugation. All signs therefore point to the erroneousness of the theory according to which the Hungarian government, worried by the close vicinity of the German Reich, is seeking political connections in the West.

"The very fear of the massive Nazi pressure, exerted both externally and internally (through Szálasi's movement), is inducing the Hungarian government to draw ever closer to that of Germany, in the belief that friendly relations will dissuade the latter from actions detrimental to Hungary's independence or territorial integrity. . . . Even Imrédy—for all his statements when he came to power—gives signs of being ready to shift from his constitutional and Christian position to a more conciliatory attitude toward the ideology and aspirations held across the Leitha River.

"The new prime minister can indeed choose but between two paths: he can either take a hard line against Nazi encroachment, in which case he will at some point be overthrown by the Germans, or he can integrate himself in the current stemming from Berchtesgaden, in which case he will be backed in his external, as well as internal, policies. There are many indications that Imrédy has chosen this second path. He will no doubt point out to Berlin that, in the event Germany wanted to establish in Hungary—be it openly, or under the convenient cloak of Budapest parliamentarism—an authoritarian regime in order to enforce its political and economic will, it would be best to forgo a risky solution such as that of Szálasi in favor of a much more reliable Imrédy solution. It is certain that such an evolution, were it to occur, would take place step by step, respecting all the appearances so dear to the prime minister's heart. I am saying 'appearances' because, at bottom, Imrédy is totally won over to authoritarian methods. Even before he came to power he often told me of his admiration for Salazar, whom he considered the finest figure of contemporary European politics. He takes pride in his nickname, 'Hungary's Salazar.' There is no doubt that he would view with relief the formation in this part of Europe of a bloc of countries determined to resist intrusions by neighboring great powers, especially if Italy were to direct from behind the scenes the formation of such a 'Helsinki-Ankara axis.' But he will refrain from any move that could be taken by the Führer to mean that Hungary was joining a grouping in the least opposed to German interests.

"In that respect, Kánya has the mission of discreetly keeping abreast of developments, following Italy's extremely prudent movements but without losing a single inch of the ground gained with Germany. Indicative of this is Kánya's agitation at the slightest irritation arising in Berlin, as well as the care with which he smooths away anything that might displease the Wilhelmstrasse. . . . It is therefore clear that in the present international situation official Hungary follows without wavering the German political line. Even in those quarters that, for ideological or traditional reasons, regret this cooperation with the Hitlerian Reich (the case of Count Bethlen or of Tibor Eckhardt), it is acknowledged that this is the only policy possible for a Hungary that does not want to give up its revisionist claims."

Even though they felt compelled by circumstances to embrace Hitler's policy, the Hungarian leaders were nevertheless fearful of the threatening German giant at their border. They were scared stiff by the mission of the German minister plenipotentiary Martius in the Danubian capitals, starting with Budapest. The mission had the transparent aim of replacing the International Danube Commission with a so-called technical commission of the riparian states. As a matter of fact, the Hungarians feared with good reason, since this would have left all of us, the nations of the Danube Basin, in tête-à-tête with Germany on Danubian matters. The Hungarian government therefore sought to oppose, as much as it dared, Hitler's plan of dominating the Danube, being secretly encouraged in this by Italy, which was at risk of losing its seat on the International Danube Commission. Kánya confirmed to me his preoccupations in this regard, and hoped that we too would turn down Martius's proposal, so that Hungary might maintain the pretext of the solidarity of riparian states in support of its opposition.

✧ ✧ ✧

The true purpose of Imrédy and Kánya's visit to Rome—forerunner of Horthy's to Berlin—was to determine to what extent they could count on the Duce's political assistance in the face of Hitler's rapacious tendencies. They wanted to find out, shortly before the face-to-face meeting with the Führer, what political aspects of the old relationship between Italy and Hungary still remained operative after the collapse of the Rome Protocols. When the Protocols had come into force, the Hungarian government's difficulty had been to keep an even balance between Rome and Berlin—to draw the maximum political and economic benefit from the Danubian arrangements set up by Mussolini, but without, for all that, endangering the traditional relations with the Reich. It might therefore have been expected that the abandonment of the Stresa policy line, marked at first by the sanctions against Italy and later by the formation of the Berlin-Rome Axis, would have smoothed the way for Hungarian diplomacy, which, having now its two protectors in the same camp, would no longer be exposed to the risks inherent in an unstable equilibrium. As paradoxical as this may seem, the difficulties had actually increased, not on the surface—for all the appearances of a perfect German-Italian solidarity were observed—but deep down, where Hungary found itself caught in the interplay of the two powers' hidden Danubian rivalries.

The abiding objective of Hungarian policy was to gain, on the one hand, the support of Germany, whose forcefulness represented a hope for Hungarian revisionism; and on the other hand, to win Italy's help in ensuring its freedom of action, so as to ward off the danger of Hitler's imperialism. From the time of the constitution of the Berlin-Rome Axis and of Italy's gradual withdrawal from the Central European scene, the part assigned in Hungarian diplomacy to the alliance with Rome had come to an end. And after the Anschluss, the close links with Italy seemed for a time to lack any political usefulness in the face of the pressure exerted by the Reich, which had become Hungary's direct neighbor. What assistance could the Italians still provide the Hungarians against the groundswell of German expansionism, public opinion asked itself, when they had looked on impassively—and, indeed, even collaborated indirectly—to Austria's collapse? The reality of economic statistics (45 percent of Hungarian exports went to

Germany and only 15 percent to Italy) helped emphasize the relative importance for Hungary of the Italian versus the German influence.

To these must be added the fact that, though Italy did not impinge on Hungary's domestic politics, the whole internal life of Hungary was bedeviled by the "Hungarist" tendency, which was nothing more than a tributary of the Hitlerian movement.

Imrédy's position was therefore somewhat akin to that of Chancellor Schuschnigg before Berchtesgaden. The situation, however, was obviously not the same. For the head of the Austrian government, Hitler represented solely a huge threat. For Hungary's prime minister—and especially for public opinion, nurtured for two decades on illusions—Hitler also represented the possibility of territorial gains in Slovakia and Ruthenia, and perhaps even of the fulfillment of other revisionist aspirations in the future. Nevertheless, in order to keep his administration in power, Imrédy, just like Schuschnigg, had to fight against some political organizations openly encouraged and supported by Berlin. At the same time, he was seeing his country gradually sliding toward the status of a German colony.

On the eve of the Kiel and Berlin meetings, Imrédy must surely have been advised moderation in Rome. He was certainly urged to appear as conciliatory as possible, so as to stay in the Führer's good graces in those times of anxiety, but still remain in favor of replacing the Italo-Austro-Hungarian protocols by a new and more flexible scheme that would leave the door open to other adhesions.

The Italian game was interesting to follow in the then prevailing situation: absolute solidarity with Germany on major international problems so as not to weaken the effectiveness of the Berlin-Rome Axis, but, on the other hand, an attempt to bring the Danubian countries together in a bloc capable of counterbalancing the German powerhouse in Central Europe. The place Austria had held in the triangle of the Rome Protocols could now be filled, and with more authority, by Yugoslavia. Kánya told me later that Ciano had warmly suggested to him a rapprochement with Belgrade, and had expressed high regard for Stoiadinović. But Kánya added that the Magyaro-Yugoslav relation was not of a kind to allow closer ties between the two countries. It was no less true, however, that the inclusion of Yugoslavia in the scheme envisioned by the Duce could have attracted at a later date the adhesion of Romania and of the Balkan countries—hence the efforts of Italian diplomacy to secure the adhesion of Yugoslavia. In his toast at the Palazzo Venezia, Mussolini had stressed "good relations with Yugoslavia," placing that country almost at the level of the Berlin-Rome Axis. But Kánya told my Yugoslav colleague that Budapest would not agree to Yugoslavia's admittance to an Italo-Magyar-Yugoslav tripartite agreement until some problems had first been resolved. It was apparently understood that "problems to be resolved beforehand" meant territorial revisions, said to be "essentially symbolic," concerning areas at the junction of the Drava with the Danube, and just south of Burgenland. The Germans, however, reportedly pleaded with Stoiadinović not to join that new triangle with its anti-German connotations, but to propose instead the formation of a Berlin-Rome-Belgrade-Budapest quadrangle, which, obviously, would be led not by Rome but by Berlin.

This was, therefore, a decisive moment for the Imrédy government, for it had to end its tergiversation and adopt a clear-cut position. Either it had to follow without reservations the German line, or it had to embrace Italy's equilibrium policy, with the prospect of signing agreements with its neighbors. In the latter case, however, German support for the achievement of Hungarian claims would become more problematic.

ROMANO-HUNGARIAN NEGOTIATIONS CONTINUE

On July 13, the Romanian government sent to the Hungarian government, through Bárdossy, a formula in which the Little Entente would recognize Hungary's parity of rights concerning armaments, both parties undertaking not to have recourse to force in the relations between them. The following draft of a declaration for the Romanian and Hungarian governments was appended: "In its wish to improve and consolidate good neighborly relations between Romania and Hungary, the Romanian (Hungarian) government has studied all the elements capable of contributing to that end and has decided on its own to take within its full sovereignty all the necessary administrative measures aiming at eliminating any difficulty that might hinder the development of friendly relations with Hungary (Romania)."

A decree of August 3 established in Romania a Commission for Minorities, with Silviu Dragomir, a Transylvanian, as commissioner general. Kánya told me that the statute granted to the minorities by the Romanian government had made a deep impression on him, and had been received with the highest satisfaction by the public. "Frankly," he added, "I would never have thought that you would make such a gesture." He considered that negotiations between us would be much easier now, and thought we would be able to agree on a formula almost identical to that proposed by Romania. He would only want to have the qualitative adjective "administrative" removed from the word "measures" so as not to establish a precedent, since in the case of Czechoslovakia the measures in favor of the minorities would be of a constitutional and legislative nature. In any case, he was going to consult his department's lawyers.

This point settled, Kánya said there would still remain for the Hungarian government the difficulty of signing an identical text with Czechoslovakia. Hungarian public opinion would never understand how a simple innocuous statement such as this could be considered acceptable, when the Runciman mission opened such broad prospects to the minorities in Czechoslovakia and when all Magyardom was demanding autonomy, and even more, for their brothers in the north. I took advantage of the occasion to stress the imperative necessity for Hungary, in its turn, to improve the conditions of its Romanian minority if a real détente between the two countries were to be reached. Kánya objected that the number of Romanians in Hungary was not large enough to be granted exceptional concessions. I replied that there was no question of exceptional concessions, but of a minimum of measures, rejected until now, to enable them to maintain their ethnic individuality. I reserved the right to tell him in detail, on another occasion, the main demands that should be satisfied. As I was leaving, Kánya stressed our countries' common interest in defending themselves against the Bolshevik peril. I agreed, and contented myself with noting that, in the face of such a danger, all expansionist dreams ought to be abandoned.

In accordance with my government's instructions, I informed Kánya on August 16 that Romania accepted the modification of its formula proposed by Hungary—that is, leaving out the adjective "administrative" from "administrative measures." The Hungarian foreign minister stated that then "everything is in order" regarding Romano-Yugoslav-Hungarian declarations.

In a report to the Romanian Minister of Foreign Affairs, on August 19, I summarized my latest negotiations with Kánya, on the eve of the Little Entente's meeting in Bled.[2]

THE LITTLE ENTENTE'S LAST MEETING

I was instructed by the government to participate in the meeting of the Council of the Little Entente, which was to open in Bled on August 21. On the evening of August 20, as per the instructions received, I drove from Budapest to Timişoara, where I boarded the Romanian ministerial railway carriage. When I left, Apor had wished me "Pleasant journey

[2]The report is set forth in Appendix C.

and good luck," and so did Gascoigne and Charmasse. Petrescu-Comnen had apparently not seen my latest cables and was amazed when I told him of the success of our negotiations: the acceptance by the Hungarian government of the notion of a common communiqué by the three members of the Little Entente and Hungary, stating clearly that the contracting parties are in agreement on the parity of rights and on a nonaggression declaration, with no mention of the other issues that remained unsettled. He couldn't believe his eyes when he read the Hungarian draft of the communiqué, and congratulated me warmly and thanked me for the "victory" I had won. He at once cabled the king. He just asked me whether I thought it possible to have the text, unaltered, initialed by all four governments. I replied that I doubted the Hungarians would be willing to initial it, at least not with Czechoslovakia, in view of the hopes they lulled themselves with.

At Jimbolia, Stoiadinović's ministerial carriage was attached to the train, which wasn't really needed since our delegation was traveling in the Romanian ministerial carriage. The director of Yugoslav protocol, Frangeo, invited me to occupy the prime minister's compartment until Bled, which I accepted with alacrity so as to rest a bit, spared from my compatriots' gossiping. At Ljubliana, Krofta's carriage was also attached to the train.

The next morning, August 21, at ten o'clock, we arrived in Bled. We were received at the station by Stoiadinović, an honor guard, and a multitude of young Slovene women in their beautiful national costumes, tossing flowers. After settling down in the pleasant Toplice Hotel and signing the royal family's registers, the three foreign ministers began their meeting. I took advantage of the respite to gaze at the enchanting views around me: the clear lake and its island with a monastery, the surrounding mountains, and the castle's ruins on a hill. I even had the time to cool off with a swim in the lake.

I got in touch with my old colleague, Bessenyey,[3] now Hungary's envoy to Belgrade, and tried to sound him out on some modifications to be brought to the text of the communiqué, as well as on the possibility of having it initialed without any change. He promised to phone Apor for instructions, Kánya being in Germany with Horthy.

In the evening, Stoiadinović hosted a so-called "informal" dinner on the hotel's terrace, from where we had a magnificent view of the lake. Fireworks shot through the sky, and searchlights illuminated the monastery and the castle. After dinner I had the opportunity of holding a conversation with Krofta. I told him how much we admired him and his

[3]George Bakách-Bessenyey.

fellow countrymen for the quiet courage and remarkable moral elegance with which they awaited the unfolding of events and were steeling themselves to meet them. Krofta replied that since this was a matter of life or death, all Czechoslovaks realized they had no choice of alternatives. The path was already traced out for them; their easy consciences thus led to their calm attitudes. They would make the maximum of concessions compatible with the preservation of the country's independence and integrity.

The morning of August 22 was devoted to the meeting of the Permanent Council of the Little Entente. Andrić, undersecretary of state of the Yugoslav Ministry of Foreign Affairs (whom I was to find again three years later in Berlin), delivered to Bessenyey the text of the communiqué we had agreed upon. The Hungarian envoy had been authorized by Apor, by phone, to initial the unaltered text, preferably with Stoiadinović, who was now taking over the presidency of the Council of the Little Entente. As for the final wording of the communiqué, Apor would consult by telegram with Kánya, who was now in Kiel with the regent.

The ban of the Drava hosted a luncheon at Bohinje, near Bled. High mountains and an alpine lake. Exchange of toasts between the ban (in Slovenian) and Krofta (in Czech), their languages being almost identical. After lunch, a walk to the source of the Savitza and its impressive cascade.

Petrescu-Comnen was scheduled to give a speech at that evening's banquet. He told me he planned to say that the Little Entente had not yet reached an agreement with Hungary. I advised him to sound a more optimistic tone in view of the impending success of the negotiations, but I got the impression he was scared of appearing optimistic about an agreement with the Budapest government. Before we entered the banquet room, Bessenyey approached and informed me he now had the necessary clearance to accept our wording for the communiqué, with the only condition that the term "difficulties" be maintained. I whispered this information to Petrescu-Comnen, and asked him to modify his speech. He was unwilling to do so, on the grounds that he had not yet spoken to Stoiadinović and Krofta, but he promised me to add a sentence indicating that "an agreement will be reached sooner than might be expected." It was clear to me that Petrescu-Comnen feared the reaction of our public opinion and wanted Stoiadinović to take the lead. Petrescu-Comnen's fear was, however, totally groundless, since everyone knew he would proceed only under the orders of the king, who sincerely wanted a détente between us and the Hungarians. Besides, Hungary had in fact exercised parity of rights for quite some time, and it was better for us to extend our recognition than for Hungary to proclaim its parity unilaterally.

After dinner there was a concert and a ball. All then joined in a kolo (a Serbian variety of our Romanian hora), except for Petrescu-Comnen, who found this to be below his dignity. Andrić, Bessenyey, and I proofread the texts on a corner of the bar. Then Stoiadinović, in the name of the Little Entente, and Bessenyey, for Hungary, initialed the texts. The job had been done. Bessenyey and I shook hands. Petrescu-Comnen congratulated me anew and thanked me warmly for "your dedication in bringing these negotiations to a head." The next day the meeting ended, and I returned from Ljubliana to Budapest.

In spite of all this, the Hungarian government was soon to give proof of its bad faith. The Budapest government's requests to the governments in Bucharest and Belgrade that the Bled agreement be put into effect were meant to throw doubt on the legal validity of the document. Imrédy as well as Kánya did not shrink from stating, without any juridical argumentation, their opinion that solely the item referring to Hungary's parity of rights in armaments had been irrevocably endorsed, while the reconfirmation of the nonaggression commitments would become effective only after the settling in Hungary's favor of the question of its minorities. When I drew Kánya's attention on September 2 to the biased interpretation given to our agreement, he gave an evasive reply, saying it would be best if, from now on, we all refrained from commenting on the Bled communiqué. He added he would try to avoid having the question discussed in Parliament, Hungarian public opinion becoming explosive as soon as there was talk of a détente with Czechoslovakia. Hungary's belief was that, with Hitler's help, its aspirations regarding Slovakia would be met in the near future.

Kánya was reticent regarding the impressions he brought back from Germany, and not very optimistic. He expected a military intervention by the Reich, and said no one knew how all this would end.

✧ ✧ ✧

While passing through Budapest, Radu Djuvara, our envoy to Berlin, disclosed that at the presentation of his credentials, Hitler had told him that if in the event of a conflict Romania barred the Russian armed forces from crossing its territory, Germany would guarantee the integrity of all its borders. "May I convey this officially to His Majesty?" Djuvara had asked. "You have my word," Hitler had replied. "Were I unable to keep my word, I would not give it. So if I give my word, it means that I can keep it and that I will keep it." The future was to show how he kept his word. Göring, too, had asked whether we would allow the Russians to pass through. Djuvara had explained that we could not prevent airplanes from passing at an altitude of 3,000 meters. “There obviously is no question of that,” Göring had replied, adding that all the Reich was asking was that we do not permit Russian troops to transit by land. Ribbentrop, on the other hand, complained to him that Romanian public opinion, instead of drawing closer to Germany, was moving away from it. Lipski, Poland’s envoy to Berlin, was insistently urging the Bucharest government to declare officially that it would not consent to the transit of Russian troops through Romania. The danger of war was considered imminent in the diplomatic circles of Berlin.

SLIDE TOWARD MUNICH

During the course of September the outlook got darker and darker. With revolting aggressiveness and vulgarity, Göring called the Czechs in a speech “ridiculous dwarfs,” boasting that Germany had thirty years’ supplies and that it was so formidably armed that no country in the world would be able to pierce its borders—a prophecy history was to belie. Equally arrogant and vulgar was the speech in which Hitler accused *dieser Herr Beneš*[4] of being a “liar.” Hard to believe that this was a head of state speaking of another head of state. There was talk of a plebiscite the Germans would impose for the Sudeten. In that case, my Polish colleague Orłowski told me, the Hungarians would demand a plebiscite in Slovakia, and the Polish government for one in the Teschen region.

Events began moving quicker and quicker. The German minority in Czechoslovakia became so arrogant and menacing that the government in Prague proclaimed martial law in the areas inhabited by the Sudeten, but the Sudeten Germans reacted by giving Beneš an ultimatum for rescinding the measure, in the absence of which they “would no longer be responsible for the situation.” The Prague government, obviously, disregarded the ultimatum and took severe measures to reestablish order in the rebellious region. Chamberlain, recognizing the seriousness of the situation, flew to meet Hitler. In the meantime, the Hungarian minority in Slovakia published a resolution demanding the right to self-determination. The Hungarian government then announced, in an official communiqué of September 18, that it would have recourse to all the means at its disposal to secure the fulfillment of that demand. Orlowski asked me what we would do if the Hungarian army, along with the German one, crossed the Czechoslovak

[4]This Mr. Beneš.

frontier, since the Budapest government feared a Romanian intervention, which could end with the Soviet army encamped at the Hungarian border. I told him he could find a clear answer in our treaties of alliance, which were in the public domain.

When Henlein issued a manifesto proclaiming it was an absolute necessity for the Sudeten to be attached to the Third Reich, London and Paris were rattled and started to yield. The two capitals began advising Prague to prepare to cede the region of the Sudeten to Germany. How could such an action, unworthy of the histories of France and Britain, have ever been taken! Paris had apparently been frightened by a report of its minister of foreign affairs, Georges Bonnet, who is said to have asked Litvinov, in Geneva, what Soviet Russia's attitude would be in the event of a German attack against Czechoslovakia. The Soviet foreign minister is said to have answered that Moscow would limit itself to what its international obligations required—that is, it would intervene only if France was attacked or if the League of Nations declared Germany an aggressor. Disheartened by such a weak reaction, Bonnet, on his return to Paris, described the general situation to the Council of Ministers in gloomy terms: Italy hostile, as Mussolini had declared in his speech in Trieste; Poland doubtful; Russia reticent; Britain willing to contribute only with its air force and navy—which meant that the French, standing alone, would be the ones to die on the Maginot line.

Terrified, the Council of Ministers decided not to start a preventive war. It was also encouraged in this by an adroit speech by Hitler in Nuremberg, in which he declared that, for him, the question of Alsace was a closed one (two years later, it became clear how closed that question had been!), and that he would limit his navy to 30 percent of the British one. Professor Barthélemy wrote in *Le Temps* an appalling article: "*Peut-on mourir pour la Tchécoslovaquie?*"[5] in which he argued that it would not be possible to galvanize the French nation to keep under Czech sway three and a half million Germans. The only thing Daladier could do was to call London for help. At Berchtesgaden, Hitler stated the conditions under which he would refrain from military intervention, and Chamberlain vowed to secure them for him, relieved not to have to endanger the lives of his fellow citizens "for a country so far from our shores, and about which we know so little."

Horthy and Kánya, in turn, also hastened to Berchtesgaden to obtain from Hitler the promise that the Hungarians in Slovakia would benefit

[5]Is it conceivable to die for Czechoslovakia?

from a treatment similar to that of the Germans of Sudetenland. My Czechoslovak colleague, Kobr, advised me that, faced with the Anglo-French pressures, Prime Minister Hodža had agreed to the territorial surrender to Germany. Kobr expected that similar territorial surrenders would have to be made in Slovakia to the Hungarians, and in Teschen to the Poles. What grief for Czechoslovakia, he added, and what a disgrace for its allies. Léon Blum summed the situation as follows: "One feels full of cowardly relief and of shame." Prince Karl-Emil Fürstenberg, former envoy of Austria-Hungary to Bucharest and later ambassador to Madrid, called on me. He told me that as much as he hated the Czechs, "who have destroyed my fatherland and its dynasty," he realized how tragic Hodža's position was. He told of the unspeakable suffering of the Austrians under the Nazi heel. He believed that if Hitler pushed things too far, he would end up by unleashing a worldwide war from which he would not be able to emerge successfully.

My Italian colleague, Vinci, told me that the Romanian press's sympathy for Czechoslovakia had left a very bad impression in both Rome and Berlin, since it denoted hostility toward the Axis. I replied that it was morally understandable that the press would express its admiration and pity for a nation that had been our ally for two decades.

I wrote in my diary:

September 24, Dramatic days. The Czechoslovak government has issued a proclamation that was read on the radio by Propaganda Minister Vavrečka (former envoy of Czechoslovakia to Vienna during my time, between 1931 and 1932), with the following content: "Just as Christ sacrificed himself for mankind, so we too are sacrificing ourselves for peace. Like Him, we have remained abandoned and alone. The responsibility will fall on the countries that have abandoned us. We are not naming them, but history will judge them."

The Hodža government had resigned. General Jan Sirový, inspector general of the armed forces, was appointed prime minister, with Krofta at the Foreign Ministry. It is a government of technicians, with some people close to Beneš. Sirový is popular and energetic, which is why Berlin and Rome criticize his government. Chamberlain flew to Godesberg and returned to London after two days, during which he wrote to Hitler more than he talked with him. Beneš seeks to hearten his people by assuring them that he has "his plan," and last night he ordered a general mobilization. This morning, France announced a partial mobilization, while Britain called up its navy's reservists. At Padua, Mussolini gave a true hysteric's speech, in which he violently attacked "the enemies on the other side of the Alps." It sounded almost as if he were declaring war on France. All mankind must perish so that two paranoiacs may relieve their nerves!

Japan's new envoy paid a courtesy call on me. He stated that his country, in the midst of a conflict with China, would remain neutral in the war that is menacing us, even if the Soviet Union joined in. Vukicević severely criticized France and England for abandoning their Czechoslovak ally; if war broke out, they would be starting with a moral defeat. As for his country, caught in a pincer between Italy, Germany, Bulgaria, and Albania, he doesn't believe it will be able to intervene to defend Czechoslovakia, despite all the provisions of the Little Entente treaty. Poland seems on the point of siding with Germany and Hungary. Maugras is very depressed: "The war of 1914–1918, compared with the one that is on the point of breaking out, will prove to have been *une guerre en dentelles*—a war in tuxedos; now, it will be a gangsters' rough-and-tumble." He seems convinced that, along with Germany, Poland as well as Hungary will attack Czechoslovakia.

I had a long conversation at the Ministry of Foreign Affairs with Istvan Csáky, its political director. He asserts categorically that the day the German armed forces enter Czechoslovak territory, the Polish army will begin its offensive against Czechoslovakia. He knows this with certitude, being in permanent touch with Orlowski: "At this very moment, for instance, he is in the office next door, where I introduced him to our economic director, for he was asking me details I do not know." I asked Csáky if the Hungarian government continues to wish to remain neutral as long as possible. He replied he was unable to answer that, since if the Germans and the Poles intervened to take possession of areas inhabited by their people, the Hungarian government would obviously have to do the same as soon as the question of dismembering Czechoslovakia was raised. I explained to him what a danger this would be for Hungary, and that it would be more prudent to let "the big ones" quarrel among themselves than to plunge the population into blood and ruins. He replied on a lyrical tone that Hungary could not fail to respond to a Czechoslovak aggression. I asked him if he could really believe that Czechoslovakia, in its present predicament, would plan to attack anybody. He maintained that Czechoslovakia had at the border four times more men than Hungary did. I then put forward the opinion that France, Britain, and the United States were a trio that, ultimately, it would be impossible to defeat. "Even in the event of their victory," Csáky replied haughtily, "Czechoslovakia shall not rise again, because there will no longer be any Czechs. The Germans will exterminate them. Only stones will remain there." (At a later date, Orlowski was to repeat to me that very same sentence.) From that conversation, I drew the conclusion that Hungary was preparing to attack Czechoslovakia at the same time as Germany and Poland, probably giving as pretext an imaginary aggression.

I am copying here selected notes made in my diary of conversations held during those tension-filled days:

September 25. Highly agitated, Orlowski came to see me. He is of the opinion that Czechoslovakia should be reduced to the smallest size possible, since it is nonviable and in the future would only be a Prussian springboard against Romania and Poland. Romania, he advised, "ought to buy Hungary at the expense of Czechoslovakia," allowing Subcarpathian Russia to be ceded to Hungary so as to establish a common border between it and Poland. He went on to tell me that "one should not help the weak, but only the strong and fit" and, in consequence, that "Romania should support Hungary, a country of the future and a powerful people who will certainly forget their former dreams." I pointed out that, for the time being, the Hungarian government does not demand the Ruthenian region. He retorted: "The government, *no,* but the general staff, the economic circles, and a large part of public opinion, *yes.*" I asked him whether Poland would still go to war, in view of today's news that Czechoslovakia was willing to make concessions to it. He thought it wouldn't, but the Czechoslovak proposals will have to be carefully studied, to see "whether they are sincere and complete." I have the impression that he would have preferred a forceful solution. I then asked him whether, this being the Polish stand, he thought the Hungarians would nevertheless go to war along with the Germans. "They would be insane not to do so," Orlowski said, "this is a unique opportunity for them. Without war, they will get at most territories in southern Slovakia; with war, they will also be given Subcarpathian Russia." Quite a warlike fellow, my Polish colleague! The British envoy has the impression that Poland is pushing Hungary to enter into military action at the same time as Germany.

September 26. Maugras came to report on a conversation he had had with Csáky, who told him that in the case of a localized conflict, Hungary would have to intervene along with Germany. In the case of a generalized war, however, Hungary would try to remain neutral as long as possible, "to join this time the victors, not like in 1914." At least Csáky is truthful, if not overly crafty. I found Maugras highly worked up against Hitler and Mussolini—"these frenzied fanatics"—and against Beck—"what madness to have resurrected Poland."

Knox shares our French colleague's feelings. Talking of Beck, he told me: "He's the man I most despise in Europe." I also had the visit of the eternally optimistic and fanciful Vinci. He seems persuaded that Britain will not intervene, and that Germany *and Italy* would defeat France in three weeks! I replied quietly that Britain would intervene, as would the United States, and that in the end Germany would be utterly defeated. But he retorted, "Don't forget the Italian army and the fact that France will have to fight on three fronts: Germany, Italy, and Franco's Spain." How ludicrous, if it were not so tragic. I then explained to him what madness it would be to end up with the destruction of Cologne, Paris, Venice, as well as with the slaughter of millions of young men, only because Hitler wants to occupy by armed force on October 1 territories that would be peacefully turned over to him a few days later, when the evacuation will have been carried out in a civilized manner. But poor Vinci is blinded by the passion of exacerbated nationalism. Besides, independent reasoning is prohibited in authoritarian states. In the evening, I listened to the broadcast of Hitler's brutal speech, with coarse insults toward Beneš.

September 27. Apor assures me the required orders have been given for the Romanian tugboats and barges stopped by the Hungarian authorities to be allowed to proceed on their course. The Portuguese envoy came to ask me for the latest news, and did not hide his indignation toward Hitler. We all listened with emotion to Neville Chamberlain's short radio address. In an almost inaudible and tired voice, seemingly nearly overwhelmed by tears, he was preparing his fellow countrymen for the prospect of war. Even though Britain has vouched that the territories promised to Hitler would be surrendered to him after their evacuation, he even having the right, as a symbolic gesture, to occupy Asch on October 1, the Führer wants to have recourse to force so as to prevent the Czechoslovak army from salvaging its ammunitions and the Czech refugees their possessions. The dividing line imposed by Hitler transfers 800,000 Czechs to German rule, contrary to the Nazis' vaunted ethnic theories. The British, declared Chamberlain, will thus fight not only for Czechoslovakia's freedom but also against a domination of Europe by force. This was said in a dignified and civilized voice, contrasting strikingly with the brutish screamings of Hitler and of his followers, who are seized by collective hysteria.

September 28. Britain has put its navy on war footing, and Germany's mobilization is expected for today. Pipinelis came to tell me of a conversation he had this very morning with Csáky. Csáky told him Hungary would try to remain neutral as long as possible. However, were Czechoslovakia to disintegrate under German pressure, Hungary would occupy the territories in southern Slovakia inhabited by Hungarian majorities. He considers that Krofta made a mistake by not immediately "offering" the region claimed by Hungary, which would have ensured Hungary's neutrality. Yugoslavia, he said, was urging Prague to make that sacrifice, but not so Romania. Talas, my Finnish colleague, also came to see me, seeking information; he forecasts that the countries neighboring Russia will remain neutral. Orlowski, still railing against France, admits that Hungary has now decided not to move immediately, "even in the event of a German and Polish attack against Czechoslovakia." He revealed to me that President Moscicki asked Beneš to cede to Poland the entire former duchy of Teschen, including the part inhabited by Slovaks, "but this last point could be negotiable." If this district were ceded at once, Poland would remain neutral. However, were France to demand that Russian troops pass through Poland and were an attempt made in that direction, Poland would cross to Germany's side. He later phoned me, saying that although optimistic until now, he was at present "scared because events are getting out of hand." The sensational news of the day: Hitler, at Chamberlain's urging, has invited Chamberlain, Daladier, and Mussolini to Munich, to confer tomorrow about the situation. At the Duce's insistence, the Führer has agreed to put off general mobilization by twenty-four hours. Hitler was no doubt also influenced by Roosevelt's message, in which he held him responsible for breaking off the negotiations and for a possible recourse to arms, with unforeseeable consequences (perhaps American intervention). The House of Commons was reportedly transported with joy when, at the end of a long speech accusing Hitler, Chamberlain announced the news (just handed to him) of the Munich Conference. An ephemeral feeling of relief, probably to be followed by a painful future disillusionment.

September 29. In Munich, the "Big Four" sign at the height of euphoria the agreement that dismembers Czechoslovakia. Germany undertakes to occupy only gradually areas less extensive than those it had demanded, by ultimatum, in Godesberg. A mixed French-Italian-German-Czechoslovak commission will be established to oversee the transfer of territories, a referendum, and the actual delineation of the border. Germany and Italy undertake to guarantee, along with France and Britain, the new borders of Czechoslovakia, once the claims of the Polish and Hungarian minorities have been resolved. The gullible Chamberlain, cheered on his return to London, was able to announce "peace for our time."

SPAT WITH KÁNYA AND CONTINUED NEGOTIATIONS

Following a meeting with Kánya on September 30, I immediately sent the following confidential letter to Petrescu-Comnen (written in French, so as not to have to translate the words used by Kánya and me): "A few days ago, my Italian colleague, Count Vinci, who had called on me, asked if I had seen Kánya recently. I replied that I had refrained from doing so during the present acute international crisis, the more so since we had nothing in particular to tell each other. 'You should nevertheless go see him,' said Vinci, 'you know he always talks approvingly of you.' Acting on this advice—I did not know to what extent it might have been suggested by Kánya—I took the opportunity of a phone conversation with the undersecretary of state, Baron Apor, on September 27, to tell him that, without insisting in the least, I would be pleased to chat with the minister of foreign affairs when he had the time.

Yesterday, September 29, I was told that Kánya would like me to come to see him today. When I got there, Kánya met me with a sullen countenance and an icy reception. He said he had made a proposal to Yugoslavia concerning the entry into force of the Bled agreement. Stoiadinović accepted it immediately, asking only that the same proposal be made to Romania. Pursuant to the Yugoslav prime minister's wish, Bárdossy reportedly made a similar démarche in Bucharest eight days ago, but has so far received no reply.

I explained that because Mr. Cancicov was serving only in an acting capacity, it made sense to wait for your return, and that such ticklish issues could not be decided instantly. He then asked me why Mr. Stoiadinović had been able to agree immediately. I pointed out that I did not know he had agreed, and in any case, even though we were allies, we were not a single country and that certain circumstances—if even only of geographic nature—were not identical. Besides, I added, I had no instructions concerning this matter and we would have to wait until our minister of foreign affairs reached a decision.

Kánya then raised his voice and began to vociferate that 'we are being mocked,' that 'we are treated as if we were slaves or scum,' and that 'when one is asked something, one has the courtesy of answering.' Even though I find it most embarrassing, I feel duty-bound to let you know he uttered personal attacks against you, which soon became quite sharp. He reproaches you for 'not having deigned to receive Bárdossy' and for having 'intrigued against Hungary' in all the capitals and in Geneva, thus 'striving to fill in for Beneš.'

Twice I had to interrupt him, saying that if he continued to speak in that tone, our conversation would have to come to an end, and that I was astonished to see him adopt the new practice of attacking a man personally instead of conferring from government to government. The conversation was taking a most unpleasant turn and I was preparing to get up and leave the room so as not to say something irremediable. But I managed to keep my temper, remembering and applying Ionel Brătianu's saying: 'A diplomat must seek to smooth out incidents, not to provoke new ones.'

Kánya undoubtedly also saw the danger and checked himself suddenly. He told me that it was not you as a man he had attacked, but the head of the Ministry of Foreign Affairs, and he subsequently refrained from taking you personally to task.

He told me that since the Czechoslovak issue had been raised—by Germany, not by Hungary—he did not see why Hungary alone should be 'excluded from the rewards.' Yugoslavia, according to him, was at present kindly inclined toward Hungary, whereas Romania showed 'all its hostility.' He therefore proposed once more his wording, or an equivalent one, for a direct agreement between Romania and Hungary (with no mention of Czechoslovakia), on the basis of 'the first step taken in Bled.' 'But this is a take it or leave it proposition, since Hungary can do without it.'

I replied that if Hungary could do without Romania, Romania could all the more do without Hungary, but that I found it totally unreasonable that after all the efforts exerted to arrive at this 'first step,' we would throw overboard this modest but real result in order to tell each other unpleasant things rather than discuss things calmly.

The conversation ended on a normal tone, but this bodes ill for the future. If Kánya persists in taking this attitude, I am determined to stand up to him."

On October 2, Petrescu-Comnen sent me the following reply: "On my way home from Geneva, Stoiadinović met me and said, among other things, that the Hungarian envoy to Belgrade had informed him two days earlier that the Hungarian government considers the Bled agreement to be in force. Stoiadinović took note of this, enquiring whether a similar representation had been made to Bucharest. The Hungarian envoy (Bessenyey) answered that he did not know. Next day Bessenyey called him to say the representation had also been made to Bucharest. Since I was unaware of the representation, Stoiadinović suggested that after I had examined the matter we should agree on a common position.

When I arrived in Bucharest, the international situation was such that I had to have daily meetings with cabinet members or audiences with the king in order to take the measures required by events. The Hungarian envoy (Bárdossy) then phoned to say that even though he had nothing to convey to me, he was at my disposal "as a courtesy gesture." Concomitantly, Raczynski, Poland's ambassador, asked my opinion about Bárdossy's representation concerning the Bled agreement. I answered that I didn't quite understand the meaning of the Hungarian representation, since I had considered that agreement to have been binding from the very moment of its initialing. I then let Hungary's envoy know that I expected him next morning. That day, however, he announced that he was unwell and couldn't come to see me. Today he asked to be received and I received him immediately. I told him what I had told the Polish ambassador: Romania and Yugoslavia never doubted the validity of the Bled agreement, which they have considered binding from the day it was initialed. Romania and Yugoslavia—with whom we did not cease to be in agreement for a single moment—sincerely wish to have the best of relations with Hungary, but fear that an ill-advised act on its part could reignite the just-calmed-down crisis."

October 2. *Le coup de pied de l'âne:*[6] the Poles sent Czechoslovakia an ultimatum on September 30, demanding the Teschen area. How elegant! The poor Czechoslovaks, abandoned by all, have today accepted the Poles' conditions. At the Hungarian Ministry of Foreign Affairs, I noted dissatisfaction and irritation at the outcome of the Munich meeting, for the officials had expected the Hungarian claims to be more forcefully endorsed by Hitler and Mussolini. There were some disappointed references to "the abandonment of the weak by the powerful." The deadline of three months set for Hungary and Czechoslovakia to reach an agreement was considered to be too long and to allow the negotiations to drag on and on. Apor told me, "In a period of three months, we will have the time to quarrel, rather than to bury the hatchet."

The reason for Kánya's annoyance at Petrescu-Comnen has become clear. Raczynski passed on to Bárdossy only the first part of his comment that he "didn't understand the meaning of the Hungarian representation," without adding the second part, "since the Romanian government has considered the Bled agreement binding from the very moment of its

[6]"The donkey's kick." Common French reference to La Fontaine's fable *The Aged Lion.* Crippled by age, the lion is set upon by his rebelling subjects. He is gored by the ox, mangled by the wolf, and as he lies awaiting death in stoic silence, here comes the donkey to give him a cowardly kick.

initialing." Being the foreign minister of a small country, and thus suffering from an inferiority complex, Kánya, according to Apor, thought he had received a "slap on the wrist," and was deeply offended. After the meeting between Petrescu-Comnen and Bárdossy, things were clarified and the incident declared closed. But at a luncheon at Orlowski's I told Apor that I had twice been on the point of getting up and bringing to an end the conversation with Kánya when he had launched such violent personal attacks against Petrescu-Comnen; whatever one may think of him, he was after all my country's foreign minister for the time being. Apor smiled: "Don't take this too tragically; Kánya is a man of seventy, with a quick temper, and all on edge in these days of crisis. You are well aware that he likes you a lot, he says so to everybody." In other words, he likes me, but can't stomach Petrescu-Comnen.

October 3. Meeting with Kánya. Courteous and formal atmosphere. I told him that Romania wishes, as does Yugoslavia, to have the best of relations with Hungary, but has some apprehensions, in view of Hungary's excessive military measures on its border with Czechoslovakia, as well as of the note it sent to Prague demanding the right of self-determination "for all of the Danube Valley's nationalities." Kánya told me that, with respect to the last point, it had resulted "from a blunder committed in my department." As soon as he had discovered it, he had cabled the Hungarian envoy in Prague instructing him to make it clear to Krofta that the note referred only to the Hungarian minority in Slovakia. He repeated officially the same statement to me, a statement of which I took cognizance. I then told him that Stoiadinović had not accepted the Hungarian proposal of putting into effect the Bled agreement, limiting himself to taking cognizance of it prior to reaching a common position with the Romanian government. Subsequently, our wording was adopted: "the agreement came into force at the time the communiqué was initialed." Indeed, the communiqué was the embodiment of a gentlemen's agreement reached between Kánya and me. But Kánya continued to assert that the Yugoslav response differed from ours by showing more good will, since he said Stoiadinović told Bessenyey: "It is with satisfaction that I take cognizance of your proposal, and I shall adapt my foreign policy to the Bled agreement." As for the Hungarian government, it considers that the agreement came into effect only with Romania and Yugoslavia, the only countries with which the three points were settled. I reminded him that any discrimination was out of the question, "the gentlemen's agreement applying to all the established points."

I gave a luncheon in honor of Vukiçević, who is being transferred to Warsaw, even though he reportedly hatched various small intrigues, telling for instance the Hungarians that Yugoslavia and Romania were opposed to the giving of Subcarpathian Russia to Hungary because of the Bucharest government's flat opposition. After lunch, Orlowski talked to me at length about the necessity of forming a Warsaw-Budapest-Bucharest bloc in order to stem German advances. For that reason, Hungary must be strong. Ergo, it must have a common border with Poland. He feels that Romania ought to help Hungary acquire Subcarpathian Russia, against a Hungarian undertaking—guaranteed by Warsaw—to give up its revisionism toward Romania. "You are forgetting our alliance with Czechoslovakia," I broke in. "Oh, that is of no consequence," replied Orlowski, "one must be broad-minded."

FUTILE DRIVE FOR A COMMON BORDER BETWEEN HUNGARY AND POLAND

October 4. Nicholas Bánffy and his niece, Cecilia Teleki, came to lunch. He acknowledged our good intentions toward our minorities, but nevertheless complained about some local difficulties that, after Carol's abolition of political parties,[7] minority members are no longer able to bring to the government's attention. I suggested a solution that could fill the gap, namely, that at the initiative of the Commission for Minorities, a consultative committee be established for each of the minorities. In the case of the Hungarians, for instance, one could appoint to that committee leading Hungarian personalities such as himself, bishops, and so forth. The idea appealed to Bánffy and he told me he would enlarge upon it in a memorandum to the regent.

In the evening, I went to see Kobr. It felt like entering a house in mourning. Poor Czechs! It is confirmed that the Slovak Catholic party has demanded complete autonomy for Slovakia in an ultimatum that expires this midnight. The Hungarians are raising preconditions to their participation in the negotiations of the Czechoslovak-Hungarian joint commission (freeing of prisoners and discharging the Hungarians serving in the Czechoslovak army). They want the joint commission to convene on October 6, but the Prague government, which is fully occupied with the Germans and the Poles, proposes the 15th. The Imrédy government, hemmed in by extremists who want to replace it with a right-wing regime favorable to Hitler and who compete by making exaggerated patriotic promises, has decided to "become activist." Prompted by Poland

[7]In February 1938.

(which wants a common border with Hungary), it is now demanding all of Slovakia and Subcarpathian Russia, which were in no way mentioned in Munich. And the press has been instructed to adopt the same position. Military forces are massed in the north, to show that Hungary does not exclude having recourse to force in order to secure its demands. Actually, the Hungarians know that they would not be able to occupy the territories they covet, but they hope to provoke a new crisis that would lead the "Big Four" to impose a plebiscite also for Slovakia and Subcarpathian Russia.

October 7. I lunched one-on-one with Maugras, who told me he had been instructed to draw the Hungarian government's attention to the dangers that would be entailed by a sort of "putsch" by Hungary and Poland to occupy Subcarpathian Russia. Apor had seemed to him evasive and had made no reassuring statement. Kobr came to tell me that the negotiations between Czechoslovakia and Hungary (represented by Kánya and Teleki) will begin the day after tomorrow. Slovakia, now totally autonomous, will send its own delegation, headed by Tiso, and the Ruthenes will send their minister, Parkany. It is likely that epic quarrels will arise among all of them. Meanwhile, the Hungarians were indignant to find out that the Germans had occupied Bratislava's bridgehead, a strategic emplacement formerly belonging to Burgenland and on which the Hungarians had an eye.

October 8. The Imrédy government is passing through critical moments because of the right-wing opposition that cannot forgive it for having lacked the courage to occupy militarily the territories claimed in Slovakia and Subcarpathian Russia. But Imrédy is not a man prone to such reckless actions, the more so since the British government had informed him that it considered itself bound by the guarantee it gave in Munich to defend Czechoslovakia's territorial integrity. Orlowski came to argue once more for the necessity of annexing Subcarpathian Russia to Hungary, and this for the following reasons:

1. It would be possible to form a Warsaw-Budapest-Bucharest bloc as a protection against both Russian and German imperialism, for a territorially expanded Hungary would have a common border with Poland and would become an element of stability in the Danube Basin.
2. It would be possible to reach a permanent Romano-Hungarian arrangement, Romania receiving the part of Subcarpathian Russia

> through which the Halmei-Sighetul Marmaţiei railroad passes, while Hungary would solemnly renounce any territorial claims against Romania, the agreement being guaranteed by Poland and, eventually, by Germany and Italy.

I assured my Polish colleague that Romania would never consent to annex even the minutest parcel of land of a country it was allied to, and especially of such a close friend as Czechoslovakia. [Had poor Orlowski foreseen that in less than a year's time his own country would be carved up between the Germans and the Russians, he would no doubt have refrained from repeatedly advocating the dismembering of Czechoslovakia.]

October 13. Knox came to see me and expressed his conviction that the Hungarians would obtain, in the Komárom (Komárno) negotiations, neither Bratislava, nor Kosice, nor Subcarpathian Russia. And they would not dare attack Czechoslovakia because of the Anglo-French guarantee, the perfect validity of which was personally confirmed by Kánya. I asked my British colleague how this guarantee would be carried out in the event of a Hungarian attack against Czechoslovakia. He answered that Hungary, which needs London's financial support, would not defy Britain's will. Czechoslovakia would be helped through Romania and Yugoslavia, if the latter decided to act. Knox told me he had explained to his government that in no case could Hungary be seen as a dam against German imperialism, and that Germany's border extended virtually to the Iron Gates.

October 14. After the collapse of the Komárom negotiations, Darányi went to Germany to seek Hitler's support, while Csáky went to Italy to ask for Mussolini's help. Bánffy came to read to me the text of the memorandum in which he fleshed out the idea I had given him of proposing the appointment of consultative bodies to the Commission for Minorities, one for each of the nationalities. The Hungarian commission would be composed of the bishops and leading personalities, among whom Bánffy and Pál Szász.

October 18. The statement given by Prime Minister Imrédy to the semi-official news agency M.T.I. means, in effect, Hungary's definitive adhesion to the Berlin-Rome Axis. Until now, Imrédy had not wanted to commit himself completely to the Axis, so that he could continue maintaining bonds with the Western democracies. But following Darányi's visit to Hitler, the Hungarian government has become convinced that it has to outbid Czechoslovakia in making advances to Germany, so as not to lose

Berlin's support, which is essential for the realization of its territorial demands. My German colleague, Erdmannsdorf, tells me he was present at the meeting of the German and Czechoslovak foreign ministers in Munich, after the meeting between Ribbentrop and Darányi. . . . Ribbentrop told the Czechoslovak minister of foreign affairs that Germany would not be in a position to guarantee Czechoslovakia's borders if these only reflected what had been proposed by the Slovak delegation in Komárom. Chwalkowsky replied that he placed the highest value on Germany's guarantee and that he would see if additional concessions could be made. But he noted that difficulties would arise from the Slovak and Ruthene representatives, who showed themselves uncompromising in order not to lose the popularity they had gained by securing the autonomy of their areas. As for the Czechs, as Counselor Fiša of the Czechoslovak legation had already told me, they are resigned to any new sacrifice. What a contrast between their despair and the mentality of "victors" of the Slovaks and Ruthenes, intoxicated by the glory of their autonomy!

My German colleague considers the Hungarian claims to be preposterous and put forward only for domestic political reasons. They will have to be substantially scaled back. Berlin considers worthless the arguments brought forth to show the necessity for a common border between Poland and Hungary. As for the economic arguments adduced to justify the annexation of Subcarpathian Russia to Hungary, they are not to be taken seriously, since they boil down to the need of importing wood from there! Erdmannsdorf is convinced that the Hungarians, who have received from Poland only a promise of diplomatic support, will not take the risk of undertaking alone a military adventure against a Czechoslovak army that is much superior in equipment and fortifications. (This information was given to him by Dörnberg, who, even though only head of protocol, is one of Ribbentrop's close friends.) According to Erdmannsdorf, Darányi, although a decent fellow, did not leave too brilliant an impression in Berlin, owing to his lack of geographic knowledge about the claimed regions and to his imperfect mastery of the German language. Ciano reportedly argued for a meeting of the "Big Four" foreign ministers, but the Germans were against it, in the belief that the differences could be settled through negotiations.

October 20. I received a letter from Gafencu, announcing his visit for the end of November and asking me to help him meet the top people of the Hungarian press. He says he needs "prodigies of prudence and balance" to write his daily column in *Timpul.* The Budapest press sees Beck's visit to Romania, and that of his chief of cabinet, Lubienski, to Hungary, as a final effort by Poland to bring the Romanian and

Hungarian viewpoints closer together and to win over the Bucharest government to the idea of a common border between Poland and Hungary.

October 21. My British colleague, Knox, read to me a cable he had received from Palairet, Britain's envoy to Bucharest, concerning Beck's sudden trip to Galaţi, where the king was watching military maneuvers, and with whom he met for three and a half hours. Beck had pleaded with insistence for a common Polish-Hungarian border, not to seek our advice but to explain a firmly taken position. From our side, it was explained to Beck that we were even more in need of a common border with Czechoslovakia, so as to ship directly to that country the cereals it would badly need now that it had lost its agricultural areas to Hungary. Besides, Romania did not want to extend along a Hungarian border expanded by 150 kilometers the costly fortifications it had had to erect on its western borders. Furthermore, the Romanian inhabitants of Subcarpathian Ruthenia did not want to fall under Hungarian domination. Beck apparently did not dare mention the offer of a territorial transfer to Romania, knowing that it would be turned down. Neither did he speak of a "bloc of resistance against Germany." At his departure, Beck would have promised he would undertake nothing that could be against Romanian interests. The reply was reportedly that only the Romanians were in a position to know what their own interests were. Rašić, the new Yugoslav envoy, called on me. He told me that Stoiadinović had authorized him to state that the Belgrade government was opposed to the establishment of a common Polono-Hungarian border.

October 22. Orlowski tells me that the purpose of Lubienski's visit to Budapest was to inquire about the tactics the Hungarian government intended to adopt in order to obtain its territorial claims in Czechoslovakia. He was reportedly told that Hungary was waiting for a new development before resuming negotiations with Prague. The new development could be a new Czechoslovak proposal capable of becoming the basis for discussion. If nothing new occurs, the Hungarian government will turn to the great powers to arbitrate the dispute. Lubienski had the task of advising against having recourse only to the powers that signed the Munich agreement, which would exclude Poland. Were Poland included, it was said that Czechoslovakia would ask for the inclusion of Romania among the arbitrators.

With respect to Beck's mission to Galaţi, my Polish colleague believes its purpose was to explain to the Romanian government Poland's crucial interest in the annexation of Subcarpathian Russia to Hungary, as well as to assure Romania at the same time that nothing would be undertaken in Warsaw to the detriment of our interests. And then Orlowski pleaded once more the case for a common Polish-Hungarian border; and I again underscored the necessity of a Romanian-Czechoslovak border.

October 29. My German colleague, Erdmannsdorf, considers it absolutely impossible for Hungary to obtain a common border with Poland, since the frontier is to be drawn on the basis of ethnic principles. The Polish newspaper correspondents in Budapest seem already to be preparing the public, saying that the issue of Subcarpathian Russia cannot be resolved now, but possibly later, if that region obtains its independence and wants to detach itself from Prague. My Italian colleague, Vinci, seems downcast by the diminishing prospect of a common border between Poland and Hungary.

November 2. We hear in Budapest the results of the Italo-German Vienna arbitral award, which gives Hungary substantial and unjustified territorial gains. Uzhorod and Munkacevo are not inhabited by Hungarians, and yet they will be attached to Hungary. Deprived of its plains, Subcarpathian Russia becomes nonviable, and the Hungarians hope, with Poland's help, to take it over in time. For the Hungarians, this is the starting point for the revision of the Treaty of Trianon. My Czechoslovak colleague, poor Kobr, whom I went to see, was dejected by this cruel and unjust sentence from the Belvedere Palace. He told me that Orlowski had stepped out on the Polish legation's balcony to pledge to the cheering crowd that a common border between Poland and Hungary would be achieved.

November 8. Before his departure from Moscow the French ambassador, Coulondre, told an Allied colleague that France would wish to maintain its treaty with Soviet Russia—even though it did not attach much value to it—so as to prevent a Russo-German rapprochement. But it was now Moscow that was seeking to denounce the treaty, precisely in order to be able to reach an understanding with Berlin, realizing that the French army would never budge to come to its aid. Asked on what basis such rapprochement would be conceivable, Coulondre replied that he was thinking of the Polish question. Along the same lines, Csáky ascribed Germany's concessions at the Vienna arbitration to the Italian point of view, after a new cooperation proposal made to Mussolini by Ribbentrop during his visit to Rome. What did this cooperation proposal consist of? After some hemming and hawing, Csáky hinted that it was related to the resolution of problems in the relations between Germany and Poland.

November 12. Rašić has been instructed by Stoiadinović to say—when asked—that, personally, he feels the system of the Little Entente will probably be altered in view of the guarantees given to Czechoslovakia by the great powers. He also tells me the Hungarian government would like to carry out the Bled agreement only with Yugoslavia, signing a protocol exclusively with that country. This is the tactic adopted in the past to isolate Czechoslovakia. But, added Rašić, as Prince-Regent Paul had told King Carol and as Stoiadinović had told the Romanian government, Yugoslavia will sign no agreement with Hungary without Romania (this was also confirmed to me by our foreign ministry).

November 19. A new Imrédy government has been formed, without the right-wing elements accused by the prime minister of obstructing the social reforms (particularly the agrarian ones) he wants to implement.

Returning from London, where in his capacity as foreign minister he had accompanied the king on his official visit, Petrescu-Comnen passed through Hungary, and I had the opportunity of having a long conversation with him between the stations Komárom and Budapest. He considers Carol's visit to have been a political success, of which he seems delighted. Carol asked Prime Minister Chamberlain whether it is true that Britain is trying to withdraw from Central and Eastern Europe. Chamberlain denied this: "It is a German fabrication." Petrescu-Comnen found the cabinet members eager to strengthen relations with Romania, but the experts seemed more reticent. He had two interesting conversations with Lord Halifax, principal secretary of state for foreign affairs. (From what his associates revealed to me, it seems that he began by asking Halifax where he bought such excellent tea, a question that apparently astonished the minister, who replied that he was not the one charged with provisioning the Foreign Office in tea.) Petrescu-Comnen told me he had emphasized to Halifax the imperative necessity for the four signatory powers of the Munich agreement to extend to Czechoslovakia the guarantees they had promised. Otherwise, their pledges would be seen to be worthless. Halifax then called Cadogan in, and they decided this was to be one of the first points of discussion with the French government at their meeting in Paris the following week. With regard to Anglo-Romanian relations, Petrescu-Comnen asked whether Great Britain would be willing to cooperate with Romania in economic matters, but of course without diminishing the role of Germany, with which we wanted—and were compelled—to live on friendly terms. Halifax seemed favorably inclined; Leith-Ross less so, however, explaining that in Britain it was not possible to impose a certain direction to economic life, as could be done in countries under a totalitarian regime. Petrescu-Comnen told me he remarked: "Some sort of accommodation will have to be found, however, otherwise all of Europe will become Germany's." Changing subjects, Petrescu-Comnen told me he had been informed that the Berlin government was opposed to the annexation of Subcarpathian Russia to Hungary. . . . Finally, he had a few kind words to say concerning me: only I, and perhaps another two of my colleagues, are valuable envoys on whom the king and the government can rely: "All you have done will be taken into account." He knows how difficult my mission to Budapest is. He also let me know in confidence that Hory, Hungary's envoy to Warsaw, proposed to Franassovici, our ambassador to Poland, that Romania and Hungary get together unofficially to see whether they could reach an agreement. Bethlen might negotiate for the Hungarians. The king is pondering which Romanian statesman without an official position he might select to negotiate with Bethlen.

November 21. I learned from Maugras and Pipinelis, who came for lunch, that Erdmannsdorf went to the Ministry of Foreign Affairs and, as instructed by his government, advised the Hungarian government not to push too hard on the question of Subcarpathian Russia, so as not to risk placing Hungary in a dangerous position.

The news began to transpire in diplomatic circles that Rosenberg may be working on a plan for a possible partition of Russia, including a "German Ukraine." [In 1941 this project was going to serve as the basis of Hitler's Eastern policy.]

November 24. The Imrédy government has resigned, mainly because Hungary has not succeeded in annexing Subcarpathian Russia, owing to Berlin's firm opposition, and later even to that of Italy.

I note a fairly significant response to Hory's proposal for nonofficial negotiations between Romania and Hungary. A leader of the Hungarian minority, Pál Szász, president of the Hungarian cooperatives in Transylvania, asked to see me on behalf of Bethlen. He began by saying that autonomy for Transylvania was a totally unachievable utopia because of the opposition of the Romanian majority in the province. Border rectifications are likewise out of the question, and besides they would reduce the Hungarian presence in Romania. The only solution would be the gradual fulfillment of the promises made in Alba-Iulia on December 1, 1918. To achieve that goal, it would be necessary to have nonofficial meetings between influential personalities from both countries, to clear the way for a détente in the relations between Bucharest and Budapest. Once the bases for an understanding have been reached, the nonofficial personalities would step aside and official organs would conclude the agreement. It would be helpful if Romania could delegate a person in all ways of the same stature as Bethlen. I replied that as envoy of Romania to Hungary, I could only applaud any endeavor seeking a rapprochement between our countries, which—beyond their temporary dissensions—are bound by so many common interests. I also said I would report these suggestions to my government.

November 25. Gyarfas, a former Magyar party senator in the Romanian Parliament, came to talk to me about the minorities question. He asserts that in the event of the establishment of a consultative committee for the Hungarian minority, recourse should not be made to "my friend Szász" or to the bishops, but rather to the former leaders of the Magyar party (that is, to himself).

November 26. Baron Joseph Iosika also came to see me and, like Gyarfas, he spoke against Szász. The Hungarian minority can be validly represented only by the *grofs*,[8] its traditional leaders. Apart from that, he was a refined man with apparently conciliatory views.

November 27. The regent having rejected Imrédy's resignation, the cabinet remains unchanged, except for Kánya, who persists in his resignation.

Rašić came early in the morning to tell me that Stoiadinović had drawn Bessenyey's attention to the dangers that could result from a direct action in Subcarpathian Russia.

I went to Hegyeshalom to join Carol, who was returning to Romania. I boarded his carriage, and we spoke for two hours, until our arrival in Budapest. He was most cordial and seemed highly interested in what I was telling him about the internal crisis in Hungary and the Polish-Hungarian scheming with regard to Subcarpathian Russia, which had led to tensions between us and the Hungarians, embittered by our continued firm loyalty to our Czechoslovak ally. I also told him of the Germans' unpopularity in Hungary because of their opposition to the annexation of Subcarpathian Russia, and of the ensuing strain in the relations between Berlin and Budapest. I also mentioned the grievances of the Hungarian minority in Transylvania, and made various suggestions for calming things down; on the other hand, I likewise mentioned the miserable conditions of the Romanian minority in Hungary, and what could be done to improve them. I then reported what I knew on the state of the Hungarian army, on the cutting by the Hungarians of railway traffic between Halmei and Sighet, and on their propaganda effort, as well

[8]Hungarian noblemen.

as on ways of fighting it. At the king's request, I described the leading personalities in Hungary, and we spoke about the various archdukes who dwelt there. The king asked what chances the legitimists had, and I said none, although monarchist sentiments do linger on in certain sectors of the population.

The king seemed highly satisfied by his visits to London, Brussels, Paris, and Berchtesgaden. When he asked Hitler what Germany would do in the case of a conflict between Romania and Hungary, Hitler replied categorically: "We would remain indifferent, since our border ends at Hungary's." Hitler assured him that Germany had no intention of smothering Romania economically, but wished to collaborate with our industry, extending it long-term credits for the purchase of machinery from Germany. Negotiations are to start shortly, but in Bucharest "so as not to be too obvious." If we are to draw closer to Germany, Carol told me, we will do so directly, without having recourse to Italian or Polish intermediaries. He was particularly indignant about the Poles' behavior: "Beck conducted himself toward us as he has conducted himself toward France. Allied with France, he abandoned it in order to pass on Germany's side. Allied with us, he worked with our Hungarian adversaries." The king showed himself favorable to my suggestions with regard to the Hungarian minority. He considers Bánffy "their best mind." As for the idea of nonofficial negotiations proposed by Istvan Bethlen, he will consult the government. The raising of the French legation in Bucharest to the rank of embassy visibly elated him.

Just before the train pulled into the Budapest station, I exchanged a few words with Urdăreanu. He said, "I don't know whether His Majesty thanked you, as he had intended to, for your cables during the crisis; they were the only solid information in the chaos that surrounded us." Grand Voevod Michael was also in the carriage, a rather handsome boy, but too serious for his age. He asked me whether it was true that the Hungarians booed when they saw an automobile from Romania, and whether the staff in hotels behaved politely. I reassured him on both counts, and told him various local anecdotes to bring forth a smile in his solemn countenance.

November 29. Erdmannsdorf came to see me and told me how furious the Hungarians are that Germany prevented them from annexing Subcarpathian Russia. But their bitterness is even greater toward Italy, which, after encouraging them both diplomatically and through its press, delivered to Budapest a note identical to that of Germany, "to tell them: Stop!"

November 30–December 2. Gafencu and Tilea's stay in Budapest was darkened by the tragic news of the assassinations in Romania and of the executions without trial of Corneliu Codreanu and thirteen other members of the Iron Guard (the murderers of Duca and Stelescu). [This ushered in an era of bloodshedding as had not been witnessed in our history for ages, and was to plunge the country into brutal internal violence, the prelude to our entry into the war and to all the endless calamities of the Romanian people, including the rending of the nation's territory.] We organized for Gafencu and Tilea a luncheon at the legation, which was also attended by Tibor Eckhardt, Baron Lang (president of the parliamentary commission for foreign affairs), Otlik (editor in chief of the *Pester Lloyd*), Bálogh (editor in chief of the *Nouvelle Revue de Hongrie*), and so forth. Gafencu told me he would soon be appointed foreign minister, replacing Petrescu-Comnen (who had fallen out of favor for trying to get elected president of the League of Nations against the king's wishes), so I set up a meeting between him and Bethlen, who seemed delighted to be able to confer—unofficially—with a Romanian politician to prepare the ground for an agreement between the official organs of the two countries. But in his new capacity as foreign minister of Hungary, Csáky told all of us that the question of a Romano-Hungarian rapprochement was not yet "ripe," and had therefore to be dealt with "with much caution and patience." At bottom he was scared of the Germans, skittish as soon as a step was taken toward a "Danubian bloc." Their motto—like that of the ancient Romans—seems to be *divide et impera*.

✧ ✧ ✧

On December 3, I sent the government the following report on Hungarian foreign policy in the current international situation: "Emerging from the severe crisis that shook the very foundations of European peace with an unexpected and in part unjustified increase in territory, and backed by what it believed to be the unwavering friendship of the Berlin-Rome Axis, Hungary all of a sudden turned its old inferiority complex of vanquished country into the mentality of a victorious state, the expansionist tendencies of which no longer met any opposition. The barriers to its wildest aspirations seemed to have been lifted by Poland's encouragements. With a political romanticism reminiscent of Napoleon III, but without his underpinning of international fairness, a new map of Europe was being designed in Warsaw, chopping off districts here to attach them there, assuming possibilities of voluntary territorial concessions, and, finally, knitting together vast blocs of states, without inquiring about their people's wishes or the desirability of the goals that were to be revealed to them in time by Mr. Beck. In this political system, a key role was to be played by a powerful Hungary designed on the one hand to link with Southeastern Europe—possibly through joining the Balkan Entente Treaty—and, on the other, to smother the slightest wish by Subcarpathian Russia to become Ukraine's 'Piemonte.'

"Even though the Budapest government, more realistic and level-headed than the one in Warsaw, did not give full credence to the vast schemes that were being proposed, it was nevertheless enticed by the prospects offered to it in Subcarpathian Russia. This was both because of its own public opinion and because of urgings by Italy and Poland, which the government believed to be tied to Germany by detailed understandings concerning all issues. Because the semi-official Italian, and especially Polish, presses were filled with appeals or even summonses for the establishment of the common Polish-Hungarian border, and because Mr. Beck was continuously accusing the Hungarian government of lack of resolution, the latter organized a violent press and radio campaign against the alleged 'terror' in Subcarpathian Russia. It also infiltrated into that region numerous agents provocateurs and some detachments of volunteer soldiers disguised as guerrillas, all of them in collusion with agitators coming in from Poland. Meanwhile, the Hungarian army, mobilized without any plausible reason and at a huge financial cost, was reinforced by a series of call-ups. There were reports of movements of military units to serve as cover for the northern forces, earmarked for action in Subcarpathian Russia. Tension was rising by the day. German agents were telling Berlin that Hungary and Poland were going to launch their military action between November 20 and 27. November 20 and 21 were undoubtedly the most crucial days.

"Then, to the amazement of the Hungarian government—as well as no doubt of the Polish one—the German government made its representation, friendly in tone but comminatory in essence. My German colleague, Erdsmannsdorf, stated to Kánya—at that time still minister of foreign affairs—that 'the German government counsels the Hungarian government to cease its actions toward the annexation of Subcarpathian Russia, since such an attitude, which besides is an affront to the great powers that passed the Vienna arbitrational sentence, could create for Hungary a dangerous situation, in which it could not count on Germany's support.'

"The communication was obviously received with great bitterness by Kánya. His bitterness increased only further when my Italian colleague, Vinci, handed him a note with an identical content—which Vinci himself considered 'rather harsh,' since his instructions until then had been to support Hungary's claims without reservation. Kánya could not help pointing out to him that the German government had at least been more consistent, since it had prohibited its press from creating an atmosphere favorable to the Hungarian demands, contrary to what the Italian government had done.

"Concurrently, my French colleague, Maugras, had been instructed to make representations to the Hungarian government, recommending that it stop its agitation with regard to Subcarpathian Russia. 'I was charged with making representations to Your Excellency on this matter,' he told Kánya, 'but I suppose it has become unnecessary, since my German colleague has attended to it.'

" . . . Prime Minister Imrédy's speeches . . . have finally made public opinion understand . . . that the Hungarian government, 'because of foreign policy intelligence it is privy to,' is not in a position to undertake 'a hasty action that would have no lasting result.'

" . . . The Hungarians must have found particularly distressing the passage in Count Ciano's speech in which he stated: 'With regard to the situation in Subcarpathian Russia, there has always reigned a complete unity of views among the two powers of the Axis, even though a certain well-known press has tried to prove the contrary. The question of the borders . . . cannot again be brought up for discussion.'

"Italy's attitude caused the most astonishment and sorrow, but it can at least be explained by the pressure exerted by the Wilhelmstrasse. . . . The greatest animosity, barely concealed in official circles, was directed toward Germany. The police must constantly prevent hostile demonstrations in front of the German legation. There are almost no Hungarians, except for those having fallen prey to Nazism, who do not criticize Germany's attitude toward Hungary and who do not advocate the cementing of a Danubian bloc for 'the defense of the independence of small countries.' And since in Germany there is deep displeasure at the policy pursued in the last weeks by the Budapest government, the coolness arising in the relations between the two countries can no longer be concealed. . . .

"Kánya's departure [I added on December 5] is the reflection of political undercurrents. Following Hungary's setback with regard to Subcarpathian Russia, Imrédy accused him of having become a tool of Polish policy, and apparently depicted him to the German government as the only one responsible for pushing for a common Polish-Hungarian border, which as a matter of fact is untrue. Being made a scapegoat must have been that much more distressing for Kánya because he had been constantly attacked by Beck during the crisis for his bureaucratic approach and lack of ardor."

December 16. First meeting with Csáky in his new capacity as minister of foreign affairs. We reminisced about the time when we were both legation secretaries in Rome (1921–1923), he at the Vatican and I at the Quirinal. We had then found each other again in Bucharest (1924–1926). He asked me to come often to see him. I talked to him about the restitution of the Transylvanian archives and about the ratification of the convention concerning the Gojdu foundation. He promised to study the questions in a conciliatory spirit.

I sent our Foreign Ministry the following report concerning Csáky's appointment: "Following the territorial gains made at Czechoslovakia's expense, Kánya submitted his resignation as Hungary's minister of foreign affairs. He expected his resignation to be again rejected, as in the past, or, in the event of its acceptance, that his exit from the government would be the occasion of a true apotheosis of his diplomatic accomplishments, to which Hungary doubtlessly owed its unexpected success.

"Circumstances, however, decreed that Kánya's departure should resemble more a rout than an apotheosis. This surprising reversal was due both to clashes between the head of Hungarian diplomacy and the prime minister and to the policy followed by Kánya in the last few weeks.

"Indeed, two natures as authoritarian and willful as those of Imrédy and Kánya could work together only with great difficulty. Moreover, under the pressure of public opinion and Warsaw's incessant urging, Kánya ended up by following too submissively Beck's directions in the question of Subcarpathian Russia, thereby causing tensions with Germany.

"This being the situation, Imrédy did not hesitate to make his colleague in the Foreign Ministry the scapegoat for the unsuccessful attempt to annex Subcarpathian Russia. He depicted him to Hitler and Ribbentrop as the only person responsible for the ill-considered campaign against the borders drawn by the Vienna arbitration. Though the prime minister's dissociation from his principal colleague could be criticized as to its elegance and even truthfulness, it is nevertheless certain that it served him to regain Berlin's favor, thereby enabling him to be seen by Regent Horthy as the government head preferred by Germany.

"The replacing of Kánya therefore also had to have a symbolic meaning, his successor having to represent a firm guarantee of the alignment of Hungary's foreign policy with that of the Axis. . . . Hungary's powers to be then decided to entrust the Foreign Ministry to Count Istvan Csáky, deemed to be the candidate most agreeable to Palazzo Chigi . . . and the best exponent of the policy of rapprochement with Italy. . . . The new foreign affairs minister incessantly emphasizes that, for him, the only great powers that should play a role in Central Europe are those of the Berlin-Rome Axis. He stresses that under his tenure at the ministry, Hungary will lean exclusively on Italy and Germany."

NEW VISIT BY CIANO TO BUDAPEST

December 19. Evening reception given by Imrédy for Ciano, who has come for a few days to Hungary "for a hunting party." I had the opportunity of talking briefly with him. He was very pleasant, but stayed clear of any political question.

The Romanian cabinet was reshuffled on December 21. Gafencu replaces Petrescu-Comnen at the Foreign Ministry—a change that is all for the better. I sent him the following report regarding Ciano's visit to Budapest: "In order to avoid losing time with the customary receptions and banquets, Ciano's stay in Hungary has been advertised as a hunting trip. In daytime, the two foreign ministers left for the countryside 'to hunt' or, more likely, to confer in a hunting lodge while the fans of the sport shot, in their name, the regent's game. . . . The general impression is that the topic of the Ciano-Csáky talks was of a most ticklish nature: Italy's attempt to put together, in the area defined by the Axis, a group of countries that would rely more on the Rome 'pole' than on the Berlin one. Mussolini wanted to know as soon as possible whom he could count on for that purpose, and in exchange for what commitments, so that he could decide what position to take during Neville Chamberlain's imminent visit to Rome. The Duce seems to have reached an agreement with Yugoslavia some while back, but Warsaw and Budapest still had to be approached. Hence the plan for Ciano's trip to Poland, which was postponed only in order not to irritate Germany. . . . There thus remained Hungary. Mussolini forced his son-in-law to accept immediately, shortly before Christmas, the invitation extended to him, with no specified date, by Regent Horthy. . . .

"It is generally believed that Ciano, without giving advice on domestic policy to the Hungarian government, put at its disposal . . . 'the treasure of experience of the Fascist regime.' Translated into more straightforward language, it is thought he suggested that the Hungarians take as model the Italian corporative system in carrying out social reforms and in reorganizing the state, rather than the principles of narrow Hitlerism.

"With regard to external matters, Hungary was advised to show even more clearly its alignment to the Berlin-Rome Axis, because it is only within the political framework of the Axis that the Fascist government would be able to work in favor of Hungary. The clearest statement of Hungary's affiliation to the Axis would be its adhesion to the tripartite Anti-Comintern treaty. Csáky agreed to carry out this adhesion at the earliest date.

"But there still remained one point to make absolutely clear in order to remove any possible misunderstanding on Hungary's adhesion to Axis policy. It was necessary for Hungary to accept Germany's opposition to the establishment of a common border between Hungary and Poland. The Hungarian government consented to no longer insist on historical and political principles in the drawing of borders, but finally to accept the ethnic principle. . . .

"In order to link Hungary to the group of countries meant to gravitate around Rome, Ciano fervently advocated a closer rapprochement between Hungary and Yugoslavia. He stated even in his official speech that 'Italy's policy in Central Europe is based on the Rome-Berlin Axis, on friendship with Hungary, and on the Belgrade agreement.'

"It is believed that during his imminent visit to Belgrade Ciano will endeavor to prepare the ground for the conclusion of a significant agreement between Belgrade and Budapest."

December 23. Meeting with Pipinelis, Orlowski, and Rašić. They told me they had been informed that, following the killing of Codreanu, Germany was extremely angry at the Romanian government. Hitler was said to be furious that, shortly after Carol's visit to Berchtesgaden, a bloody repression was undertaken that could be seen as having been agreed to by him, the natural protector of extreme right-wing movements. The Hungarians, I am told, would like to take advantage of this strain to bring forward their revisionist claims against Romania.

III. 1939

This was the year worldwide tragedy began. It was also a year of familial sorrow for me (the loss of both my beloved parents) and, on a professional plane, the year my mission to Budapest came to an end with my transfer to Rome.

An important political issue had to be looked into by the Romanian government: former Prime Minister Bethlen's proposal that nonofficial negotiations be started between leading personalities from Romania and Hungary, in view of preparing the ground for the initiation of official negotiations aiming at a détente between the two countries. Returned suddenly to Bucharest because of my father's illness, I was invited by Gafencu to a luncheon also attended, among others, by Tilea, Victor Bădulescu, and Cretzianu. We debated which Romanian personality should be put in touch with Bethlen. In Gafencu's view, the most appropriate person was Vaida-Voevod, also a former prime minister and he, too, a Transylvanian. At any rate, I was authorized to inform Bethlen that we were willing to undertake nonofficial talks.

We also spoke at that luncheon about the general political situation. Gafencu confirmed the straining of our relations with Germany, since Hitler was not forgiving Carol for the bloody repression of the Iron Guard so soon after the Berchtesgaden meeting. Göring and Ribbentrop returned the decorations the king had given them. The Hitlerian diplomatic corps was inciting the Hungarians and Bulgarians against us, and the German press was attacking us ceaselessly. It was clear that Hitler wanted at all cost to get rid of Carol. "But we too can play tit-for-tat with the Germans," said Gafencu, "for we will seek to draw closer to

Italy, which is covertly endeavoring to put together a bloc of countries that would resist German hegemony." He said he had evidence of Germany's incipient "jealousy" at our good relations with Italy and was therefore expecting imminent reactions.

Cretzianu drew me aside and said he knew for a fact, in his capacity as secretary-general, that I would be immediately entrusted with an embassy were Budapest not so important a post in the present circumstances that no replacement for me could be found. "If I could," he added, "I would cut you in slices, you and Radu Crutzescu, one slice for each important post, for you two are the aces of our diplomacy."

Returned to my post, I attended Regent Horthy's traditional New Year's reception. Stopping in front of me, he asked—for the first time—for news of the king, with whom he told me he had exchanged telegrams. But he did not say a word to the Czechs, a pettiness I had not expected of him.

Interesting conversations at a dinner party given by former finance minister Fábinyi. Archduchess Anna related to me some details about Carol's visit to Germany, for she was staying at that time with her sister, Princess Margarete von Hohenzollern. The king, it seems, had been highly offended by the German authorities' lack of consideration. Hitler did not come to greet him at the railroad station, sending Meissner in his stead, and he went no further than meeting Carol at the Berghof's entrance. And even though the king had requested a one-on-one meeting, Hitler received him in the presence of Ribbentrop. Carol was unable to be alone with Hitler for a single minute, which irked him no end. As for Göring, he had the pretension that the king come to him, though protocol required the opposite. After lengthy negotiations, a compromise was reached: they met halfway, in Göring's parlor car. "That is how the Nazis are," sighed the handsome archduchess, née princess of Saxony. "Were I to tell you all they did to my brothers, I would go on forever."

Imrédy, who also attended the dinner party, drew me aside to ask why we, the Romanians, had been so opposed to the annexation of Subcarpathian Russia by Hungary, which would in fact have represented a safeguard for our country. I replied that it was not we who had thwarted Magyar aspirations, but Germany. I added with a slight smile: "If Berlin allows you to establish a common border with Poland, I daresay we would probably also let you do so." "Thanks a lot," he retorted, laughing, "but you see, the rub is precisely that Berlin does not allow us to." I retorted in my turn, "Then why do you reproach us, rather than the Germans?"

Also at that dinner party, Baron Váy, secretary of state to the Presidency of the Council, came to thank me for my intervention, following which the

Romanian state had paid his wife and her sisters the due compensation for the expropriation of a plot of land next to the Mureş River, where an airport was being constructed.

The next day, I had a long talk with Csáky at the Ministry. He seemed to appreciate the Romanian government's conciliatory approach with regard to relations with Hungary and on the minorities issue. He wanted as considerable an improvement in Romano-Hungarian relations as possible, but the improvement would have to be made gradually and discreetly so as not to give Germany the impression that we wanted to constitute a Danubian bloc directed against its interests. He believed this was also Rome's view, but without telling me what his belief was based on. He also disclosed that the Hungarian government would soon adhere to the Anti-Comintern Pact and quit the League of Nations, the required "baptism" for those who wanted to join the Axis. "One cannot belong simultaneously to two denominations, and Hungary's denomination is that of the Berlin-Rome Axis." He then asked me whether Romania would eventually also adhere to the Anti-Comintern Pact. I replied by showing him on a map our country's geographical position.

PROPOSED TALKS WITH COUNT ISTVAN BETHLEN

Bethlen came to see me at the legation on January 11. He let me know he had got in touch with Csáky, who fully agreed to begin nonofficial and preliminary talks between the Bucharest and Budapest governments. He asked me if the Romanian government was willing to designate a person knowledgeable about the situation in Transylvania with whom he might start the conversations.

Gafencu conveyed to me the government's intention of designating Vaida-Voevod as Bethlen's "partner" and asked me to sound Vaida out in this connection. I arrived in Cluj on February 17, and Vaida kept me in his house—lunch and tea—from ten in the morning to seven in the evening. He agreed to talk with Bethlen and proposed as a meeting place Nicholas Bánffy's castle in the vicinity of Cluj. Then he reminisced about the past, about his friendships before the war with the *Grossoesterreich*[1] groups, about his frequent meetings with Archduke Franz Ferdinand in Vienna's Belvedere palace, and about his activities in the Budapest parliament. He once read in the packed Chamber a series of epigrams against the Hungarians, written by himself, on the pretext that the

[1]Greater Austria.

deputies had to be aware of "the discontent in Hungary against the dominant nation." Another time, he was prevented from speaking by three deputies who sat around him and belabored him with insults. After Romanian rule was established in Transylvania, one of them, Sebestyen if I'm not mistaken, kept dropping in on Vaida to ingratiate himself. Vaida told me he had always endeavored to be impartial and generous toward members of the Hungarian minority. He derided Carol's regime with gusto and ridiculed the uniforms of the National Revival Front.[2] He saw the killing of Codreanu as a political mistake of major proportions. There had been talk of Vaida's appointment as envoy to Berlin, but the project was abandoned in view of Wilhelmstrasse's reserved response. All during this long conversation in his house facing the National Theater, Vaida, surrounded by old engravings of Horia, Cloşca, and Crişan, showed himself to be full of geniality, simplicity, and humor.

I informed Bethlen that Vaida would be his interlocutor. I added, according to instructions from Gafencu—who did not place too much confidence in Vaida's negotiating subtlety—that, irrespective of these talks, the Romanian foreign minister would always be willing to examine favorably any definite proposal conveyed through me. With regard to the meeting with Vaida, I asked Bethlen to come to an understanding directly with Bánffy, in whose home they were to meet.

But Bethlen came again on February 24 to tell me that, after reflection, he didn't believe that Vaida's suggestion of meetings at Bánffy's was appropriate, for the following reasons. First, Bethlen was so well known in Transylvania that his presence there would prevent maintaining the secrecy that had to surround the talks. Second, Bethlen feared that if it became known that these nonofficial talks were being held in the home of the Hungarian minority's leader, Romanian public opinion would be aroused. Bethlen added: "Suppose that we Hungarians were to hold negotiations with the Germans concerning the German minority in Hungary. Our public opinion would never accept that the negotiations take place at Basch's [the leader of the German minority]." A third reason adduced by Bethlen—and confirmed the same day by Bánffy—was that Bánffy was not willing to put his castle near Cluj at the disposal of the two negotiators, not wishing his name to be mixed up in the matter. "I have the good fortune of being well thought of by the Romanian government," Bánffy told me, "and I don't want to run the risk of losing my standing were the

[2]A movement recently established by Carol II to replace all political parties and support his dictatorial rule.

negotiations, held in my home, to fail." Bethlen therefore proposed that he and Vaida meet somewhere in Italy. I of course reported these two conversations to my government. Another possible solution was then proposed, which should be acceptable to the two parties: namely, that the Vaida-Bethlen meeting take place at Mocsonyi's, in the Transylvanian countryside.

On May 24, however, Bethlen told me that, in view of Csáky's latest speeches, in which he proposed to the Romanian government direct negotiations for an agreement on minorities, it was necessary for him to get in touch with Csáky to find out whether the Hungarian government still wanted him to negotiate for Hungary. In any case, he felt it would be preferable if his eventual talks with Vaida were to take place in a neutral locality, for instance in Italy.

The truth must have been that, informed of Hitler's ulterior designs in Czechoslovakia, and foreseeing that other changes might take place in Central Europe, the Hungarian government deemed it safer not to tie its hands by negotiating with Romania.

It is thus that negotiations with Bethlen were nipped in the bud.

CSÁKY'S FOREIGN POLICY

Csáky's policy ever since he took over the Ministry of Foreign Affairs had as its objective the closest possible alignment with the Axis—hence the haste with which, at his instigation, the Hungarian government joined the Anti-Comintern Pact. Hence, likewise, his attempts to cement the rapprochement with Belgrade through a diplomatic instrument—rejected by Yugoslavia in the absence of Romania's participation—so as to please Italy in particular, for he considered himself to be a great favorite of the Palazzo Chigi. From Ciano's memoirs, however, it is clear that Csáky was far from being valued in Rome as highly as he imagined. What stood in his way was the disapproval of the foremost statesman of Hungarian political life, Count Istvan Bethlen. Bethlen was worried by Germany's growing influence over Hungary, and he strongly disapproved of Imrédy's anti-Jewish bill, which revealed to what extent Hungary had become servile toward Hitler. The government—and especially Csáky—argued, however, that the closer Hungary hewed to the Reich's line, the greater were the prospects of seeing all its claims satisfied. But Bethlen and Eckhardt were determined to fight the anti-Jewish bill, being secretly supported by Regent Horthy himself, who disclosed to my British colleague, Sir Geoffrey Knox, that he would refuse to sign such a law.

At that time, Britain's ambassador to Berlin reported to the Foreign Office that, at the exhortation of other Nazi leaders, Hitler would have reached the conclusion that he had to unleash war at short notice and before the Western powers had completed their rearmament. I had, in this connection, interesting exchanges of information with my new British colleague, Owen St. Clair O'Malley.

At the beginning of January, I received the visit of Labour M.P. Arthur Henderson, son of the leader of the same name (former chairman of the Disarmament Conference), who handed me a letter of introduction from Sir Geoffrey Knox. He told me he had seen Horthy, Bethlen, Eckhardt, and Csáky, and that he would now like to go to Romania to meet with the king and with our political leaders. He would deliver to the king a message from Horthy. He was panic-stricken by Germany's advances and would have liked to see the countries of the Danube Basin closely united to form a barrier.

Eckhardt seemed to share the same illusion. He told me the only hope he had, given Imrédy and Csáky's opportunistic policy of drawing close to Germany, was that once decisively tied to the Axis, Hungary would have more possibilities of permanent contacts with the other countries of the area, with a view to forming a group of states that could act as a counterbalance to the growing pressure of the Nazi Reich. Eckhardt also told me that both he and Bethlen were highly satisfied with the new policy we had adopted toward minorities. They were both convinced of the necessity of clearing the air between our countries. But a rapprochement between us could not be cemented by a legal instrument, or even by an official pronouncement, because of the categorical opposition of Germany, always worried by the possible formation of a Southeastern European bloc that might hinder its expansion. Hitler would tolerate only a rapprochement between Hungary and Yugoslavia, perhaps because of the personal friendship between Göring and Stoiadinović. Kánya disclosed to Eckhardt that his departure from the government had been imposed by Hitler, who apparently did not forgive him for the conclusion of the Bled agreement or for the presence of the Romanian and Czechoslovak envoys at the Berlin railway station at Regent Horthy's arrival. In the present circumstances, and so as not to awaken the Führer's ire, all that could be done would be a de facto strengthening of Romano-Hungarian relations on the basis of a tolerant policy toward minorities that would end up being a sort of "moral and cultural condominium in Transylvania."

On his return from Bucharest, Henderson came to lunch at the legation, as did Bánffy. Henderson continued to strive for a Romano-Hungarian rapprochement. He was disappointed that Imrédy had refused to receive him after his stay in Romania, for fear that he, prime minister of Hungary, might be thought of as acquiescing to a plan that displeased Berlin. In exchange, he was received for the second time by Horthy, who apparently showed himself in favor of a détente with Romania. He, too, recognized that the rights of the crown of St. Stephen to Transylvania did not form a practical basis for discussion, which rather should be sought in guarantees for minorities. Horthy declared himself satisfied by the Romanian government's efforts in that regard. On the other hand, he complained about Germany's demands in favor of its nationals in Hungary—which, Henderson observed with a chuckle—were identical to those demanded by Horthy for the Hungarians in Transylvania!

✧ ✧ ✧

On January 18, I sent our Ministry of Foreign Affairs the following report on the then current phase of Romano-Hungarian relations: "Even though Hungary's basic policy is directed equally against all successor states of the Dual Monarchy that are ruling former territories of St. Stephen's crown, and regardless of the fact that the final objective of Hungarian foreign policy is the recovery of as many of the lost territories as possible, Budapest knows how to tailor its diplomatic actions to the needs of the day and according to where the wind blows. This is why, striving to isolate Czechoslovakia, which it saw as doomed by Hitler's unyielding will to annihilate it, Hungary sought at Bled a rapprochement with Yugoslavia and Romania. Similarly, after settling accounts with Prague, it has adopted a hostile attitude toward our country, not so much as vengeance for its failure at establishing a common border with Poland, which it blames for the most part on our opposition, but because it feels that Romania, situated on one of the channels of German expansion toward the Ukraine, will inevitably come to a clash of interests with the Reich. And Hungary, having resolved to submit to—if not even to assist in—the fulfillment of Germany's aspirations, expects to draw substantial benefits from that clash. Romania has therefore to be isolated and, to that end, Yugoslavia won over and Bulgaria roused. At the same time, the friendship with Germany has to be firmly cemented—the cement being Hungarian internal and external concessions and unambiguous German commitments. The Budapest government's attitude toward Romania therefore depends in the first instance on the extent to which it believes—or imagines—that Wilhelmstrasse supports it. One could thus say without exaggeration that more solid and lasting relations between Romania and Hungary will originate not in Budapest but in Berlin. . . .

"Even so, the full-scale panic at Germany's encroachments that I discern more or less everywhere here is leading Hungarian political circles . . . to seek nonofficial contacts with Romania, since certain interests might be induced to make common cause. The Romanian government's conciliatory policy toward the Hungarian minority has been seen in Budapest as providing a welcome argument to explain to public opinion the reason and usefulness of a détente with Romania. The idea has caught on more strongly within the ranks of the opposition (Bethlen, Eckhardt) because, not having to face the worries of governing, it can disregard Germany's testiness. The government, and the press it influences to such a large extent, do not seem opposed to a discreet movement toward rapprochement, provided it does not run against the broad lines of German policy, that it is looked upon favorably by Rome, and especially were events to prove there was no prospect of realizing certain aspirations, the anachronism of which is at times recognized by the more enlightened minds. . . .

"Without wanting to draw hasty conclusions . . . it must be noted that a slight détente in Romano-Hungarian relations is taking place right now. An obviously temporary détente, temporary as are all political positions, but which, if peace is maintained, could constitute a favorable step toward the development of relations between the countries of the Danube Basin."

NEW PRIME MINISTERS IN HUNGARY AND ROMANIA

After a sad stay in Bucharest at the time of my mother's death, I returned to Budapest, where, in the meantime, a new government had been formed under the presidency of Count Paul Teleki, a well-known geographer, a man of high moral standing but lacking the wide-ranging background required of a prime minister. The dignity of his life and the lack of sharply defined political positions made him look more like an umpire than a leader. The future was going to show that this man of great integrity would prefer death to breaking his given word. When I lunched with him at Regent Horthy's, he assured me he would do the utmost for a rapprochement with Romania. He also included a passage relatively friendly to our country in the speech in which he presented his program.

Around that time, I received a letter from Count Széchenyi, the head of that family, thanking me for having been instrumental in the reinstallation at the Iron Gates[3] of a memorial plaque recalling his ancestor's role in the building of the Iron Gates highway.

As for Csáky, he no longer wanted to hear of the Bled agreement, which had offended the Germans because it had been concluded during Horthy and Kánya's visit to Berlin and could therefore be taken for an act of defiance. But on the basis of that agreement it would have been easy to push forward the negotiations between our countries. Poor Csáky proved to be a fallible prophet: he assured me, on the basis of his recent conversations in Berlin, that at least in this year 1939 there would be no war!

On March 7 Patriarch Miron died in Cannes, and Armand Călinescu replaced him as prime minister. There was in the air a sniff of détente between Romania and Hungary. Would it last? Bánffy came to see me, highly flattered by the consideration with which he had been received in Bucharest. At a luncheon at the Palace, he was seated immediately below the former ministers, and the king spoke with him for ten minutes, *in German,* urging him to present his grievances to Călinescu. This he did, being received by the prime minister in a most friendly manner. In turn, Teleki, the Hungarian prime minister, received me most courteously and told me he had drawn up the bill for the ratification of the agreement concerning the Gojdu Foundation.

Among diplomatic envoys, some were optimistic, others not. The first group included my new French colleague, Guerlet, who saw in the formation of the Teleki government a distancing from the Axis, and Rašić, who saw signs of an imminent "incipient friendship" between Romania and Hungary. He told me "you are so loved in Budapest," that all the Hungarians had only good to say about me and that "you have all my sympathy for your delicate mission here." In the group of the pessimists—and therefore of those who foresaw future developments more clearly—I must mention my friend Pipinelis, especially worried by Bulgaria's territorial claims.

Pessimism about the international situation, which I unfortunately had to share, seemed warranted. Indeed, on March 14 Slovakia, encouraged politically and financially by Hitler through the intermediary of Tiso, Karmasin, and Tuka, declared itself independent and the German army invaded what it called "Czechia," occupying Märisch-Ostrau and the important Wittkowitz industrial center (on which Poland had had its

---

[3]A scenic but hazardous gorge on the Danube near Orşova, and a place of historical significance dating to Roman times, now partly drowned by a dam and hydroelectric power plants, a joint undertaking of Romania and Yugoslavia in the 1960s.

eye). Hacha, the Czech president, and his foreign minister Chwalkowsky, were summoned by Hitler to Berlin, and it almost looked as if the Berchtesgaden tragedy with Schuschnigg was being repeated. The Hungarian government was overcome by an anxiety close to panic, panic at seeing one's country surrounded by Nazi Germany. At the same time, however, covetousness was reawakened toward Subcarpathian Russia, which now remained isolated. An unobtrusive partial mobilization toward that border was undertaken.

That same day I saw Vörnle, undersecretary of state at the Ministry of Foreign Affairs, and told him on behalf of my government, "Romania takes a close interest in the fate of Subcarpathian Russia and could accept a change in the present situation, established by the Vienna arbitral award, only following agreement between all interested countries, Romania obviously included." Vörnle took written notes of what I was telling him, showing, however, some surprise: "But Romania was not party to the Vienna award." I retorted, "Neither was Poland, but I am sure you will not dispute that it, too, has a stake in Subcarpathian Russia." I then counseled that the Hungarian troops that were advancing into Subcarpathian Russia not go beyond the Hust-Vizkov line. I added that the Romanian troops massed at the northern border would not cross the border unless our interests were endangered. My démarche was made in a friendly tone and was accepted as such by my interlocutor.

On the way out, I learned of the demise of our faithful ally, Czechoslovakia, purely and simply annexed by Hitler. The unfortunate Hacha and Chwalkowsky were forced, on March 15, to sign their own country's death certificate. As for lonely Subcarpathian Russia, it appeared that Berlin was now consenting to its being taken over by Hungary.

THE MARCH CRISIS: SUBCARPATHIAN RUSSIA AND THE HUNGARIAN MOBILIZATION

Undersecretary of State Vörnle asked me to come see him on March 16 and handed me the following note, written in atrocious French: "The masses and the leaders of the people of Subcarpathian Russia have approached the Hungarian government, requesting it to occupy militarily, without delay, the land inhabited by the Ruthenes, in order to rapidly reestablish personal security and the security of property in that territory.

"The Hungarian government has acceded to this request. As ordered, the Hungarian army is leaving the positions it has occupied until now on the territory of Subcarpathian Russia and is advancing and will take up positions on Ruthenian soil.

"Our army now has at its disposal such forces that by this fact alone it has foredoomed to total failure any resistance or attacks that might occur. The Hungarian army is thus able to occupy Subcarpathian Russia and to establish normal order in the shortest possible time and, it is hoped, without bloodshed.

"Of course, during its progression [*sic*] the Hungarian army shall scrupulously respect the territories and interests in connection with the frontier of countries bordering the former Subcarpathian Russia. Moreover, it has received strict orders to avoid even the appearance of any contrary [*sic*] action."

After handing me this note Vörnle declared that the Hungarian troops would occupy all of Subcarpathian Russia and that the Hungarian government, sincerely wishing to have the closest and most friendly relations with Romania, would like the annexation of this territory to be carried out in complete understanding between the two countries. He also asked me, on Csáky's behalf, to intercede with Bucharest in order that the Romanian troops along the border be ordered, in turn, to avoid any conflict with the Hungarian troops, thereby preventing incidents that might escalate. I answered that it was precisely to avoid such incidents that I had suggested the day before that the Hungarian army not go beyond a certain line. If need be, an even shorter line might be drawn, including the Romanian townships (Apşa de Mijloc, Apşa de Jos, Ocna-Slatina, and Biserica Albă) as well as the railway line Vişăul-Iaşina toward Poland. Vörnle assured me he would convey my proposal to his government, and that once the Polish border was reached, his government would solemnly declare its intention of respecting all the borders and interests of neighboring countries. In fact, however, the Hungarian government ignored my proposal, wanting to occupy the entire district immediately.

Erdmannsdorf confirmed to me that Hungary's annexation of Subcarpathian Russia had been made with Germany's consent.

In its desperation, the government of Subcarpathian Russia, headed by Vološin, proclaimed its union with Romania and, appealing to the Bucharest government for help, took refuge in Romania. Our government in no way pursued the matter politically.

Also on March 16, Orlowski came to see me. I congratulated him ironically for the establishment of a common border with Hungary, but he complained that it had been paid for too dearly by the disappearance of Czechoslovakia from the map. Odd statement from the representative of the country that dug Czechoslovakia's grave day by day and, in the end, gave it *le coup de pied de l'âne!* My Polish colleague then launched into an attack against the Nazi Reich: "If they touch Danzig, or even Memel, it will mean war!" It was clear that the Poles felt their turn coming, despite all the apparent Lipski-Ribbentrop cordiality.

After Orlowski's departure, I went to Kobr's to let him know of my sorrow at the dreadful calamity that had befallen his country. The poor man was totally devastated. Erdmannsdorf had already come to demand the handing over of the Czechoslovak legation's building, of the coding books, of the political archives, of the consulate's cash, of the safes' combinations, and so forth. A vulgarity and lack of feelings worthy of the government that did not shrink from appointing no less than Henlein as commissioner of the "Protectorate of Bohemia and Moravia!" However, both Kobr and Fiša, the legation's counselor, admitted that Erdmannsdorf had carried out his instructions with tact and seemed extremely embarrassed by the horrible task assigned to him.

In London, Tilea told Reuters that the German government had issued an ultimatum to Romania: we either delivered to it all of our production and gave up efforts to industrialize the country, limiting ourselves to agriculture, or our borders would no longer be guaranteed. Gafencu denied the accuracy of the information, but Tilea insisted it was the truth, with the consequence that he was nearly sacked. Meanwhile, the other foreign envoys in Budapest, and especially Knox, were highly alarmed by the news of the German "ultimatum" to Romania, and viewed our situation as most "critical." We apparently gained heroes' laurels and popularity in the Allied capitals, and were acclaimed in the theaters and movie houses of America, Britain, and France.

On March 18 I was instructed by the government to protest the overflight of Hungarian aircraft that, following the upper course of the Tisza, had strayed over Romania's border, and to ask at the same time that strict orders be given the Hungarian air force to avoid such incidents in the future. In his turn, Vörnle drew my attention on March 20 to the fact that a Romanian aircraft had flown over Hungarian territory south of Debrecen. A decision was then taken that both governments would issue the required instructions for the prevention of such incidents. When Vörnle requested information about an alleged mobilization of the Romanian army, I replied that it was merely a question of some strengthening measures to maintain order at the frontier following the Hungarian army's mobilization and the massing of its troops at the Romano-Hungarian border. I added that no person of common sense would imagine that Romania would intend to, or have the least interest in, attacking Hungary, and that I could guarantee that if Hungary withdrew its forces from the border, Romania would follow suit.

This question was also discussed by Gafencu and Bárdossy, who agreed to establish direct contact between the two governments in order to clarify their respective positions with regard to the occupation of Subcarpathian Russia by the Hungarian army. In this connection, Gafencu notified me as follows: "Together, we decided that this contact should be established in Budapest, between Foreign Minister Csáky and Romania's envoy, Mr. Bossy." Actually, the essence of our position was the demand that the Hungarian government recognize that the Bled agreement had entered into force. And since the agreement prohibited the use of force under any circumstance, the two parties could begin demobilizing.

In this connection, Knox told me he had made a representation to Csáky, asking him in the name of the British government for clarifications on the purpose of the Hungarian mobilization. He then counseled that any clash with Romanian troops be avoided, since such a clash could escalate and lead to unforeseen consequences. It is impossible, Knox noted, for anyone in his right mind to believe that Romania would begin a military operation against Hungary. He thought there might also be an external factor—that is, Hitler—who could have interest in bringing about a clash between Romanians and Hungarians, so that he could then foist himself as arbitrator and pacifier, as per his recently unveiled methods. France's envoy, Guerlet, made a similar representation. And Jules Sauerwein, with whom I had lunch at Guerlet's, saw the Hungarians as being completely tied to Germany's apron strings. Even though Sauerwein was one of the best international journalists, he did not manage to be received by Horthy, Teleki, or Csáky, for fear of the Germans, "who make them dance to their tune by dangling a piece of Slovakia before their eyes."

✧ ✧ ✧

After the German annexation of Memel, the Poles began to be flustered. Orlowski told me, "In the case of Danzig it will be different; it will mean war!" As a matter of fact, he had told me the same regarding Memel. The Czechs, in contrast, were full of hope: war will break out, the Allies will be victorious, and Czechoslovakia will be resurrected. Kobr declared this at a luncheon I was giving in his honor on the occasion of his departure, and Fiša, his counselor, proclaimed it with passion.

The signing of the Romano-German economic agreement, which was named after its German signatory, Wohltut, naturally led to a détente between Bucharest and Berlin. Probably out of spite, and also so as to be seen by his fellow citizens as an energetic statesman, Csáky delivered to the Chamber's Foreign Affairs Commission a speech full of arrogance and of blatant untruths. He pretended that Romania had wanted to intervene in Subcarpathian Russia but had been stopped by the threat of a clash with the "awesome" Hungarian army. On March 24 I asked to see him, and on the following day I had a rather heated meeting with him.

I began by telling him that I wanted to see him because Bárdossy had proposed talks between the two of us with a view to clearing up the situation between our countries. I added: "He could as well have proposed that the conversations take place between Gafencu and himself, which would have made things easier, since they meet almost daily, whereas we never see each other. He nevertheless suggested, on your instructions, that the contact be established between you and me. It is for this reason that I must have given your secretaries the impression that I was forcing my way in."

Csáky replied that he had been unable to meet with me because he had been hospitalized, but that his speech in Parliament had emphasized Gafencu's endeavors to improve relations between our countries, and that he was now going to hand me a note that would satisfy us. But before letting him read the note to me I stated that, since he had broached the matter of his speech, it had disappointed and incensed my government. I went on: "Besides, you wanted to make yourself much nastier than you really are. You mentioned threats and warnings toward Romania: when were they made and by whom? Bárdossy, in his talks with Gafencu, has been careful to avoid anything that could in the least be taken as a threat; as for Vörnle, he was all sugar and honey with me. Since our benevolent neutrality was necessary, there were only smiles for us. So, when were you threatening or warning us, to which I hasten to add we would have replied in similar fashion? The truth of the matter, according to what everyone tells me, is that the Hungarian government [that is, Csáky] needed to enhance its popularity, and since it could make the most of its march into Subcarpathian Russia only by presenting it as a victory, it had to designate a vanquished enemy. This could not be the dismembered Czechoslovaks . . . and therefore it had to be the Romanians."

Csáky interrupted me: "I give you my word of honor that it was not such a reason that induced me to talk as I did. It was solely information I received from an extremely reliable source that I was duty-bound to take into account, according to which you intended to occupy the whole of

Ruthenia—information that greatly irritated our armed forces." I answered, "Could you really believe such machinations and imagine my government so lacking in sense as to want to ingest five hundred thousand Ruthenes?"

"What could have led us to believe it was your military concentration at the Ruthene border while we still had few forces there, as well as the passage in the aide-mémoire you delivered to me on March 15 through Vörnle, in which it was stated that your troops would cross the border only if your interests were injured."

"But you had Poland's guarantee that we would not attack you. Had we intended to do so, we would have done so. Who would have prevented us?"

"It would not have been that easy, our troops were there."

"Oh, we would have faced minimal risks, given the superiority of our army, the disparity of our two countries in area and population, and the fact you just brought up that at first you had very few detachments there." I also made it a point of mentioning that, if we were not thanked for our good will once the danger had passed, we should at least not be rubbed the wrong way as we had been by his speech.

Csáky then read to me the note he had prepared. It contained the following points:

1. The Hungarian government will respect the new Hungaro-Romanian border as it had respected the old one.
2. The new border will be the one that until now separated Romania from Czechoslovakia.
3. The Bled declaration also applies to this new border.
4. Twenty-four hours after the Romanian government states that it is beginning to unwind the military measures it took, the Hungarian government will undertake the repeal of its own military measures.
5. The Hungarian government is willing to discuss issues stemming from the establishment of the new border through diplomatic channels.

I immediately pointed out that the note failed to take into account, as had been promised, our interests in Subcarpathian Russia, and that in addition it did not contain the promised solemn declaration concerning the respecting of borders. The reference to the Bled agreement represented merely a reconfirmation of the nonaggression declaration, and not a declaration concerning the respecting of borders; this is a distinction that must not be overlooked. We will not be able to proceed with the disbanding of troops before Hungary does. Csáky assured me that the order to demobilize the VI Army Corps from Debrecen would be issued that very day. In turn, I assured him that as soon as our military high command was satisfied that the order had in fact been implemented, Romania would take a similar measure. At that point Csáky, beaming and all smiles, told me that upon his return from Rome and Berlin in early May he would make another speech in Parliament, this time friendly toward Romania: "You will be pleased by it."

On March 30, Bánffy and Szász came to see me at the legation to express their indignation at Czáky's speech of the preceding week. They totally disassociated themselves from his unfounded assertions of alleged persecution of Hungarians in Transylvania, which they said were based on an incendiary article in *8 Orái Ujság* by Bethlen's son, for whom Bánffy had harsh words: "This scoundrel who set his father at loggerheads with the Hungarian government."

COOLING OF RELATIONS BETWEEN HUNGARY AND ROMANIA

Called back to Budapest by his government, Bárdossy informed me that I would be received the next day, April 1, by Csáky, who would propose an exchange of notes stating that the Bled agreement (which had only been initialed) had entered into force by a gentlemen's agreement. I told him I held Csáky responsible for having sabotaged, for reasons of personal vanity (Bárdossy smiled), the détente for which we are working: "If you instead of him had been appointed last fall as minister of foreign affairs, you would certainly not have made a speech such as his." He smiled again. I got the impression that he did not have a high opinion of his minister.

In the meantime, Neville Chamberlain's speech announcing the Franco-British guarantee given to Poland seemed to have turned the Hungarians' heads. They were now anticipating events of major import, as a consequence of which they might no longer have the same interest in achieving a détente with neighboring countries. A *Pester Lloyd* editorial said that the new atmosphere brought about by the British prime minister's speech was not favorable to the policy of rapprochement between Hungary and its neighbors. In other words, the Hungarians were expecting the outbreak of a widespread war from which they would emerge victorious along with the Germans. They were in consequence less willing to negotiate with their neighbors. And this was the atmosphere in which my conversation with Csáky took place. As I entered his office, he asked me if I was coming to bring him the happy news that the Romanian army was again on a normal peace footing, since Hungary had demobilized the Debrecen army corps and had moved its troops away from the Romano-Ruthenian border. I replied that, as he knew full well, the purpose of my visit was to ask what answer he intended to give our proposal of signing the Bled agreement, a signing that would, as a matter of fact, facilitate and expedite demobilization in both countries. Without this gesture on the part of Hungary, whose army was on a war footing, I said Romania would not be able to demobilize completely and would limit itself to some possible troop movements, as Hungary had done.

Csáky then proposed a written declaration in which he would confirm that the Bled nonaggression agreement had entered into force on the basis of a gentlemen's agreement. Or, if we preferred, he could sign and publish only those parts of the agreement that, in the current circumstances, were more acceptable to Hungarian public opinion. I told him that the first alternative might suit us, but that the second one struck me as an odd innovation in diplomatic relations. To choose from an initialed text only a few passages for signature and publication would indeed be an unprecedented procedure! Csáky admitted that, in fact, it would mean relinquishing the initialed document and negotiating a new one. But he would have to wait for the prior demobilization of our troops, so as not to give the impression that the Hungarian government was negotiating "under the threat of Romanian bayonets." I retorted that the declaration that had been promised to us, and on which we insisted, would make our mutual demobilizations easier, but that he believed that an atmosphere favorable for negotiations could only be established after demobilization in both countries. In the end, Csáky accepted that the Romanian demobilization take place only after Bucharest had been satisfied that the Hungarian army had been demobilized.

Csáky gave me the following explanation for the Budapest government's changed attitude toward the Bled agreement: "Momentous events are occurring on the vast international scene, and it is not surprising that positions taken on one day have to be modified the following day because of changing conditions." It was an almost direct way of saying that the Hungarians found it preferable to temporize so as to remain uncommitted as long as the general situation was not clarified and the balance of forces in Europe was not evident. This would leave the door open for their hopes—or illusions.

✧ ✧ ✧

I arrived in Romania on April 3, recalled by cable in order to report on the situation. I had long meetings and discussions with Gafencu and Armand Călinescu. We decided together that I should ask the Hungarian government for either a note on the lines indicated above or an exchange of letters as per Csáky's proposal, acknowledging the entrance into force of the Bled agreement.

Among other issues we examined was an Anglo-French proposal for guaranteeing Romania's independence and territorial integrity, on condition that we broaden *erga omnes*[4] (that is, also against a German aggression) the obligation stipulated in our alliance with Poland, which only made provision for the event of a Russian attack. My view was sought. Cretzianu drew me aside and cautioned me to weigh my comments carefully, since my opinion "carries much weight with Gafencu." I said we could not turn down an Anglo-French pledge of assistance in the event of danger: "If on the street someone tells me that, were I to be attacked, he would spring to my defense, I cannot say, 'No thank you.'" Nevertheless, all our commitments must be kept and the usual formalities respected so as not to give the impression that we are trying to provoke Germany, with which we must keep the best of relations as long as it does not intend to dominate us politically or take us over economically. The German government could easily counterbalance the Anglo-French move by, in turn, guaranteeing that it would defend us in the event of a Russian aggression.

But Gafencu made another suggestion, namely, that Paris and London agree to the mutual Romanian-Polish guarantee being extended to cover only aggressions by "common neighbors" (that is, Russia and Hungary). In the event of a refusal, he believed it would be best to forgo the Anglo-French guarantee. For my part, I would have preferred the Poles not to agree to Gafencu's proposal, rather than for us to reject the hand held out by our country's traditional friends. Gafencu, backed by Cretzianu, wanted to avoid at any cost an attitude that could be interpreted in Berlin as a provocation. He complained bitterly about what he called "Tilea's bomb"—his statement regarding a "German economic ultimatum," which uselessly provoked the Berlin government. "We had decided to recall him," he disclosed, "and you were nearly appointed to London. Everything had been arranged, but at the

[4]Toward all.

last moment the king decided not to get rid of Tilea, who in his view represents Transylvanian youth."

Călinescu and Gafencu overwhelmed me with congratulations for my work in Budapest. I answered I did not see why, since I had been unable to bring them any favorable result. "Never mind, you are putting up a good fight with the Hungarians," the prime minister told me. Those of my colleagues who had access to my reports and cables likewise added their friendly praise. Whether deserved or not, these flattering remarks heartened me for the thankless mission that was my lot.

✧ ✧ ✧

I was back in Budapest on April 6 and was at once asked by Csáky to come see him at the Ministry. He handed me the text of a note that differed from the one I had proposed. Instead of "The Hungarian government will respect the Romanian border," I found the sentence "The Hungarian government has issued to its troops, from the start of Subcarpathian Russia's occupation, the order to respect as scrupulously as in the past all of Romania's borders." I pointed out to Csáky that it was one thing for a government to declare it will respect a border—which implies a legal and political element—and another to order its army to respect it—which is more of a technical military nature. In addition, it implied that it was a past matter: the time to occupy a certain territory. Csáky assured me that it also applied to the future. I then said I would report to my government, and, if the text was acceptable, we would acknowledge receipt of it and the notes would be published simultaneously.

Turning to the attitude of the Budapest press toward Romania, I compared it with our newspapers' patience and fairness when mentioning Hungary. Csáky acknowledged that feelings were running high in Hungary, especially because of turmoil flowing in from abroad, each group of powers trying to attract the smaller countries to its side. I observed to him that Romania for its part had no need to join blocs, since it did not feel threatened by anyone. We had very good relations with Germany, sanctioned by the recent economic agreement, and were tied by alliances with Poland and Yugoslavia and by nonaggression treaties with Hungary and Bulgaria. We therefore had nothing to fear. As for Hungary, I added, it was well known, in London as well as in Paris, that it was indissolubly tied to the Axis, and therefore neither Britain nor France was seeking to detach it from its allies. Csáky appeared embarrassed, but did not dispute what I had told him.

APRIL 1939

On April 8 all the envoys of the Balkan Entente met at Pipinelis's to examine the grave situation that was developing in our region following the landing of Italian troops in Albania and the occupation of its capital, Tirana. Rašić told us that the Italians had informed his government that they had decided to chase away Zog, until now their protégé, and to impose an Italian protectorate on Albania. The brave Albanians fought and resisted as much as they could. We were faced with a flagrant violation of the status quo in the Adriatic, one that had been sanctioned by the Italo-Yugoslav agreement of March 1937 as well as by the Italo-British agreement that provided for respecting the status quo in the eastern Mediterranean, to the east of longitude 20, which passes through Corfu. Pipinelis was worried because he felt that Corfu was directly threatened by Italy. According to the latest news, Zog had taken refuge in Greece. We asked Rašić what position Belgrade was taking. He replied that Yugoslavia would remain neutral, since Ciano had given "the most categorical pledge that all Yugoslav interests in Albania will be respected." Exactly which interests? Neither he nor Andrić, the new envoy to Berlin who was passing through Budapest, was able to throw light on this. Both were of the opinion that Yugoslavia was now completely blocked by Germany and Italy, and therefore unable to react even in the event of a generalized war. In any case, Pipinelis was certain that Britain would defend Greece.

The international situation was becoming more and more dangerous. My British colleague, Knox, told me he was certain of an imminent world war, in which Romania, in its own interest, should side with Britain and France. Bucharest was extremely careful not to provoke Hitler needlessly. The Rador agency denied the news of a German economic ultimatum spread by Tilea in London, and Gafencu instructed all our legations to disseminate the denial broadly, adding that the German negotiator, Wohlthat, had never exceeded the bounds of state-to-state commercial negotiations. At the same time, Armand Călinescu and Gafencu sent Cretzianu to London and Paris to find out the status of the guarantees that had been offered to Romania.

On his return, Cretzianu stopped in Budapest to bring me up to date on the results of his mission. He told me that in London he had been received by Halifax, who had roared with laughter when he was shown the text of the note Csáky had handed me on April 6. "Instead of giving you a guarantee concerning the respect of borders," Halifax said, "they merely conveyed to you a 'technical' order they issued to their troops." Halifax would have wished us to extend *erga omnes* our treaty with Poland, so that it might also be valid against Germany. Beck, however, told him this was an issue he would discuss directly with us, but that he had "not yet been approached by Bucharest"; he hoped that Romania would broach the topic, so that the Warsaw government would not appear to be the one that sought Germany's encirclement. On the other hand, Halifax promised a unilateral guarantee for Romania and Greece, to which would be added a similar guarantee from France. From a practical point of view, he said, he urged us to reach an understanding with the Poles, and this in our own interest. Were we to be attacked by Hitler, only Poland and Russia could effectively come to our assistance, and the British navy could only go to the help of Greece. How naïve this reasoning is in light of what was to happen! The Poles were able to resist the Germans for only a few days and then took refuge in Romania, while Russia was already planning the conquest of our country.

In Paris, Cretzianu was received by Daladier. Daladier would have liked us to conclude a four-party treaty—France, Britain, Romania, and Poland—but was also agreeable to the notion of a unilateral guarantee. He admitted that in September, in their attitude toward hapless Czechoslovakia, the Poles had been "*ignobles.*"[5] He had no confidence in Yugoslavia and vehemently attacked Stoiadinović. At the Quai d'Orsay, Secretary-General Léger told Cretzianu that the Germans would be unable to wage war for more than three months without our oil.

In conclusion, Cretzianu returned with the impression that the aggressive attitude of Germany and Italy was only bluff. The Germans as well as the Italians, he said, realized that for every million they spent on armament, the British and French would spend ten or one hundred million. For that reason, they were resigned to the thought of an international conference that would impose the status quo and limit armaments. Anticipating that international arrangement, the Germans and Italians were hastening to occupy territories relatively easy to take over, such as Bohemia, Memel, and Albania. What naïveté and blindness! In Paris, as in London, the hope of peace was thus still alive, especially after Mussolini's appeal to Chamberlain. But if war was inevitable, there remained the unshakable belief in both capitals that the final victory would belong to the Western Allies.

---

[5]Despicable.

In the same order of ideas, Pipinelis revealed to me that he was against an official British guarantee for Greece, since it would compromise his country in the eyes of Berlin and Rome. Moreover, Britain would defend Greece even without a guarantee. Halifax had stated in Rome that Greece's territorial integrity was of foremost importance to Britain, and that Britain would go to war if the Italians occupied Corfu. The British envoy to Sofia notified the Bulgarian government of this fact.

✧ ✧ ✧

On April 13, Chamberlain announced in the House of Commons that in the event Romania and Greece were to deem it vital to defend their independence with all of their national forces, Britain and France would come to their assistance. Daladier made an identical statement in the French parliament. That same day—and probably for this reason—Csáky made a conciliatory speech toward Romania. But, to stress Hungary's attachment to the Axis, he also announced its withdrawal from the League of Nations. Two days later, on April 15, Roosevelt sent a message to Hitler and Mussolini, proposing a ten-year truce, a disarmament conference, and an economic one. Yet another Anglo-Saxon self-delusion!

My British colleague, Knox, came to take his farewell, having been recalled to the Foreign Office. He was certain that a world war was imminent, at the latest in the fall. He deplored Chamberlain's weakness: he should have ordered the bombing of the Italian navy on its way to Albania. Mussolini would have pulled back, humiliated, and would perhaps have been hanged by his own, "which would not have been a great loss to anybody." Knox believed Hitler would not have stirred, but had he moved, the war would have taken place in the most favorable context, with the whole world being indignant at the dictatorships.

At a luncheon organized by Orlowski in Knox's honor, a woman, Yugoslav by birth, told me that public opinion in Belgrade was unanimously against the Axis, with the sole exception of Prince-Regent Paul who, "more crafty than intelligent, tries to equivocate." My Yugoslav colleague informed me that his chief, Cinčar-Markovič, would soon go to Venice to discuss with Ciano the possibility of a rapprochement with Hungary, the end sought by Rome—but by no means by Berlin—being the formation of a satellite Budapest-Belgrade-Sofia bloc. Pipinelis repeated to me a conversation he had had with Remeny-Schneller, the finance minister, who assured him the Hungarian government would spare no efforts to remain neutral were war to break out, for if it had to choose sides, it would intervene on the side of the Axis, which was foredoomed to defeat, and Hungary would thus repeat its mistake of 1914.

At a luncheon given by the British Counselor Gascoigne, Daisy Károlyi was indignant at the lack of humaneness of the Italians, who deposed Zog the day after Queen Geraldine gave birth to a son. Geraldine (née Apponyi) had been very dignified and had turned down the refuge offered by Italy's legation. Knox, who was also present, told us that Prince Paul had confided to Campbell, Britain's envoy to Belgrade, that Yugoslavia would in no case participate actively in war on the side of Britain's enemies. In other words, explained Knox, an alliance with "those two vulgar and ridiculous corporals" had almost no takers.

✧ ✧ ✧

A pleasant, although rather anachronistic, luncheon at Archduke Joseph and Archduchess Augusta's. I was seated next to their daughter, Archduchess Magdalene, a very likable person with artistic leanings (she painted and sculpted), but somewhat stifled by *Frau Mama*. She would have liked to live in the fifteenth century, or at the time of Charles V and Francis I, both ancestors of hers. I pointed out that she would not have had a bathroom. Laughing, she gave up on that period, but complained about the current one. Archduke Joseph showed me a painting of a former castle of his in Slovakia: "I hope it will be returned to me soon." He added that, even though he was a field marshal who had commanded armies during the past war, he was utterly opposed to a new armed conflict and wished from the bottom of his heart that Hungary would remain neutral. To Knox, he had said that a Hungarian revisionist move against Romania would be madness. Archduchess Augusta was revolted that Zog, a former corporal in the Austro-Hungarian army, could ascend to a throne. I replied that the shah of Persia, Reza Pahlavi, was also a former corporal and, besides, we lived in the era of corporals: Hitler, Mussolini.

✧ ✧ ✧

The Hungarians hated Knox and at his departure on April 25, contrary to all protocol, no one from the foreign ministry came to see him off at the station. Only we, the Allied envoys, were there. This, a colleague told me, was a Hungarian snub to a man who had come to know them too well and who described them in London as they really were.

Rašić was also at the railway station; he told me Csáky had admitted to him that both in Rome and in Venice (Cinčar-Markovič's visit) it had become clear that it was impossible for Yugoslavia, Romania's ally, to sign alone an agreement with Hungary. He reportedly also expressed to Mussolini Hungary's wish to see Yugoslavia strong, within and outside, and assured Mussolini that he would prevent inasmuch as he could its unraveling or the weakening of its unity. "He was talking like a conceited cockerel," concluded Rašić laughing, "his ridiculous tone of voice totally unsuited to his minimal significance on the European scene. He wanted to appear as my country's protector! Another would have flown at him, but I let him blow his horn so as to understand his way of thinking."

In his April 28 speech, Hitler turned down Roosevelt's conference proposal and denounced the Anglo-German naval agreement and the German-Polish nonaggression treaty. He also said the only obstacle to a common border between Poland and Hungary had been "the most influential person in Romania" (that is, Carol).

✧ ✧ ✧

On April 28, I forwarded to our Ministry of Foreign Affairs the following report on the objectives pursued by the Hungarian government with regard to the Little Entente: "From the instant Italy, needing a starting point for its Central European policy, extended a hand of friendship to 'dismembered' Hungary, the Budapest government, with the help of Rome, has sought to break the unity of the Little Entente in order to take advantage of events for the gradual realization of its revisionist aspirations.

"Inasmuch as German militancy pointed to the possibility of revisionist successes against Czechoslovakia, the Prague government became branded as Hungary's 'enemy number one,' and efforts to break the Little Entente's unity were aimed against it. I thus witnessed the innumerable overtures made to Romania and Yugoslavia to induce them to dissociate themselves from their ally. 'With Romania and Yugoslavia, I would sign any treaty at any time,' Kánya used to say last summer, 'on condition that I were not obliged also to bind myself to Czechoslovakia.' This is how it became possible to conclude the Bled agreement, with Hungary hoping to be able to induce Bucharest and Belgrade to abandon Prague to its fate.

"The unfolding of events allowed Hungary to fulfill its northern territorial aspirations without Czechoslovakia's being attacked militarily and without the treaty of the Little Entente having the opportunity of being brought into action. From that moment, Romania became the 'enemy number one,' and one could immediately note Budapest's unwillingness to bring the Bled agreement into force. Its hostility was also proved by a violent press campaign against Romania, as well as by the Hungarian army's deployment at our border, owing to a wrong reading of Romanian-German relations.

". . . When the signing of the commercial agreement with Germany proved the real state of our relations with the Reich, Budapest's tone quieted down to some extent. Action has shifted from the 'loud' level of speeches, newspaper articles, and boisterous military measures, to the softer one of political intrigues. The method used for the isolation of Czechoslovakia is now used in an attempt to encircle Romania.

"Since Hungary cannot turn to Moscow, especially after the break in diplomatic relations because of its adherence to the Axis . . . all of the Budapest government's diplomatic resources are directed to parting Belgrade from Bucharest. For that purpose, the entire arsenal of temptations of the Axis, and especially of Italy, is being brought to bear. They hoped that if Yugoslavia allowed itself to be ensnared in the trap of its Adriatic friends, it would more quickly be enticed by Hungarian friendship, to which it might sacrifice the old and tried Romanian alliance.

"This, however, appears to have been a miscalculation, and the complicated scheme did not succeed. During the meetings between Mussolini, Teleki, and Csáky, as well as during the Cinčar-Markovič–Ciano conversations in Venice, note was taken of the Yugoslav government's unflinching determination not to overlook the letter of the agreements that tied it to Romania. As the Hungarian minister of foreign affairs summarized the situation to some of my colleagues: 'Hungary is willing to sign on the spot any agreement with Yugoslavia, forgoing all the conditions it had raised at the beginning; Italy is most eager to see a Belgrade-Budapest agreement concluded, but Yugoslavia refuses to sign any separate instrument because of its alliance with Romania.'

"Prime Minister Teleki put an end to the hopes raised in Hungary by the Venice meeting, to which a particular significance had been attached after the Hungarian visit to Rome, by saying in a speech: 'We all have the same dream; unfortunately, however, we cannot live in dreams, but only in reality.' As for Csáky, he personally wrote a commentary on the official communiqué of the Venice meeting, which appeared on the first page of *Pester Lloyd's* evening edition of April 24 and of which I extract the main passage:

'Hungary, filled with the greatest patience . . . will on its part also take advantage of all the possibilities opened by the auspicious development of relations between Belgrade, Berlin, and Rome. It appears that the

Yugoslav people have an increasingly better understanding of Hungary's wish to see the Yugoslav state strengthened internally and externally within its present diplomatic relationships. During this consolidation period we are willing to give proof of the required tact . . . toward Yugoslavia's most eminent personalities. We will thus enable Yugoslavia, after a meeting of minds in all fields, to reach, as we did, a sincere understanding between the two countries.'

"The order of the day seemed to be as follows: Given the Romanian-Yugoslav alliance, the Budapest government would show the required tact toward the personal obligations of the Yugoslav head of state not to insist on the signing of a Hungarian-Yugoslav treaty. For the time being, it would content itself with the actual deepening of relations between the two countries."

LATE SPRING, EARLY SUMMER 1939

On his way back from Berlin, Gafencu stopped over in Paris. From there, he cabled me to meet him in Venice so that he might bring me up to date on the results of his trip and to find out from me the true position of the Budapest government. I arrived in Venice on May 3 and checked in, as usual, at the Danieli. Until the arrival of the foreign minister, I wandered through the old and entrancing alleys so dear to me. I also had the opportunity to visit at the Cà d'Oro its magnificent Veronese collection.

The next day, Gafencu alighted from his train. During our stroll at the Lido and our lunch at the restaurant La Fenice, he told me the impressions he had gathered during his trip. Toward evening we boarded the Simplon and set out for Yugoslavia, continuing the conversation in our compartment. He gave me to read his summary of the talk he had had with Hitler. Hitler had stated that all he was asking Romania was compliance with the commercial agreement, that we refrain from transforming the British and French unilateral guarantee into a bilateral agreement, and that we do not link up with the Soviet Union. As for the Hungarians, Hitler asserted he had made no promises to them, and that even so, too much had been granted to them. "I told Horthy and Teleki, and more recently Csáky, all of whom sat in the very same armchair you are sitting in now," added the Führer, "that neither the German population in Romania nor that in Yugoslavia wanted to fall back under Hungarian domination, and that in Central Europe I adhere to the policy favored by my Germans." Hitler conversed with Gafencu in a courteous manner, very outspokenly, and with a certain appearance of sincerity. He let Gafencu explain for a quarter of an hour Romania's policy, and then held forth for an entire hour. Ribbentrop, obviously, spoke to him to the same effect, but in more detail. Göring, on the other hand, was quite unpleasant. He seemed to warn Romania not to join the policy of encircling Germany, or else! Toward the end, he seemed to grow mellower. Gafencu gave an interview to the *Essener Nationalzeitung,* which quoted him as saying that Romania would under no circumstances join a coalition directed against Germany. Gafencu authorized Tilea to deny this alleged statement, which could have damaged the favorable atmosphere we enjoyed in London. "Instead," Gafencu told me, "Tilea denied the entire interview, which led the paper to publish an article headlined 'Mr. Tilea Lies Once More.'"

Gafencu seemed particularly pleased with his stay in London, where, he told me, he had been warmly received by all. "With Halifax, I even can say we became friends," added Gafencu, delighted. Those he talked with seemed to understand the difficulty of Romania's international position. As in the past, the British persisted in wanting us to broaden the provisions of our treaty with Poland *erga omnes* (that is to say, *erga Germaniam*). Gafencu argued that, in fact, the treaty was *erga omnes,* but that "the technical agreement foresees only the Russian hypothesis." Nothing precluded, however, that at a favorable moment other "hypotheses" might also be foreseen. But it would not be wise to provoke Germany uselessly in the present circumstances, a point of view that Halifax understood. Gafencu seemed convinced that London was preparing to conclude treaties with Ankara and Moscow.

In Paris as well as in Rome, Gafencu told me, the conversations were most harmonious. Mussolini stated flatly to him: "Transylvania is Romanian, and any territorial revision is unacceptable. There is but a minority problem, which you are trying to settle." Subsequent developments were to show how little the Duce was to keep to his statement. Gafencu replied that we endeavored to resolve the minority problem as best we could, but only internally, since we could not concede an oversight right to the Budapest government, so irremediably hostile to us. Mussolini regretted we had consented to a unilateral guarantee from Britain and France, "which smacks of a protectorate."

Arrived in Ljublijana, we separated; Gafencu proceeded to Belgrade, I returned to my post.

✧ ✧ ✧

I had the opportunity of seeing Gafencu again in May, in Bucharest, where I stayed for two weeks to attend the last moments of my father, who died on May 15. Gafencu told me he returned from Belgrade with the impression that the Yugoslav government wanted to withdraw from the Balkan Entente, under the pretext that the conclusion of the Anglo-Turkish treaty infringed on the basic principle of the Entente, which prohibited joining a great-power bloc. Gafencu hoped he had succeeded in convincing Cinčar-Markovič that the Anglo-Turkish treaty referred only to Turkey's Mediterranean role, and not to its existence as a Balkan power. Always Belgrade's concern to ingratiate itself with the Axis!

Back in Budapest, I found Rašić with similar worries about the Anglo-Turkish treaty, worries he believed were also shared in Athens. But Pipinelis knew nothing about these alleged "worries" of his government. He pointed out that Athens was tied to Ankara in regard not only to Balkan events but also to Mediterranean ones.

✧ ✧ ✧

Hungarian revisionist propaganda was continuing apace, even though Csáky maintained that it was only concerned with the improvement of the Hungarian minority's condition in Transylvania. In a Chamber of Deputies speech Gafencu declared that "none of the major powers supports Hungarian revisionism," and that "we are undertaking no new foreign commitments regarding minority issues." My friend Christian de Charmasse, France's chargé d'affaires, told me that, basing himself on Halifax's proposal for resolving current problems through negotiations, Barcza, Hungary's envoy to London, informed Britain's foreign minister about the Hungarian claims on Transylvania, asking him at least to facilitate a resolution of the minority question. The Foreign Office sent a written reply to Barcza, stating that the British government saw no territorial problem in Transylvania, and that additional details would be required in order to examine the validity of complaints concerning the treatment of the Hungarian minority.

✧ ✧ ✧

At the end of my summer vacation I stopped in at the Ministry in Bucharest. The political director, Cretzianu, full of praise for my work, told me I could soon expect one of the highest positions: an embassy or one of the major legations before the end of the year. He then informed me that Prime Minister Călinescu was asking me to participate in a meeting of heads of mission from important capitals on July 25. Attending the meeting, in addition to myself, were Călinescu and Gafencu, Radu Crutzescu (Berlin), and Filotti (Sofia) and, from central administration, George Grigorcea, Cretzianu, and Davidescu. Călinescu asked all of us to report on the situation in our respective areas. Crutzescu said he did not believe war would break out, since there were nine chances out of ten that the Germans would be defeated. Hitler, who had to be aware of the situation, had therefore no incentive to trigger the catastrophe. True, he added, neither Hitler nor Ribbentrop was sufficiently informed about the international situation: they never saw foreign diplomats, and the foreign press was summarized tendentiously for them by Dietrich. The Germans seemed not to fear the Russians in the least. Large troop movements were going on all over Germany, Crutzescu said, which seemed to refute his contention that Hitler was not considering war. Crutzescu was never able to meet with Ribbentrop, and was only received by Weizsäcker. Nor had he been able to meet Göring, even though he had four times requested an audience. On the other hand, even Britain's ambassador in Berlin, Nevile Henderson, did not grant Cretzianu an interview, and he could only meet the embassy's counselor. Crutzescu regretted the Anglo-French guarantee we received—which made us look bad in Berlin—as well as the tone of our press, so hostile toward Germany. His opinion was that we should withdraw into our house, "like a snail," so as not to offend the Reich, because in the event of war we could only lose.

When my turn came to speak, I explained that the Hungarians were totally bound to the Axis. If the Germans don't attack us, the Hungarians, too, will remain neutral. But if the Germans were to try getting to our oil by force, the Hungarians would volunteer to be their vanguard in an attack on Transylvania. The German military attaché in Budapest went daily to the Hungarian general staff, which had become an annex of the one in Berlin. At the diplomatic level, Csáky flirted with London in case an international conference was held, or as reinsurance in the event of an Axis defeat. The purpose of the Hungarian press campaign against Romania was to call the British public's attention to the Transylvanian issue.

Poor Filotti was upset by the behavior of the Bulgarians, who no longer shook hands with him and sang the "Dobrudjan hymn" as soon as they saw him. No matter how many concessions were made to

Bulgaria, it would still not join the Balkan Entente. It was therefore useless to talk with them. Nevertheless, it was not out of the question that they might remain neutral in the event of a generalized war. They would also be influenced to a large extent by Yugoslavia's attitude.

Gafencu maintained that, in spite of appearances, Yugoslavia would not adhere to the Axis. Prince-Regent Paul had stated this to him most categorically: he detested equally the Italians and Bulgarians, and of King Boris, he had said, "He is a chip off the old block, the greatest liar to sit on a throne." The Yugoslav armed forces were pro-French and hostile to the Germans and Italians. The Bulgarians had fallen out with all their neighbors. Bulgaria's envoy to Ankara told Gafencu that even were they to be given Western Thrace, Yugoslav Macedonia, and the Quadrilateral,[6] they would not cooperate militarily with the Balkan Entente; at most, they would remain neutral. This confirmed what Vinci had been telling me in Budapest. Regarding our relations with Germany, Gafencu feared—in his own word—two major "hurdles": the conclusion of the Anglo-Turkish and Franco-Turkish treaties, and the conclusion of Anglo-Soviet and Franco-Soviet treaties, which would probably also provide for assistance to Romania.

Călinescu was extremely worried. Like all of us, with the sole exception of Crutzescu, he expected a major war to break out at any time. He saw as a premonitory sign the increasing boldness of the German minority, which had proclaimed Fabritius[7] as their *Landesführer*.[8] He asked us to give him, as soon as we were able to, the answers to two questions that preoccupied him: where will war break out? When will it break out? The atmosphere in Bucharest seemed very tense to me.

✧ ✧ ✧

Back in Budepest, I had a long meeting with Csáky, who took pains to make it as cordial and conciliatory as possible. He told me he disapproved of the anti-Romanian press and radio polemics and that he had now instructed the newspapers to put an end to them. With apparently great feeling, he assured me he wanted to have the same good relations with us as Yugoslavia did, but we imagined that Hungary had hidden designs against Romania, which prevented building up an atmosphere of

[6]Area of Dobrudja that Bulgaria had to cede to Romania in 1913, after the Second Balkan War.

[7]The German envoy to Bucharest.

[8]Regional leader.

trust between us. I expressed my satisfaction at his statements, which I heard for the first time out of the mouth of a Hungarian foreign minister, and I assured him of our wish for a détente. But I drew his attention to some signs that seemed to contradict his good intentions. For instance: the continuing violent anti-Romanian press campaign, the scheme of periodically raising internationally the issue of Romano-Hungarian relations, the shutting down of all Romanian schools in Subcarpathian Russia, the prohibition of printing any textbook in Romanian, the firing of all Romanian teachers, the nonratification of the agreements concerning the Gojdu Foundation and the restitution of the Transylvanian archives, and so forth. Csáky took notes of what I was telling him and promised to look into it and take the measures required to correct any mistakes that might have been committed. Obviously, one of the objects of this new attitude was the wish that Romania sign an agreement on navigation on the Tisza River, which would serve Hungarian interests. There may also have been another purpose: a relative détente with Romania would give Csáky more freedom of maneuver during his upcoming talks with Ribbentrop and Ciano.

THE RIBBENTROP-MOLOTOV PACT

August 22 brought the unexpected and sensational news of Ribbentrop's arrival in Moscow to conclude a German-Russian nonaggression treaty. And this while Franco-Anglo-Russian negotiations were under way! The bombshell obviously unleashed passionate discussions. Among the Allied envoys there was great indignation at this about-face by Hitler, who was seen as capable of any shameful bargain in order to reach his objectives, as well as at Stalin's unheard-of treachery. Guerlet, my French colleague, remarked, "A betrayal more or less, what does it matter in Moscow?" The balance of power had now shifted in the Axis's favor. My Italian colleague Vinci told me that if Germany wanted its army to cross Hungary in order to attack Poland, the Budapest government wouldn't hesitate a second to obey this injunction, being tied hand and foot to Berlin (but not to Rome!).

The Labour M.P. Arthur Henderson was at that time in Budapest, on his way to Romania, and came to have lunch with me. He, too, expected war to break out at any moment. The Hungarians he had met complained about the discriminatory treatment allegedly faced by the Hungarian minority in Transylvania—the same broken old record! Henderson told them that since under no circumstance, and whatever the result of an eventual war, would they be able to regain Transylvania, the best thing would therefore be to come to an understanding with the Romanians, which would then be reflected in the treatment of their fellow nationals.

✧ ✧ ✧

August 24. Ribbentrop and Molotov signed, in Stalin's presence, the German-Soviet nonaggression treaty. I listened on the radio to Chamberlain's and Halifax's speeches declaring that Britain would stand by Poland. War is drawing near and an atmosphere of panic reigns. The French and British legations are beginning to evacuate their nationals from Budapest. Slovakia's new envoy, Spisiak, who spoke to me nostalgically of the former Czechoslovakia (from which the Slovaks had torn themselves off only so as not to be surrendered to Hungary), disclosed to me that the Germans were massing troops in Slovakia and eastern Prussia.

Toward evening, Henderson came to tell me that, owing to the tense situation and following the British legation's advice, he was giving up his trip to Romania in order to return to London. Tilea, who was passing through Budapest on his way to rejoin his post, told me no one in Bucharest doubts anymore the imminence of war.

Before leaving, Henderson asked me to convey a message from him to the Romanian government: Teleki told Eckhardt that this very day, Erdmannsdorf had invited him to ally himself officially with Germany and to cooperate actively with it; Teleki refused, stating that Hungary wanted to remain neutral. So, added Henderson, "Csáky had his knuckles rapped," since he had overcommitted himself in Salzburg in the hope that, seen as "Hitler's man, he would succeed Teleki as prime minister." In his conversation with Henderson, Teleki reportedly showed himself in favor of nonofficial talks between Bucharest and Budapest; Regent Horthy told him he would oppose the crossing of German troops to attack Romania.

I remained until late at night at the legation with my staff, in permanent contact with Gafencu and the foreign ministry's code room.

August 25. The atmosphere of panic is intensifying. Cristea, who has arrived with an economic delegation to negotiate some custom tariff matters, wanted to break off the talks and return immediately to Bucharest. But I stopped him, so as not to give the impression that we could not control our nerves or that we anticipated a major strain in our relations with Hungary.

The correspondent of the Havas press agency came to ask me whether there was any chance of reaching a nonaggression treaty between Romania, Yugoslavia, and Hungary—a sort of resuscitation of the Bled agreement. At the Hungarian Ministry of Foreign Affairs, where he had also sought an answer, they had told him "neither yes nor no." In reply, I said, "For once, I am in full agreement with them, and answer you the same way."

I went to see Orlowski, who expects a German attack at any moment. I asked him if Poland has massed substantial troops at the border. He replied that he did not believe so, since "this will be a war of movement and the Polish army will be in Berlin in three weeks' time." [Poor Orlowski. Three weeks later, the Polish commanding officers were going to be not in Berlin, but in Cernăuţi.[9]]

August 26. Rüstü Aras, who was passing through Budapest, assured Pipinelis that since a secret clause in the Italo-German military treaty stipulates that the two contracting parties will not declare war for a period of three years, Italy will remain neutral, and has so forewarned Germany. The secretary of our legation in Berlin, Rădulescu-Pogoneanu, on his way to Romania, gave me the same information. This might explain why Hitler, faced by Mussolini's refusal to enter the fight, yesterday proposed to London negotiations aimed at avoiding a military conflict.

Deep disagreements have arisen within the Hungarian government. Horthy and Teleki want at all costs to maintain Hungary's neutrality, while Csáky, impressed by Germany's military might and believing in its ultimate victory, inclines toward an intervention alongside the Axis; since he considers himself to be Hitler's favorite, such a course would also serve his ambition of becoming prime minister.

✧ ✧ ✧

August 27. Hitler's demands are unacceptable: Danzig, the Polish Corridor, border rectifications in Upper Silesia. The atmosphere reeks of war. Romanians are passing through Budapest in a hurry, in order to catch "the last train" homeward. The Germans have occupied Slovakia. There were demonstrations of support by Hungarians in front of the German and Italian legations.

---

[9] City in northern Romania, later annexed by the Soviet Union and renamed Chernovtsy.

August 29. The exchange of letters between Chamberlain and Hitler continues, through the medium of the British ambassador in Berlin. On the other hand, neither do the phone calls between Mussolini and Hitler slow down. A French publicist, Georges Oudard, intelligent and impassioned, told me that all of France, as a single man, was determined to fight the Hitlerian tyranny. Vinci, returned from Rome where he has seen Ciano, likewise came to see me. He was no longer bellicose and talked to me about the Duce and the pope's feverish efforts to preserve peace; this seems to confirm the indication that Italy does not intend to enter the war at the same time as Germany. The Italian military attaché told his Romanian counterpart, "We can't start a war just for Hitler's glory."

August 30. The Chamberlain-Hitler correspondence has not stopped, but neither must it have gone too well, since Poland has ordered general mobilization. Italy's noncommittal attitude seems to indicate that Hitler has agreed it should remain neutral in the first phase of the war, as long as the Germans have to deal with the Poles. When—as hoped in Berlin—the German army will have successfully completed its Polish campaign, other army corps will be able to move westward, and that would be the time for Italy to enter the fray, without incurring excessive risks.

WAR BREAKS OUT

September 1. Outbreak of the German-Polish war. Without a declaration of war, Germany attacked Poland, bombing Warsaw, Krakow, and other cities. Hitler's vociferations could be heard on the radio. General mobilization in France and Britain. The ambassadors of France and Britain in Berlin warned the German government that if it did not immediately cease hostilities against Poland and withdraw its troops from Polish territory, France and Britain would defend Poland in accordance with their commitments. In the event of a negative reply, the ambassadors will demand their passports back. Italy, as was to be expected, has not moved, stating it would not initiate hostilities. It is obviously preparing itself for a long neutrality and will intervene only in the event of a German victory, in order to "fly to the assistance of the victor." In his speech to the House of Commons, Neville Chamberlain placed the entire responsibility of the catastrophe on Hitler's insane ambition.

September 2. The Germans attack on all the line, but the Poles defend themselves bravely. Turkey's new envoy, Rusem Estef Ünaydin, called on me and confirmed his country's will to abide by its commitments toward Britain, France, and the Balkan Entente. In the afternoon, I went to shake Orlowski's hand and to tell him how close we feel to Poland in these days of great ordeal. He had seen Csáky and found him deeply depressed by the events, for he had thought that, in view of Italy's neutrality, Hitler would have hesitated to unleash the war.

September 3. Britain declared war on Germany at 11 A.M., and France at 5 P.M.

September 4. The Germans have sunk the British passenger ship *Athenia.* There were some three hundred Americans on board. It is a repetition of the *Lusitania* incident of the last war. The British have captured the German ship *Bremen.* Roosevelt made an uplifting radio speech in which, behind the screen of neutrality, one could feel the revulsion of the Americans. I had at lunch Spisiak and Milecz, Slovakia's new envoys to Budapest and Bucharest. Both described to me the mood of their fellow countrymen: like the Czechs, the Slovaks were awaiting their deliverance by the Allies, but until then, in order to live from day to day, they have been obliged to turn themselves into tools of the Germans.

September 6. The Germans have occupied Krakow. The French are advancing toward Saarbrücken.

I had a meeting of more than an hour with Csáky. Following instructions received from my government, I drew his attention to the grave consequences that could ensue from the massing of Hungarian troops at our border and the calling up of three army corps, that is, of 400,000 men. Csáky phoned the army's chief of staff in front of me, asking for an explanation. He was told that only one regiment with its reservists was stationed at Bekesczába, on our border, and that only the army corps VI and half of the army corps V had been called up, or 160,000 men, who had been ordered to remain in their garrisons and not to move to the Romanian frontier. Csáky admitted that his government was under pressure from the general staff, whose chief was saying that he could not take responsibility for the situation if he was not allowed to take the measures made necessary by the massing of Romanian troops. Csáky believed this was a reference to the transfer of the Romanian army corps I from Craiova to Timişoara and of the Botoşani regiment to Braşov, on its way northward.

I replied that the entire world knew we did not covet the possessions of others, and that we therefore had no reason to attack Hungary. Smiling, I added—with the exception of St. Margaret Island,[10] which we would wish

[10]Danube island between Buda and Pest, known for its excellent restaurants.

to annex to our colonial empire since Romanians love it madly. "That is probably the reason why it is guarded by your sentries," I went on. Csáky laughed. Also, I said, "It's the same for the Ritz; why have antiaircraft guns been hoisted to its roof? Since I dine there almost every evening, that is, after all, an assurance that Romanian aircraft won't bomb it!"

"I know, since I am staying at the Ritz. But you are joking, for we are informed that you intend to invade and annihilate Bulgaria with the help of the Turks, and then turn on us and advance up to the Tisza!"

"Now it is you who are joking by attributing to us such vast Napoleonic designs."

I then drew his attention to the brazen irredentist campaign conducted in Hungary against us: newspaper articles, postage stamps with views from Transylvania, irredentist maps, and so forth. Csáky took the pertinent material I handed him and seemed impressed. He apologized, attributing this campaign to the extreme right. He promised to take measures through the minister of the interior and to personally take over the censorship of articles on foreign policy.

We pledged ourselves to work for the improvement of the atmosphere between our two countries. I said that the clearest proof of our peaceful intentions was our offer to sign a nonaggression treaty, an offer that had been rejected by Budapest. Csáky explained this rejection by the absence of a protocol concerning the treatment of minorities, which the Hungarian government had proposed to Yugoslavia and, through its intermediary, also to Romania. He said the suggestion had been made on August 25 to Rašić, who was even offered to have Cinčar-Marcovič draft a text that would also suit us. Since they had received no response, he said Bessenyey had been instructed to "return to the charge." I replied that Rašić had distinctly assured me that he had never received such a proposal from the Hungarian government, and not even a hint had been made to him. Where was the truth? With Csáky or Rašić? With neither? Or half with the one and half with the other? In any case, I concluded, please don't always talk to me of alleged persecutions, because our minorities are satisfied with their situation and have expressed their thanks innumerable times to the government. "Thanks given by minorities to governments mean nothing," Csáky replied. "If you want, I could show you entire files with Maniu and Vaida's thanks for the good treatment Romanians received under Hungarian rule. As a matter of fact, we exhibited those files at Trianon."

We then talked of broader political matters. Csáky believes that Mussolini has reached an agreement with Hitler for Italy not to move at present, since it constitutes the weak flank of the Axis. But should Hitler at one point ask Mussolini for military assistance, the Duce would provide it—without enthusiasm, but resolutely. It was not in Hitler's interest to accept military cooperation from Russia, Csáky said, so as not to bring a competitor into Central Europe and the Balkans. Such cooperation—should it ever take place—would be a catastrophe for Hungary and for its neighbors. The two great powers would allocate each other zones of interest in our region, with the two proletarian regimes fighting against the capitalist ones. Poland's heroic resistance was to be admired, and even Ribbentrop had paid tribute to it in a conversation with Sztojáy, Hungary's envoy to Berlin. As we parted, Csáky told me: "This war is a thirty-year war, and I shall not see its end." [The second part of the prediction turned out to be true, for Csáky died during the war.]

September 8. Gigurtu, a businessman with good connections in Germany [who was later to become prime minister in tragic days for Romania] is passing through Budapest on his way to Berlin, where he tells me he is to see Göring and Ribbentrop, and perhaps even Hitler. Göring apparently suggested the meeting, in order to receive through Gigurtu assurances concerning Romania's neutrality. In exchange for our shipments of petroleum and wheat—in accordance with the agreement concluded—Romania would receive the assurance that Germany would not attack it. Hitler would apparently even tolerate the transit through Romania of munitions for Poland, in accordance with the provisions of the 1907 Hague Convention (Convention V, art. 7). The transit of troops, however, would not be allowed. Even so, Gigurtu remarked, what the Germans give us is much less than what we give them: petroleum. What we might ask in addition is that Berlin rein in Budapest and bring to an end Hungary's mobilization preparations. Gigurtu believes that something like that could be obtained. He does not rule out the possibility that Hitler might force the Hungarians to conclude a nonaggression treaty with us, which would consolidate our neutrality. The only hitch is that Fabritius, the German envoy to Romania, complains that we are not neutral, and gives as proof the fact that British aircraft flying to Poland are allowed to refuel in Constanţa. Fabritius would have liked Gigurtu to carry a handwritten letter from the king to the Führer to dispel his mistrust, but, rightly so, Carol refused.

September 11. A very heavy day. I had meetings with the envoys of the United States, Yugoslavia (twice), Greece, and Poland, and with the chargé d'affaires of the Netherlands.

I was told that, called by Ribbentrop last Thursday, Csáky flew off in a German aircraft sent for him. Csáky claimed he had been struck by the lack of warlike enthusiasm in Germany, not only among the population at large but also among the leaders. Through Csáky, the Hungarian government was asked to grant the German army free passage to cross its territory toward Poland in order to cut off the retreat of the Polish army toward Romania. Being weak-willed and under the thumb of the Germans, Csáky would have been prepared to give in, but he had received clear instructions from Horthy and Teleki to resist the demand. Having no choice, all Csáky could do was to plead insistently with Ribbentrop that the Germans give up this demand that would drag Hungary into the camp of the enemies of Poland, a country with which the Hungarians were tied by a traditional friendship. Ribbentrop tried to explain to him that if the Polish army succeeded in crossing into Romania, it could form there, with the help of a Franco-British expeditionary corps (probably the one organized by Weygand in Syria), a new "Salonika front," as during World War I.

The issue has remained open, but in order to put pressure on Budapest, at German instigation the Slovak press has begun an anti-Hungarian revisionist campaign asking for the return of the territories lost at Munich and Vienna. The fact that these articles were reprinted in the German press indicates that Berlin wants to force Hungary's hand and compel it to yield on this point. The only hope the Hungarians could still muster is that the German army will advance so rapidly toward the south of Poland that it will cut off the Polish army's retreat between Przemysl and Lwów, thus avoiding the need to cross through Hungarian territory. [This did indeed occur.]

Government circles in Budapest seem very depressed. Even Ullein-Reviezky, the archenemy of the Romanians, exclaimed in front of Pipinelis, "It is the eleventh hour to reach an understanding with the Romanians." What a state he must be in to have been driven to such an extremity! However, I was assured that Erdmannsdorf had informed Csáky of the German government's will that Hungary participate in no bloc—not even a bloc of neutrals—because the Reich did not tolerate blocs, which at some time could turn against it.

September 12. Vinci came to see me, pro-German as always. Italy, he declared, is tied to the Axis more closely than ever. The Italian people, he claimed, while grateful to the Duce for having so far spared them from war, are nevertheless ready to take up arms at his call if Hitler so demands. And other absurdities of that nature. Rašić also came to see me. He, too, is pro-German, but more fearful—that is, more of a realist, less *comediante*.

TRANSFER TO ROME AND FAREWELLS

On September 13, I gave a dinner in honor of the Romanian and Hungarian economic delegations, which were in the midst of negotiations. I was called away from table for an urgent phone call from Bucharest. Gafencu, at the other end of the line, told me: “I have good news for you.” (Good news was hard to come by at that time—nowadays as well.) I urged him to explain. “Well,” he said, “the government is asking for Rome’s assent to your becoming Romania’s accredited envoy to Italy. Naturally, I wanted to be the first to tell you and also to offer you my warmest congratulations.” I thanked Gafencu for his friendly message and the trust he showed in me. When was this new appointment to take place? “As soon as possible,” came the reply: the idea was to be ready for a swift move. We hung up.

Distinctly mixed feelings took hold of me. Was this really what one would call “good news”? From a career point of view, it was. The same was true in regard to personal pleasure. I loved the beautiful country of Italy, where I had been stationed already twice, where I had grown fond of so many landscapes, monuments, and old works of art, where I had become attached to so many friends. Yet from the professional point of view, how many responsibilities awaited me! The Fascist government belonged to the Axis, which had started the war and wanted to rule and impose its will over all of Europe. Besides, hadn’t Mussolini championed Hungary’s border revisionism, a country that after lending a hand to the partition of Czechoslovakia was now intent on making Romania suffer the same fate? Nothing good awaited me in my new posting. In Rome the die had already been cast, as it had in Berlin. I knew I would undoubtedly experience bitterness and disappointment, and that it would take all the dazzling Roman sunshine, all the flowers layered up on the steps of Trinità dei Monti, all the *gentilezza* of my Italian friends to brighten up the somber days before me. Yet heeding William the Silent’s advice, I was determined to undertake even without hope, and to persevere even without victory.

September 14. Again a heavy day, with visits from Pipinelis, Guerlet, and Rašić. Csáky denied to Guerlet that he had gone to Berlin, but that very same day he admitted the fact to Orlowski. No comment. He told Guerlet it was possible, once they had wound up the war with Poland, that the Germans would attack Romania by crossing the Dniester in Bukovina. My French colleague asked him whether it would not be easier to launch such an attack through Hungary. Csáky had replied, “We would never accept that.” Yet today his speech to the parliamentary foreign affairs commission did not lack in polemics against us. The only conciliatory note was the repetition of the pledge that Hungary would at last ratify the Gojdu Foundation agreement that had been concluded with Romania two years earlier. [The pledge has never been carried out, and I still have in my personal archive the full powers signed by the king authorizing me to proceed with the exchange of ratifications—full powers I never had the privilege of using.]

I also received the visit of the German journalist von Michaelis, grandson of the former German chancellor and correspondent of the dailies *Kölner Zeitung* and *Neues Wiener Tagblatt.* He claimed the Hungarians "are now detested in Germany's leading circles because, after having proclaimed themselves for years the most loyal friends of the Reich, they are now trying to hedge their bets." In Berlin, he said, there continued to be fear of a new "Salonika front," led by General Weygand for the purpose of keeping the Italians at bay in Albania and unleashing an attack against Germany through Yugoslavia. The sympathies of the Serbs, and especially of the Croats, being undeniably in favor of the French and the British, it was not impossible, Michaelis said, that the Yugoslav army would rally to an expeditionary corps under Weygand in view of an attack against the Reich, in the direction of Carinthia. In such an event, Hitler would find himself compelled to unleash a Blitzkrieg against Yugoslavia, and Belgrade would fall more rapidly than had Warsaw. After that, according to my interlocutor, it would be the Führer's "painful duty to occupy all the countries of this region in order to secure the sources of Southeastern European production [that is, Romanian oil] in view of a possible long-lasting war of economic attrition." I pointed out to Michaelis that the entire structure of his argument was based on a single and unlikely hypothesis, but I could not help thinking that this might have been a discreet warning I was expected to transmit to Bucharest. In the rigid discipline of the Nazi Reich's press system, it seems indeed inconceivable that the Budapest correspondent of a German paper would request an audience with the envoy of Romania only in order to expound the fruit of his own cogitations.

September 16. I was received by Csáky, whom I informed that I was being transferred to another post, and whose assent I sought for my successor, Gheorghe Crutzescu. We took this opportunity to talk about the relations between our two countries. I confessed that I found his recent speech rather "bellicose." He replied that the press must have misstated his words, because he had specifically intended to show himself conciliatory—the more so, he emphasized, since in their present phase the Romano-Hungarian relations had "clearly improved." He promised anew that he would recommend that Parliament ratify the Gojdu agreement and that he would make a suggestion for the resolution of the Transylvanian archives issue.

In response to my question he did not deny that he had been to Berlin, where he got the impression that it was Ribbentrop, not Hitler, who had initially had the idea of a Germano-Russian rapprochement. As things now stood, I told Csáky, "Why don't you propose, you the Hungarians who were made to sign the Anti-Comintern Pact, that *anti* be changed into *pro,* so that it may from now on be called the Pro-Comintern Pact?" Csáky laughed: "I have a better idea: let's have Stalin join the Anti-Comintern Pact."

I asked Csáky whether he thought the Germans and Russians would again divide Poland between themselves.

"It is by no means out of the question if the English and French push Hitler into the Russians' arms. The Soviet Union would then take possession of White Russia and of the area inhabited by Ukrainians, and would thus reach the border of our Carpathia [Subcarpathian Russia]." He made an expressive face.

"In that case, we would have even more interests in common."

"Certainly, I have always been of the opinion that it was not negotiations that would draw us to each other, but external circumstances and dangers." We parted company in a very friendly fashion.

In conclusion, I saw Hungary's political position in the international crisis as follows: Hungary was asserting its friendship with Germany and did not want to declare itself neutral, so as to show Berlin its solidarity with the Reich. At the same time, however, Hungary was avoiding any gesture that might draw it into a generalized war it was striving to stay out of. In the event of a German victory, it trusted it would be able to avail itself of this friendship to cash in on its revisionist claims. In the event of a German defeat, the Budapest government hoped that London would credit it with the Brownie points earned by resisting German pressures and refusing to be dragged into a war against the Allies.

Cretzianu asked Dinu Hiott, who was on the point of returning to Budapest, to tell me, since I was a "historian," the mystery of how the Germans had found out that, in contrast to the British, the French had been willing to accept Mussolini as a mediator. Mussolini was proposing a cease-fire between Germany and Poland, a freezing of the current military positions, and the convening of an international conference. This was the key to the mystery: because the Germans had cut the direct line between Paris and Warsaw, Georges Bonnet, the French foreign minister, phoned Adrien Thierry, France's ambassador in Bucharest, asking him to instruct the French ambassador in Warsaw, Noël, to advise Polish Foreign Minister Beck to accept the proposal of Mussolini's mediation. But because the Paris-Bucharest phone wire also crossed Germany, the Germans were able to listen in on the Bonnet-Thierry conversation.

September 17. The Russians informed the Poles that "since the Polish state no longer exists," the Russo-Polish treaties had lapsed and their army would enter Polish territory in order to protect their White Russian and Ukrainian fellow countrymen. Our envoy in Moscow was informed at the same time that the USSR would remain neutral toward Romania. What neutrality, since we are not at war? Poles en masse are taking refuge in Romania, where they are being received like brothers. Among them are even President Moscicki and Field Marshal Smigly-Ridz, as well as other government members. They brought with them their country's gold reserves and political archives.

September 18. The advance of the Soviet army into Poland causes intense anxiety in all Budapest circles. Ghiczy, the political director, seems frightened by the Russian army's approach toward the Hungarian border, the more so since, after Hungary's adhesion to the Anti-Comintern Pact, diplomatic relations between Moscow and Budapest have been cut.

September 21. Cretzianu phoned to tell me the Italian government has assented to my appointment as Romania's envoy to Rome and that the king has signed the decree appointing me. I am appointed as of September 26, and have therefore to hasten the preparations for my departure.

I received the new draft of the text of a Romano-Yugoslav-Hungarian declaration proposed by Bucharest and Belgrade.[11] But Csáky told Rašić that he could not sign off on this formula, which contained "too precise a commitment." Csáky was reportedly terrified by the presence of Russian troops at the Hungarian border. "We expected to meet Russian soldiers," he lamented, "but we encountered Bolshevik gangs."

The situation of the Polish legation in Budapest is rather ticklish. If Orlowski and his collaborators do not leave willingly, Csáky fears the Germans will compel him to evict them forcibly.

At noon, I heard tragic news from Bucharest: Prime Minister Călinescu has been assassinated by the Iron Guard. That evening, the murderers were executed at the scene of the crime. We are entering a horrible and bloody phase of our national history.

---

[11]The text is contained in Appendix E.

September 22. Vörnle, undersecretary of state at the Hungarian Ministry of Foreign Affairs, came to offer me condolences for Romania's heavy loss in the person of its prime minister. I received condolence visits from the British, Greek, and Polish envoys, as well as from my other colleagues. In Romania, frightful reprisals are visited upon the Iron Guard. A new government was formed, headed by General Argeşanu. It differs from the preceding one only by new faces taking over the portfolios held by Armand Călinescu (Generals Argeşanu, Marinescu, and Ilcuş).

On his way back from Berlin, Gigurtu stopped in Budapest and came to see me. He found the Germans most considerate; they had received him with full honors, "as if I were an envoy of the king." Göring assured him that Germany would tolerate no aggression against Romania. He also gave him formal assurances with regard to Bessarabia, "provided, of course, you do not attack the Russians on the basis of your alliance with Poland, which would be senseless since that state no longer exists." [It was on the eve of the Soviet army's entry into Polish territory. As was to become known later, Göring's assurances were lies, since in the Ribbentrop-Molotov agreement the Reich had given the Russians a free hand with regard to Bessarabia.] Göring had also been reticent at the mention of a nonaggression treaty between Romania and Hungary, which could be a first step toward the setting up by Britain of an anti-Axis bloc. Gigurtu insisted, however, that this would only be to strengthen Romania's neutrality, which seemed to convince Göring. Although he is our envoy in Berlin, Radu Crutzescu has been kept in the dark about the purpose of Gigurtu's mission to Germany. Reportedly, Göring himself seemed surprised by the rapidity of Germany's victory in Poland.

September 24. In a conversation with Csáky, Hitler revealed to him that his scientists were preparing an arm that could destroy entire populations [Hitler's first intimation of research for the production of an atomic bomb]. However, he said Germany would use it only if the military situation were to become so disastrous for Germany that, in extremis, the use of this new weapon would become compelling.

Vinci came to tell me he was at my disposal to help in any way with my transfer to Rome. He told me he had heard from Csáky that the German government probably had asked the Soviet one what intentions it had regarding Southeast Europe; the Soviet government would have expressed "reassuring" intentions concerning Bessarabia, stating it wished to respect the status quo.

September 26. After a good-bye dinner offered to my collaborators, I got caught up in a series of farewell luncheons and dinners given by my foreign colleagues. Today, Rašić gave a luncheon for eighteen in my honor; attending were the heads of mission of Great Britain, France, the United States, Greece, Turkey, Switzerland, the Netherlands.

In the afternoon, I went with my wife to Gödöllö for our farewell call on Regent and Mrs. Horthy. The regent conferred on me the Great Cross of the Order of Merit. We had a friendly and informal conversation with this decent and well-bred couple. Horthy, as a matter of fact, is Austrian from head to toe, and I am told he speaks Hungarian with a Viennese accent. We spoke in German. He evoked old memories, especially from the time of the last war. Foch, he said, had proposed in 1918 that the Allies and their adversaries join forces to fight Bolshevik Russia. What a pity this suggestion was not heeded, Horthy remarked sadly, because a sentiment of comradeship between nations would have been created and there would have been no *Diktat*. But Clemenceau, he concluded, preferred to have a climate of hatred and discord continue, and that is why he gave Poland Danzig, the Corridor, and so forth. This was followed by some rather transparent allusions, such as that the League of Nations should be reformed so that it could indict those who are guilty of territorial annexations and bring them to justice. I replied, "First, it would have to be determined who were those who stole territories they were not entitled to, and when such illicit appropriations took place." Another allusion by Horthy: "Let's all of us in Europe bury the hatchet, sit around a conference table, and eliminate intolerable situations." My reply: "First of all, let's create among us a friendly and frank atmosphere, and then examine eventual intolerable situations. Otherwise, it is possible that because of hatred and resentment some situations may be characterized as intolerable when in reality they are perfectly justifiable." Apart from that, however, both our hosts were most considerate. As we were leaving Horthy, shaking my hand, said: "You are now going to climb a step. I wish you to climb all of them and to have a brilliant career that brings you to the very top, because I know we would then be able to reach an agreement." The Horthys accompanied us to the door, and we returned to Budapest in a rose-colored twilight enwrapped in a slight mist or veil of dust. It was perhaps, I thought, a veil that was falling on a difficult, but action-filled and interesting chapter of my life.

On the road, we passed the mournful and endless file of Polish cars, carrying the multitude of refugees, fugitives after the annihilation of their homeland, fleeing the terror of bombings and of Bolshevik rule.

September 27. Leave-taking audience with Prime Minister Paul Teleki [who a few years later was to commit suicide in order not to break his promise to Yugoslavia as he was being urged by Hitler to attack it by occupying the Bačka region]. My last meeting with him confirmed, once more, the opinion I had of this true aristocrat, the son of a Greek woman (the Muratti cigarettes) and married to the daughter of a Romanian woman (Mocsonyi). He avoided political topics in this conversation, except for his fear at Russia's penetration in our area, which he felt would be permanent. Later, my wife and I had tea with Countess Teleki, in a most pleasant and amiable atmosphere.

September 30. My foreign colleagues have given us a series of farewell parties: Guerlet, Montgomery [whom I was to find again, in such changed circumstances, in the United States], Pipinelis, Erdmannsdorf, Vinci, and so forth. I went to say good-bye to Vörnle at the Ministry. He was full of flattering praise and assured me that "your mission has been an undeniable success." Finally, I went to the Ritz to take leave of Csáky, who, being unwell, was resting in his hotel room. He received me in his dressing gown, "since we know each other for close to twenty years." He told me all sorts of pleasantries and compliments, adding: "You have been very skillful and you have been very successful in Budapest; my sister almost burst into tears when she heard of your departure. Give my best regards to Gafencu, in whom we all have confidence. Tell him not to judge us only on the basis of our speeches—which are on the whole directed to the domestic audience—but also on our actions; he will then see that we are reasonable. We will never let ourselves be dragged into adventures. The common external danger brings our countries closer together, more so than negotiations. The proximity of the Russians is no cause for rejoicing, but it will at least enable us to adopt a balancing policy, similar to that which you Romanians have used for centuries between the Slavic and Germanic nations."

We had our last lunches at friends', Ferry Hunyady and Franz Hohenlohe-Waldenburg.

October 1. At the crack of dawn, we left Budapest by car, returning to Romania. Another chapter in my life had ended.